1994

The world fame of Samuel Beckett is due to a combination of high academic esteem and immense popularity. An innovator in prose fiction to rival Joyce, his plays have been the most influential in modern theatre history. Beckett's celebrated refusal to 'explain' his work, allied to his indifference to the rewards of celebrity, made him seem a 'difficult' author. Yet, when pressed, Beckett's own emphasis fell on the 'fundamental sounds' he was seeking to express.

As an author in both English and French and a writer for the page and the stage, Beckett has been the focus for specialist treatment in each of his many guises, but there have been few attempts to provide a conspectus view. This book provides thirteen introductory essays on every aspect of Beckett's work, paying particular attention to his most famous plays (e.g. *Waiting for Godot*, and *Endgame*) and his prose fictions (e.g. the 'trilogy' and *Murphy*). Further essays tackle his radio and television drama, his theatre directing and his poetry, followed by more general issues such as Beckett's bilingualism and his relationship to the philosophers. Reference material is provided at the front and back of the book, in the form of a chronology of Beckett's career, a list of French and English titles and a list of books for further reading.

THE CAMBRIDGE
COMPANION TO
BECKETT

Cambridge Companions to Literature

The Cambridge Companion to Old English Literature
edited by Malcolm Godden and Michael Lapidge

The Cambridge Companion to Dante
edited by Rachel Jacoff

The Cambridge Chaucer Companion
edited by Piero Boitani and Jill Mann

The Cambridge Companion to English Medieval Theatre
edited by Richard Beadle

The Cambridge Companion to Shakespeare Studies
edited by Stanley Wells

The Cambridge Companion to English Renaissance Drama
edited by A. R. Braunmuller and Michael Hattaway

The Cambridge Companion to English Poetry, Donne to Marvell
edited by Thomas N. Corns

The Cambridge Companion to Milton
edited by Dennis Danielson

The Cambridge Companion to British Romanticism
edited by Stuart Curran

The Cambridge Companion to Ibsen
edited by James McFarlane

The Cambridge Companion to James Joyce
edited by Derek Attridge

The Cambridge Companion to Beckett
edited by John Pilling

The Cambridge Companion to Brecht
edited by Peter Thomson and Glendyr Sacks

THE CAMBRIDGE
COMPANION TO
BECKETT

EDITED BY

JOHN PILLING

University of Reading

CAMBRIDGE
UNIVERSITY PRESS

Published by the Press Syndicate of the University of Cambridge
The Pitt Building, Trumpington Street, Cambridge CB2 1RP
40 West 20th Street, New York, NY 10011–4211, USA
10 Stamford Road, Oakleigh, Melbourne 3166, Australia

First published 1994

Printed in Great Britain at the University Press, Cambridge

A catalogue record for this book is available from the British Library

Library of Congress cataloguing in publication data

The Cambridge Companion to Beckett / edited by John Pilling.
p.   cm. – (Cambridge Companions to Literature)
Includes bibliographical references and index.
ISBN 0 521 41366 4 (hardback) – ISBN 0 521 42413 5 (paperback).
1. Beckett, Samuel, 1906–89 – Criticism and interpretation –
Handbooks, manuals, etc. I. Pilling, John. II. Series
PR6003.E282Z585 1993
848'.91409–dc20 92–47287 CIP

ISBN 0 521 41366 4 hardback
ISBN 0 521 42413 5 paperback

CE

CONTENTS

CONTENTS

CONTRIBUTORS

H. Porter Abbott is Professor of English at the University of California, Santa Barbara. He has published many essays on Beckett in journals and is the author of *The fiction of Samuel Beckett: form and effect* (Berkeley and Los Angeles: University of California, 1973) and of *Diary fiction: writing as action* (Ithaca, NY: Cornell University Press, 1984).

Ann Beer teaches at the Center for the Study and Teaching of Writing, Faculty of Education, McGill University, Montreal, and has published essays on Beckett in the *Journal of Beckett Studies* and *The Southern Review*.

Paul Davies is Lecturer in English at the University of Ulster, Coleraine and the author of *The ideal real: Beckett's fiction and imagination* (forthcoming from Fairleigh Dickinson University Press). His essays have appeared in *Temenos* and the *Yearbook of English Studies*.

Keir Elam is Professor of English Language and Literature at the University of Pisa and the author of *The semiotics of theatre and drama* (Routledge and Kegan Paul, 1980) and *Shakespeare's universe of discourse: language games in the comedies* (Cambridge University Press, 1984). With Alessandro Serpieri and others he co-edited a four-volume study of Shakespeare's dramatization of his historical sources, *Nel laboratorio di Shakespeare* (Pratiche, Parma, 1988).

Jonathan Kalb is Assistant Professor of Theater at Hunter College, City University of New York and a regular theatre critic for *The village voice*. His book *Beckett in performance* (Cambridge University Press, 1989) was the 1991 winner of the George Jean Nathan award for Dramatic Criticism, and Limelight Editions have published *Free admissions: collected theater writings*.

Paul Lawley is Senior Lecturer in English, University of Plymouth. His essays on Beckett have appeared in *Modern Drama, Modern Fiction Studies* and the *Journal of Beckett Studies* and have often been reprinted in collections.

Roger Little occupies the oldest chair of French in the world in the department at Trinity College, Dublin where Beckett was successively a student and an assistant lecturer. He has written books on Rimbaud, Apollinaire, Saint-John Perse and André Frénaud and edited several selections from the modern French poets.

Anna McMullan is Lecturer in Film and Drama at the University of Reading and the author of *Theatre on trial: the later plays of Samuel Beckett* (Routledge, 1993). Her essays on Beckett have appeared in *Modern Drama*, the *Revue d'esthétique* and the *Journal of Beckett Studies*.

P. J. Murphy teaches English at the University College of the Cariboo, British Columbia. He is the author of *Reconstructing Beckett: language for being in Samuel Beckett's fiction* (University of Toronto Press, 1990) and of *Beckett as critic* (forthcoming from Routledge and Kegan Paul). He has co-authored (with Konrad Schoell, Rolf Breuer and Werner Huber) a *Critique of Beckett criticism* (forthcoming from Camden House).

John Pilling is Professor of English and European Literature and Director of the Beckett International Foundation at Reading University. He edited the *Journal of Beckett Studies* from 1979 to 1985. His books include: *Samuel Beckett* (Routledge and Kegan Paul, 1976), *Frescoes of the skull: the later prose and drama of Samuel Beckett* (with James Knowlson; John Calder, 1979) and *Fifty modern European poets* (Heinemann, 1982). He co-edited (with Mary Bryden) *The ideal core of the onion: reading Beckett archives* (Beckett International Foundation, 1992).

Andrew Renton teaches Fine Art and History of Art at Camberwell College of Art, The London Institute and Goldsmith's College, London University. He has curated numerous exhibitions of contemporary art throughout Europe. He co-edited (with Liam Gillick) *Technique anglaise: current trends in British art* (Thames and Hudson, 1991) and has published essays on Beckett in *Performance* and *The ideal core of the onion: reading Beckett archives*, ed. John Pilling and Mary Bryden (Beckett International Foundation, 1992).

Rupert Wood is Lecturer in French at St John's College, Cambridge. He is currently writing a book on the decay and implosion of philosophical and critical language in Beckett's writing and the development of the ways in which his prose and drama present world-pictures, which grows out of a

1990 Ph.D. thesis, 'Aesthetics and ascesis: Schopenhauerian structures in the later prose of Samuel Beckett'.

Michael Worton is Senior Lecturer in French at University College, London and is co-editor of the Bloodaxe French Poets series. He has co-edited (with Judith Still) *Intertextuality: theories and practice* (Manchester University Press, 1990) and *Textuality and sexuality: reading theories and practices* (Manchester University Press, 1993) and is currently writing a study of the novels of Michel Tournier.

PREFACE

By the time of his death in 1989 Samuel Beckett had emulated the fame of his sometime mentor and lifelong model of excellence as a writer, James Joyce. Beckett had, indeed, gone one better in terms of public recognition and the visible signs of its rewards, and been awarded the Nobel Prize for Literature in 1969. Yet, much like Joyce, Beckett had remained a writer working at the limits of the possible, always experimenting beyond his audience's expectations, indifferent to the imperatives of the market-place. Beckett's adamant refusal to become a commodity – he never willingly gave interviews, and shunned publicity to the point where it became inevitable he would attract it – created misconceptions about the man, and an aura of 'difficulty' and 'unapproachability' attached itself to his writings. Thirty years of expert commentary have seen the creation of an enormous secondary literature with almost a life of its own – so much so that interested parties may find themselves sufficiently hard-pressed on the way to Beckett never to encounter him directly, in the way Beckett himself (above and beyond his self-punishing disaffection at being a focus for debate at all) would have wished. A reader could be forgiven for feeling that there is just not enough shelf space for much more interpretation of a figure intent upon eluding definition, whose profound pull towards, if not into, silence has nevertheless been the occasion for millions of words in addition to his own.

But it is not so. For as the critical literature has grown, it has naturally become more specialized and stratified, an outcome in part provoked by Beckett having written in both English and French, and for both the page and the stage. The very possibility of an overview seems to have been imperilled by the expansion of critical perspectives, which paradoxically has also led to narrower views and a tendency to tunnel vision. Hence this *Companion*, an 'addition to company'[1] of a distinctive kind, designed to supply what is perhaps no longer within the compass of a single commentator, if it ever was. It is in the very nature of such an enterprise that we should hear voices of different timbres, occasionally discordant one with another, generating material not meant to facilitate what Beckett dismissed as mere 'book-keeping',[2] but rather to supply a general reader's needs. The multiplicity of aspects reflects and respects a multiplicity originating in Beckett himself, and in texts that are cunningly designed to mobilize as much expressive power as possible, even as the means to do so seems (either because of intrinsic shortcomings in a given medium or because past precedents operated actively against Beckett repeating himself) to dwindle almost to nothing.

The topics within these essays suggest themselves as areas worthy of focus, which is not to say that thirteen other frames of reference could not have been brought to bear upon an exceptionally rich body of work, for all its author's insistence on poverty and 'indigence'.[3] The corporate aim is in no way to limit discussion by presupposing that these readings might be definitive and 'proof against enduring tumult',[4] but rather to provoke it, as posterity proceeds to decide for itself where the best of Beckett is to be found. As seems proper in the circumstances, these essays are offered in a companionable spirit, but not a complacent one. In rising to a challenge they seek also to perpetuate it, without foreclosing upon readers discovering the work of Beckett for themselves.

NOTES

1 *Nohow on (Company, Ill seen ill said, Worstward Ho)* (London: John Calder, 1965), 22.
2 Ruby Cohn (ed.), *Disjecta: miscellaneous writings and a dramatic fragment* (London: John Calder, 1983), 19.
3 Ibid., 141.
4 *Collected shorter prose 1930–1980* (London: John Calder, 1984), 146.

CHRONOLOGY OF BECKETT'S LIFE

This chronology has benefited greatly from the expert attentions of Beckett's official biographer, James Knowlson, whose willingness to help is very much appreciated.

1906 (13 April)	Samuel Barclay Beckett born at Cooldrinagh, his parents' house in Foxrock, south of Dublin, on Good Friday.
1911	Attends Ida Elsner's private academy (cf. Moran on the Elsner sisters in *Molloy*) and Earlsfort House School in Dublin, with his elder brother Frank.
1920	Follows Frank to the distinguished Portora Royal boarding school at Enniskillen, County Fermanagh, Northern Ireland, where he throws himself vigorously into the life of the school, excelling at cricket and showing signs of considerable scholastic potential.
1923 (October)	Enters Trinity College, Dublin, where he studies Modern Languages (French and Italian) and in his leisure hours goes to plays at the Abbey Theatre.
1926 (June)	Awarded a Foundation Scholarship on the basis of exceptional academic performance. First visit to France, a month cycling in and around Tours.
1927	Vacation trip to Florence, visiting churches and museums.
(December)	Graduates B.A., first in the First Class. Awarded the Gold Medal.
1928 (January– September)	Takes up post as teacher of French and English at Campbell College, Belfast. First visit to Germany, to stay with his cousin Peggy Sinclair and her family in Kassel.

1928 (October)	Installed as *lecteur* at the Ecole Normale Supérieure in Paris, as successor to Thomas MacGreevy. MacGreevy becomes a close personal friend and introduces Beckett to James Joyce and the Joyce circle.
1929 (June)	Publishes his first essay ('Dante...Bruno.Vico..Joyce') and his first short story ('Assumption') in the *émigré* magazine *transition*.
1930 (Summer)	Composes *Whoroscope*, his first separately published creative work (Hours Press). Reads Proust's *A la recherche du temps perdu*. Translates Rimbaud's *Le bateau ivre*.
(September)	Returns to Trinity to a post as lecturer in French.
1931 (February)	*Le Kid* (a parody of Corneille's *Le Cid* co-written with his friend Georges Pelorson) performed by the Modern Language Society.
(March)	*Proust* published (London: Chatto and Windus) to largely favourable reviews.
(September)	First Dublin publication, the poem 'Alba'.
(December)	Christmas in Kassel (as also in 1928, 1929, 1930). Resigns his lectureship.
1932 (February)	First serious attempt at a novel, *Dream of fair to middling women*, written in Paris on returning from Germany.
(December)	Publication of the story 'Dante and the lobster' in *This Quarter* (Paris).
1933 (May)	Death of Peggy Sinclair from tuberculosis.
(26 June)	Death of Beckett's father after a heart attack.
1934 (January)	Takes up residence in London, seeking medical advice to temper mourning and melancholia.
(24 May)	*More pricks than kicks* published (London: Chatto and Windus).
(Summer)	Working on poems later published as *Echo's bones and other precipitates* (Paris: Europa Press, 1935). Reviews in London literary magazines.
1935 (Summer)	*Murphy* begun.
(Autumn)	Attends one of C. G. Jung's Tavistock lectures (cf. *All that fall*).
1936 (26 June)	*Murphy* completed in typescript.
(29 September)	Leaves Ireland for Germany.
1937	First serious attempt at a play based on Dr Johnson and his circle (*Human wishes*). *Murphy* turned down

by a succession of London publishers. Beckett becomes 'the bawd and blasphemer from Paris' in the *Irish Times* after being cross-examined during a Dublin libel action. Brief love affair with the American heiress and 'art addict' Peggy Guggenheim.

1938 (7 January)   Stabbed by a pimp in Montparnasse. Visited in hospital by Suzanne Deschevaux-Dumesnil, later his companion for life.

(March)   *Murphy* published (London: Routledge).
Working with Alfred Péron on a French translation of *Murphy*.
Writing poems directly in French.

1939   Joyce's *Finnegans wake* published.

(3 September)   England declares war on Germany.

1940   Fall of France. Beckett travels south as part of the exodus from Paris (June). Returns to his apartment (October) and a year later, joins the Resistance.

1941 (January)   Death of James Joyce in Zurich.

(February)   *Watt* begun.

1942 (16 August)   Alfred Péron arrested. Beckett and Suzanne go into hiding.

(6 October)   Arrival at Roussillon, after crossing clandestinely into Vichy France.

1944 (24 August)   Liberation of Roussillon.

1945 (March)   Awarded the Croix de Guerre for his Resistance work.
Watt finished in manuscript after three years of intense but spasmodic writing 'to get away from war and occupation'.

(August)   Arrives at devastated St-Lô in Normandy to take up his duties as storekeeper–interpreter at the Irish Red Cross Hospital, a job for which he had volunteered.

1946 (July)   First publication of short fiction in French. First novel in French (*Mercier et Camier*) begun.

(Autumn–
Winter)   Writing the four *nouvelles*.

1947 (January)   First play in French, *Eleuthéria*, begun.

(2 May)   *Molloy* begun.

(27 November)   *Malone meurt* begun.

1948 (9 October)   *En attendant Godot* begun.

1949 (29 March) *L'Innommable* begun.

1950 (Spring) Completes translations from the Spanish for *Anthology of Mexican poetry* (Bloomington: Indiana University Press, 1958). Translates Apollinaire's *Zone*.

(25 August) Death of Beckett's mother.

(24 December) *Textes pour rien* begun.

1951 (March) *Molloy* published (Paris: Editions de Minuit).

(October) *Malone meurt* published (Paris: Editions de Minuit).

(December) *Textes pour rien* completed in manuscript.

1952 Buys land at Ussy-sur-Marne with the legacy from his mother's estate. Ussy subsequently becomes Beckett's preferred location for writing.

(October) *En attendant Godot* published (Paris: Editions de Minuit).

1953 (19 January) First performance of *Godot* under Roger Blin's direction at the Théâtre de Babylone in Montparnasse.

Watt published in Paris (Olympia Press).

Translation of *Godot* into English begun.

1954 (September) Death of Beckett's brother Frank.

1955 (March) *Molloy* (in English) published in Paris (Olympia Press).

(April) Best man at Joyce's son Stephen's wedding.

(Summer) First version of *Fin de partie* finished.

(3 August) First English production of *Godot* opens.

(November) *Nouvelles et textes pour rien* published (Paris: Editions de Minuit).

1956 (3 January) First American production of *Godot* in Miami.

(February) First British publication of *Waiting for Godot* (London: Faber and Faber).

(June) One-act version of *Fin de partie* finished.

(July–
September) *All that fall* written.

1957 (3 January) First radio play (*All that fall*) broadcast on the BBC Third Programme.

(March) Death of Jack B. Yeats.

(May–
August) Translates *Fin de partie* into English.

1958 (February)	*Krapp's last tape* begun.
(October)	First performance of *Endgame* at the Royal Court Theatre.
(December)	*Comment c'est* begun.
1959 (June)	Honorary D. Litt. degree ceremony at Trinity.
1960 (Summer)	*Comment c'est* finished.
(Winter)	Moves to new apartment on the Boulevard St Jacques, Montparnasse, his Paris address for the rest of his life.
1961 (March)	Solemnization of marriage to Suzanne at Folkestone, Kent.
(May)	Shares Prix International des Editeurs with Jorge Luis Borges. *Happy days* finished.
(December)	First radio play in French (*Cascando*) written.
1962 (July)	*Play* begun.
	Translating *How it is*.
1963 (May)	*Film* and *Play* finished. Beckett assists with the German production of the latter, and from this point onward is invariably closely involved with the major productions of his plays.
1964 (Summer)	First and only visit to the United States, to assist with the realization of *Film*.
1965 (Spring)	*Imagination morte imaginez* and *Eh Joe* written, the latter his first television play (first broadcast BBC2, July 1966).
(Autumn)	*Assez* written; *Le dépeupleur* begun.
1966	Translation of *Textes pour rien* into English. Helps with the translation of *Watt* into French.
1967 (Spring)	Glaucoma diagnosed. Death of Thomas MacGreevy.
1969	Writes *Sans* and translates it as *Lessness*.
(23 October)	Awarded the Nobel Prize for Literature. Beckett in Tunisia in flight from the world's press.
1970 (October)	First of two successful eye operations (second operation, February 1971).
	Consents to the long-delayed publication of *Mercier et Camier* and *Premier amour*, both written in 1946.
1972 (Spring)	*Not I* written, after a trip to Morocco in February.
(April–May)	Translating *Premier amour*.
(June–July)	*Still* trilogy begun.
1973 (January)	Successful London production of *Not I*, with Billie Whitelaw as Mouth. Translating *Not I* into French.

(August)	*As the story was told* written. Translation and re-casting of *Mercier et Camier* finished.
1974 (Summer)	*That time* begun. Translating *Still* into French.
1975 (March)	Directs *Godot* in German at Berlin. *Footfalls* begun.
(April)	Directs *Pas moi* in Paris.
(December)	*Pour finir encore* written.
1976 (Autumn)	Television play *. . .but the clouds. . .* begun.
1977	*Company/Compagnie* begun.
1980	*Mal vu mal dit* begun.
1981	Writes and translates *Rockaby* and *Ohio impromptu.* *Worstward Ho* begun.
1982	Writes and translates *Catastrophe. Nacht und Träume* written.
1989 (July)	Death of Suzanne Beckett.
(22 December)	Death of Samuel Beckett. Burial in Montparnasse Cemetery.

ABBREVIATIONS

Except in the case of the following abbreviations, full details of works referred to are given after each essay, either in the endnotes or in the checklist of recommended reading.

AST   *As the story was told: uncollected and later prose*, London: John Calder, 1990.

CP   *Collected poems 1930–1978*, London: John Calder, 1984.

CSP   *Collected shorter prose 1930–1980*, London: John Calder, 1984.

CSPL   *Collected shorter plays*, London: Faber and Faber, 1984.

D   *Disjecta: miscellaneous writings and a dramatic fragment*, ed. Ruby Cohn, London: John Calder, 1983.

Dream   *Dream of fair to middling women*, Dublin: The Black Cat Press, 1992.

E   *Endgame*, a play in one act, followed by *Act without words*, a mime for one player, London: Faber and Faber, 1958.

HD   *Happy days/Oh les beaux jours*, a bilingual edition ed. James Knowlson, London: Faber and Faber, 1978.

HII   *How it is*, London: John Calder, 1964.

LO   *The lost ones*, London: John Calder, 1972.

MPTK   *More pricks than kicks*, London: John Calder, 1970.

Mu   *Murphy*, London: John Calder, 1963.

NO   *Nohow on (Company, Ill seen ill said, Worstward Ho)*, London: John Calder, 1990.

PTD   *Proust* and *Three dialogues with Georges Duthuit*, London: John Calder, 1965.

T   *The Beckett trilogy: Molloy, Malone dies, The Unnamable* London: Pan, 1979.

W   *Watt*, London: John Calder, 1963.

WFG   *Waiting for Godot*, second edition, London: Faber and Faber, 1965

A NOTE ON TITLES

The two columns below list all substantial Beckett works, providing a conversion table between them. In relatively few cases no equivalence exists. English titles are given in alphabetical order.

ENGLISH	FRENCH
	Abandonné
Act without words I and II	*Actes sans paroles I and II*
All strange away	
All that fall	*Tous ceux qui tombent*
As the story was told	
Breath	*Souffle*
...but the clouds...	*...que nuages...*
Cascando	*Cascando*
Catastrophe	*Catastrophe*
Come and go	*Va et vient*
Company	*Compagnie*
Dream of fair to middling women	
Eh Joe	*Hé Joe*
	Eleuthéria
Embers	*Cendres*
Endgame	*Fin de partie*
Enough	*Assez*
	La falaise
Film	*Film*
Footfalls	*Pas*
For to end yet again	*Pour finir encore*
From an abandoned work	*D'un ouvrage abandonné*
Ghost trio	*Trio du fantôme*
Happy days	*Oh les beaux jours*
How it is	*Comment c'est*

ENGLISH	FRENCH
Imagination dead imagine	*Imagination morte imaginez*
Ill seen ill said	*Mal vu mal dit*
Krapp's last tape	*La dernière bande*
Lessness	*Sans*
The lost ones	*Le dépeupleur*
Malone dies	*Malone meurt*
Molloy	*Molloy*
More pricks than kicks	
Murphy	*Murphy*
Nacht und Träume	*Nacht und Träume*
Not I	*Pas moi*
Ohio impromptu	*L'impromptu d'Ohio*
A piece of monologue	*Solo*
Ping	*Bing*
Play	*Comédie*
Proust	*Proust*
Quad	*Quad*
Rockaby	*Berceuse*
Rough for radio I and II	*Esquisse radiophonique; Pochade radiophonique*
Rough for theatre I and II	*Fragments de théâtre* I and II
Still	*Immobile*
Texts for nothing	*Textes pour rien*
That time	*Cette fois*
Three dialogues with Georges Duthuit	
The Unnamable	*L'Innommable*
Waiting for Godot	*En attendant Godot*
Watt	*Watt*
What where	*Quoi où*
Words and Music	*Paroles et Musique*
Worstward Ho	*Cap au pire*

I

RUPERT WOOD

An endgame of aesthetics: Beckett as essayist

Whilst it is easy to see where Beckett's discursive writing begins, it is difficult to see where, or how, it ends. It is possible to outline the loose assemblage of aesthetic theories and philosophical ideas that form their point of departure, but it is extremely difficult to see what happens to these ideas and where they end up. Beckett's two major early essays, 'Dante. . .Bruno. Vico. .Joyce' (1929) and *Proust* (1931) are founded upon fairly coherent systems of philosophy and aesthetics. The rest of his pre-war discursive writing, which consists mainly of short literary reviews, can with care be unpicked to reveal developments of the same ideas. After the war, Beckett's critical attention switched to painting. Despite their highly stylized manner and ironic tone, his first two essays are in many respects logical extensions of his pre-war ideas, and they can readily be labelled 'discursive'. Yet these pieces represent the start of a deconstructive process whose logical conclusion is not to be found in recognizably discursive writing at all, but in dramatized dialogue and in the condensed lyricism of the *témoignages* and later prose.

There are several totally different ways in which the reader can tackle Beckett's discursive writings. Perhaps the most obvious strategy is to attempt to tease out an aesthetic which may then serve to elucidate Beckett's other works. In this way, his discursive writings are read as if they contained an aesthetic theory or even a philosophical doctrine which underpins his drama, fiction and verse. Much critical attention has been devoted to uncovering these supposed theories or doctrines. Given Beckett's reluctance to discuss his work in these terms, and given the elusiveness of any kind of systematic thought in his literary output, it is easy to see why one might wish to claim the discursive writings as some kind of critical key. It is particularly tempting to see Beckett's discursive writing occupying a clearly demarcated position; like the key to a map, it sits aloof in the margins, yet remains indispensable for deciphering the map itself.

A completely different strategy – one which is often ignored in the rush to locate a system – is to judge these texts according to the criteria by which we conventionally judge introductions to texts or pieces of literary journalism.[1] After all, however self-revealing we imagine them to be, Beckett's critical works are not about his own work, and they are often not even about writing at all. *Proust* was intended, ostensibly at least, to serve as an introduction to *A la recherche du temps perdu*, and its informativeness in this respect is often overlooked. Indeed, one should overlook neither the fact that Beckett dismissed most of his discursive writing as the result of friendly obligation or economic need, nor the fact that the work of some of his friends seems to provide unlikely objects for Beckett's high-flown praise. Beckett's long resistance to the republication of these articles, and his eventual choice of the title *Disjecta* for the collection that contains these various discursive writings, might suggest that these pieces are of rather marginal importance. Yet this 'throwaway' status would hardly put *Disjecta* (1983) in a unique position within Beckett's work, littered as it is with abandoned texts, fragments, '*têtes-mortes*' and fizzles. Like his heroes' bodies, the Beckettian corpus is dismembered; in its wake this particular body leaves behind the *disjecti membra poetae*.

Whilst it is possible to find within Beckett's discursive writings a logical development of aesthetic theory (and much else to interest students of the various branches of philosophy), that is not a sufficient reason to marginalize them as keys to Beckett's work. Too often these pieces are regarded as philosophical or aesthetic credos which give meaning to the rest of his work. Beckett's discursive works, like his prose works, chart a course of contraction and the abandonment of various possible ways of expressing. Beckett's work is negatively defined; he described it as the work of a 'non-knower, a non-can-er'.[2] In the discursive pieces, Beckett toys with, and eventually tries to abandon, those very things which, as critic or as writer, he cannot do, say, or know. The most obvious of the things that it turns out he cannot do are philosophy and aesthetics, at least in any systematic or serious sense. However, in later pieces Beckett undermines the foundations upon which anything serious can be written by the critic. The increasing difficulty Beckett has in being 'serious' means that the artists he chooses to write about begin to resemble, in terms of their function within the texts, characters in his fiction. Thus, as I hope to demonstrate, Beckett's discursive writings lie on a continuum with at one end relatively stable and systematic philosophy, and at the other a continuously self-deconstructing and self-consciously fictive residue of philosophizing.

'Dante. . .Bruno.Vico. .Joyce', which traces James Joyce's indebtedness in his 'Work in progress' (the future *Finnegans wake*) to Dante, Giordano Bruno and Giambattista Vico, is perhaps rather unrepresentative of

Beckett's ideas and interests for two reasons: the philosophical angles were in fact Joyce's idea, and the essay was written at Joyce's behest in order to publicize his forthcoming work. The essay nevertheless prefigures some tendencies in Beckett's own critical writing, perhaps most interestingly in the way that Beckett uses Vico to elaborate his own concerns with the relation between content and form. Vico's empirical investigation of the development of religious language into poetic and philosophical language temporalizes philosophy by relegating it to a stage in the historical development of natural languages. Thus philosophy is robbed of its transcendent status, and form and content become inseparable. Beckett then goes on to apply Vico's insight to Joyce's work: 'Here form *is* content, content *is* form [...] His writing is not *about* something; *it is that something itself*' (D, 27). These statements can, no doubt, be applied to tendencies in Beckett's literary output, yet they also prefigure tendencies in his critical writing. The privileged position that philosophy assumes for itself will gradually disappear in Beckett's later discursive texts. Moreover, it will become clear that the philosopher's untenable position is also that of the critic who sees himself as writing *about* something. Philosophy and criticism share the same assumed perspective, and both imply the same distance between the writer and what he writes *about*. The direction that Beckett's critical writings take gradually serves to demonstrate the untenability of the metatextual status they have apparently assumed for themselves, and which the Beckett scholar may be tempted to claim for them.

Beckett sets about his introduction to Proust by attempting to outline the quite formal philosophical considerations (aesthetic, ethical and metaphysical) that he regards as the foundation of Proust's novel. Proust himself considered *A la recherche* to be 'un ouvrage dogmatique',[3] and Beckett clearly considers it to be founded upon quite clear conceptions about the status of art, habit, memory and time, as well as about the value of existence itself. Yet the origins of the ideas that Beckett plays with are never made clear in *Proust*. Much of the material that Beckett uses in order to create an account of Proust's aesthetic comes from the wealth of comments made by Proust in his novel. However, in addition to this, Beckett draws heavily, throughout *Proust*, on the writings of the nineteenth-century German philosopher Arthur Schopenhauer; Schopenhauer's name, though, is mentioned only four times. The result is that *Proust* often reads like an encounter between Beckett and Schopenhauer, with Proust's novel supplying pertinent material for a philosophical essay. *A la recherche* is filtered first through Proust's own comments, but, more significantly, through Schopenhauer's most important work, *Die Welt als Wille und Vorstellung* (*The world as will and representation*). Beckett's use of quotation marks and page references is decidedly unscholarly, and by blurring the distinction between quotation, paraphrase and his own material, Beckett gives the impression that he sees the aesthetic and ethical systems of Proust and Schopenhauer as virtually identical.

The broadly Schopenhauerian filter that Beckett uses to sift *A la recherche*, while far from arbitrary (Proust does undoubtedly make use of Schopenhauer), is only one of several plausible philosophical filters he might have used. For the Beckett critic, the choice of filter is of greater interest than the matter to be filtered, and it is perhaps methodologically dangerous to dwell too long on the 'treasury of nutshell phrases' (*PTD*, 29) he has gleaned from the novel itself. There is an obvious pitfall in seeking affinities between a critic and his subject; Beckett's admiration for many of the artists he writes on does not necessarily mean that their concerns are the same. The Schopenhauerian filter that Beckett uses is a well-structured combination of pessimism and a tragic view of existence. The Schopenhauerian system, moreover, offers a convenient epistemological 'geometry'. It offers, through artistic contemplation, the possibility of an aloof and stable perspective from which things can be seen in their true essence (in their Ideal form, as Schopenhauer puts it), and ultimately from which the sheer awfulness of the life of the body on earth can be seen. Artistic contemplation is, then, the sole redeeming feature of our existence, because in the disinterested aesthetic experience, we step outside our existence, and outside the futile and endless cycles of willing that characterize it. This heady mixture of idealism and pessimism provides the starting-point to much of Beckett's subsequent discursive writing.

Beckett's analysis of the Proustian aesthetic is centred around an account of the workings of habit upon memory, and the consequences these have for the subjective experience of time. The (Proustian) individual is afflicted by time, for in effect the 'individual' is nothing but a series of individuals. Thus, Beckett states, the desire of an individual at time A cannot be satisfied at time B, for the individual at time B will no longer be the same individual. These individuals are, moreover, afflicted by habit, which, among other things, packages the sensory impressions that the individual receives as motives. The habit-determined mental 'attention'[4] which the subject pays to the object means that his perceptions are ordered in time and space, and assigned a place in a causal chain. The purity of the thoughtless, motiveless impression is thus reduced to the baseness of a utilitarian concept. Indeed, according to Beckett's analysis, voluntary memory, direct perception, conception and even imagination provide nothing but façades which disguise the object. Beckett correctly points out that the only exit that the Proustian subject has from this habit-bound existence is one over which the subject has no control: involuntary memory. For the Proustian subject, the moment of involuntary memory is a moment when, through some external stimulus, circumferential phenomena, stored away in the back of the memory in unconceptualized form, rush back to engulf the subject in their pure and timeless essence. During these miraculous moments, when habit's spell is broken, the subject, too, is liberated from the order of time.

Beckett, more of a Schopenhauerian than a Proustian, filters the whole of Proust's theorizings on time, memory and habit through the aesthetic system of his favourite philosopher. Schopenhauer calls the basic unit of the subject's consciousness *eine Vorstellung* (a representation). Representations, the sum of which constitute the subject's experience of the world, are objects *as they are* for the subject. In virtually all cases, claims Schopenhauer, representations are given shape by the 'principle of sufficient reason'; it is through this principle that the subject's representations are assigned a particular place in time and space, and in chains of cause and effect. To this extent, Schopenhauer is a Kantian. Through this individuating principle, representations are served up as motives. It is in the subject's interest to order things in this way; hence the ordinary way that we see things is in the thrall of the will-to-live. The analogy to Proust is clear, and Beckett recognizes this. He identifies Proustian habit with Schopenhauerian will-to-live. For Schopenhauer, the only way of escaping from this futile force which controls our lives lies in the aesthetic experience, the moment of will-less contemplation when the veil which disguises the object is thrown aside. In these all too rare moments, the subject can contemplate the pure timeless essences of the world, the Platonic Ideas, independently of the principle of sufficient reason. (Although, according to Schopenhauer, works of art are not necessary for an aesthetic experience, works of genius do provide the clearest window onto the Ideas.) Once again, the analogy to Proust is not lost on Beckett; Proustian involuntary memory becomes Schopenhauerian aesthetic experience. Yet here the analogy is not particularly accurate. For Proust, time in its pure state is regained through involuntary memory, whereas for Schopenhauer time is merely obliterated in the rapture of the aesthetic experience. Beckett, therefore, admits that he cannot understand the title of Proust's final book, *Le temps retrouvé* (PTD, 75). Here, as in a few other places, a little conceptual residue betrays the presence of Beckett's discreet Schopenhauerian filter.

From the lofty disinterested heights of aesthetic experience Schopenhauer sees the world as a veritable vale of tears. The world of the ordinary subject, slave as he is of the will-to-live, is one of infinitely frustrated longing. Beckett, seemingly seduced by the power of this world-picture, understands Proust to be a pessimist, an interpretation he was later to regard as 'overstated'.[5] Beckett maintains that music, for the Proustian narrator, reveals life to be a punishment, a pensum, a duty that has to be discharged (*PTD*, 93). He even goes so far as to relate Proust's novel to 'the wisdom of all the sages, from Brahma to Leopardi, the wisdom that consists not in the satisfaction but in the ablation of desire' (*PTD*, 18). The observation that Proust is detached from all moral principles turns into a reworking of Schopenhauer's point that the tragic figure represents the expiation of the sin of having been born. In this connection, he even borrows the Calderón quotation that Schopenhauer uses: '*Pues el delito mayor del hombre es haber nacido*'. Half-remembered snippets of these expressions of pessimism, all taken from Schopenhauer, reappear with some regularity in Beckett's later drama and prose.

Beckett's 'filter' has a strong philosophical structure. But what does he find praiseworthy in the way that Proust writes? Perhaps realizing how dogmatic his own analysis has become, Beckett insists, near the end of the essay, that 'for Proust the quality of language is more important than any system of ethics or aesthetics' (*PTD*, 88). For Beckett, Proust does not evade the implications of the way that those ecstatic moments of involuntary memory have been revealed to him. Proust pursues the Idea rather than the concept. He is not content merely to describe, in the form of notations, surface phenomena. Although apparently analytic, Proust's explanations are experimental; they go in search of the elusive Ideal beneath the surface of concept. His writing is therefore excavatory. In a later short review, 'Proust in pieces' (1934), Beckett writes that *A la recherche* is not the analytic statement of the search, with all its 'plausible frills', but *is* the search itself. Proust, he writes, 'communicates as he can, in dribs and drabs' (*D*, 65). The result is described in *Proust* as a sort of literary impressionism (*PTD*, 86).

Beckett takes sideswipes at contemporary realism and naturalism (which 'worship the offal of experience' (*PTD*, 78)), and at what he sees as the over-conceptualized writing of certain Symbolists. Paraphrasing another critic, Arnaud Dandieu,[6] he contrasts Proust to the classical writer who raises himself artificially out of time to give order to his work. Proust, he claims, has a strong Romantic strain, and thus writes *in* time. It is during those moments of involuntary memory that Proust discovers himself as an artist. As a writer he merely attempts to translate those experiences. Proust himself maintains that as a writer, he is not an artist, but an artisan (*PTD*, 84). Hence, whilst a way out of habit-bound perception is possible in involuntary memory, the images of involuntary memory cannot be recalled and put into words without a loss. Therefore Proust's writing has to remain 'the indirect and comparative expression of indirect and comparative perception' (*PTD*, 88). This is, perhaps, for Beckett, the central problematic of the writer, and it remains, of course, a major theme in his work right through to the 'ill seen ill said' of his late prose. It is the eventual abandonment of even the possibility of the kind of exit provided by involuntary memory, the possibility of access to another space, which determines the direction that his later discursive writing takes.

'Humanistic quietism' (1934), a review of a collection of poems by Thomas MacGreevy, represents, if anything, a more idealist account of literature than *Proust*. There is, it must be said, something rather artificial or even pretentious about the extravagant claims Beckett makes for his friend's poetry. Yet this element of pretence is significant, for the structures which Beckett uses are of the kind that are dismantled in his later writings on aesthetics. According to Beckett, what distinguishes poetry from other literary forms is that it represents the only way out of the prison formed by ordinary or non-poetic language. MacGreevy's poetry, a kind of 'prayer', simultaneously opens up a space beyond language and condemns ordinary language, 'the tongue-tied profanity' (*D*, 68), to a secondary and impotent status. The article is constructed on the same philosophical 'geometry' as *Proust*. It consists of a first space which is the conceptual prison of language, and a second space, arrived at almost miraculously through the power of poetry, which is like that of the Schopenhauerian aesthetic experience. This second space is not only one which affords a sort of clarity of vision, but one which condemns ordinary language to an enfeebled status.

This geometry is developed much further in the highly revealing letter Beckett wrote (in German) in 1937 to Axel Kaun. In this letter, Beckett sets out what he thinks ought now to be the aims of writing: he wishes to see a kind of writing – a 'Literatur des Unworts' (a 'literature of the unword') (*D*, 54) – that can penetrate the veil of words. Beckett's ideas, which here have an apparently Modernist edge, still derive their shape from the Schopenhauerian aesthetic of *Proust*. Ordinary language, like any form of representation, is but a veil, but poetic language should be able to tear aside the veil and point to a space beyond representation, thus revealing words for what they are: merely a veil. What lies beyond this veil, though, remains unknown. It may be nothingness, and art in general may only be able to point to the opaque nature of representation rather than to any real object beyond it. Beckett is now noticeably more reserved about the kinds of art that can escape the impositions of representation. Music, he claims, is able to penetrate its own surface: he cites Beethoven's Seventh Symphony as an example. Literature, however, has been unsuccessful, although he does believe that Gertrude Stein's 'logographs' have revealed a certain 'porous' nature in language. Beckett suggests that ironically drawing attention to this closed nature of language might be a necessary stage in undermining old forms of writing. This may not be enough, though, and he wonders whether the irredeemably corrupted game should be given up altogether. The tension between making the game work and giving up, with its ethical overtones, reappears both in later discursive writings and in his later literary output, most noticeably in *L'Innommable/The Unnamable*.

The Axel Kaun letter is ostensibly a programme for a future mode of writing, and it marks a break with earlier, more optimistic, views about the power of poetry. Yet despite that break, Beckett's views are still dogmatically sceptical with regard to language; his philosophical vision still encompasses spaces both inside and outside the prison of words. What bars us from the second space seems almost impenetrable, yet the more impenetrable it becomes, the more Beckett blocks off his own justification for using the picture in the first place. If the subject can have no conception of anywhere else, how can it know it is trapped? Hence his position seems somewhat ironic, for the aesthetician is assuming for himself the very powers he has denied the artist. This position, which had seemed unproblematic when there was a means of access from the first space to the second, now begins to look a little shaky. Up until the Axel Kaun letter, Beckett's discursive writing focuses almost exclusively on the expressive possibilities of art, and in particular literary language. His increasing pessimism in this respect means that a second dimension to his discursive writing has to develop. This will, in post-war articles, take the form of a steady ironization of the critical perspective itself, and an undermining of the possibility of saying anything serious about art.

Meanwhile, the definition of an art more restricted in its scope continues in journalistic reviews. In 'Intercessions by Denis Devlin' (1938), Beckett identifies qualities in Devlin's poetry that he sees in *A la recherche*: he praises Devlin's highly imaged writing, and the minimal interference of the rational. The suggestion that any form of art has a privileged position is now firmly rebuffed. 'The time,' he writes, 'is perhaps not altogether too green for the vile suggestion that art has nothing to do with clarity, does not dabble in the clear and does not make clear' (*D*, 94). Art is now trapped in the world, and is no longer an alternative space. Exits to a space where the subject can have complete access to the object have disappeared. There is no way out for the artist, and, since art represented the only way out of the conceptual prison short of total silence, the human condition possesses no way out either. This sense of being trapped is articulated in 'MacGreevy on Yeats' (1945), a review of MacGreevy's study of the painter Jack B. Yeats (W. B. Yeats' brother), where Beckett describes Yeats as bringing light to the 'issueless predicament of existence' (*D*, 97). The predicaments of the artist and the human being are thus the same: both issueless, they are without exit, solution or outcome.

On a less abstract level, 'MacGreevy on Yeats' demonstrates Beckett's rejection of the nationalistic side of much contemporary Irish writing. He denies that Yeats' true importance lies in his supposed position as 'the national painter' of Ireland. An earlier article, 'Recent Irish poetry', pseudonymously published in 1934, contains a diatribe against the 'antiquarian' Celtic twilighter tendency of many of his contemporaries in the Irish Free State; Beckett rounds on these poets for ignoring the twentieth-century 'breakdown of the object' and for 'delivering with the altitudinous complacency of the Victorian Gael the Ossianic goods' (D, 70). That Beckett believed politicians should not interfere in art is undeniable; he praises Proust's detachment from moral considerations, but rounds on him for occasionally raising his voice with 'the plebs, mob, rabble, canaille' (PTD, 66f.). That is not to say, however, that Beckett's discursive writing never has a direct political edge, for he launches a scathing attack on the parochialism and philistinism of Ireland's censorship laws in a commissioned yet unpublished article 'Censorship in the Saorstat' (1935) – now available in Disjecta.

'MacGreevy on Yeats' marks several points of change and departure in Beckett's discursive writing. First, most of the subsequent texts are written, initially at least, in French, Three dialogues with Georges Duthuit (1949) being a notable exception. Second, it is perhaps the last piece where the critical voice stands aloof from the aesthetic problematic, before being caught up in its own inexorable deconstructive logic. Third, Beckett switches his attention, in this and subsequent essays, away from literature and towards painting. The initial aim of these pieces is to give an account of particular explorations of the expressive limitations of painting. However, they also explore language's impotence in the face of visual images, and the instability of the philosophical foundations upon which art-criticism of this kind is built. The result is that whilst the logical centre of the essays may be the painters and their paintings, these can seem curiously absent. Just as Mr Knott's world – the logical centre of Watt – becomes a sort of hidden vehicle for an exploration of the communicative failings of language, so painting gives way to the word in essays that are ostensibly about painting. Once again, we can see that Beckett's works are not really about something; they are that something themselves.

Beckett's next two essays, 'La peinture des van Velde ou le monde et le pantalon' (1945) and 'Peintres de l'empêchement' (1948), are written on his friends the brothers Geer and Bram van Velde, two Dutch painters working in Paris during the post-war period. The first of these essays is a long and uncomfortable mixture of disparate elements: an anti-intellectual defence of the art-world's *petit peuple*, obscurantist sideswipes at critics and criticism, and a highly ironic piece of speculative aesthetics. At least Beckett recognizes this, calling it 'un bavardage désagréable et confus' (D, 119). It is nevertheless possible to discern that the essay revolves around the discussion of two subject–object relations: that between the viewer (or critic) and the painting, and that between the painter and his object.

Beckett starts from the premise that the painting is a pure object, which, as it were, waits to be disfigured by human attention. It is, in its pristine state, 'un non-sens'. The disfigurement is 'un double massacre' perpetrated by perception and conception; the 'risible imprinte cérébrale' is disfigured even further by the 'assassinat verbal' (D, 124). The object is ill seen, the image ill said. Beckett holds out the faint hope of a pure subject, for he praises the simple *amateur* who might wander into the gallery off the street, and who is ignorant of the advice given by legions of aestheticians, art-historians and critics. This, however, is hardly a convincing model for the disinterested subject of aesthetic perception, and further scattered comments throughout the essay suggest that Beckett is not convinced either. What he seems to be after is less a simple art-lover than a will-less deaf-mute with an incapacity to differentiate time: a sort of ascetic simpleton.

The van Veldes, Beckett claims, realize the impossibility of representation. In the irreparable breakdown of subject and object, he goes on to claim, Geer's paintings somehow escape from the condition of space, and Bram's from the condition of time. By exploring the boundaries of art, they are exploring the boundaries of the human condition, which interests them more than painting. How, though, can Beckett as critic, know this, say this, write this? He, like the loquacious *amateurs* he describes, cannot leave the art-object alone. He too must drag it into 'une sorte de ronde syntaxique' (D, 125). So the essay struggles frantically with the illegitimacy of its own philosophical conceptualization, which allows the critic the transcendent perspective that it has disallowed everyone; everyone, that is, except perhaps for Bram, who, far from being 'un cochon d'intellectual', has no idea about what he has done in painting until about ten years after the event.

The problem Beckett faces now is how to find any stable background against which to write about art. In 'Peintres de l'empêchement', Beckett tries a different approach. Instead of continuing the impossible search for a philosophical justification, he suggests that the critic might attempt to *create* one. By affirming something, and remaining faithful to it through constant repetition, one can hold a solid opinion on just about anything, he claims, tongue half in cheek. Beckett seems to be asking whether a conscious forgetting of the necessarily self-undermining element in any adopted system of aesthetics might be possible in order to get on with the business of describing modern paintings. Thus Beckett's attempts to describe the subject–object relation dissolve into an attempt to create a definition of the crisis inherent in modern art: philosophical statement becomes a declaratory speech-act aimed at *creating* a philosophical stability. The single constative gives way to the reiterated performative. The creation of a stable background, though, has no more truth-value than any piece of fiction. Yet, Beckett suggests, philosophical foundations are not, and never have been, anything more than this anyway. So what is undermined in 'Peintres de l'empêchement' is not merely the philosophical structure Beckett has been using, but the last possibility of any *seriousness* of philosophical intent. The philosopher, it seems, cannot be serious, because the language he uses is unstable. Under the old certainties of the Schopenhauerian system, it was art that provided access to a stable position which made things clear and guaranteed seriousness. That channel (or door, or issue, or borehole, or any other metaphor Beckett uses in his philosophical geometry) is now closed as much for the philosopher/aesthetician as for the artist himself. This does not mean, however, that the essay is reduced to the level of a joke. Despite the apparently fatal blow to seriousness, the essay seems to cling to the hope of stability, and desperately struggles to remain upright. So the serious aesthetician in Beckett's discursive writings finds himself in that familiar Beckettian position of 'I can't go on, I'll go on'. He is once again left in an essentially ethical dilemma, torn between the hopeless desire to bring the philosophical game to an end and the equally hopeless desire to make the game work, and once again all that is left in his wake is an accumulation of words.

What Beckett puts forward in this half-serious manner in 'Peintres de l'empêchement' is an attractively symmetrical piece of idealist aesthetics. His 'argument' is as follows. The essence of the object of representation in art is its unrepresentability. The van Veldes, he maintains, are resigned to this. Nevertheless, they do end up representing something as if by chance. The new object of Geer's painting consists in those qualities of the object ('l'empêchement–objet') that prevent him from seeing it. The new object of Bram's painting consists in the subjective conditions of representation ('l'empêchement–œil') that prevent him from seeing the object. Beckett suggests that there are now three routes open to art: to return to an old and discredited naïvety and to ignore the subject–object problematic; to continue to struggle with the old subject–object relation; or the van Veldes' way, which admits defeat but finds a new object in the conditions of unrepresentability. In this respect, something is salvaged from the old subject–object crisis, and so the paintings of Geer and Bram van Velde might be described as successes. The description of total capitulation and its conditions is left until *Three dialogues with Georges Duthuit*.

Beckett remarked to the critic Martin Esslin that he had written the *Three dialogues up* rather than *down* (D, 14). He described them as a very free reflection of the conversations he had had with Georges Duthuit, the then editor of the Parisian review *transition* (D, 14). This dramatization makes the simple identification of the two interlocutors B and D as Beckett and Duthuit problematic. The title of course means that on one level this identification is possible, but the reduction of names to initials also implies that the aesthetic theory is held at arm's length: it becomes less serious, more fictionalized. By distancing himself from B, Beckett can avoid some of the deconstructive irony of the two previous essays, and avoid the implosions inherent in trying to write from the point of view of the serious philosopher. So the *Three dialogues* enjoy a status somewhere between philosophical aesthetics and dramatized repartee. The dialogue form leaves no space for 'serious' authorial intervention, either to come to the aid of or to ironize B's theorizing. In the less confined space of the dialogue form, the contradictions and lacunae of B's theorizing can be highlighted.

Overall, what has happened in Beckett's aesthetic theorizing looks like a sort of Derridean manoeuvre. The deconstructive logic that undermines the marginal space *within* Beckett's theory (the space of the aesthetic experience) has been turned inside out to undermine the marginal space that Beckett himself occupies *outside* his own theory. Its clarity and seriousness are undermined, but not destroyed. So the drama we are presented with in the *Three dialogues* is a kind of endgame of aesthetic theorizing; it is a drama which is neither entirely serious nor entirely playful, but one where playfulness and seriousness continuously infect one another.

The *Three dialogues* represent something of a terminus in Beckett's discursive writing. They are a recapitulation on the failings of modern art, but unlike his earlier essays, they no longer point a way forward, however limited, for Western art; instead they appear to recommend total capitulation. In the first dialogue, B rejects the view, held by D and most commentators, that painters such as the early Matisse and the Breton Tal-Coat (Pierre Jacob) deviate from the path so far taken by Western art. B sees Tal-Coat's painting as 'thrusting towards a more adequate expression of natural experience'. According to B, all Western artists have struggled, in one way or another, to make representation work and thereby to 'gain' something. Their concerns have been with the possibilities of art. Some, like Tal-Coat, may have 'disturbed a certain order on the plane of the feasible', but they have never 'stirred from the field of the possible'. B speaks of a new (and apparently logically impossible) art, which has finally abandoned feasibility, 'an art turning from it in disgust, weary of its puny exploits, weary of pretending to be able, of being able, of doing a little better the same old thing, of going a little further along a dreary road' (D, 138–9). Whilst Tal-Coat and the early Matisse cling to a belief in the possibilities of art, André Masson, according to B, tries to salvage something from the wreck of the subject–object relation. He does not try to make representation work, but attempts instead to operate from the occasion of its impossibility. Even Masson, says B, 'continues to wriggle' (D, 140).

Bram van Velde (Geer having been jettisoned) represents a totally new direction for B: so different, in fact, that his work has taken him into waters that are not so much uncharted as logically unchartable. B's view of Bram van Velde's work has gone beyond the views expressed in Beckett's earlier essays, where both van Veldes were pushing the subject–object relation to its limits. Bram van Velde has, according to B, accepted, apparently unknowingly, the impossibility of any degree of adequacy of expression in art. Yet his paintings are not *about* that impossibility either: he does not even possess the certitude that expression is impossible. As an artist, Bram van Velde simply *fails*. In a clear example of that ambiguously playful quality, B comes to the logically absurd conclusion, only after a fortnight's deliberation, that van Velde's paintings are inexpressive. B's only means of justifying this self-falsifying claim is that van Velde's paintings are just very different from any paintings that precede them.

From what B says in the dialogues, van Velde comes over as a species of total ascetic, who lives in an impenetrable world, and whose paintings are wholly inexpressive. Like a hermit, or a Schopenhauerian 'saint' wearily abandoning the will-to-live, he turns his back in disgust on the world, which, in his case, consists in nothing more than the endless strivings of modern art. In these dialogues, painting is van Velde's whole way of being. As a painter, he is obliged to paint as much, and as little, as a human is obliged to live. Yet his painting is impossible; 'can't' meets 'must' head on, and the inevitable result is failure. Van Velde is, according to B, the only artist brave enough to admit, albeit apparently unknowingly, that 'to be an artist is to fail, as no other dare fail' (D, 145). Thus his whole way of being is as much in his failing as in his painting.

There is, of course, an almost overwhelming temptation, especially since Beckett once stated 'I'm working with impotence, ignorance',[7] to read what B says about van Velde as a literary credo on Beckett's part. It is not; brushstrokes are not words, and words, even Beckett's words, are not inexpressive in that sort of way, nor could they be. Beckett's works bear tribute to the fact that words can never undo themselves and turn into a 'literature of the unword', however desirable this may seem. *Three dialogues with Georges*

Duthuit is not simply a metatext. The world of the Bram van Velde of the dialogues (rather than the real-life person) is a totally closed world, and because of this, he plays the same role in the *Three dialogues* as do, for example, Mr Endon in *Murphy* and Mr Knott in *Watt*. Bram van Velde is perhaps the last in the series of total ascetics whose world is unsuccessfully transmitted through the mediating figures of reporters, narrators and critics.

The total inaccessibility of Bram van Velde's vision (as portrayed by B) completes the separation (started, perhaps unwittingly, back in the Axel Kaun letter) of the artist's and the critic's zones. Communication between one and the other has become impossible. B cannot understand van Velde ultimately because he is not van Velde. B can offer no more than a picture of what he is 'pleased to fancy he [van Velde] does' (*D*, 144). He admits that *what* van Velde is and does is more than likely quite otherwise. Thus we come to the unhappy conclusion that the *Three dialogues* are not about van Velde (or Tal-Coat, or Masson) at all, but are merely a statement of B's fancy. The critic cannot step outside his own prison of words. Art, in the earlier essays, had provided access to a common ground where subjectivity could negate itself and step outside itself. The transformation could not be more total, for now every subject is trapped inside its own world.

How van Velde sees the world is inaccessible to B; so, too, is how B sees the world to D who, like the psychiatric nurses at Murphy's mental hospital, functions as a 'sane eye'. B's views neither make sense to D, nor, ultimately to a reader looking for a stable argument. When B does attempt to outline the philosophical framework that he uses, it collapses into a jokey non-seriousness. Even in a quasi-dramatic form, Beckett fails to draw up stable, coherent ground-rules for discussing the subject–object relation. We are shown the impossibility of foundation; there is nowhere to start, for as B's admission that he cannot properly say anything about van Velde shows, the real discussion never got started anyway. What van Velde in fact is and does was never really on the agenda, and so the whole text has been circling around an absent centre.

However deconstructive the logic of his philosophizing may be, Beckett can never quite stop playing the game; he cannot bring himself to turn from it in disgust. That sense of having to go on, whatever the odds, continues beyond the *Three dialogues*, which is as much an acceptance of the contra-dictions of systematization as a signal of its end. A tone of weary acceptance creeps into 'Henri Hayden, homme–peintre' (1952), when Beckett writes, 'elle n'est pas au bout de ses beaux jours, la crise sujet–objet' (*D*, 146). Traces of Beckett's earlier idealist 'geometry' reappear in *témoignages* such as 'Hommage à Jack B. Yeats' (1954) and in 'Pour Avigdor Arikha' (1966). In these *témoignages* and in the later short prose texts, the narrating voice struggles to capture evanescent images, yet underneath these assaults on the image, the voice makes desperate attempts to provide the text with a solid enough basis to last for a paragraph or the space of a sentence. (An example of this compulsion can be found in 'Se voir', written in the 1960s, which opens 'Tout ce qu'il faut savoir pour dire est su', a phrase reduced to its desperate minimum in the opening phrase of *Bing*, 'tout su'.[8]) In the later prose, snatches of philosophical/aesthetic discourse reappear as paragraphs, sentences or short phrases in almost neurotic attempts to provide the text with a stable self-containment. The following paragraph from *Worstward Ho* (1983) can be read as an attempt to create or reaffirm foundations for the text. Yet it is also a passage which retraces, from the writing subject's eventual isolated position inside the first space, the course, both described and enacted in Beckett's discursive writing, of the gradual abandonment of the second space, that of the philosophical/aesthetic/critical perspective:

> A place. Where none. A time when try see. Try say. How small. How vast. How if not boundless bounded. Whence the dim. Not now. Know better now. Unknow better now. Know only no out of. No knowing how know only no out of. Into only. Hence another. Another place where none. Whither once whence no return. No. No place but the one. None but the one where none. Whence never once in. Somehow in. Beyondless. Thenceless there. Thitherless there. Thenceless thitherless there. (*NO*, 104)

NOTES

1 This was John Fletcher's warning, in 1964, in 'Beckett et Proust', 90.
2 Israel Shenker, 'An interview with Beckett', *New York Times*, 5 May 1956, reprinted in Lawrence Graver and Raymond Federman (eds.), *Samuel Beckett: the critical heritage* (London: Routledge and Kegan Paul, 1979), 148.
3 Letter to Jacques Rivière, 7 February 1914, in Philippe Kolb (ed.), *Correspondance de Marcel Proust* (Paris: Plon, 1970–), vol. XIII, 98f.
4 Beckett's use of the word 'attention' seems to owe something to his reading of the nominalist philosopher Fritz Mauthner. 'Attention' seems to correspond to Mauthner's use of the term 'Aufmerksamkeit', which distorts perceptions and turns them into motives, in his most important work, of 1901–2, *Beiträge zu einer Kritik der Sprache* (Hildesheim: Georg Olms Verlagsbuchhandlung, 1967–9).
5 See John Pilling, 'Beckett's *Proust*' in *Journal of Beckett Studies*, I (1976), 24.
6 As John Fletcher points out in 'Beckett et Proust', Beckett paraphrases material he has taken from Arnaud Dandieu, *Marcel Proust, sa révélation psychologique* (Paris: Librairie de Paris, 1930).
7 Shenker interview in Graver and Federman (eds.), *Samuel Beckett: the critical heritage*, 148.
8 'Se voir' in *Pour finir encore et autres foirades* (Paris: Editions de Minuit, 1976), 51, and 'Bing' in *Têtes-mortes* (Paris: Éditions de Minuit, 1967), 61. (English versions: 'Closed space', 199, and 'Ping', 149, in *CSP*.)

RECOMMENDED READING

Acheson, James, 'Schopenhauer, Proust and Beckett', *Contemporary Literature*, 19 (1978), 165–79.

Fletcher, John, 'Beckett et Proust', *Caliban*, 1, Toulouse: Université de Toulouse le Mirail (January 1964), 89–100.

Harvey, Lawrence, *Samuel Beckett: poet and critic*, Princeton University Press, 1970, chapter 10.

Karátson, André, 'Le Nirvana comme supplice de Tantale: note sur Beckett et Schopenhauer', *Roman 20–50*, 6 (December 1988), 117–23.

Miller, Lawrence, *Samuel Beckett: the expressive dilemma*, London: Macmillan, 1992, chapter 2.

Morse, J. Mitchell, '"The ideal core of the onion": Samuel Beckett's criticism', *French Review*, 38.1 (October 1964), 23–9.

Pilling, John, 'A poetics of indigence', in James Knowlson and John Pilling, *Frescoes of the skull: the later prose and drama of Samuel Beckett*, London: John Calder, 1979, 241–56.

Pothast, Ulrich, *Die eigentliche metaphysiche Tätigkeit: über Schopenhauers Ästhetik und ihre Anwendung durch Samuel Beckett*, Frankfurt-am-Main: Suhrkamp, 1983.

Read, David, 'Artistic theory in the work of Samuel Beckett', *Journal of Beckett Studies*, 8 (1982), 7–22.

Rosen, Steven, *Samuel Beckett and the pessimistic tradition*, New Brunswick, N.J.: Rutgers University Press, 1976, 123–230.

Zurbrugg, Nicholas, *Beckett and Proust*, Gerrards Cross: Colin Smythe, 1988.

2

JOHN PILLING

Beckett's English fiction

Les formes sont variées où l'immuable se soulage d'être sans forme.

(Malone meurt)

Beckett could hardly perhaps have more perfectly exemplified Malone's dictum – 'The forms are many in which the unchanging seeks relief from its formlessness'[1] – than by choosing both French and English as expressive mediums, and then translating from one to the other. In so strikingly hybridized a context even to speak of 'the English fiction' runs the risk of seeming simply a convenient construct ill-adapted to what is in reality, if not a confused, then at least a potentially confusing state of affairs. But even Beckett's extraordinary writing career began with due deference to the compromise of composing in his mother tongue, so that for all practical purposes there is a kind of logic in reserving 'the English fiction' for the body of work he produced before turning forty. The work in question comprises three novels – *Murphy, Watt,* and *Dream of fair to middling women* (the last to surface but the first to be written); three stories – *Assumption, A case in a thousand* and *Echo's bones* (none of them strictly part of the corpus as Beckett came to conceive it); a book of prose fiction that is not quite a novel and not quite a collection of short stories – *More pricks than kicks*; and a scatter of non-fictional items more or less ancillary to his narrative enterprises.[2] Even within the restricted focus of this English fiction, however, the forms – as Malone the writer was well-placed to recall – were many and various; so numerous, indeed, that it remains a moot point whether they can reasonably be said to have brought complete relief from 'formlessness', or to have offered unambiguous evidence on the matter of 'the unchanging', itself an ill-defined notion at best. What is certainly clear is that the young Beckett and the Beckett of early middle-age, though greatly gifted, suffered from a fiction-making impulse or compulsion that was constrained to flow, in part at least, in conventional channels, even as it manifested itself in a more or less heterodox fashion which threatened to exhaust, expose and, in due course, dispense with all conventions whatsoever.

Beckett's English fiction, for all its many virtues (some of which are in shorter supply later), can legitimately be seen as a forced growth: extremely ambitious, courageously experimental, but a little too exotic (with the obvious exception of *Murphy*) to take root and be widely admired. Even *Murphy*, as some letters from Beckett to his friend Thomas MacGreevy indicate, left its author feeling that 'the difficulty and danger' of it all had not been wholly successfully negotiated (*D*, 102). However, both before and beyond *Murphy* Beckett faced difficulties and dangers less amenable to solution; and he was impelled – as his recalcitrant temperament operated on intrinsically refractory materials – to thrive as best he could with the residue of unresolved problems. Though his difficulties remain very visible in a number of the early fictions, they are nowhere better indicated than in a brief book review of 1934, which appeared almost a month to the day after Beckett's first appearance before the general public with creative work in prose: *More pricks than kicks*. In assessing an academic study of how Proust had composed *A la recherche du temps perdu*, and in finding its author deficient in preferring 'the narrational trajectory that is more like a respectable parabola and less like the chart of an ague', Beckett observed:

> If there is *mésalliance*, as for the purists there must be, it was there from the start. And is it not precisely this conflict between intervention and quietism [...] and its statement without the plausible frills that constitute the essence of Proust's originality? (*D*, 65)

In these comments the very fervency with which Beckett rushes to Proust's defence – no doubt partly prompted by the feeling that his own 1931 study of the subject ought to have dispelled such misapprehensions – is an index of the man behind the reviewer, or rather the creative artist very much, and in some ways very justly, in thrall to his own originality. Appropriately enough, on the dust-jacket of *More pricks* – its full title perfectly foregrounding a *mésalliance* carefully framed to upset 'the purists' – Beckett's blurb-writer perpetrated a common enough cliché which posterity at least could wholeheartedly subscribe to: 'Here is a new independent spirit at work.'[3]

Beckett's book review of 1934 is surprisingly consonant with at least the language, if not the tone, of his *Three dialogues with Georges Duthuit* published fifteen years later.[4] In the first of the *Three dialogues* Beckett finds the painter Pierre Tal-Coat 'straining to enlarge the statement of a compromise' (*PTD*, 102), a strategy he by no means deplores, although he emphatically registers the shortcomings of any such confinement to 'the field

of the possible' (*PTD*, 103). Much like his comments on Proust, this judgment can easily enough be applied to his own creative predicament in the
fiction of the 1930s, a period decisively supplanted in his own mind, by the
time of his conversations with Duthuit, by four feverish years of writing in
French. In his English fiction Beckett is continually chafing against the
boundaries of 'the field of the possible' without finally transcending them;
some strain, and some compromise, naturally eventuate. It is as if, in spite of
believing that 'statement without the plausible frills' (*D*, 65) is all that
matters, Beckett cannot quite free himself of recidivist tendencies.

Though the general reader is as yet in no position to pursue the issue fully
– even with *Dream of fair to middling women* at last available – Beckett's
earliest fictional impulses were statemental with a vengeance, almost as
though any statement would serve his purpose so long as it was he himself
making it. His first published story, *Assumption*, opens with a typically disquieting and destabilizing stab at possibility and impossibility: 'He could
have shouted and could not.' The two 'could's are grammatically and semantically incommensurable, though lexically identical. And though there is
much else of more substantive interest in this (very) short story, nothing else
in it is quite so linguistically riveting. Beckett seems almost to be exploiting,
or at least exploring, the ambiguous area in English – much more clearly
defined in modern Romance languages – where subjunctives and modal
auxiliaries tend to become confused. The sentence in question acts as a kind
of call to attention, or as an invitation, not easily avoided, to the reader to
re-read and unscramble it; its very brevity seems to conspire in this miniature drama of pre-emptive activity. (Since the production of fiction pre-
cludes the 'relief' that in real life could be obtained by shouting, Beckett
needs to do something comparable to feel comfortable at all, even at the
expense of discomforting the reader.) After this first sentence, however, he
abandons this mode, necessarily perhaps, since it threatens to issue in statements that cannot easily be got beyond. In the rest of *Assumption* he writes
principally as if on his mettle to emulate the notoriously long sentences
characteristic of Proust, a task to which Beckett, at the age of twenty-three,
cannot really be said to be suited, as this curious first sentence has already
obliquely indicated. In the ensuing rhetorical flux, which absolutely lacks
the clarity upon which Proust's elephantine utterances depend, desperation
and perspiration are uppermost, and communication comes to seem a
secondary or tertiary matter.

Assumption is a most curious affair. After the galvanizing precision of its
opening (disguised as a confusion), it leaves its reader with a cluster of hazy
impressions that are the product of abrogating the end-stopping tactic with
which it has begun. Of the impressions with any real claim upon us the most

important is perhaps the unnamed protagonist's profound, but obscure, need to transcend the mundane world. This need, a need not quite vigorously enough engaged in to be called a quest, is given a quasi-mystical aura, but without any accredited mystical base being provided as a context. The very catholicity of the emblems of transcendence generated – the 'blue flower' of German Romanticism (and specifically Novalis), the star Vega and GOD in full capitals – is an index of the desperation that this figure, and by extension his author, is feeling. Yet the prose employed to convey this is flabby and turgid, a poor substitute for the shout which, as the first sentence tells us, has been stifled from within or without. *Assumption* is best read as wish-fulfilment rather than achievement, even in the most limited sense of the word. But perhaps its principal claim to a residual kind of fame is as Beckett's first attempt to write against the empiricist grain of the English language, the outcome of which is to make the piece read as if it had been translated out of some other tongue. It certainly resonates disconcertingly with the claim Beckett made – and in the same issue of the magazine *transition* – in the essay 'Dante...Bruno.Vico..Joyce': 'No language is so abstracted as English. It is abstracted to death' (*D*, 28). *Assumption*, very ironically in the circumstances, offers an English too abstracted to be vivid, whatever virtues of momentum its free-wheeling syntax may possess, and in human terms a figure, the first of many, ruefully but mercifully resolving his predicament by the way of the rare (in Beckett's world) benediction of death.

Assumption is a 'finished' work in terms of its minimal plot, if in no other respect. Beckett's first attempt at a novel, *Dream of fair to middling women*, has much more subject-matter (though even less plot in a teleological sense), but was never finished. *Dream* is a pot-pourri of volatile but irreconcilable elements, part-autobiography, part-fiction, and part-looseleaf folder for any passing expressive gesture. By comparison with *Assumption* it is undoubtedly a kind of 'shout' conducted – if the word is not too strong – against all the mysterious odds that seem to be marshalled to prevent it. A useful thumbnail description of *Dream* occurs in a poem ('Alba') written shortly after the novel was abandoned, and prosaically prefigured in the torso we have: 'a statement of itself drawn across a tempest of emblems' (*Dream*, 181).[5] It is *Dream*'s 'tempest of emblems' aspect that will most strike anyone coming to it sixty years after it was first committed to paper; but only as something akin to a 'total object, complete with missing parts' (*PTD*, 101) does it seem to approach the self-standing condition of being 'a statement of itself'. *Dream* illustrates the degree to which the young Beckett felt a compulsive need to dramatize his life, combined with a no less pressing urge to conceal himself from the public gaze. In *Dream* he accomplished the second of these largely, one suspects, by default; for surely no publisher would have scrupled to encourage him in the first. In the event, with an unfinished work on his hands, Beckett was offered the opportunity to stand back and assess the damage, and then to mine *Dream* for whatever might pass muster under the aegis of *More pricks than kicks*. As the dramatization of a life, however, *Dream* is an endlessly fascinating document, embodying the *Angst* of a young man who had thrown up a potentially brilliant academic career for the very much less secure world of creative (or, as Beckett saw it, 'uncreative' and 'discreative') writing, and it also offers us our first glimpse of some of the fictional prophylactics that would later temper, if not entirely remove, his anguish.

Even with *Dream* now public property, *More pricks than kicks* can still be seen as the book that launched Beckett's unusually brief career as an English writer. *More pricks*, although as 'independent' in spirit as any blurb-writer could wish, is relatively conventional in other respects, a surprisingly speedy compromise having supplanted the virtuosic frenzy of *Dream*. The fictional domain that emerges is in fact more formally and more decently colonized than Beckett's outrageous title might incline one to expect. Gone, or more carefully recessed, are the *obiter dicta* on a multiplicity of subjects that make *Dream* dizzying and indeed dream-like; Beckett remains for the most part on his fictional best behaviour, whilst from time to time indicating how irksome he finds it. The radical oddity of *Dream* – written in the belief that 'Here form *is* content, content *is* form' (D, 27; in reality a licence for content to roam free and far afield, with form spluttering to keep up) – is reduced in *More pricks* by the expedient of imposing a distance between the authorial presence and the characters, of whom only Belacqua, a survivor from *Dream*'s practice-pad, along with some incidents in which he participates, really matters. With the introduction of the kind of settled perspective that *Dream* disavows and disregards, Beckett is forced to kowtow to some traditional imperatives: meaningful interaction between distinctive personalities, and a shaped plot illustrating and elaborating a paraphrasable truth. Where *Dream* buried telling local effects in a welter of endless flow, *More pricks* applies the brake, manufacturing 'a hitch in the lyrical loinstring' (as an early poem[6] puts it), and actively soliciting the attention of the careful and patient reader. Having established a much more instrumental evenness of tone, Beckett can situate his idiosyncratic proclivities where they will do least damage: as constitutive elements of the character Belacqua (the 'reasons' why he is so and not otherwise) and as intriguingly enigmatic plot-lines freighted with loaded, not to say coded, messages. *More pricks* disperses *Dream*'s high-pressure compounds, in which generic considerations principally provide a focus of parody, and redistributes Beckett's scepticism in such a way that it seems fruitless to inquire whether we have to do here with a collection of ten semi-congruent short stories, or with ten episodes of a life which have somehow failed to compose themselves into a novel. 'The danger', Beckett had written a few years before (in the programmatic opening to 'Dante. . .Bruno.Vico. .Joyce'), 'is in the neatness of identifications' (D, 19), and More pricks remains something of an affront to neatness even as if seeks to respect the terms of a truce hastily drawn up to end hostilities.

The material in More pricks which survives transplantation from Dream – 'The Smeraldina's billet-doux' verbatim and 'A wet night' with relatively minor revision – stands up well enough when divorced from its matrix, which speaks volumes for the endlessly disintegrative potential of the earlier experiment. Yet neither of these items, nor the longest sustained story ('What a misfortune'), represent More pricks at its best, and perhaps only real Beckett devotees – reinforced by acquaintance with the excised eleventh story ('Echo's bones') – can feel comfortable with the otherwise lame coda to the collection ('Draff'). The remainder – the first three stories, the fifth and sixth, and the last but one – are of variable quality, both as a group and in themselves, but they benefit from Beckett confining the action to two principal individuals ('A wet night' and 'What a misfortune' have large cast lists), and concentrating on the perenially interesting differentials of l'amour and la mort. These traditional bedfellows are foregrounded by way of a line from the poet Ronsard in the story whose very title ('Love and Lethe', MPTK, 105) insists upon their association, and indeed effectively offers them as the categories most applicable to the book as a whole. La mort proves (even without 'Echo's bones') uppermost in Belacqua's destiny, although l'amour gives him plenty of problems before death supervenes. The dominance of la mort over l'amour – momentarily suspended at the end of 'Love and Lethe' – is obliquely prefigured from the outset, in the conclusion to the first and best-known story, 'Dante and the lobster'. Belacqua, already identified as a person fastidious to a fault where food is concerned, has arrived for dinner with his 'lousy old bitch of an aunt', having brought with him a lobster ordered early in the day, which he has collected for her from the fishmonger's. The verbal exchanges between them in the kitchen establish Belacqua's ignorance of (and his aunt's insensitivity to) the fact that lobsters must be cooked live, with the story ending at a point of suspension just previous to the demise of the crustacean:

> She lifted the lobster clear of the table. It had about three seconds to live.
> Well, thought Belacqua, it's a quick death, God help us all.
> It is not. (MPTK, 21)

'It is not' represents Beckett at his most statemental, and it is the most extreme instance in *More pricks* of the 'intervention' that Beckett needed to instil vigour into his 'quietism', to borrow the key terms of his 1934 book review (*D*, 65). It also re-animates, though this time (and more aptly) at the end rather than at a beginning, the 'not'-factor evident in *Assumption*. Also, although the link is more tenuous, it prefigures the 'Parthian shot' of Christ on the cross ('it is finished': *consummatum est*) which exercises the thoughts of Murphy in Beckett's first published novel (*Mu*, 52). But beyond its quantitative importance 'It is not' is a somewhat crude weapon, a brazenly partisan QED following upon discriminations of much greater finesse early in the story. An inkling of the author of *Murphy*, or a poor relative of him, is more discernible elsewhere, as in the following passage, which describes Belacqua's preparation of a text from Dante's *Paradiso* for his Italian lesson:

> For the tiller of the field the thing was simple, he had it from his mother. The spots were Cain and his truss of thorns, dispossessed, cursed from the earth, fugitive and vagabond. The moon was that countenance fallen and branded, seared with the first stigma of God's pity, that an outcast might not die quickly. It was a mix-up in the mind of the tiller, but that did not matter. It was good enough for his mother; it was good enough for him.
>
> (*MPTK*, 11–12)

This passage illustrates a pervasive fault of *More pricks* that *Murphy* triumphantly corrects: over-elaboration in a context Beckett understands better than any reader could. But what is impressive here is the management of sound and syntax, 'interventionist' activity of a much more subtle order. From 'mother' to 'moon' to 'mind' to 'matter', and back to 'mother' again, a kind of circular contour emerges: an equivalent, perhaps, at the linguistic level, of Belacqua's 'quietism'. *Murphy* refines this imaginative strategy still further, generating book-long ironies for which a single story like 'Dante and the lobster', even with nine companion pieces, could obviously not provide much preparation. But it is at moments like this that *More pricks* harnesses the dynamism of *Dream*, without falling foul of the disadvantages which attend it.

'Dante and the lobster' also gave Beckett room (not that *Dream* had lacked this commodity) to develop what would, by the time of *Murphy*, have become a brilliantly sharp tool of dramatization: the cut-and-thrust, usually with an involuntary or deliberate quotient of misunderstanding, of conversational exchange. But the underestimated story 'Fingal', second in the collection and inevitably therefore somewhat overshadowed by its forebear, is even more adventurous in this respect, and points forward to *Murphy* even more clearly in presenting the landscape near the Portrane

Lunatic Asylum (an Irish foretaste of the Magdalen Mental Mercyseat in *Murphy*) and a pair of ill-matched and eccentric lovers not unlike Murphy and Celia. 'Fingal', like 'Dante and the lobster' (and like most of the other *More pricks* stories that work well), seems to hinge on moments when all the usual fictional categories – of time, or space, or 'human interest' in the accepted sense – are suspended, with vivid verbal items called in to occupy the otherwise denuded foreground. In 'Fingal' there is just such a moment when an *idiot-savant* figure in 'shirt sleeves and slippers', a figure who knows his Swift (or at least his life of Swift) by rote, trots out, Ancient Mariner-like, a tale that stops at least one of the three principals whom the narrative has locked together in a Beckettian version of the eternal triangle:

> '[. . .] you might have heard tell of Dane Swift, he kep a' – he checked the word and then let it come regardless – 'he kep a motte in it.' [The Portrane house where Esther Johnson, Swift's 'Stella', resided with her companion Mrs Dingley.]
>
> 'A moth?' exclaimed Winnie.
>
> 'A motte' he said 'of the name of Stella.'
>
> Winnie stared out across the grey field. No sign of Sholto [her doctor 'friend'], nor of Belacqua, only this puce mass up against her and a tale of a motte and a star [i.e. 'Stella']. What was a motte? ['A girl' or 'a harlot' according to Eric Partridge's *Dictionary of historical slang*, although only a distinctively Irish usage in the first case.]
>
> 'You mean' she said 'that he lived there with a woman?'
>
> 'He kep her there' said the old man, he had read it in an old Telegraph and he would adhere to it, 'and came down from Dublin.'
>
> Little fat Presto [Swift's nickname for himself in correspondence with 'Stella'], he would set out early in the morning, fresh and fasting, and walk like camomile.   *(MPTK*, 34–35)

In this exchange one enigma generates another, and the reader is very much kept on his toes (like Swift), not least by the eccentric punctuation. But Winnie – who is doomed not to 'win' Belacqua – is stalled sufficiently long, much like the narrative impetus of the story, for her intended to make good his escape from her. A single word, as it were, gangs up on her as if it had the same right to behave as independently as the vanished gallant. And even though Dr Sholto ('master of the situation' as Beckett ironically dubs him) returns to express his confidence that Belacqua can be retrieved from the various sanctuaries (snugs mostly) which he employs as bulwarks against emotional imbroglios, the conclusion of the story casually confirms that Sholto and *his* putative 'motte' have an exceptionally slippery customer to deal with:

A young man on a bicycle came slowly round the corner from the Donabate direction, saluted the group and was turning into the drive of the asylum.

'Tom' cried Sholto.

Tom dismounted. Sholto gave a brief satirical description of Belacqua's person.

'You didn't see that on the road' he said 'did you?'

'I passed the felly of it on a bike' said Tom, pleased to be of use, 'at Ross's gate, going like flames.' [i.e. *presto*]

'On a BIKE!' cried Winnie. 'But he hadn't a bike.'

'Tom' said Sholto 'get out the car, look sharp now and run her down here.'

'But it can't have been him', Winnie was furious for several reasons, 'I tell you he had no bike.'

'Whoever it is' said Sholto, master of the situation, 'we'll pass him before he gets to the main road.'

But Sholto had underestimated the speed of his man, who was safe in Taylor's public house in Swords [i.e. some three miles away], drinking and laughing in a way that Mr Taylor did not like, before they were well on their way. (MPTK, 35–6)

Although this is admittedly a far cry from the developed forms of *Murphy* and *Watt*, we have here what is perhaps the first failed quest for someone in Beckett's *œuvre*, with the whole situation symptomatic of what can happen when a character of 'quietist' tendencies (outside of public houses) breaks away from the chains and claims that his sometime friends have 'kep' for him.

There is more happening in the best episodes of *More pricks* than immediately meets the eye, as some of my own 'interventions' in quoting from 'Fingal' are intended to indicate. Indeed, one begins to see here what Beckett must have meant when he promised himself in *Dream* that 'the experience of my reader shall be between the phrases, in the silence, communicated by the intervals, not the terms' (*Dream*, 137). A splendid communication by 'intervals' – which is an aptly musical term in the circumstances – occurs in the story adjacent to 'Fingal', the otherwise rather desultory 'Ding-Dong'. Once more ensconced in the 'crapulent den' of a pub (MPTK, 44) – much as Cooper will be at the end of *Murphy* – Belacqua, or it may be his 'sometime friend' the narrator (MPTK, 39), waxes lyrical about the pleasant instances to be found there of 'machinery decently subservient to appetite' (MPTK, 45). Belacqua's pleasure principle reaches its apogee in a long sentence much more exactly calibrated than anything in *Assumption*, though still sufficiently awkwardly phrased to compel a reader to look more closely. The pub is summed up as:

A great C major symphony of supply and demand, effect and cause, fulcrate on the middle C of the counter and waxing, as it proceeded, in the charming harmonies of blasphemy and broken glass and all the aliquots of fatigue and ebriety.   (*MPTK*, 45)

And later in the story, in the single and most conclusive threat to Belacqua's bower of bliss encountered two pages further on, an itinerant female pedlar, apparently even more inarticulate than the old man in 'Fingal', sells Belacqua two seats in heaven, and two more by defaulting on the change ('"make it four cantcher, yer frien', yer da, yer ma an' yer motte"'; *MPTK*, 48). From the outset we have known that Belacqua's 'last phase of [. . .] solipsism' has been 'enlivened [. . .] with the belief that the best thing he had to do was to move constantly from place to place' (*MPTK*, 39). Here he has been decisively cornered. Yet as a kind of recompense this old woman's description of a place she has not yet visited (and may never arrive at) offers Belacqua the even more pleasant illusion of constant motion that is at the same time perfect inertia:

> 'Heaven goes round' she said, whirling her arm, 'and round and round and round and round.'
>   'Yes' said Belacqua 'round and round.'
>   'Rowan' she said, dropping the d's and getting more of a spin into the slogan, 'rowan an' rowan an' rowan.'   (*MPTK*, 48)

This is as subtle as it is funny. The blend of a folksong-like refrain and 'mere' local colour articulates the view later to be memorably expressed in *Molloy*: 'would not the beatific vision become a source of boredom in the long run?' (*T*, 154). In the much shorter run of this story, however – and 'Ding-Dong' is perhaps the most static in a collection where plot is at a minimum – it also reveals, or *almost* reveals, what was left unsaid in the 'great C major symphony' sentence earlier. For in 'dropping the d's' on a piano one comes inevitably to C, 'the middle C of the counter', and – after the 'interval' in which one has digested this point – it suddenly becomes clear that the whole latter half of 'Ding-Dong' is a kind of extended gloss on Schumann's famous description of the 'heavenly length' of Schubert's 'great C major' symphony (no. 9). This is why 'Ding-Dong' ends with Belacqua 'listen[ing] to the music', just as 'Love and Lethe' ends with a one-line prayer (once again prompted by a homage to Schubert) for Belacqua and Ruby Tough: 'May their night be full of music at all events' (*MPTK*, 105; the reference is to the *Lied* 'An die Musik'). 'Music' will once again be much in evidence in *Murphy*, published four years later, nominally to avoid outraging the public with inflammatory material (*Mu*, 55), but from the aesthetic point of view adumbrated in *Dream* more precisely to communicate by way of intervals, and so keep silent about other things.

There is at least one other feature of the *More pricks* experiment which helps to make *Murphy* seem less of a quantum leap than it would otherwise be. It is best illustrated by way of a remark made to Belacqua by his Italian teacher in 'Dante and the lobster':

> 'It occurred to me' she said 'apropos of I don't know what, that you might do worse than make up Dante's rare movements of compassion in Hell. That used to be' her past tenses were always sorrowful 'a favourite question.'
>
> He assumed an expression of profundity.
>
> 'In that connexion' he said 'I recall one superb pun anyway: "qui vive la pietà quando è ben morta ..."' [*Inferno*, XX, 28]
>
> She said nothing.
>
> 'Is it not a great phrase?' he gushed.
>
> She said nothing.
>
> 'Now' he said like a fool 'I wonder how you could translate that?
>
> Still she said nothing. Then:
>
> 'Do you think' she murmured 'it is absolutely necessary to translate it?'
>
> (*MPTK*, 18)

Here, as elsewhere in *More pricks than kicks* (not excluding its title), we are invited to look at words which have the disturbing property of looking back at us. Dante's pun on 'piety' and 'pity' remains untranslated, but it is nudged gently in the direction of 'compassion' by an author who, like Belacqua's teacher, is intent on studiously maintaining silence. Too often in *More pricks* Beckett rather laboriously demonstrates his need to lambast conventional social norms with a battery of sophisticated weapons, a tendency much better controlled in *Murphy*. But here Beckett's ability to convey compassion, which will later be crucial to his presentation of the prostitute Celia (and which is a quality immensely successfully developed in the much later fiction and drama), is also in evidence, as it is again in the story 'Yellow', the penultimate story in *More pricks*, during which Belacqua dies:

> An asthmatic in the room overhead [cf. *Murphy*, chapter 5] was coughing his heart up. God bless you, thought Belacqua, you make things easier for me. But when did the unfortunate sleep? During the day, the livelong day, through the stress of the day. At twelve sharp he would be sound, or, better again, just dozing off. Meantime he coughed, as Crusoe laboured to bring his gear ashore, the snugger to be.
>
> Belacqua made a long arm and switched off the lamp [cf. *Murphy*, chapter 10]. It threw shadows. He would close his eyes, he would bilk the dawn in that way. What were the eyes, anyway? The posterns of the mind. They were safer closed [cf. *Murphy*, chapter 10].   (*MPTK*, 173)

Within two years of 'Yellow' appearing in print Beckett was writing to Thomas MacGreevy about 'the risk of taking [Murphy] too seriously and separating him too sharply from the others' (D, 102); Belacqua's for the most part successful withdrawal from social constraints had obviously convinced Beckett, under the influence of his own 'movements of compassion' (MPTK, 18), that some of the shortcomings of More pricks could be attributed to too sharp a separation of elements. At the same time Beckett emphasized to MacGreevy that what was needed was 'the sympathy going so far and no further'. A less extravagant, more classical, balance was in the offing. But Murphy, obviously enough, posed much greater problems of organization than Beckett had encountered in More pricks than kicks. And the figure at the centre of its plot, if not always at the centre of the scenes which enable the plot to advance towards a vanishing-point, is problematic in ways that his predecessor Belacqua – only seen in a succession of episodic vignettes – could never aspire to, and would never measure up to. Even so, without the experience of More pricks, for all its shortcomings – in his maturity Beckett roundly, but unfairly, condemned it as a 'fiasco' – Murphy would have been still more difficult to accomplish. Indeed, it is doubtful if 'the mixture of compassion, patience, mockery and "tat twam asi"' (D, 102; with the 'thus thou art' Sanskrit phrase borrowed from Schopenhauer) which makes Murphy what it is would have been anything like as compelling had Beckett not struggled with the intrinsically baser alloy of Belacqua.

Even though it had been crafted in a mood of compromise consequent upon the collapse of Dream, More pricks proved too much a 'statement of itself', with or without the 'tempest of emblems' aspect voiced in 'Alba', to satisfy the public taste of the time. There were few reviews, and sales were poor. In the wake of another failure, this time a public one, Beckett was forced to confront the problem of possessing an 'independent spirit' with no material gains to guarantee its continuance. Ironically, as his personal circumstances worsened, Beckett's capacity to live vicariously proved surprisingly resilient. Out of crisis, and doubtless as a consequence of crisis, came achievement. In the composition of Murphy, easily the most labour-intensive enterprise he had thus far undertaken, Beckett effectively sacrificed the cavalier and facile manner which had privileged 'expression' (suitably disguised as 'form' and 'content') over anything so mundane as purpose. Hindsight perhaps revived memories of 'the many concessions required of the literary artist by the shortcomings of the literary convention', which Beckett had tacitly lamented as early as the second paragraph of his Proust book (PTD, 11). In finding himself – much like the Proust he had been keen to imagine without the trappings of a 'legendary life and death' (PTD, 9) –

'not altogether at liberty to detach effect from cause' (*PTD*, 11), Beckett admitted the force of conventional imperatives for what it was. *Murphy* could be written because he could 'accept regretfully the sacred ruler and compass of literary geometry' (*PTD*, 12). Though he had not much enjoyed the role of literary critic, Beckett could derive from his one serious attempt at a sustained piece of literary evaluation the benefit of a programmatic, self-administered discipline: 'it will be necessary [. . .] to interrupt (disfigure) the luminous projection of subject desire with the comic relief of features' (*PTD*, 11–12).[7] His sterner stance in the face of necessity is fascinatingly confirmed in the letter to George Reavey of 13 November 1936, in which Beckett emphatically states that 'the relief has also to do work and reinforce that which it relieves' (*D*, 103). (There is, of course, a pre-echo of Malone here.) Unabashed by the *limae labor* of *Dream* (*MPTK*, 153) – also a pre-echo, but of the 'labour lost' in the late Beckett text *Company* (*NO* 52) – he put his trust in work, very prolonged and concentrated work, and was rewarded with *Murphy*, which he was not unnaturally then disinclined to alter at the behest of publishers, as the letter to Reavey indicates.

Murphy, in addition to its intrinsic merits, is an example without parallel of Beckett co-ordinating means and ends in a way designed to make them reciprocally interactive, and mutually supportive, as if there were really no divorce between form and content once inspiration had given way to method. A kind of 'moral law' emerges (partly, notebook evidence suggests, as a consequence of re-reading Kant), which runs counter to the 'pure subject . . . almost exempt from the impurity of will' vigorously championed in *Proust* (*PTD*, 90). Whereas in 1931 Beckett could speak scornfully of 'the vulgarity of a plausible concatenation' (*PTD*, 81–2), by 1935, the year *Murphy* was begun (or at least by 1938, the year *Murphy* was published), he was ready to put 'concatenation' first and foremost, and to keep 'vulgarity' at bay by making everything, as he told George Reavey, 'essential to the whole' (*D*, 103). And whereas *Proust* had spoken of 'impressionism' (*PTD*, 86; and had simultaneously generated and sought to make an impression), *Murphy* gravitates towards 'intelligibility' and integration, qualities governed by – though Beckett admits to Reavey that they may also be imperilled by – 'compression' (*D*, 103). It was precisely to subserve the 'chain of cause and effect' (*PTD*, 86), though the latter is often (as legitimated by conventional narrative practice) the trigger inviting further investigation, that Beckett adopted pre-existent structures and strategies, almost all of which can be found in Cervantes and the English novelists of the eighteenth century for whom Cervantes was so beguiling a model. It must have given Beckett a wry pleasure to reflect that the framing elements of his opening sentence in *Murphy* – 'The sun shone [. . .] on the nothing new'

(*Mu*, 5) – tacitly indicated what he was up to: scouting the very idea of *the novel* as '*something* new', whilst nevertheless seeking at some level to put new wine in old bottles.

In *Murphy* the 'intervention' and 'quietism' of which Beckett had spoken in his 1934 book review are redistributed, with Murphy the character inheriting the passive quietist role, and his narrator behaving in an exceptionally active interventionist manner. The narrator relishes every opportunity to participate or, in the terms offered by the prologue to *Proust* proper, 'to interrupt (disfigure)'. Murphy the 'hero', struggling as he is to figure forth a philosophy of sorts, is disadvantaged from the outset, both narratively and (the more subtle factor) perspectivally. In the first half of the novel, which Beckett himself justly considered 'plain sailing enough' (*D*, 103), Murphy's disadvantaged, and indeed expropriated, status is not perceived as a liability. The frequent interruptions of temporal sequence are paradoxically felt – as perhaps they are at the deferred 'turning point' of chapters 37 and 38 in *Great expectations* – to be indices of a free flux operating objectively, even when strictly non-equivalent narrative elements are shown to echo one another. Throughout the first half of *Murphy* the idea that all lines culminate in the titular hero ('everything led to Murphy', *Mu*, 49) is always interpretable as fundamentally a device of structuration, the 'scaffolding' as Beckett calls it in *Proust*. As plot convergence becomes imperative, however – effectively from the point in the plot where a real *peripeteia* must occur, and Murphy's adoption of 'asylum' proves stronger than his experience of 'exile' (*Mu*, 53) – the narrator's deterministic view of human interaction prevails. The very quest structure on which Murphy depends, an inheritance from picaresque tradition, threatens the hero's ambition to be 'a point in the ceaseless unconditioned generation and passing away of line' (*Mu*, 79). Even the pastoral elements which periodically occupy the foreground – at their most poignant perhaps at the very end of the novel – cannot do more than suggest how an essentially conservative narrative might be given a mildly progressive or utopian colouring.[8] Yet there are also contrary indicators, or what seem on first encounter to be so, notably two priceless relics of eighteenth-century fictional practice: the horoscope of chapter 3 and the whole of chapter 6. These work much like the interpolated episode or moral essay which proved so useful to eighteenth-century novelists; the suspension of narrative momentum unexpectedly promotes narrative continuity, and at the same time offers a forum in which discursive, or even specifically dogmatic, issues can be raised.

The horoscope (or 'Bull of incommunication'; *Mu*, 25) and the unusually communicative '*bull*etin' devoted to Murphy's mind (*Mu*, 80) make for a multiplication of aspects and – even if the latter does come from the horse's mouth – they are of a piece with Murphy's need to feel free, even if this is only an illusion. A similar effect results, against all the odds, from the narrator's obvious affection for maxims, apophthegms and items of folk wisdom. As conscious extrapolations from the prevailing mode of reportage – and, as such, contingent upon frankly partial evidence, and very insecurely based on what passes for 'reality' – these are liberating forces, as for an instant a wide-angle lens is used, and the appeal to a kind of universal truth provides a window of ventilation. Indeed, as these instances of non-specific truth diminish, Murphy's plight worsens. In generic terms the unruly realm of comedy is tamed by the darker tones of 'elegy'. The narrator interrupts the narrative at one point to emphasize that Murphy is not a puppet (*Mu*, 86); but as the plot unfolds he becomes more like a marionette.[9] In systematically doing his duty at the Magdalen Mental Mercyseat, Murphy is effectively conceding that he has become more a function than a person. On reflection it becomes clear that the narrator's overwhelming superiority – best epitomized by the barrage of filters employed in chapter 6 – has worsted the cracker-barrel philosopher of the opening chapters. The 'plain sailing' of the beginning can be seen retrospectively as much more catastrophic than the experience of first reading it through suggests it will be. From this perspective the mock gravity of the 'bulletin' which occupies chapter 6 masks a real change in tone and direction. Beckett's subtlety, and the new flexibility that a modicum of compromise has generated, is epitomized by the fact that the 'shocking thing' (*Mu*, 75) apparently deferred until chapter 7 has actually come and gone without our being, on first reading, in any position to register how shocking it is, even though the narrator insists that we take note of it.

'There seemed to me', Beckett wrote to MacGreevy, 'always the risk of taking [Murphy] too seriously and separating him too sharply from the others' (*D*, 102). Yet in the event *Murphy* does neither of these things. So many absurd shenanigans occur around, or because of, Murphy that his own intrinsically peculiar behaviour can never seem other than a more extreme example – though conducted with some dignity and integrity – of what falls within a fairly circumscribed continuum. Moreover, whilst Murphy (or his narrator) separates himself successfully for the most part from a number of 'the others' – and necessarily so from the Neary–Wylie– Miss Counihan group, or there would be no plot to unfold – his dealings with Celia, not to mention hers with him, occupy a considerable amount of fictional time and space early on, and continue to matter even after they have ceased to live together and, unknown to themselves, will only ever meet again with the great divide of death between them. Beckett subtly underscores this privileged relationship, a relationship which becomes increasingly poignant the less time they are allowed to spend together, by drawing a structural parallel between Celia's acceptance of her isolation (chapter 10, *Mu*, 159) and Murphy's more turbulent recognition that his chess-playing partner, Mr Endon, effortlessly achieves the closed-circuit transactions with 'the big world' he himself is denied (chapter 11, *Mu*, 165). The narrator describes Celia's recognition in his most recondite manner, attempting (unsuccessfully as usual) to diminish her to the level of puppetry that 'the others' rarely rise above. But the 'protasis' (*Mu*, 159) which, for the narrator, signals the end of all love whatsoever, is applied as a defence against Celia's simple, straightforward, eminently human sentiments and sentimentality. Celia's heroism is heightened by what the narrator seems ready to despise. By contrast, Murphy's 'afflatulence' (*Mu*, 171), whilst testifying once again to the narrator's penchant for abstraction and pigeon-holing, is a much more complex affair, befitting the character and the pretensions of the figure giving voice to it. The vertigo this induces is an important preparatory element prefiguring the 'chaos' (*Mu*, 173) into which Murphy will shortly be delivered. Yet it is precisely the shape of this coda that brings Celia's 'protasis' to mind, generating a very telling contrast between her ability to hypothesize a future without Murphy – one meaning of 'protasis' is 'a stretching towards', and Celia is certainly stretching towards the life she will henceforth live – and Murphy's complete inability to recollect a past, though he has never quite weaned himself of his need to revive it. In his *Proust* period of the early 1930s Beckett had adhered to a 'statemental' aesthetic of limited liability, and form became overburdened with content. In *Murphy* the balance between them is helped by their more visible separation, creating ironies, contrasts and resonances that are invariably subtle and suggestive. It is as if Beckett had found it both expedient and profitable to reaffirm his early conviction (as expressed in *Dream*) that 'the experience of my reader shall be [...] communicated by the intervals, not the terms' (*Dream*, 123), but had improved the outcome by thinking of the 'intervals' as attributes intrinsic to an overall structure, rather than as merely local instances of relative or absolute autonomy. *Assumption*, when it speaks of an 'explosive feat [...] commanding undeserved attention because of brilliance' conveys the proper tone of censure, but lacks the resources to implement more durable alternatives, a deficiency still present in *More pricks*. *Murphy*, though full of 'brilliance', and with a real explosion at the climax of its plot, abjures all talk of 'whispering the turmoil down' – the faculty most prized in *Assumption* – but gets on with the business of demonstrating how it can be accomplished.

Murphy is an immensely rich novel, a quantum leap above the intriguing but scattered debris of Beckett's earliest English fiction. Though the provision of 'demented particulars' (as Celia's paternal grandfather Mr Kelly calls them; *Mu*, 13) must have seemed to Beckett a considerable climb-down from the aesthetic ideals he had set out to animate, he clearly possessed a representational gift which craved satisfaction along the broadly 'realist' lines that most novelists find it convenient to respect. In the opening pages of *More pricks* (*MPTK*, 10–13) the business of Belacqua's lunch is very fully particularized for its own sake, and not simply because his lobster supper is to follow; and throughout *More pricks* one comes across pages of essentially 'descriptive' writing designed to constitute 'reality' rather than contest it. *Murphy* builds handsomely on its predecessor in its presentations of what Murphy calls 'the big world' (*Mu*, 123), a world actually felt to be quite small, for all practical purposes bounded by West Brompton, South Kensington, the Caledonian Road and – full of Eastern promise – the mental asylum 'a little way out of town [...] on the boundary of two counties' (*Mu*, 109; in real life the Maudsley Hospital at Beckenham). All the key locales in *Murphy* are vividly portrayed, as if Beckett's sojourn in London had compelled him, in spite of his personal difficulties there, to register its existence. (Beckett's native Dublin, by contrast, is merely a shadowy elsewhere, honour of a sort having been satisfied – though Joyce's *Dubliners* left little room for it – in *More pricks than kicks*.) *Murphy*, in fact, could be called 'a novel of London' in much the same way as T. S. Eliot's *The waste land* can be seen as 'a poem of London', and there is perhaps no other single work of Beckett's that fosters, though very much as an incidental by-product, the possibility of a 'literary pilgrimage' to the places mentioned in it. Some of the apparent strangeness, for example, of Murphy encountering sheep in Kensington Gardens, vanishes once one discovers that this was quite usual in the years before the Second World War; and this cannot be the only case in which the few first readers of *Murphy* were better placed than we now are. Without such representational, solid points of reference – quite as important in their way as the 'points' which both the characters and the narrator insist we take note of (*Mu*, 19) – Murphy's desire to elude definition would itself lack definition. It would be difficult to see the Beckett of *Murphy* as an 'artist of the void' in the way commentators on the later fiction (perhaps misguidedly) have tended to do, when even Murphy himself is obliged by his narrator to accept that 'to see nothing [...] is such a rare postnatal treat' (*Mu*, 168).

It is Beckett's regulated distribution of 'realist' elements in *Murphy* which, sixty years on and in a world struggling to come to terms with 'virtual' realities, guarantees it as wide a readership as any of his prose fictions can hope to command. Yet *Murphy* is obedient to the conventional novelistic pieties the better to expose them, out of their own mouths as it were, for the frauds they are, or as the more or less cunning ruses of an author with some major axes to grind, and only the relatively obtuse materials of a plot to sharpen them on. The competing impulses, the moves both away from and towards time-honoured narrative tactics, give the novel its hard-won, but remarkably well-sustained, vitality. The kinds of conflict that are indispensable to the provision of audience 'interest' (as customarily supplied by what Beckett elsewhere summarily dismisses as 'chartered recountants'; *D*, 89) are abundantly present in *Murphy*, at the level of the plot, at the level of the narrator's wry commentary upon the action, and – insofar as we can reconstruct it – at the biographical level. (From what we can tell, or can now be told, Beckett was experiencing even more personal distress during the writing of *Murphy* than at most other points in a life far from the bourgeois norms of contentment; yet it would be impossible to guess as much from a novel so full of knockabout humour – so much so, indeed, that it seems sensible to regard *Murphy* as, at least in part, therapeutic activity, as its successor *Watt*, in more trying times globally, certainly was.) Beckett's adherence to the intrinsically dynamic principle of conflict left him, paradoxically perhaps, free to function for the first time in a spirit of play, with a positive attitude to the removal of any obstacles to the exercise of a kind of narrative 'pleasure principle' that was not merely high-handedness. Indeed, he must have been struck by the peculiar reciprocal relationship which permits any predominantly 'rule-bound' narrative to include aberrant elements, and so save itself from becoming 'bogged' (like Belacqua at the beginning of 'Dante and the lobster'; *MPTK*, 9) in inertia. Perhaps this is why Beckett tells us that Murphy 'never ripped up old stories' (*Mu*, 16), and why the narrator effectively disclaims this book's 'novel' status in his first sentence.

Ironically, one of the most obviously innovative gestures in *Murphy* (and rendered the more obvious by appearing at the head of chapter 2) – the dismissal of several categories of Celia's physiognomy as 'unimportant' (*Mu*, 11) – proves in the event to have been merely local in effect. Our impression of her as immensely important in areas far more crucial than those which this narrator documents grows stronger as the book unfolds. The price that Beckett had (and was perhaps content) to pay for his bi-focal presentation of the nominal hero Murphy was the elevation of his heroine Celia to the still centre of the novel. The 'old boy' whom Miss Carridge describes as 'never still' (*Mu*, 50) is a mere bit-part player, a kind of surrogate Mr Kelly, by comparison with the young woman who inherits his room in the Brewery Road kip. In the last paragraphs of *Murphy* (*Mu*, 191–2) it is Celia – by way of the rallentandos applied to the prose, concealing emotion the better to move readers more deeply – who is allowed, redemptively as it were, to lapse into silence. The wailing of the park rangers anxious to close the park echoes wearily, much like the 'ellipses' (*Mu*, 97) Murphy foists on Suk's horoscope. If silence is only Murphy's 'fourth highest attribute' (*Mu*, 31), what price Celia's assumption of a strict non-combatant stance in this connection? (Murphy, by contrast, is very prone to finding situations 'irksome beyond endurance'; *Mu*, 6). The impressive thing about the concluding paragraphs of *Murphy* – a novel which for a number of reasons presents determinism as more powerful than free will – is that Celia's emotions seem to well up within her, free of any extrinsic imposition from without. It is precisely in approaching fixed goals, however free-floating they may be, that Murphy makes a number of tactical errors and desperate compromises, all of which are summed up by his conduct during his game of chess with Mr Endon. It falls not to Murphy but to Celia to become, or rather for the novel to suggest that she might become, 'a mote in the mind of absolute freedom' (*Mu*, 79). It could almost be said that, without Celia, *Murphy* would have had no real plot above and beyond that which could be borrowed from 'old stories' (*Mu*, 16). Yet it was by way of Celia that Beckett moved towards the plotlessness of *Watt*.

Much as those in quest of Murphy ran him to ground in the end, Beckett finally found a publisher for his novel. But *Murphy* – though never a mouth-watering prospect from a commercial point of view – had remained this side of an imaginary line dividing innovative novels and experimental prose fictions. Beckett composed its successor *Watt* between 1941 and 1945, but the book only found a publisher in 1953, and in Paris rather than London – the Paris which had responded positively to Beckett's French 'trilogy'. The extrinsic conditions which summoned *Watt* from oblivion not unnaturally prompt the question why – given the mood of 'fatigue and disgust' recorded in the footnote to the novel's 'Addenda' (W, 247) – it survived as an entity at all. Yet although the circumstances in which *Watt* was written were extremely unpropitious, with Beckett hiding from the Gestapo in the mountainous Vaucluze above Avignon, there is abundant manuscript evidence that he laboured at *Watt* with his characteristic diligence and fortitude.[10] The end product is certainly, by any standards, distinctly odd, arguably the oddest of all Beckett's works, whether in prose or drama (though *Quad* runs it a close second). So peculiar is it that one may find oneself imagining a personal crisis comparable with that for which *Murphy* served as a partial remedy, though the biographical evidence is at best ambiguous in this connection, and in fact offers some proofs to the contrary. It was Europe, rather than Beckett, that was in crisis; and whilst, by Beckett's own admission, he wrote *Watt* 'to get away from war and occupation',[11] more than a tincture of the times affected its composition. Against the background of an epoch given over to irrational barbarism posing as the saviour of civilization, *Watt*'s mobilization of ridiculously 'rational', and hence utterly deranged, strategies, looks almost perfectly emblematic. Though there is no trace of the global conflict in *Watt*, it reads very much as if it could only have emerged from a world gone mad.

In *Watt* all the effort which, in *Murphy*, had been expended on making episodes either more dense or more specific, is turned topsy-turvy. Having for the purposes of this enterprise reduced incidents to a minimum, Beckett further subjects them to isolation one from another, in order to envelop each event in a mist of enigma. The focus falls almost (but not quite) exclusively on Watt's mental habits, which are at once prompted by, and independent of, any particular location that presents itself. The most obvious consequence of Beckett's systematic reduction of what would ordinarily be considered meaningful and purposeful utterance is that only four spatial contexts – keyed in to a book fourfold in structure – assume anything like the typical 'reality' quotient of fiction. In themselves these four locations could hardly be more ordinary: a city street, a two-storeyed house, a garden and a railway station. But they strike us as quite other than ordinary because any co-ordinates which could situate these items in relation to one another appear to have completely vanished. This said, and this degree of incongruity once granted, it seems apt that two of the most intrinsically memorable incidents in *Watt* should occur effectively *nowhere*: one in a railway compartment whilst the train is in motion (W, 25ff.), and the other on an intermediate road from a house to a railway station (W, 224ff.), for neither of which any useful map reference could ever be supplied. These events may suggest a kind of residual nostalgia for purposeful movements towards, or away from, specified focal points. But their principal effect is to leave things in suspension, as if encounters could only occur 'off the ladder' (W, 53) which, in a conventional fiction, subordinates one thing to another. Though there are indicators in the 'Addenda' to *Watt* that Beckett considered reintroducing perspective later on – 'Note that Arsene's declaration gradually came back to Watt' (W, 248) – even these are submerged by the mysterious 'soul-landscape' in which contours and features disappear (W, 249), and by the picture of Erskine's room, which runs counter to its artist's 'love of significant detail' (W, 251) – the description is appropriately detailed – when *Watt*'s author (or editor) casually neglects to elicit any significance from it.

Having abandoned almost all the perspectival devices which *Murphy*, even as it mocks them, depends on, the narrative agent of *Watt* also refuses to endorse any other principal of coherence, except *en passant*. The last entry in the 'Addenda' – 'No symbols where none intended' (W, 255) – looks helpful, but there is of course no authenticated ambience in which it could be so. Almost every object in *Watt*, and almost every moment of narrative production, *could* be received as symbolic, but need not be. There is, however, a pervasive impression that things in general matter less for what they are (or, in a context of 'pseudo-statements', might be) than for what they can be translated into, at some unspecified, but obviously *non-narrative*, level of classification or taxonomy. *Watt*, as the name of the figure central to its existence serves to remind us, is an investigation into the possibility of 'what'-ness. Yet at the same time the investigation is conducted with such a manically intransigent set of weapons that anything which promises to illuminate items of 'what'-ness (or even 'what'-ness itself) begins to immaterialize before our very eyes (cf. *Mu*, 43). This, aptly enough in the circumstances, is precisely what happens to Watt himself in the splendidly funny opening scene of the book, where he is 'witnessed' by Mr and Mrs Nixon and Mr Hackett, but not in any meaningful sense actually *seen*. It is also what happens – almost as if Beckett were reluctant to abandon circularity of form (the first picture Watt discovers in Erskine's room is of a broken circle; W, 127) – when Watt in his turn 'witnesses' a figure approaching the railway station at the end (W, 225–7), only for this 'particular hallucination' to grow fainter and fainter, and finally disappear. In the final tableau of all, Watt, having laboriously attempted to purchase 'a ticket to the end of the line' (W, 244), also disappears. But a no less questionable item, and by implication a no less useless one, replaces him:

> Not many minutes later the six-four entered the station. It did not take up a single passenger, in the absence of Mrs Pim. But it discharged a bicycle, for a Miss Walker.
> (W, 244)

The train schedule can only matter if there is someone waiting for it, in which case readers might feel they have a right to know *how many* minutes later the six-four arrived. And to pause to record 'the absence of Mrs Pim' is beside the point when it is the absence of Watt that might legitimately be noted. The 'discharged' bicycle is a narrative prop with considerable comic potential, but principally designed to illustrate the fact that the narrator has in no way discharged his narrative duties. We are left to muse upon whether Watt's walking days – his strange walk has occasioned bemused comment earlier (W, 28) – are over. Or to set the final tableau of bit-part players – Mr Case, Mr Gorman and Mr Nolan – against Mr and Mrs Nixon and Mr Hackett whom we met for the one and only time two-hundred-and-fifty pages earlier, since there is not even any evidence at the end that Watt so much as haunts these new (but absurdly belated) denizens of the 'real' world in spirit.

A decade and more before *Watt*, Beckett had dissociated himself from the 'double-entry book-keeping' – doubly hyphenated – of allegory (*PTD*, 79), even as practised by his beloved Dante. Yet in *Watt* Beckett is at least in part re-animating allegory (which is classically fourfold!), as he would later do again in *The lost ones*. But Beckett is also intent on exploding any potential dynamic interplay between what is said and what is implied, which makes allegory as conventionally understood impossible to achieve. As the insistent surface of the book implies, *Watt* is all surface, with larger horizons inter-mittently hinted at, but with access to them foreclosed. Very typically, Beckett's attempts – notably in part three (especially *W*, 162–7) – to mediate matters stereoscopically, or more properly telescopically, founder and peter out. Increasingly enigmatic data are elicited from strategies which have only a weirdly systematic self-consistency to recommend them, and not even the kind of minimal self-evidence which narrative discourse conventionally confers. In Part III 'Sam' inherits something of Mr Hackett's need to translate Watt into a tangible entity. Yet neither Sam nor Mr Hackett pos-sesses the single-minded persistence and imaginative ingenuity which are the hallmarks of Watt's need to make something of Mr Knott. In the end the efforts of everyone generate more heat than light, and more attributes than any substance could tolerate. No quest is successful, but there is so much information in the foreground that the very idea of a point to aim for atom-izes into nothing. In *Watt* to ask 'What?' seems to be synonymous with saying farewell to any tranquillity of spirit which might have survived all previous challenges to its continuance. And yet in the 'intervals' between asking such a question and a satisfactory answer to it there are some con-solations to be found. Watt increasingly learns to 'provide [his] own aspirin' (*D*, 109) on encountering baffling matters that do not easily yield up their meaning:

> [...] there were limits to what Watt was prepared to do, in pursuit of infor-mation (*W*, 110–11)

> [...] there were many things that Watt could not easily imagine (*W*, 118)

> Watt could not counterfeit obscure keys [...] (*W*, 122)

Critics of *Watt* have been most adept, and necessarily so, in imagining, counterfeiting and pursuing information. But for the general reader who, in spite of all the provocations to do otherwise, perseveres with *Watt*, there is much to be said for adopting Moran's stance on encountering his bees at the end of *Molloy*: 'Here is something I can study all my life, and never understand' (*T*, 156). And when study stales, there is the considerable consolation of watching, or 'witnessing', Beckett writing by no means his best book, but arguably his funniest.

Only in the most extended sense of an infinitely elastic term can *Watt* usefully be described as a 'novel', even if it does begin as if it might consent to be one. Though it has no real antecedents, and certainly no progeny, *Watt* is a kind of tale, fable or parable that looks a little less bizarre when compared with *Candide* or *Rasselas* rather than, say, *Middlemarch* or *Great expectations*. (Ironically, its message, if it can be said to have one, is not far removed from that of the last-named.)[12] Beyond *Watt* Beckett's fiction in English supplants 'the English fiction', being either translated from French originals (the *nouvelles*, the 'trilogy', the *Texts for nothing, How it is* etc.) or difficult to disentangle from French equivalents (especially in the case of *Company*). Yet *Watt*, a story which stops but has no end, is not quite the end of the story as far as 'Beckett's English fiction', in the restricted sense of the phrase, is concerned. In the mid-1950s, some ten years after the abandonment of *Watt* to its 'Addenda', Beckett began a work similar in tone and style to his French trilogy, and presumably intended to be of something like the length of each of the constituent components of the trilogy. Shortly before the point where work on this was also abandoned – without it being taken up again, though the nonce-title *From an abandoned work* misleadingly suggests otherwise[13] – Beckett wrote 'awful English this' (*CSP*, 137),[14] a severe self-judgment added after having seen the fragment printed in the magazine of his old university.[15] The comment presumably reflects his fear that – a decade having passed since his last serious attempt to write in his native language, and with the enormous stimulus of having switched to French still active – his expressive capacities in his mother tongue had atrophied in the interim. If so, very ironically, Beckett's anxieties were without foundation, since *From an abandoned work* indicates most impressively what could have been achieved in English, and very much prefigures what was to follow by way of self-translation. What is most striking in *From an abandoned work* is its quality of *voice*, the *sine qua non* of monologue. Its ventriloquism apart, *From an abandoned work* also possesses a flexibility of rhythm and a suggestive scope never evident in the juvenilia and prentice-work of twenty and thirty years earlier, though *Murphy* made great amends and was strikingly mature. *From an abandoned work*, though a mere torso (and hence in no position to challenge *Murphy*'s pre-eminence amidst Beckett's English fiction), makes one faintly regretful that he should ever have abandoned his first expressive medium, even if the alienation of a foreign tongue enabled him surreptitiously to repossess it.

NOTES

1 Beckett's own translation (*Malone dies*; *T*, 181) of the sentence I have adopted as an epigraph (*Malone meurt*, Paris: Editions de Minuit, 1951, 42).

2 The three stories are, at the time of writing, uncollected. *Assumption* appeared in *transition*, 16 and 17, Paris (1929), 268–71, and is too brief to warrant the pagination of citations. *A case in a thousand* was published in *The Bookman*, 86 (1934), 241–2, and is not referred to here. *Echo's bones* is at present unpublished, although there is a helpful account of it in Rubin Rabinovitz, *The development of Samuel Beckett's fiction* (Urbana and Chicago: University of Illinois Press, 1984).

3 Raymond Federman and John Fletcher, *Samuel Beckett: his works and his critics* (Berkeley and Los Angeles: University of California Press, 1970), 13.

4 In *transition 49*, 5, 97–103; reprinted in *Proust* and *Three dialogues with Georges Duthuit*, and *Disjecta*.

5 The phrase occurs in *Dream of fair to middling women* as part of Belacqua's meditation on the woman he calls Alba Perdue.

6 'Casket of pralinen for a daughter of a dissipated mandarin', *The European caravan* (New York: Brewer, Warren and Putnam, 1931), 476–8.

7 In a notebook kept during the composition of *Murphy* Beckett associates the opposite, 'tragic relief', with the Mozart–da Ponte opera *The marriage of Figaro*. See my 'From a (W)horoscope to *Murphy*' in *The ideal core of the onion*.

8 Some of the terms of my argument here are gratefully borrowed from Michael McKeon's *The origins of the English novel* (London: Radius Hutchinson, 1988).

9 See *Disjecta*, 66, and James Knowlson's 'Beckett and Kleist's essay "On the Marionette theatre"' in Knowlson and Pilling, *Frescoes of the skull*, 277–85.

10 See Ann Beer, '*Watt*, Knott and Beckett's bilingualism', *Journal of Beckett Studies*, 10 (1985) 37–75.

11 Beckett is quoted in John Fletcher, *The novels of Samuel Beckett* (London: Chatto and Windus, 1964), 59.

12 Beckett speaks warmly of Dickens, and specifically of *Great expectations*, in 'Dante...Bruno.Vico..Joyce' (*D*, 28), and there are moments in Part III of *Watt* (e.g. the bottom of 161) which quite resemble Pip's narrative manner in describing his childhood and young manhood.

13 See Federman and Fletcher, *Samuel Beckett: his works and his critics*, 28.

14 Cf. Paul Auster, 'From cakes to stones: a note on Beckett's French': 'However stripped his style in French may be, there is always something a little extra added to the English renderings, some slight twist of diction or nuance, some unexpected word falling at just the right moment, that reminds us that English is nevertheless Beckett's home.' *The art of hunger and other essays* (London: Menard Press, 1982), 54.

15 *From an abandoned work* first appeared in *Trinity News*, 3 (7 June 1956).

RECOMMENDED READING

Acheson, James, 'Murphy's metaphysics', *Journal of Beckett Studies*, 5 (1979), 9–24.
Bair, Deirdre, *Samuel Beckett: a biography*, London: Jonathan Cape, 1978, chapters 5 to 15.

Chalker, John, 'The satiric shape of *Watt*' in Katharine Worth (ed.), *Beckett the shape changer*, London: Routledge and Kegan Paul, 1975.

Coe, Richard, *Beckett*, Edinburgh: Oliver and Boyd, 1964, chapters 2 and 3.

Culik, Hugh, 'Mindful of the body: medical allusions in Beckett's *Murphy*', *Eire–Ireland*, 14.1 (Spring 1979), 84–101.

'The place of *Watt* in Beckett's development', *Modern Fiction Studies*, 29.1 (Spring 1983), 57–71.

Cousineau, Thomas J., '*Watt*: language as interdiction and consolation', *Journal of Beckett Studies*, 4 (1979), 14–34.

Farrow, Anthony, *Early Beckett: art and allusion in 'More pricks than kicks' and 'Murphy'*, Troy, N.Y.: The Whitston Publishing Company, 1991.

Federman, Raymond, *Journey to chaos: Samuel Beckett's early fiction*, Berkeley and Los Angeles: University of California Press, 1965, chapters 2 to 4.

Harrington, John P., *The Irish Beckett*, Syracuse University Press, chapters 2 to 4.

Harrison, Robert, *Samuel Beckett's 'Murphy': a critical excursion*, Athens, Ga: University of Georgia Press, 1968.

Harvey, Lawrence E., *Samuel Beckett: poet and critic*, Princeton University Press, 1970, chapters 8 and 9.

Henning, Sylvie Debevec, *Beckett's critical complicity: carnival, contestation and tradition*, Lexington, Ky: University Press of Kentucky, 1988, chapter 2.

Hill, Leslie, *Beckett's fiction: in different words*, Cambridge University Press, 1990, chapters 1 and 2.

Kennedy, Sighle, *Murphy's bed: a study of real sources and sur-real associations in Samuel Beckett's first novel*, Lewisburg: Bucknell University Press, 1971.

'"The simple games that time plays with space": an introduction to the manuscripts of *Watt*', *Centrepoint*, 2.3 (Fall 1977), 55–61.

Kroll, Jeri, 'The surd as inadmissible evidence: the case of attorney general v. Henry McCabe', *Journal of Beckett Studies*, 2 (1977), 47–58.

'Belacqua as artist and lover: "What a misfortune"', *Journal of Beckett Studies*, 3 (1978), 10–39.

Lees, Heath, '*Watt*: music, tuning and tonality', *Journal of Beckett Studies*, 9 (1984), 5–24.

Mays, J. C. C., 'Mythologized presences: *Murphy* in its time', in Joseph Ronsley (ed.), *Myth and reality in Irish literature*, Toronto: Wilfred Laurier, 1977, 197–218.

Mood, John J., 'The "personal system": Samuel Beckett's *Watt*', *PMLA* (1975), 255–65.

Moorjani, Angela B., *Abysmal games in the novels of Samuel Beckett*, Chapel Hill: University of North Carolina Press, 1982, 23–39, 68–93.

Murphy, P. J., *Reconstructing Beckett: language for being in Samuel Beckett's fiction*, University of Toronto Press, 1990, chapter 1.

Pilling, John, *Samuel Beckett*, London: Routledge and Kegan Paul, 1976, chapter 3.

'*Dream of fair to middling women*', in James Knowlson and John Pilling, *Frescoes of the skull: the later prose and drama of Samuel Beckett*, London: John Calder, 1979, 3–22.

'From a (W)horoscope to *Murphy*', in John Pilling and Mary Bryden (eds.), *The ideal core of the onion: reading Beckett archives*, Reading: Beckett International Foundation, 1992, 1–20.

'A "short statement" with long shadows: *Watt*'s Arsene and his kind(s)', *Samuel Beckett Today* (forthcoming).

Power, Mary, 'Samuel Beckett's "Fingal" and the Irish tradition', *Journal of Modern Literature*, 9.1 (1981–2), 151–6.

Rabate, Jean-Michel (ed.), *Beckett avant Beckett: essais sur le jeune Beckett*, Paris: Presses de l'Ecole Normale Supérieure, 1984.

Robinson, Fred Miller, 'Samuel Beckett: *Watt*', in *The comedy of language: studies in modern comic literature*, Amherst, Mass.: University of Massachusetts Press, 1980.

Robinson, Michael, *The long sonata of the dead: a study of Samuel Beckett*, London: Rupert Hart-Davis, 1969, part two.

Stevenson, Kay Gilliland, 'Belacqua in the moon: Beckett's revisions of "Dante and the lobster"', in Patrick A. McCarthy, (ed.), *Critical essays on Samuel Beckett*, Boston: G. K. Hall, 1986, 36–45.

Zurbrugg, Nicholas, *Beckett and Proust*, Gerrards Cross: Colin Smythe, 1988, chapters 9 to 11.

3

PAUL DAVIES

Three novels and four *nouvelles*: giving up the ghost be born at last

I'm locked up, I'm in something, it's not I.   (*The Unnamable*)

If Beckett had written no other works than the four *nouvelles* and the 'trilogy' of novels, these alone would have secured for him in this century the eminence won in earlier times by Dante for the *Divine comedy*, by Milton for *Paradise lost*, and by Goethe for *Faust*. Those works expressed the unspoken consciousness of their age as Beckett's trilogy speaks to ours. They all describe a borderline between the salvation of an epoch and its destruction.

Beckett's fictions confront a civilization which is the theatre of (amongst other things) a conflict between two powerful forces. One is the rational-(izing) principle, *cogito*, abstract reasoning, the conscious mind, will and design, determinism, positivism, the imposition of extrinsic order. The historical index of this force is the Cartesian Enlightenment and the empirical tradition.[1] Its reflection in world-view is the 'scientific' concept of the universe as a mechanism. In psychology it is apparent in Freud's view of art and religion as the 'symptoms' of neurosis. Philosophically, it is a force of materialism, the physical brain being seen as the producer of thought, consciousness and psyche, and the conventions established between separate brains in the interests of survival being seen as the social order.

Beneath, above and against this force, is the opposite force, often hidden, as yet inaccessible to conscious will: a sense of the primordial spring of life, which does not respond to analysis; the stream of which the archetypes are the only fit indicators; the mystery of birth and death, of which biology illustrates only the grossest mechanism; the actual *unfoldment* of existence, that is, something which we know, as living beings, but which is beyond our powers of comprehension. Its expression can only be in organic or symbolic forms; for instance, the life principle can only be experienced in its becoming, manifesting as, human, animal or plant, but not as a concept or structure of ideas. In psychology, this force was the province of Jung's theory. Its

world-view is the synergetic, integral or holistic. Its philosophy is the eso-
teric tradition. Jung's understanding of the unconscious saw it as empower-
ing the whole cosmos, whereas Freud's reduced the unconscious to the individual alone.

Beckett's writing career was auspiciously launched from the midst of one
of the most exciting attempts in the world of the arts to come to terms with
what this conflict of forces means for the creatively minded. In the late 1920s
Jung and Beckett amongst others found themselves in a loosely knit community of intellectuals contributing to a journal called *transition: an International Quarterly for Creative Experiment*, which ran for eleven years.
Some of Beckett's first published poetry appeared in the same issue (no.
19/20) as Jung's seminal lecture on 'Psychology and poetry',[2] where his
views on creativity were first communicated to the English-speaking world.
A few years later Beckett heard Jung lecture at London's Tavistock Clinic.
Like Jung, Beckett was preoccupied by the manner in which some literary
works seemed to write themselves. It can hardly be doubted that Beckett
read Jung's theories, since they accord so closely with his own: 'Art . . .
seizes a human being and makes him its instrument, one who allows art to
realise its purposes through him . . . He is subordinate to it, and we have no
right to expect him to interpret it for us. He has done his utmost by giving it
form'.[3] Beckett rarely went further in explaining his work than to say: 'It
means what it says'. Jung, as a psychologist opposing Freud, and Beckett as
a writer, angrily denouncing determination of symbols and the 'vulgarity' of
literary realism (*PTD*, 81), were, whether or not confessedly, in deep agreement. For Jung, the work of art in the imagination of the artist manifested
the creative principle just as a child does in the womb of the mother. Jung
saw art as reconnecting humans, rationalistically separated from the universe, with the ground of the universe, its principial energy. Beckett had
begun postgraduate life by attempting a thesis on Descartes, but had abandoned it upon realising that Descartes' search for systematic clarity was
foreign to his nature. For Beckett 'art has nothing to do with clarity, does
not dabble in the clear or make clear [. . .] Art is the sun, moon and stars of
the mind, the whole mind' (*D*, 94). This holistic view of 1938 is anticipated
in the 1932 'Poetry is vertical' manifesto, devised by *transition*'s editor
Eugene Jolas and signed by Beckett, which consciously dissociates itself
from 'a world ruled by the hypnosis of positivism, [. . .] the sterilisation of
the living imagination'.[4]

For the *transition* writers, speakers on behalf of the 'a-logical movement
of the psyche', the Cartesian Enlightenment was actually a darkening (*D*,
94). Descartes's effort had apparently been to introduce clarity into what he
thought was a confused picture. Earlier world-views had suggested the

'world' or 'outer' was as much a matter of consciousness as the 'self' or 'inner'; animism is an example of this perspective, as was the work of Jakob Böhme, writing at the same time as Descartes but as an adept of the older tradition: 'The life of man is the formed word of the divine knowledge.'[5] Or, in the form of the Neoplatonic tradition, 'the Cosmos is the Great Man'.[6] But for Descartes, the guarantee of a clear philosophy could only be found by trying to isolate the individual consciousness, the observer, from everything else. Sequestration led soon enough to separation, to treating the physical world, things, creatures, as *not-man*, and man as 'other than' world. As the physicist Fritjof Capra has observed:

> Descartes' famous sentence *Cogito ergo sum* – I think, therefore I exist – has led Western man to equate his identity with his mind, instead of with his whole organism. As a consequence of the Cartesian division, most individuals are aware of themselves as isolated individual egos existing inside their bodies. The mind has been separated from the body and given the futile task of controlling it, thus causing an apparent conflict between the conscious will and the involuntary instincts [...] this inner fragmentation of man mirrors his view of the world 'outside' which is seen as a multitude of separate objects and events.[7]

Beckett's narrators embody the spiritual emergency of the Cartesian consciousness, split off not only from the environment but also from its own organism, so that all it is left with is 'thinking, if that is the name for this vertiginous panic as of hornets smoked out of their nest' (*T*, 322). No image of panic could be more panic-stricken than that. The Cartesian split goes against the spiritual ecology of the human mind just as the smoke does against the delicate equilibrium of the baleful insects. Beckett's lost, blind, will-less, impotent, dried-up tramps and wanderers are the casualties of Cartesianism. We see Beckett's tramps meandering from name – Molloy – to name – Malone – to namelessness – the 'Unnamable' – withering as the severance of self from world takes its effect. Under the 'hypnosis of positivism', or the rule of mechanistic reason, there can be no answer to the question *What am I?* other than 'I am a thinking machine whose disintegration is inevitable and utterly gratuitous.' What Beckett is really doing is probing the mechanistic postulate and exposing its rotten, even dead, heart. He gives no easy answers not because the predicament is doomed and issue-less (cf. *D*, 97), but because no conceptual prescriptions could meet the force of 'something strange that derives its existence from the hinterland of man's mind, as if it had emerged from the abyss of prehuman ages, [...] a presentiment of incomprehensible happenings in the pleroma, [...] a glimpse of the psychic world that terrifies the primitive and is at the same time his greatest hope'.[8] Beckett's trilogy resounds constantly with this strangeness. Just as Jung called art 'a glimpse into the unfathomable abyss of the unborn and things yet to be', so Beckett writes in *The Unnamable*, a story of 'your time, others' time, the time of the ancient dead and the yet unborn' (*T*, 358).

Anguish closes in on the person who, hypnotized by positivism, cut off from the living mystery, feels himself to be nothing more than an isolated thinking machine. So Beckett's characters are mostly homeless, culturally and physically, and move just like machines, 'their great balls and sockets rattling and clacking' (*T*, 214). It is made clear that they once had a home, a culture, education and parentage, not to speak of a metaphysical or spiritual 'home'. Just as the word *homeless* has the ghost of home in it, so the people of Beckett's lost world faintly hear the breath of the pleroma and feel its unseen immensity. Their isolation is not that of never having been or never having had, but the isolation of separation – the *lessening* of contact, the *weakening* of musculature, the *wandering* of mind, the *fading* of destination. The emphasis on separation leading to isolation is crucial, and is imaged and discoursed upon constantly by Beckett's narrators. Their predicament is epitomized in the person of Molloy, whose relations with other people are drained of sentiment, but who still has a glimmer of attachment to material, inanimate, objects. He shuns everyone he meets, especially his mother (whom he actually meets only in reminiscence), but fondles the pebbles in his pocket and jealously guards his knick-knacks.

The chronological history and surface contents of these seven narratives are quickly told. All first written in French, beginning with the *nouvelles*, between 1945 and 1950, and later translated, they tell, in somewhat varying styles, of what is essentially the same character. He has many different incarnations and names, as he goes from story to story. But in the final novel, *The Unnamable*, they are all declared to be 'vice-existers' (*T*, 289) for the one self who speaks, either about them, or out of their own mouths. Here even the protagonists from Beckett's earlier fiction join in the chain of vice-existers, from Belacqua, through Murphy, Watt, Mercier, Camier, Molloy, Moran, Malone, Saposcat, Macmann, Mahood, to Worm, the last in the line, shorn of all identity. The I-narrators of the *nouvelles* have no name but they are equally members of this chain of nearly identical characters.

In the prose and plays alike, the same description fits them all: the homeless, wandering, ageing male, with hat; boots; long coat; infected scalp; speech impediments; general sensory confusion; a special fondness for small objects; sensitivity to animals and plants and dawn/dusk twilights; a tendency to aporia (purposiveness without purpose); hatred of sexuality, conception and birth; isolation from relationships with human beings; varying degrees of cripplement; and a rarely failing sense of humour in the midst of these deprivations. By describing what seem to be distinct individuals who are ultimately re-reflections of the same human state, Beckett is able to illustrate the human consequences of a philosophical perspective, without naming it directly. This is what makes him a literary artist, someone who has rendered the consciousness of an age – which in the hands of the philosopher cannot move beyond the discourse of rational exposition – into an *impression*, the story he tells, the images he brings before the mind's eye of the reader. So the isolation of the Beckett character speaks for itself: it is not talked *about*, but *inscribed* (by the author as writer) and *envoiced* (by the author as speaker). Unlike a tract or commentary, a work of art, said Jung, 'acts upon us as it acted upon the artist. To grasp its meaning we must allow it to shape us as it shaped him'.[9]

Three aspects of the Cartesian separation spring from Beckett's pages with exceptional force. The first is in the realm of the storyteller's discourse, the question as to whether words can tell the truth or not; whether they, as well as the mind, are forever separate from the world. The second is in the realm of the storyteller's images: Beckett's celebrated evocation of humans shut up in a small circular space – be it dustbin, urn, jar, log-hut, bone of the skull, pile of sand. The third is a ruthless rhetorical arsenal, constantly speaking of the supposed 'not-man' part of existence in terms of mud, slime, excrement, that is, of formless, undifferentiated matter, the manifest correlative of what in traditional philosophy used to be called *prima materia*. Beckett's language relates this matter to the sexual function.

These three issues run deep in all Beckett's poetry, drama and later fiction. But it is in the trilogy that they make their most obvious and memorable, not to mention accessible, impression. The Cartesian split is particularly evident here because the chosen form – a solitary self speaking about itself – perfectly matches the philosophical concern and agony of the post-Cartesian world: a concern with self and its supposed separability from not-self.

The rambling, formless appearance of the *nouvelles* and *Molloy*, *Malone dies* and *The Unnamable* is only skin-deep. They are cohered by a compelling cyclic or circular logic which turns into one process the three themes briefly introduced. There are two cycles, or to be more precise, one process seen in two different ways. The first is the negative one which Beckett's people are in as they narrate: from sexuality arises the sin and pain of birth, and then during life the fear of engagement with further generative sexuality. Language tries to confirm a false independent personality which does not really exist, and so doubts itself all the time. Birth, relationships and language being felt as sinful or futile, the only refuge is death, oblivion, never having been. The second cycle is the one which the characters dimly remember and sometimes long for, the non-Cartesian one. Here they recall, and glimpse now and then, a state where the circle was positive instead of negative and consisted of the primordial identity of I and not-I, followed by descent into matter via the fluids of conception and birth, with a sense during physical existence that language once was and could still be able to tell the truth and so work as a conscious link to the originary top of the circle again. Only by exploring Beckett's parallel account of both these cycles can the depth of his imaginative resources be understood.

Our study of this circle, like Beckett's evocation of its stages, could join it at any point, but since the stories are about humans, birth is the place to begin.

Beckett's evocations of mud, slime, mucus, sexual love and birth are linked inexorably together; they symbolize human existence in matter. His 'heroes' often speak as though birth is something that happens *to* them; that, therefore, individuation as a person was somehow an event which the pre-existent being might have avoided or postponed. Beckett speaks, notoriously, of the *sin* of having been born (*PTD*, 67). Jung's Tavistock lecture, heard by Beckett, related the case of a girl who had not been properly born, that is, not become fully agreed to the fact of being incarnate.[10] All Beckett's people echo this, from first to last. The hero of *First love* is appalled to the point of nausea by his girl-friend's pregnancy, while she celebrates it. He leaves her, hearing her cries as she gives birth, which 'pursued him down the stairs and out into the street [...] As soon as I halted I heard them again, a little fainter each time, admittedly, but what does it matter, cry is cry, all that matters is that it should cease. For years I thought they would cease. Now I don't think so any more' (*CSP*, 19). The whole story pivots on this: the father wishes birth would cease, even that it had never been caused, but knows that conception has bound the mother, the child and him. Conception and birth cannot be undone; so whoever has not been fully born, that is, not fully forgotten where he came from, will feel revulsion, the pull away from incarnation (the will to non-existence) and at the same time the pull towards it (from sex). So Malone calls the womb of his mother 'putrid mucus' (*T*, 207); Molloy feels 'remorse at having begotten' his son (*T*, 96), just as the teller of *The end* unexpectedly, with horror, catches sight of 'his son, the insufferable son of a bitch' (*CSP*, 59). The defiant narrator imagining non-existence says in *The Unnamable*: 'The slut has yet to menstruate capable of whelping me [...] a sperm, dying of cold in the sheets, some people are lucky, born of a wet dream and dead before morning. I must say

I'm tempted . . .' (*T*, 349). This same self, incarnated as Macmann, wonders 'if it was really necessary to be guilty in order to be punished but for the memory, more and more galling, of his having consented to live in his mother, then to leave her' (*T*, 220). Molloy longs to see his testicles 'gone, from the old stand where they bore false witness, for and against, in the life-long charge against me' (*T*, 34). *The Unnamable*'s Mahood describes himself as having, by way of killing his parents and family, 'been delivered of a pack of blood relations, not to mention the two cunts into the bargain, the one forever accursed that ejected me into this world and the other, infundibuliform, in which, pumping my likes, I tried to take revenge' (*T*, 296). Beckett's narrators often give way to this cruelty when the subject of birth comes up: 'I'm looking for my mother to kill her. I should have thought of that a bit earlier, before being born' (*T*, 360). Molloy is kinder to his mother: 'I know she did all she could not to have me, except of course the one thing' (*T*, 19). Macmann, in *Malone dies*, is imagined childless, so as to escape the pain: 'His semen had never done any harm to anyone. So his link with the species was through his ascendants only, who were all dead' (*T*, 221). For Beckett's heroes, the harm is in the descendants. Descent, literally, is the hated tragedy, the descent into flesh via the slime and mucus of generation. His characters are explicitly horrified by the phenomenon known to the Neoplatonists as the descent of the soul.[11] The speaker of *The Unnamable*, diminished almost to annihilation, wishes 'If only I were not obliged to manifest'; and, imagining himself having taken leave of the world, he says, 'There will never be another woman wanting me in vain to live' (*T*, 271, 317). Lulu in *First love* was just this woman, inviting him to a relationship and a child. Thus, each story tells the same story.

As if this way of describing reproduction were not enough to make the point, Beckett goes a stage further. This view metaphorically transposes itself into a view not only of children but of all material existence, the physical world. And on top of that, the whole thing is given a name, the shit, the apotheosis of the unwanted. It shows up everywhere, in signs like the hovel in *The end* where the wandering hero finds a mess – excrement, rubbish, vomit, used condoms, along with 'a cowpat in which a heart had been traced, pierced by an arrow' (*CSP*, 61). Here the formless detritus of humans and animals is equated with the potential for generation out of formless fluids presented in sexual love. Molloy manages still further to stress this equation of maternal/material generation with refuse and elimination in an extraordinary disquisition on the 'arsehole [. . .] Perhaps it is less to be thought of as the eyesore here called by its name than as the symbol of those passed over in silence, a distinction due perhaps to its centrality and its air of being a link between me and the other excrement'

(T, 73). So each human born is an addition not only to the sum of the physical world, but also to the pile of shit represented by it and by life to a man like Molloy (and, as likely as not, like Beckett, who as critic had already used Leopardi's line *E fango è il mondo* (the world is mud) as the epigraph to his 1931 essay *Proust*).

This rhetorical equation is increasingly hammered home, in case the reader should miss it: 'if ever I'm reduced to looking for a meaning to my life, it's in that old mess that I'll stick my nose to begin with, the mess of that old uniparous whore' by which Molloy (T, 19) means his mother. *The Unnamable*'s narrator speaks of 'not knowing how to move, either locally in relation to myself, nor bodily, in relation to the rest of the shit' (T, 322). The outgoings of the womb and of the rectum are indissolubly confused; and the equation fits the colloquial description of life in the world – the shit – just as well as it does the like equation of generation with failure in the phrase 'making a balls of it', a pun which Molloy does not miss his chance to brandish (T, 34). *The Unnamable*'s narrator, sitting in his own excrement in a jar opposite a café in Paris, voices this disgust subtly from another angle: 'In the morning, when she has rattled up her shutters, the first look of her eyes still moist with fornication is for the jar' (T, 304).

This equation is not a trick or diversion; it is ingrained in Beckett's prose language. It puts the Cartesian division of self from not-self into instinctual, sexual, physical terms, which feel at once more unanswerable and more disturbing than a philosophic precept could possibly seem. Peter Conrad saw the pitched battle against *mess* implicit in advertisements for household cleaning agents as another figuration of Cartesian isolation of self from surrounding world.[12] *First love*'s hero distinguishes between himself on the one hand, and on the other, 'that residue of execrable frippery known as the non-self, or even the world, for short' (CSP, 6). Like the hovel's contents in *The end*, the world itself is seen as execrable residue. Molloy calls the surroundings 'muck': 'if all muck is the same muck that doesn't matter, it's good to have a change of muck, to move from one heap to another, a little further on' (T, 39). Already in *Watt*, in Arsene's twenty-five page 'short statement', Beckett had described the earth and the earthly life as 'excrement [...] a turd [...] a cat's flux' (W, 45–6).

Common to all these various descriptions is that they rigorously exclude the world from the self, and at the same time term it a *mess*, a mess connoted by mud, vomit, excrement, sexual fluids and afterbirths (which many characters scattered over the six decades of Beckett's writings see left by sheep on hillsides); a mess which could otherwise be described as matter with the potentiality to produce form, but not yet having produced it. So

Beckett's men fear women for their reproductive capability, envy them for their mercy, and blame the fertility of both sexes for being drawn towards conception. Similarly, shit and mud can otherwise be called fertilizer and soil, supporting potential form into manifestation. Simply reversing the perspective makes all the difference.

This 'mess' is the *prima materia* of the alchemists;[13] the common etymological root of *materia* and *maternal* is no coincidence. William Blake called it the 'Vegetable Universe'. And Beckett's characters, like Jung's 'unborn' girl, cannot assent to this incidence of form from the formless, this descent of the soul, especially when it takes the form of new human life. Malone describes the Lambert family as an example of people who *have* assented totally, even too much, to having been born: 'men and women embedded deep in life, hoping for nothing more, for themselves or for others' (*T*, 183). The hint is that they lack aspiration, and compassion for others, and it is no coincidence that this family are animal slaughterers by profession. The scene of the life lived around Beckett's narrators is always a scene overrun with slaughterhouses, they are round every corner. Sapo's playground is adjacent to one (*T*, 195); Molloy says 'the country is full of them' (*T*, 28); *The Unnamable*'s narrator lives in a jar opposite a restaurant on the way to an abattoir – 'here all is killing and eating', he says (*T*, 313). This compassion for animal life, which Beckett, like the Buddhist, feels, becomes less the more embedded in physical life you become. Like Plato's reborn souls who have drunk the Lethean waters (forgetfulness of past state), the Lamberts can be absorbed in matter without problems. Being fully born is fully to forget. But most of Beckett's people who have 'never been properly born' as *Watt*'s Addenda say of Watt (*W*, 248), cannot properly forget: whence their agony and fear in relation to growth, sex, generation, and their arrogant attempts to rule themselves out as independent of the shit.

It is here that the Beckett characters' peculiar love for inanimate objects begins to make sense. Such things are the furthest from fertility: stones, metal knife-rests, wooden objects. *First love*'s callous protagonist, while verbally excoriating the pregnant woman, tells the reader: 'it was things made me weep' (*CSP*, 11). It is as though love is only reserved for things, which have no choice about coming into manifestation. Animals are accorded some sympathy, then, but humans not, because they have the choice whether or not to bring about more of their kind. But still, an impulse of perplexity, possibly shame, causes Malone to identify his emotion as a 'foul feeling of pity [...] in the presence of [...] little portable things'. It is as though he senses this response to objects is not quite in order, but does not know why, just as he feels slightly rueful about 'never having really evolved in the fields of affection and passion, in spite of my experiences' (*T*, 227).

The 'mess', *prima materia*, is at once hated for its ability to produce more matter, and yet attractive, perhaps as a reminder of what precedes manifestation: 'the calm that precedes life ... it's like slime, paradise, but for this noise, it's life trying to get in, no, trying to get him out' (*T*, 335). The next stage in the cycle will make more apparent why *life* comes to be seen as such an adversary.

Beckett's depictions of confinement within a closed space are known even amongst those who have never seen a Beckett play, or read his novels. Here we are faced with a complex of images unique to Beckett; in the trilogy the image is of a jar enclosing the narrator. Sometimes it is merely a thought or comparison in the narrator's imagination; sometimes, as in *The Unnamable*, the narrative image itself is of a being, a person, trapped in a jar constantly. Being shut in a jar is the final physical expression of a state which begins merely as a thought, the thought of 'the régime of systematic doubt prescribed by Descartes, in which everything potentially deceptive, the external world, memory, the senses themselves, is ruled inadmissible [...] until all the philosopher is left with is the flicker of doubt itself, the self-reflexive *cogito* which is the ground and guarantee of being'.[14] The external world is *ruled out*; from there it is a short step to being *shut out*. And what must come of this is less than a step away: the very moment the external world is shut out, the 'cogitator' is *shut in*. The enclosure is complete, the jar, its perfect symbol, is in place, with its victim inside. The jar prison is imaginally[15] equivalent to the Cartesian *cogito* or mind, due to Beckett's celebrated play on colour, sound and image which suggests by turns that the prison is a room, the bone of the skull, the ratiocinative mind, and a jar-like container. Each trope embodies the same state of being, the cut-off-ness, to which Jung, R. D. Laing and Owen Barfield, amongst others, attribute the phenomenon of schizophrenia. Beckett's gamut of figurations of this state is endless; in the trilogy the following deserve especial notice:

I woke up in a bed, in my skin. (*T*, 36)

In that block the prey is lodged and thinks himself a being apart. (*T*, 102)

A head, but solid, solid bone, and you imbedded in it, like a fossil in a rock. (*T*, 362)

I say to myself I am in a head. (*T*, 322)

Back to this foul little den all dirty, white and vaulted. (*T*, 217)

I was a solid in the midst of other solids. (*T*, 99)

I see at the confines of this restless gloom a gleam and shimmering as of
bones. (T, 205)

Enormous prison, and in it, somewhere, riveted, tiny, the prisoner. (T, 377)

This inexhaustible variety of descriptions is characteristic of the *mundus
imaginalis*, what Henry Corbin has called the imaginal world, in which sensible images take on meaning, and meaning clothes itself in imagined
forms.[16] Jung would say that at such a point an archetype becomes intelligible: and this is more than a metaphor as conventionally defined, which
would simply speak of one thing in terms of another regardless of whether
the link between them is intrinsic or extrinsic.

For Beckett the confinement of the thinker does not stop at itself. It subtly
but inevitably leads him to total self-centredness: 'I on whom all dangles,
about whom all turns' (T, 342); 'perhaps that's what I am, the thing that
divides the world in two, on the one side the outside, on the other the inside
[...] I'm the tympanum, on the one hand the mind, on the other the
world', says the narrator of *The Unnamable* (T, 357). 'Anything is prefer-
able to the consciousness of third parties, and more generally speaking of an
outer world' (T, 359).

Not only this: there is a wretchedness about this condition of confinement
to the 'ancient head abandoned to its solitary resources' (T, 332), revealed in
the Beckett hero's infected scalp and the shame he feels doffing his hat: 'I
slipped it smartly forward, held it a second poised in such a way that the
person addressed could not see my skull, then slipped it back.' 'I could not
go about bare-headed, with my skull in the state it was' (CSP, 51).

These are all variations on the main image of the imprisoning jar and its
confined, stranded or islanded consciousness. Seventeen pages of *The Unnamable* (T, 378 ff.) are given over to it, 'lashed to a rock, it's a body, it's
not I, I'm not outside, I'm inside, I'm inside something, I'm shut up'. The
anguish is obvious here: this confinement is not a consolation, nor a guarantee of being, nor any of the things Descartes perhaps hoped it could be. The
speaker here even tries to propose, frantically, that his confined consciousness is 'not I', even though his educators, the post-Cartesian civilization,
have brought him up with the teaching that it is. 'I'm locked up, I'm in
something, it's not I' (T, 373). Here is a hint of the true nature of identity,
dropped in the heat of the moment.

Such hints are followed up by the Beckett hero at times of lesser anxiety.
One of the most revealing of all the trilogy's jar images occurs at a point
where the Cartesian prison gives way to an altogether different state of being. Molloy is standing in a garden, listening to the 'sound the earth makes,
that far unchanging noise which other noises cover, but not for long':

There was another noise, that of my life become the life of this garden, as it rode the earth of deeps and wildernesses. Yes, there were times when I forgot not only who I was, but that I was, forgot to be. Then I was no longer that sealed jar to which I owed my being so well preserved, but a wall gave way and I filled with roots and tame stems, for example, stakes long since dead and ready for burning, the recess of night and the imminence of dawn, and then the labour of the planet rolling eager into winter, winter would rid it of these contemptible scabs. Or of that winter I was the precarious calm, the thaw of the snows, [...] But that did not happen to me very often, mostly I stayed in my jar which knew neither seasons nor gardens.   (T, 46)

This is a perception opened from its isolation and confinement and explicitly contrasted with them. What a far cry it is from Malone's 'I am far from the sounds of blood and breath, immured' (T, 171), the state which Beckett's characters are usually in. Significantly, and touchingly, Molloy's state of mystical identity with the surrounding world is only allowed with plants, 'roots and tame stems'; the pain and guilt of birth has prevented him from mingling with the feminine principle in women and sexual love. 'Blood and breath' are too much for him, reminding him of his absolute dependence on the *prima materia* and his complicity in conception, whether as transmitter or as recipient.

The immolating isolation of being in the jar, despite its all too brief relief, inevitably means that relationships are impossible for the Beckett heroes. From *First love* to *The Unnamable*, all the narrators without exception have forgotten how to communicate: 'When asked something, I take time to know what' (T, 27); 'So far from words so long', in his 'rare conversations with men', Molloy has to 'avoid speaking as much as possible' (T, 30, 33). Then it is no wonder that they all with one voice echo Malone's: 'I never knew anyone' (T, 217). Human relationships are replaced by relationships with stones, plants and animals, from which even the Cartesian duality cannot estrange these characters completely.

This would explain their unusually careful and tender observations of plants and animals. 'I have always loved skinning branches and laying bare the pretty white glossy shaft of sapwood. But obscure feelings of love and pity for the tree held me back most of the time', says Moran. 'Personally I just liked plants, in all innocence and simplicity. I even saw in them at times a superfetatory proof of the existence of God' (T, 138, 91). The *nouvelles'* narrators share this dispassionate yet wholly sympathetic understanding, of animals this time: 'Toads at evening, motionless for hours, lap flies from the air. They like to squat where cover ends and open air begins, they favour thresholds', says the narrator of *The end* (CSP, 66). The Expelled, likewise sensitive, 'several times during the night [...] felt the horse looking at me through the window and the breath of its nostrils' (*CSP*, 32). Moran, again, meditates on 'flies, I like to think of those that hatch out at the beginning of winter, within doors, and die shortly after. You see them crawling and fluttering in the warm corners, puny, sluggish, torpid, mute. That is you see the odd one, now and then. They must die very young, without having been able to lay. You sweep them away, you push them into the dust-pan with the brush, without knowing. That is a strange race of flies' (*T*, 153). There is no anguished temper in Beckett's writing at these points, where suddenly the observer is not cut off from the observed, but one life with it, in calm and compassion. This respect for animals is very deep, like the Buddhist's; Moran has no greater satisfaction than to contemplate the honey-bees' dance (*T*, 155–6), and no wording could make clearer the contrast between this participation in the complex life of the universe and the dry Cartesian mind Moran has been brought up with: 'For me, sitting near my sun-drenched hives, it would always be a noble thing to contemplate, too noble ever to be sullied by the cogitations of a man like me, exiled in his manhood. And I would never do my bees the wrong I had done my God, to whom I had been taught to ascribe my angers, fears, desires, and even my body' (*T*, 156). It is no coincidence that the honey-bee is the mystics', not the conventional religions', symbol of divine wisdom in the life of the universe; nor is it by accident that Beckett echoes Descartes' *cogito*, speaking here in the voice of the exiled Moran.

I said earlier that the trilogy's evocations of the self could be seen in terms of two cycles, one of them describing existence as guilt and separation, with oblivion the only solution; the other cycle seeing birth as the descent into manifestation, and consciousness as bearing the purpose of returning a manifest being to its source having realized its essential *identity with* its source, not its separateness as per the dualist view. When Molloy sees the 'walls giving way' in his moment of inspired perception (*T*, 46), at that moment the dualist cycle has also given way and he participates in the cycle of union or mystical awareness, and the Cartesian error is suddenly healed. The self suddenly sees that being born does not have to mean being shut up, immured in 'the skull, seat of all the shit and misery' (*T*, 245). There is another way, and to find it is to answer the question, *What am I?*

The prisoner's desire, *per se*, is for liberation, and it is this which the self, or soul, of Beckett's fiction continually strives for. In the consciousness of liberation we are returned to the ancient concept of Pythagoras, Plotinus, Paracelsus, Böhme, Coleridge and George Russell, to name six exponents of the *philosophia perennis* – a perspective in which the human ('little man') is in the image of the cosmos ('great man') and in which the problem of self and world is explained thus: the microcosm (human) is neither separate from nor other than the macrocosm (deity); it is merely distinguished and individuated by its mode of manifestation, just like the hand of a person or the leaf of a tree. This holistic vision is shared by mystics and researchers into physics such as David Bohm, Fritjof Capra and Danah Zohar.[17]

Malone, too, sees a profound vision of the self's essential, if not apparent, identity with his environment and the cosmos:

> [...] the eyes stare into the space before them, namely the fulness of the great deep with its unchanging calm [...] But at long intervals they close, [...] Perhaps it is then he sees the heaven of the old dream, the heaven of the sea and of the earth too, and the spasms of the waves from shore to shore all stirring to their tiniest stir [...]   (*T*, 214)

It is important that Malone's eyes are closed: instead of physical observation of the natural events, Malone is conscious with, his mind is animated with, the relation between sea, earth, waves and shore. The 'heaven of' these is the identity of self and cosmos, all too soon aggressed upon by

> the so different motion of men, [...] who are not tied together, but free to come and go as they please. And they make full use of it, and come and go, their great balls and sockets rattling and clacking like knackers, each on his way.   (*T*, 214)

The root of the evil is pointed to in this phrase 'free to come and go as they please'. According to the *philosophia perennis*, if humans do not use their freedom to align themselves with or harmonize with the cosmos/'great man'/deity, as the sea does with heaven in Malone's vision, then their freedom becomes self-will or egotism, and their surrounding world and universe merely something to exploit, a mine to plunder. Hence the deep regret felt in Malone's saying 'And they make full use of it' and the death-ridden cruelty haunting his comparison of men with 'knackers'.

In the 'heaven of the old dream' Malone reminds us all of the ecology of the psyche or soul. Mind is as much an ecosystem as is the biosphere, soil, sky or ocean. In fact it is no other than that, just as it is no other than God. And here we begin to see yet another element in the grim background to the Beckett heroes' fear of sexual love. For if no-one has this harmonizing knowledge, what can further births bring to the world, except more harm? In actual fact, men may be more 'tied together' than Malone thinks, and certainly so in respect of the cosmos; they are utterly dependent on earth and atmosphere for their barest survival. There is only a limited sense in which they can be 'free to come and go as they please'; and for the mystic, there can be only one pleasure, God's pleasure, just as there can be only one existence, God's existence. The application of the term *God* is wider here than the one established in the mainstream of Christianity and humanist thinking.[18]

The cycle of mystical union, then, known to the Sufis as the path of return,[19] is suggested as the alternative to the guilt-laden cycle of separation, isolated self-absorption and hatred of life. This path is mentioned at an intriguing moment in the trilogy when Malone tries to fathom his motive for choosing to be born. Somehow he feels his attempt failed – he did not really get born (into full knowledge of identity, perhaps?) but

> what I sought, when I struggled out of my hole, then aloft through the sting-ing air towards an inaccessible boon, was the rapture of vertigo, the letting go, the fall, the gulf, the relapse to darkness, to nothingness, to earnestness, to home, to him waiting for me always, who needed me and whom I needed, who took me in his arms and told me to stay with him always, who gave me his place and watched over me, who suffered every time I left him, whom I have often made suffer and seldom contented, whom I have never seen.
>
> (*T, 179*)

The 'he' here is not simply a friend, or a father, or the Christian God. Malone is also speaking of the ground of Being, and of that in it which gives expression to his hidden self; of the journey out of it into the world, manifestation by birth – 'the hole'; and then of the return to the Unmanifest. Elsewhere, *The Unnamable* puts it differently: 'Who knows towards what high destiny I am heading, unless I am coming from it?' (*T, 360*).

Beckett was familiar with mystical texts and traditions, alluding to them several times in the trilogy: generally (*T, 241*); to the tree of life (*T, 136*); to the spiritual organs or chakras (*T, 219*); to the 'carnal envelope' (*T, 303*). Malone on his deathbed says 'If I were to stand up again [...] I fancy I would fill a considerable part of the universe, oh not more than lying down, but more noticeably' (*T, 215*). Beckett may be recalling Milton here, who saw man's standing erect as a sign of his kinship with heaven, as opposed to the horizontal position of the animals and the serpent (*Paradise lost*, VII, 506–10). These visions and residual references to the identity of human, cosmos and Ipseity keep suggesting that the rationalist predicament is not solved by nihilism or pessimism, but instead by transformation of self. 'The only reality is provided by the hieroglyphics of inspired perception', wrote Beckett in the essay *Proust* (*PTD, 84*).

The Cartesian split, embodied by Beckett in the infernal jar, imprisons the soul and prevents its communion with the life which is its own essential sustenance. This is Beckett's unique picture of existential anguish. When relief comes, it is always at times when the jar's walls give way and the soul is no longer caged. The soul is indeed, as Malone says, 'denied in vain'

(T, 204): it must break out of the cage if it is not to explode with anger or wither into nothingness.[20]

I have shown how the world of the Beckett character ruthlessly exposes two links in the tragic Cartesian chain. His antipathy to conception, and his equation of new life (and the existing world) with excrement and rubbish, have put him at a hopeless distance, conferring on him a 'privilege' which is more bane than blessing: all that is not my private consciousness is shit, my private consciousness is the only existent. This can only fail him in the end, turning his antipathy into guilt, and then to grief at the resulting isolation. Beckett then figures this in the prison of solipsism, the human shut up in a jar. The rare moments when the walls dissolve and the frustration gives way to peace show his hero, and us, that the Cartesian conclusion, though entrenched, is a false one.

The third link in the chain is the attitude to language in the two cycles. Language is the medium in which the foregoing themes have been brought forth in Beckett's novels, as well as being a subject of enquiry in itself on the part of his heroes. It is obviously the most 'literary' of the three figurings of modern consciousness so far discussed.

As well as marks on a page, words are sounds. To a correspondent's enquiry about the meaning of his work, Beckett's reply – that it is a matter of fundamental sounds – has become well-known. This agrees with the voice of The Unnamable: 'I emit sounds. If that's not enough for them I can't help it' (T, 324). The relations between a word and what it stood for, between word and meaning, occupied Beckett from the beginning. In this Beckett was truly a child of his time. The rise of Structuralism derived from Ferdinand de Saussure's investigations of the same relations. But before we assume Beckett drew the same conclusions as the Structuralists have done, we should remember Beckett's own warning: 'Art has nothing to do with clarity', nothing to do with 'solution clapped on problem like a snuffer on a candle' (D, 92). If anything, Beckett's word on this issue would suggest that the Saussurean view of language disintegrates the psyche rather than answering its questions.

The language of Beckett's novels does not only tell a story, transparently as it were, but it also reflects, as it tells, on the means of telling. This trick has many names, one of which – the 'narrator narrated' – has been current since the rise of the Modernist movement. Beckett's narrations are littered with second thoughts and comments which question the validity of what was put forward first:

> He left the house with his books under his arm, on the pretext that he worked better in the open air, no, without a word. (T, 178)

Here I go, none the less, mistakenly.   (*T*, 183)

The silence was absolute. Profound in any case.   (*T*, 109)

When I think, that is to say, no, let it stand, when I think of the times [...]
                                                         (*T*, 146)

Yes, the river still gave the impression it was flowing in the wrong direction.
That's all a pack of lies I feel.   (*CSP*, 54)

This doubting comment, qualification, review, built into the story, is discussed at length in most critical works on Beckett. It is so endemic to his prose that we find ourselves tempted to agree with Malone when he says to himself: 'My notes have a curious tendency, I realise at last, to annihilate all they purport to record' (*T*, 238); and when whoever tells *The Unnamable* asks 'how proceed? By aporia pure and simple? Or by affirmations and negations invalidated as uttered, or sooner or later?' (*T*, 267), we wonder how the remaining hundred pages of that novel will make any sense. 'All I say cancels out. I'll have said nothing', says the writer of *The calmative* (*CSP*, 36).

The link with modern philosophy and linguistics could be summed up in the dictum 'all descriptions are misdescriptions'; and Beckett in his later works plays more and more on this. 'Said is missaid [...] How better worse so-missay?' asks the voice of *Worstward Ho* (1983; *NO*, 113). It is difficult to explore this aspect of Beckett's style without discussing his whole *œuvre*. But the trilogy gives especially vocal doubts as to the ability of language to tell the truth – from, at one extreme, 'All lies, invented to explain I forget what' to 'I simply believe I can say nothing that is not true' at the other (*T*, 278; 216). The novels also dramatically evoke the psychic state of a person who makes this odd discovery about language. Put as briefly as possible, if words are labels, then each label describes properly only its difference from the next label, rather than describing the thing which it is supposed to label. And if a label is stuck too permanently on its thing, that thing is spoiled. This is what leads Beckett to speak of language so used as 'this long sin against the silence that enfolds us' (*T*, 345). Molloy reflects:

> My sense of identity was wrapped in a namelessness hard to penetrate [...] and so on for all the other things [...] when all was fading, waves and particles, there could be no things but nameless things, no names but thingless names. What do I know now about then, now when the icy words hail down upon me, the icy meanings, and the world dies too, foully named.   (*T*, 31)

If it is true, as positivism holds, that words only have an arbitrary relation with what they name, a relation established only by convention and for convenience, then anyone who has an experience, of a colour, say, or a sound, or any other event, will find the words for that experience no sooner said than dismissed as partial, non-essential, extrinsic, useless. Named, the world dies. So we sympathize with Molloy's 'whatever I said was never enough and always too much' (*T*, 33).

The agonies consequent on this feeling could be recounted *ad infinitum*, or at least *ad nauseam*. *The Unnamable* is really about nothing else; its self tries to find itself in speech, fails, and hopes for nothing more than to 'go silent'. Beckett's heroes denounce language as 'clatter', 'fatuous clamour', a 'frenzy of utterance', 'little phrases that [. . .] pollute the whole of speech' (*T*, 177). 'Ideas are so alike, when you get to know them' (*T*, 207), 'the same old thing, always the same wrong thing said always wrong' (*T*, 344).

These people sense that words and their meanings, as usually understood, do not help to explain existence. They do not relate to what they name except in an arbitrary and deadening way. Molloy desperately concludes that the only choice is 'to lie or hold your peace' (*T*, 81).

Their predicament is the formation in art of the tremendous question underlying language: the question about the true function of the human being. The characters, though often frustrated and angry, constantly speak of 'a passion for truth', 'in the frenzy of utterance, the concern with truth'; 'within me the wild beast of earnestness padded up and down, roaring, ravening, rending' (*T*, 179). 'I whose soul writhed from morning to night, in the mere quest of itself' (*CSP*, 23); 'I seek, like a caged beast' (*T*, 356).

Freedom cannot be found by trying to define the self in concepts. It has to be sought by other means than the discursive language which, naming experience, kills it. Just as the caged beast has another life which the cage denies it, so the self has another vital mode of existence denied by the positivist view of language. Simply speaking and hoping for the best is not enough. 'I tell myself so many things', says Malone. 'What truth is there in all this babble?' (*T*, 216; punning on Babel, the confusion of tongues). The question is put finally, in view of all this: 'Would it not be better if I were simply to keep on saying babababa, for example, while waiting to ascertain the true function of this venerable organ?' (*T*, 283). The question is understandable. I think Beckett came close to indicating the way this question could be answered, but he cannot spell it out because 'spelling out' is perhaps not the true function of 'this venerable organ'. 'What can be said of the real silence' (*T*, 376)?

Ways to the answer are implicit, I believe, in Beckett's reference to 'fundamental sounds' (*D*, 109); and in the curious observations Molloy and Malone make on the nature of silence, and its *hearability*: 'the noise you hear when you really listen, when all seems hushed [. . .] the far unchanging noise the earth makes and which other noises cover' (*T*, 46); what Beckett's *Ill seen ill said* (1982) calls 'silence merging into music infinitely far and as unbroken as silence. Ceaseless celestial winds in unison' (*NO*, 83). Molloy drops hints constantly about these sounds, when he does not mention them directly. 'I seemed to hear a distant music', he says, apparently *à propos* nothing in particular. Half a page later, having left Lousse's house, he directly connects music, in his mind and in ours, with the cosmos and its movements, something which in the perennial philosophy was known as the music of the spheres: 'I am going towards the sun', he says, 'out in the heart again of the pre-established harmony, which makes so sweet a music, for one who has an ear for music' (*T*, 58). He is echoing Leibniz, and also Plotinus and Pythagoras, whose doctrines of music in the forces of the universe entered Europe through the Florentine court of Marsilio Ficino.[21] Beckett's heroes are very strongly attracted to the gleams of dawn and twilight, where the rays of the sun, moon and planets are at their most conspicuous because in transition. 'When I am abroad in the morning I go to meet the sun, and in the evening, when I am abroad, I follow it, till I am down among the dead.' That is how the Expelled finishes his story (*CSP*, 33).

In this miraculous music, which Beckett refers to without seeking too closely to define it, sound and vision are united, and reveal the secret meaning of *sounds*, a meaning which discourse can hardly touch. Cartesian perceptions of language see sounds as tokens which in combination add up to knowledge, but only in the conceptual realm. The ancient theory of planetary music, and sound's relation to it, suggest something much more integral. Sound, hence also the root of speech, not only links humans to the universe, but is the very energy of its grounding and motion. In *The candle of vision*, which Beckett knew, George Russell restated this traditional knowledge: 'The roots of human speech are the sound correspondences of powers which in their combination and interaction make up the universe.'[22] So did Gerhart Hauptmann, whom Jung quotes as saying that 'poetry evokes out of words the resonance of the primordial word'. *transition*'s Verticalist Manifesto alludes to this tradition consciously in its promotion of language as a 'mantic instrument', and of 'Orphic creativity'. (And Beckett returned to this theme in a short piece called *Sounds*, a companion to *Still* and *Still 3*.[23])

It is here that Beckett's seeker, the desperate soul, the caged beast, begins to feel what it is that Cartesianism blocked from the awareness of eighteenth-century philosophy, art and cultural life, and that a still prevailing positivism continues to obscure from us now. Beckett undoes the Cartesian perception, exposes it as 'spatter', 'fraud', a false view 'rammed down my gullet' by 'a dirty pack of fake maniacs' (*T*, 338). He shows the situation of one under its illusion to be tragic, or at best ridiculous.

It is through his intimation of the cosmology described in terms of the music of the planets and the mystic path of return that Beckett exposes the shortcoming of the positivist Cartesian system. Although 'spelling out' is not in the nature of this kind of awareness, Beckett is as near to explicit about it as it is possible to be. 'Homo mensura can't do without staffage', says Molloy, giving the empiricist his due. 'But to be beyond knowing anything, to know you are beyond knowing anything, that is when peace enters in, to the soul of the incurious seeker' (*T*, 59). In this condition Molloy can also begin to feel the origins of his existence, the ground sounds of the great universe, in '*a lower frequency, or a higher, than that of ratiocination* [. . .]' pure sounds, free of all meaning' (*T*, 47; my italics). Freedom from literal, indexical meaning liberates perception of the hidden truth about oneself. It is then that 'peace enters in'.

It is this lost vision which Beckett's seekers remember dimly, with a memory much longer than the habit-forming associative memory high-lighted by Hume and Locke and the reductionist psychologies that followed in their wake (cf. *T*, 45). It is for the sake of this vision that Beckett's wanderers, bereft of nearly everything they could possibly lose, still seek, still – as they put it – 'go on'. In the words of Dom Sylvester Houédard, 'That question which makes all other questions possible is thus unique and unlike any other question'. Seeking is 'equally our acknowledgement that there is something to know *and* that we desire to know it'.[24] So Beckett's moribunds go on, seeking, 'clawing towards a light and countenance I could not name, that I had once known and long denied' (*T*, 137).

Beckett writes of what Jung identified in the title of one of his books, 'modern man in search of a soul'. Every literary resource at his command in the trilogy and *nouvelles*, whether of rhetoric, image or symbol, is dedicated to this end. Perhaps Beckett refused to interpret his own work for much the same reasons as Molloy feels doubtful about the value of discursive expla-nations. Whatever he said about it would have been 'never enough, and always too much'. Like Kafka and Paul Klee, both of whose work appeared in *transition*, Beckett deals with experiences that have their existence in the night-world and regions where intuition is the only guide. The works them-selves are the fullest account possible of what the artist has glimpsed, so any explanation is bound to fall short. Jung said of such works that they 'posi-tively force themselves upon the author; his hand is seized, his pen writes things that his mind contemplates in amazement. The work brings with it its own form; anything he wants to add is rejected, and what he himself would like to reject is thrust back at him. While his conscious mind stands amazed and empty before this phenomenon, he is overwhelmed by a flood of thoughts and images which he had never intended to create and which his own will would never have brought into being. Yet in spite of himself he is forced to admit that it is his own self speaking, his own inner nature revealing itself and uttering things which he would never have entrusted to his tongue.'[25]

The Unnamable is the culmination of the search, and it does reach a conclusion of sorts, not an impasse as many critics have claimed. Put simply, the conclusion is that there appear to be two I's, not one. The first is apparent only, using discursive reasoning, explanations, personal history, rhetoric and pretexts to try to bolster up the illusion that it actually exists as a separate personality. Beckett ascribes all his vice-existers, with their vague names and tattered histories, to this class. 'They have made me waste my time, suffer for nothing, speak of them when, in order to stop speaking, I should have spoken of me, and of me alone' (*T*, 278).

The second I is the real one, the consciousness of Molloy in the garden, when he 'forgets to be' (*T*, 46); it is 'the unthinkable ancestor of whom nothing can be said', the primordial Ipseity, the I AM of which Coleridge said that the universe is its 'choral echo'.[26] It is the Identity which Beckett hears speaking near the end of *The Unnamable*: 'I am Matthew and I am the angel, I who came before the cross, before the sinning' (*T*, 276). Beckett's works of imagination meet the question that can only be stilled by moving beyond discussion and explanation; a question rarely put in a way more appropriate to Beckett than by Jung in 1930:

> Do we delude ourselves in thinking that we possess and control our own psyches, and is what science calls the 'psyche' not just a question-mark arbitrarily confined within the skull, but rather a door that opens upon the human world from a world beyond, allowing unknown and mysterious powers to act on man and carry him on the wings of the night to a more than personal destiny?[27]

And we hear more than an echo of Jung's words in the final sentence of the trilogy, speaking of the narrator's own words: 'perhaps they have carried me to the threshold of my story, before the door that opens on my own story, that would surprise me, if it opens, it will be I, it will be the silence, where I am, I don't know, I'll never know, in the silence you don't know, you must go on, I can't go on, I'll go on' (*T*, 381–2). When the small I is abandoned, the door opens onto the great I.

NOTES

1 See, for example, Bertrand Russell, *The problems of philosophy* (Oxford University Press, 1967); Daniel Dennett, *Consciousness explained* (London: Allen Lane, 1991). See also relevant entries in *The Fontana dictionary of modern thought* (London: Collins, 1979).

2 Reprinted in C. G. Jung, trans. R. F. C. Hull, *The spirit in man, art and literature* (London: Ark, 1984), 65–105.

3 Jung, ibid., 104.

4 Reprinted in Dougald McMillan, *transition: the history of a literary era 1927–1938* (London: John Calder, 1975), 66.

5 Jakob Böhme, trans. J. R. Earle, *Six theosophic points and other writings* (University of Michigan Press, 1971), 190.

6 Reference to this perspective and expositions of it can be found in, for example: Muhyiddin Ibn'Arabi, trans. R. W. J. Austin, *The bezels of wisdom* (London: Society for Promoting Christian Knowledge, 1980), xii, 34–6, 51, 72, 97, 119, 198, 229; Paracelsus, trans. N. Goodricke-Clarke, *Essential readings* (Wellingborough: Crucible, 1990), 93–6, 112, 115–16; G. I. Gurdjieff, *Life is real only then, when 'I am'* (New York: Viking Penguin, 1991), 22–3; C. G. Jung, *The spirit in man, art and literature*, 9, 22; Titus Burckhardt, trans. V. Stuart and J. M. Watkins, *Alchemy* (Shaftesbury: Element Books, 1986), 168.

7 Fritjof Capra, *The Tao of physics* (London: Fontana/Collins, 1976), 21.

8 Jung, *The spirit in man, art and literature*, 96.

9 Ibid., 105.

10 C. G. Jung, trans. R. F. C. Hull, *The collected works* (Princeton University Press), vol. XVIII, 96.

11 See Plotinus, trans. Thomas Taylor, *On the descent of the soul* (Edmonds, Wash.: Alexandrian Press, 1989); Titus Burckhardt, *Mirror of the intellect* (Albany, N.Y.: State University of New York Press), 1987, 40–1.

12 Peter Conrad, *Television: the medium and its manners*, (London and Henley: Routledge and Kegan Paul, 1982), chapter 7.

13 See Titus Burckhardt, *Alchemy*, chapter 7 and passim.

14 Steven Connor, *Samuel Beckett* (Oxford: Basil Blackwell, 1988), 49.

15 See Henry Corbin, 'Mundus imaginalis, or the imaginary and the imaginal', in *Spring* (Zurich/New York: 1972), 1–19.

16 See also Corbin, trans. Philip Sherrard, *Temple and contemplation* (London and New York: Kegan Paul International, 1986), 188–9, 265; and Corbin, trans. Ralph Manheim, *Creative imagination in the Sufism of Ibn'Arabi* (Princeton University Press, 1969), 179–83, 216–20.

17 Danah Zohar, *The quantum self* (London: Bloomsbury Press, 1990).

18 See Frithjof Schuon, *Die Innere Einheit der Religionen* (Interlaken: Ansata, 1981), chapters 1 to 3, 8.

19 See Titus Burckhardt, trans. D. M. Matheson, *An introduction to Sufi doctrine* (Wellingborough: Crucible, 1976), chapters 9, 10, 13, 14.

20 See Mary A. Doll, *Beckett and myth*, chapters 1 and 2.

21 See Noel Cobb, 'Beauty and the beast', *Sphinx*, 1 (1988), 162; Joscelyn Godwin (ed.), *Music, mysticism and magic* (London: Arkana, 1987), chapters 6, 7, 27, 36; and Joscelyn Godwin, 'The golden chains of Orpheus', *Temenos*, 4 (1983), 7–24.

22 George Russell ('A.E.'), *The candle of vision* (London: Macmillan, 1918), 120. See also Martin Lings, *Symbol and archetype* (Cambridge: Quinta Essentia, 1991), chapter 6.

23 *Still, CSP*, 183 ff.; *Sounds* and *Still 3, Essays in Criticism*, 28.2 (1978), 156–8.

24 Dom Sylvester Houédard, 'The question about Questions', *Beshara*, 1 (Spring 1987), 11.

25 Jung, *The spirit in man, art and literature*, 73.

26 S. T. Coleridge, *Biographia literaria* (London: George Bell, 1894), chapter 12, thesis VI, 130, and chapter 24, 302.

27 Jung, *The spirit in man, art and literature*, 95.

RECOMMENDED READING

Abbott, H. Porter, *The fiction of Samuel Beckett: form and effect*, Berkeley: University of California Press, 1973.
  'The harpooned notebook: *Malone dies* and the conventions of intercalated narrative', in Pierre Astier, Morris Beja and S. E. Gontarski (eds.), *Samuel Beckett: humanistic perspectives*, Columbus: Ohio State University Press, 1983, 71–9.

Baldwin, Hélène L., *Samuel Beckett's real silence*, University Park: Pennsylvania State University Press, 1981.

Bataille, Georges, 'Review article, *Molloy*', in Lawrence Graver and Raymond Federman (eds.), *Samuel Beckett: the critical heritage*, London: Routledge and Kegan Paul, 1979, 55.

Davis, Anthony J., *No symbols where none intended*, Bristol: Belston Night Works, 1984.

Doll, Mary A., *Beckett and myth: an archetypal approach*, Syracuse University Press, 1988.

Erickson, John D., 'Objects and systems in the novels of Samuel Beckett', *L'Esprit créateur*, 7 (1967), 113–22.

Foster, Paul, *Beckett and Zen*, London: Wisdom Publications, 1989, chapters 8 to 10.

Hesla, David H., *The shape of chaos: an interpretation of the art of Samuel Beckett*, Minneapolis: University of Minnesota Press, 1971, chapter 4.

Hoffman, Frederick J., *Samuel Beckett: the language of self*, Carbondale: Southern Illinois University Press, 1962, chapter 4.

Kenner, Hugh, *Samuel Beckett, a critical study*, New York: Grove Press, 1961.

Miller, Lawrence, *Samuel Beckett: the expressive dilemma*, London: Macmillan, 1992, chapters 3 to 5.

Mooney, Michael, '*Molloy*, part one: Beckett's *Discourse on method*', *Journal of Beckett Studies*, 3 (Summer 1978), 40–55.

Morot-Sir, Edouard, 'Samuel Beckett and Cartesian emblems' in *Samuel Beckett: the art of rhetoric*, ed. Edouard Morot-Sir, Howard Harper and Dougald McMillan, Chapel Hill: University of North Carolina Press, 1976.

Murphy, P. J., *Reconstructing Beckett: language for being in Samuel Beckett's fiction*, Toronto University Press, 1990, chapter 1.

O'Hara, J. D., 'Jung and the narratives of *Molloy*', *Journal of Beckett Studies*, 7 (Spring 1982), 19–48.

Pilling, John, *Samuel Beckett*, London: Routledge and Kegan Paul, 1976, chapter 3.

Scruton, Roger, 'Beckett and the Cartesian soul', in *The aesthetic understanding*, Manchester: Carcanet Press, 1983, 222–43.

Sheringham, Michael, *Beckett: 'Molloy'*, London: Grant and Cutler, 1985.

Smith, Roch C., 'Naming the M/inotaur: Beckett's trilogy and the failure of narrative', in *Critical essays on Samuel Beckett*, ed. Patrick McCarthy, Boston: G. K. Hall, 1986, 75–81.

Watson, David, *Paradox and desire in Beckett's fiction*, London: Macmillan, 1990.

Wellershof, Dieter, 'Failure of an attempt at de-mythologization in Samuel Beckett's novels', in *Twentieth century views: Samuel Beckett*, ed. Martin Esslin, Englewood Cliffs, N.J.: Prentice-Hall, 1965, 92–107.

4

MICHAEL WORTON

Waiting for Godot and *Endgame*: theatre as text

Beckett once asserted: 'I produce an object. What people make of it is not my concern [...] I'd be quite incapable of writing a critical introduction to my own works.'[1] Furthermore, whenever directors and critics asked for explanations of *Godot*, he both side-stepped their questions and revealed his distrust of any kind of exegesis. Two examples will suffice here. To Alan Schneider's question 'Who or what does Godot mean?', he replied, 'If I knew, I would have said so in the play';[2] when Colin Duckworth suggested that the characters existed in a modern version of Dante's Purgatory, he responded to the 'proofs' offered to him with a dismissive, if generous 'Quite alien to me, but you're welcome.'[3] As is now clearly established, allusions to Dante are present throughout his novels and plays, but Beckett's position remained resolute; he wanted no part in the process of decoding that haunts critical work, preferring to cling to his belief that: 'The key word in my plays is "perhaps".'[4]

Yet he also said about *Endgame* that 'You must realise that Hamm and Clov are Didi and Gogo at a later date, at the end of their lives [...] Actually they are Suzanne and me.'[5] Here he was referring to his relationship with Suzanne Deschevaux-Dumesnil, whom he finally married in 1961, and to the fact that in the 1950s they found it difficult to stay together and impossible to leave each other. This statement reveals Beckett's ambivalent response to his position as playwright; he initially allows total freedom to directors, actors and critics, but then wishes to correct their interpretations. Although Beckett only once gave an official interview, his many letters and statements to friends and collaborators reveal a wish to control the performance – and therefore the reception – of his plays. His close friend Jean Martin, who played Lucky in the 1953 première of *Godot* at the Théâtre de Babylone in Paris, said of the rehearsals: 'Beckett does not want his actors to act. He wants them to do only what he tells them. When they try to act, he becomes very angry.'[6] What is most interesting is that whenever he directed or was closely involved in the production of his plays, he focused on different aspects. For example, his 1975 production of *Godot* at Berlin's Schiller-Theater pointed up the bleakness of the play, whereas in the 1978 Brooklyn Academy of Music production directed by Walter A. Asmus, who had lengthily discussed the text and production with him, there was much more comic interplay with the audience.

So Beckett's own uncertainty about his 'certain' *perhaps* may give us grounds for more interpretive hope than is usually admitted. What Beckett says outside the texts of his plays is undoubtedly worth considering, but when he comments on either texts or productions, he is just another critic, just as eligible for sceptical examination as any other interpreter. He may well have said to Deirdre Bair that 'the best possible play is one in which there are no actors, only the text. I'm trying to write one',[7] but the use of the word *text* suggests that we should focus on the text itself and not seek to make our interpretations fit with what the dramatist may have said at any particular moment.

Beckett stressed that 'the early success of *Waiting for Godot* was based on a fundamental misunderstanding, critics and public alike insisted on interpreting in allegorical or symbolic terms a play which was striving all the time to avoid definition'.[8] He is undoubtedly right, but as readers, we are bound to interpret his works within a different context from that in which he wrote them. *Ohio impromptu*, his most sustained dramatic allegory of reading, opens with the Reader saying twice 'Little is left to tell' and closes with his repeated lament 'Nothing is left to tell' (*CSPL*, 285, 288). This final expression of nothingness is, however, an ambiguous recognition of the inevitability of 'nothing', for it comes at the end of a consideration of what 'nothing' is and whether it can even exist. Following the paradoxical logic of Beckett's position as playwright, director and (anti-)critic, each of us has the right to disagree with him – and the 'obligation to express' (*PTD*, 103).

Beckett's first two published plays constitute a crux, a pivotal moment in the development of modern Western theatre. In refusing both the psychological realism of Chekhov, Ibsen and Strindberg and the pure theatricality of the body advocated by Artaud, they stand as significant transitional works as well as major works in themselves. The central problem they pose is what language can and cannot do. Language is no longer presented as a vehicle for direct communication or as a screen through which one can see darkly the psychic movements of a character. Rather it is used in all its grammatical, syntactic and – especially – intertextual force to make the reader/spectator aware of how much we depend on language and of how much we need to be wary of the codifications that language imposes upon us.

Explaining why he turned to theatre, Beckett once wrote: 'When I was working on *Watt*, I felt the need to create for a smaller space, one in which I had some control of where people stood or moved, above all of a certain light. I wrote *Waiting for Godot*.'[9] This desire for control is crucial and determines the shape of Beckett's last theatrical works; the notion that the space created in – and by – the playscript is smaller than that of the novel, however, needs urgent and interrogative attention.

It is undeniable that, having chosen to write in French in order to avoid the temptation of lyricism, Beckett was working with and against the Anglo-Irish theatrical tradition of ironic and comic realism (notably Synge, Wilde, Shaw, Behan). However, his academic studies had led him to a familiarity with the French Symbolist theories of theatre – all of which contest both French Classical notions of determinism and the possibilities of the theatre as a bourgeois art-form. Mallarmé's vision of de-theatricalization and Maeterlinck's dream of a theatre of statues, reflections, sleepwalkers and silence are undoubtedly behind his first plays, but Beckett questions even these theories in order to create his own, new form of anti-theatre.

In the context of twentieth-century theatre, his first plays mark the transition from Modernism with its preoccupation with self-reflection to Post-Modernism with its insistence on pastiche, parody and fragmentation. Instead of following the tradition which demands that a play have an exposition, a climax and a dénouement, Beckett's plays have a cyclical structure which might indeed be better described as a diminishing spiral. They present images of entropy in which the world and the people in it are slowly but inexorably running down. In this spiral descending towards a final closure that can never be found in the Beckettian universe, the characters take refuge in repetition, repeating their own actions and words and often those of others – in order to pass the time.[10] Many critics have insisted that Beckett's early plays are constructed on a series of symmetries,[11] pointing to the fact that characters are often organized in pairs, to the importance of dialogue and repetition, and to the concept of the set-design (notably in *Endgame*, with its underlying thematic and visual metaphor of the chessboard). This view is seductive, but is somewhat blind both to the problematics of the psychology of the characters, who exist as individuals and not just as cogs in a theatrical mechanism, and also to the complex web of references within the plays (*intra*textual reference) and of references to other texts (*inter*textual reference). These various references fragment the surface message of the text by sending the reader off on a series of speculations. However, this fragmentation operates (for the reader) as an opening-up of the text and therefore counterbalances the progressive closure of entropy experienced by the characters.

It cannot be denied, of course, that *Godot* and *Endgame* present many of the themes already explored in the novels, all of which centre on the complex problem of how we can cope with being-in-time.

There is the abiding concern with death and dying, but death as an *event* (i.e., actually becoming 'a little heap of bones'; WFG, 9) is presented as desired but ultimately impossible, whereas dying as a *process* is shown to be our only sure reality. Beckett's characters are haunted by 'the sin of having been born' (PTD, 67), a sin which they can never expiate. Pozzo remarks that '[...] one day we were born, one day we shall die, the same day, the same second [...] They give birth astride of a grave, the light gleams an instant, then it's night once more' (WFG, 89). Death as a final ending, as a final silence, is absent from the plays. The characters must go on waiting for what will never come, declining into old age and the senility which will make of them helpless, dependent – but decrepit – children again, as exemplified by Nagg in *Endgame* who asks plaintively for 'Me pap' (E, 15).

We have here an apparent example of the circularity of existence which was proclaimed by the pre-Socratic philosophers (such as Heraclitus and Empedocles) whom Beckett admired, the difference being that the return to childhood in *Endgame* is merely part of the diminishing spiral that will go on and on – to infinity. It is worth pointing out that Beckett originally intended to make *Godot* a three-act play, but finally decided that two acts were enough; and that *Endgame* started as 'a three-legged giraffe' which left him 'in doubt whether to take a leg off or add one on', but which ended up as a one-act play 'more inhuman than *Godot*'.[12] The reason for these decisions is important. Beckett was fascinated by mathematics (hence his love of chess) and especially by the paradoxes that can be made by (mis-)using mathematical principles. He knew that in mathematical theory the passage from 0 to 1 marks a major and real change of state, and that the passage from 1 to 2 implies the possibility of infinity, so two acts were enough to suggest that Vladimir and Estragon, Pozzo and Lucky and the boy, will go on meeting in increasingly reduced physical and mental circumstances but will never *not* meet again. The same is true of Winnie in *Happy days* who will never be completely covered by her mound, just as Achilles will never overtake the tortoise in Zeno's famous paradox. We know from our own empirical experience that Achilles would undoubtedly have overtaken the tortoise to whom he has given a head-start, but in many of his works Beckett uses the genre of paradox as a means of reminding us that in metaphysical terms we can never arrive at our chosen destination (death).

The characters are consequently engaged in a perpetual act of waiting. Much has been written about who or what Godot is. My own view is that he is simultaneously whatever we think he is and not what we think he is: he is an *absence*, who can be interpreted at moments as God, death, the lord of the manor, a benefactor, even Pozzo, but Godot has a *function* rather than a *meaning*. He stands for what keeps us chained to and in existence, he is the unknowable that represents hope in an age when there is no hope, he is whatever fiction we want him to be – as long as he justifies our life-as-waiting. Beckett originally thought of calling his play *En attendant* (without *Godot*) in order to deflect the attention of readers and spectators away from this 'non-character' onto the act of waiting. Similarly, he firmly deleted the word 'Wir' from the German translation of the title *Wir warten auf Godot* (*We're waiting for Godot*), so that audiences would not focus too much upon the individuality – and therefore the difference, the separateness – of Vladimir and Estragon, but would think about how all existence is a waiting.[13]

The title of *Endgame*, with its references to chess, articulates an equally powerful sense of waiting as reality and as a metaphor for infinity. Beckett's own comments are useful here:

> Hamm is a king in this chess game lost from the start. From the start he knows he is making loud senseless moves. That he will make no progress at all with the gaff. Now at the last he makes a few senseless moves as only a bad player would. A good one would have given up long ago. He is only trying to delay the inevitable end. Each of his gestures is one of the last useless moves which put off the end. He is a bad player.[14]

All those who people Beckett's plays attempt to delay the end and are 'bad players', but it is crucial that Hamm is conceived as a king in a chess game. When two kings are left on the board (this is possible *only* when bad players are playing!), they can never end the game but merely engage in an infinite series of movements around the chess-board. So taking Beckett's metaphor logically implies that Clov is a king – as well as a pawn. This inference accords with the fact that their relationship is one of master and slave/servant. Such relationships have fascinated philosophers from Aristotle through Hobbes, Hegel and Nietzsche to the present day, precisely because they are ambiguous; although the master has social superiority, the servant is actually more powerful, since he is more necessary to the master than vice versa. Thus Clov is stronger than Hamm because he makes his existence possible, just as Lucky is stronger than Pozzo because his apparent servility and inadequacy provide the crutch on which Pozzo constantly leans in order to create or, rather, to proclaim, a sense of his authority.

All of Beckett's pairs are bound in friendships that are essentially power-relationships. Above all, each partner needs to know that the other is there: the partners provide proof that they really exist by responding and replying to each other. In this respect, Beckett was much influenced by the contention of the eighteenth-century Irish philosopher, Bishop Berkeley: *Esse est percipi* (To be is to be perceived). This postulate, which informs much Existentialist thinking[15] and which Beckett quotes in *Murphy* and places as the epigraph to *Film*, underpins the anxious desire of his characters to be noticed: 'Vladimir: ... [*Joyous*] There you are again' (*WFG* 59); 'Hamm: You loved me once' (*E*, 14). However, Beckett drew from his – highly subjective – reading of Proust a more cynical attitude: 'friendship is a function of [man's] cowardice', and 'Proust situates friendship somewhere between fatigue and ennui' (*PTD*, 63, 64–5). There is certainly the desire to embrace and be embraced (*WFG* 9, 17, 58, 62), yet there is also a realization that friendship is based on the need to give and receive pity (*E*, 28–9).

If our one certain reality is that '[...] we breathe, we change! We lose our hair, our teeth! Our bloom! Our ideals!' (*E*, 16), this truth is very difficult to accept emotionally. The problem is aggravated by the fact that the time is always 'The same as usual' (*E*, 13) and is therefore 'abominable' (*WFG*, 89). In fact, time does not pass in this world; rather, the characters have to find ways of passing the time. One solution adopted by Beckett's characters is mechanical repetition, re-enacting situations without perceiving any significance in these repeated actions – somewhat like Pavlov's conditioned dogs who salivate when the bell rings, even when there is no food. The object of these games is not fun but defence against a world they do not and cannot comprehend or accept. In this, they are like the infant playing what Freud calls in *Beyond the pleasure principle* the 'Fort/Da game'. Freud once by chance observed a boy of one-and-a-half playing with a reel of cotton. The child threw the reel over the edge of his cot, uttering a loud, long-drawn-out 'o-o-o-o', which Freud interpreted as the German word *fort* (gone), and then drew it back by the string with a gleeful *da* (there). Freud argues convincingly that by doing this, the child was compensating for the fact that his mother left him against his will (although she would also come back). His oft-repeated game was a means whereby he himself staged the disappearance and return of an object in order to move from a purely passive situation in which he was helpless to a situation in which he could take an active part and thereby (pretend to) master reality.[16] For Freud, this fundamental defensive need to move from the passivity of an experience to the activity of a game is characteristic of much human psychology. It is certainly enacted by all the characters in Beckett's early plays.

Amnesia heightens their anxiety. As Pozzo says, memory is 'defective' (*WFG*, 38). According to Beckett:

> the laws of memory are subject to the more general laws of habit. Habit is a
> compromise effected between the individual and his environment [...] the

> guarantee of a dull inviolability, the lightning-conductor of his existence.
> Habit is the ballast that chains the dog to his vomit. Breathing is habit. Life is
> habit. Or rather life is a succession of habits, since the individual is a succes-
> sion of individuals [. . .] The creation of the world did not take place once and
> for all time, but takes place every day. (*PTD*, 18–19)

In other words, time indubitably exists as a force of which the characters
are aware in that they become increasingly decrepit, but they have no sense
of its *continuity*. If each day is like all the others, how can they then know
that time is really passing and that an end is nigh? *Godot* is grounded in the
promise of an arrival that never occurs, *Endgame* is the promise of a departure that never happens. This would seem to imply that the characters look
forward to the future, yet if there is no past, there can be neither present nor
future. So in order to be able to project onto an unlocatable – and perhaps
non-existent – future, the characters need to *invent* a past for themselves.
And this they do by inventing stories. In both plays the past is invariably
regarded with nostalgia:

VLADIMIR:	Must have been a very fine hat.	(*WFG*, 71)
NELL:	[*elegiac*]. Ah yesterday!	(*E*, 18, 20)
HAMM:	She [Mother Pegg] was bonny once, like a flower of the field. [*With reminiscent leer.*] And a great one for the men!	
CLOV:	We too were bonny – once. It's a rare thing not to have been bonny – once.	(*E*, 31)

Crucially, the various stories are never really finished – and they are told not
only to give the teller a belief that he or she does in fact have a past but,
more importantly, to convince a listener that a past, or at least 'their' past,
exists. Failure is the inevitable outcome – even the punch-lines of their jokes
fail to be properly understood. The reason is that none of these would-be
autobiographers can believe in their own tales or even invent plausible
accounts. Hamm may redefine his story as 'my chronicle', that is to say, as a
factual account (*E*, 40); however, like everyone else, he is striving not to
remember his past but to construct it. Vladimir may say ironically to Estragon, 'you should have been a poet' (*WFG*, 12), but both plays articulate a
mistrust of the adequacy of subjectivity. This explains Vladimir's violent
refusals to listen to Estragon's dream-recitals (*WFG*, 16, 90).

If both subjectivity and narration are suspect, then any and all communication becomes difficult. Beckett repeatedly addresses this problem, but he
makes clear in his plays that he believes that full communication is ultimately impossible:

HAMM: Yesterday! What does that mean? Yesterday!
CLOV: [*Violently*]. That means that bloody awful day, long ago, before this

> bloody awful day. I use the words you taught me. If they don't mean
> anything any more, teach me others. Or let me be silent.   (E, 32)

Like Vladimir and Estragon, Hamm would like to be a poetic writer and
even in his monologues he searches for the right words:

HAMM: A little poetry. [*Pause.*] You prayed – [*Pause. He corrects himself.*]
You CRIED for night; it comes – [*Pause. He corrects himself.*] It
FALLS: now cry in darkness. [*Pause.*] Nicely put, that.   (E, 52)

With no listener (in this case, Clov) the only alternative is to 'speak no
more' (E, 52–3). Desolation and isolation on Hamm's part, certainly; also an
oblique allusion to Iago's last words in *Othello*. This is one of many references to theatre and theatricality throughout the two plays: for instance,
Vladimir and Estragon squabble about whether their evening should be
compared to the pantomime, the circus or the music-hall (WFG, 35), and
Hamm speaks of his 'aside', his 'soliloquy' and an 'underplot' (E, 49; the last
term is a mischievously double reference to the subplot of traditional theatre
and to the plots or graves in cemeteries). We may consequently describe
Beckett's plays as being metatheatrical, in that they simultaneously *are* and
comment upon theatre. These texts, both in performance and when read,
challenge the traditional contract between play and spectator or reader,
since they deny and, indeed, render impossible the need for what Coleridge
memorably defines as 'that willing suspension of disbelief for the moment,
which constitutes poetic faith'.[17] We are forcibly reminded that we are being
confronted by pieces of theatre and so we seek not so much an identification
with the characters and their predicaments as an understanding of what the
plays mean and why they (can) mean in a new way.

Beckett's great innovation in *Godot* and *Endgame* is both to question the
formal structure that playwrights of previous traditions have felt obliged to
respect, and to offer a *mimesis* or representation of reality that recognizes
and inscribes the formlessness of existence without attempting to make it
'fit' any model. In 1961, Beckett wrote as follows:

> What I am saying does not mean that there will henceforth be no form in art.
> It only means that there will be new form, and that this form will be of such a
> type that it admits the chaos, and does not try to say that the chaos is really
> something else. The form and the chaos remain separate. The latter is not
> reduced to the former. That is why the form itself becomes a preoccupation,
> because it exists as a problem separate from the material it accommodates.
> To find a form that accommodates the mess, that is the task of the artist.[18]

Much earlier, he wrote in his essay–dialogue on the painter Bram van Velde
that 'to be an artist is to fail, as no other dare fail' (PTD, 125), thereby
rewriting his first artistic creed: 'There is no communication because there

are no vehicles of communication' (*PTD*, 64; see also 103). There was clearly a major shift in his critical and creative position between the 1930s and 1940s and the 1950s when he composed *Godot* and *Endgame* for, although he continued to juxtapose an acute sense of bleakness and nothingness with a desire for 'control', he discovered that the medium of play-writing afforded him greater freedom to make silence communicate.

The pauses in these plays are crucial. They enable Beckett to present: silences of inadequacy, when characters cannot find the words they need; silences of repression, when they are struck dumb by the attitude of their interlocutor or by their sense that they might be breaking a social taboo; and silences of anticipation, when they await the response of the other which will give them a temporary sense of existence. Furthermore, such pauses leave the reader–spectator space and time to explore the blank spaces between the words and thus to intervene creatively – and individually – in the establishment of the play's meaning. This strategy of studding a text with pauses or gaps poses the problem of élitism, but above all it fragments the text, making it a series of discrete speeches and episodes rather than the seamless presentation of a dominant idea. Beckett writes chaos into his highly structured plays not by imposing his own vision but by demanding that they be seen or – especially – read by receivers who realize both that the form is important and that this very form is suspect. One of his most quoted statements, made to Harold Hobson in 1956, is as revelatory in its 'scholarly mistake' as in its affirmation of a love of formal harmony:

> I take no sides. I am interested in the shape of ideas even if I do not believe them. There is a wonderful sentence in Augustine. I wish I could remember the Latin. It is even finer in Latin than in English. 'Do not despair; one of the thieves was saved. Do not presume: one of the thieves was damned.' That sentence has a wonderful shape. It is the shape that matters.[19]

The reference is to the debate about one detail of Christ's crucifixion in *Godot* (*WFG*, 12–13), where the 'wonderful shape' is deliberately presented in an amputated and hesitant way. However, it is significant that, while Beckett later said that he thought the sentence was in St Augustine's *Confessions*, scholars have been unable to find it there – although it has been pointed out that there is a possible origin in a statement in St Augustine's *Letters*.[20] What is interesting is that, like so many of his characters, Beckett has a 'bad memory' (*PTD*, 29) – or, rather, a memory that, perhaps involuntarily, alters an original sentence in order to give it greater shape than there is in the original. This suggests that, as a playwright, he considers structure to be more important than any 'message' for the communicative functioning of a play.

This does not mean, however, that he is insensitive to the directive or didactic power of many of the texts to which he alludes. Rather, he seeks to show how their very construction is what makes them suspect. In *Godot*, Estragon replies to the question 'Do you remember the Bible?', 'I remember the maps of the Holy Land. Coloured they were. Very pretty' (*WFG*, 12). In other words, the Bible is just another book for Estragon, a book that he can read or merely look at, rather than believing it to be 'Gospel truth'. It is well known that Beckett refused Christian interpretations of his work, as indeed he refused all reductive readings, but Vladimir's commentary on the Gospel accounts of the crucifixion is indicative of the seriousness of Beckett's life-long subversive meditation on the authority of the Bible. Vladimir reminds us that of the four Evangelists who 'were there – or thereabouts' only one (Luke) speaks of a thief being saved, and goes on 'Of the other three two [Mark and John] don't mention any thieves at all and the third [Matthew] says that both of them abused him.' So 'Why believe him [Luke] rather than the others?' (*WFG*, 12–13). This point is central to Beckett's attitude to all writings, be they sacred or secular: why believe any text wholeheartedly? After all, if even the Gospels provide radically different versions of one single event, why trust any chronicle (especially Hamm's) – or any fiction? As Alice and Kenneth Hamilton argue forcefully and provocatively, the playwright repeatedly refers or alludes to the Bible, especially to the New Testament, because it is one text that he knows he cannot trust: 'Beckett does not use Christian "mythology" just because he knows it, but, more particularly, because he is certain it is not true.'[21]

Important and powerful though their themes may be, what makes these plays so interesting is their exploitation of the liberating possibilities of texts that refer within and outside themselves in order to expose the instability of every apparently solid structure. The tree in *Godot* is a marvellous example of how Beckett refuses to allow concrete images to become (mere) symbols. For the 1961 Paris Odéon revival of the play, the sculptor Giacometti designed a tree that was so crucially emblematic that each evening he and later Beckett would come to the theatre before the performance to tweak a twig.[22] The appearance in Act II of four or five leaves has often been interpreted as a sign of optimism, but this interpretation must be unsatisfactory for it neglects (or forgets) that the text constantly denies time as a hopeful movement forward. The tree has no allegorical meaning – but it does have a textual function. It is first evoked (silently!) in Vladimir's thoughts on ending:

VLADIMIR: [*Musingly.*] The last moment . . . [*He meditates.*] Hope deferred
maketh the something sick, who said that? (*WFG*, 10)

While we might initially read this as just one example of Vladimir's amnesiac discourse, its rehearsal of an archaic syntactic formulation suggests
that we need to fill in for ourselves the gaps in his memory. Proverbs, 13:12
says: 'Hope deferred maketh the heart sick: but when the desire cometh, it is
a tree of life.' Not surprisingly, Vladimir forgets the heart (symbol of life
and emotion) and the tree (symbol of life and desire). All he can utter is a
half-remembered fragment. The intertextual reader, however, completes the
sentence – and is consequently alerted to the complexity of *Godot*'s tree(s).

As the play continues, the references to the tree multiply: it is successively a potential gallows-tree (*WFG*, 17, 53, 93); a paradoxical symbol of
change and stability (*WFG*, 60); an inadequate hiding-place (*WFG*, 74); the
name of a yoga balancing-exercise (*WFG*, 76); a symbol of sorrow (*WFG*,
93). Furthermore, the references to crucifixion and to hanging ironically
evoke the New Testament image of Christ hung on a tree – which is the
necessary prelude to the Resurrection. And, of course, in Genesis the fruit of
the tree of the knowledge of good and evil, while the only fruit forbidden to
Adam and Eve, gives them both their humanity and their mortality. The tree
thus means *so much* that it can have no single meaning, and we should
remember that Vladimir and Estragon are not sure if it is even a tree, suggesting it might be a bush or a shrub (*WFG*, 14).

In other words, both the denotative and symbolic functions of language
are exposed as unstable modes of communication. The many references to
the tree are not so much circular as labyrinthine. Wandering in a textual
maze with no centre, the reader follows up one reference, establishes a
sense, and then comes across another which suggests another sense. The
tree is not just 'an arbitrary feature in an arbitrary world',[23] nor is it a
symbol of hope. Rather, in its multiplicity, it serves as an indicator of
the play's strategies of saying indirectly, and functions as a 'visual' and
'concrete' representation of the essential textuality of the play.

Consider the discussion of the need to talk in Act II:

VLADIMIR: We have our reasons.
ESTRAGON: All the dead voices.
VLADIMIR: They make a noise like wings.
ESTRAGON: Like leaves.
VLADIMIR: Like sand.
ESTRAGON: Like leaves.
           [*Silence.*]
VLADIMIR: They all speak together.
ESTRAGON: Each one to itself.
           [*Silence.*]
VLADIMIR: Rather they whisper.

ESTRAGON: They rustle.
VLADIMIR: They rustle.
[*Silence.*]
VLADIMIR: What do they say?
ESTRAGON: They talk about their lives.
VLADIMIR: To have lived is not enough for them.
ESTRAGON: They have to talk about it.
VLADIMIR: To be dead is not enough for them.
ESTRAGON: It is not sufficient.
[*Silence.*]
VLADIMIR: They make a noise like feathers.
ESTRAGON: Like leaves.
VLADIMIR: Like ashes.
ESTRAGON: Like leaves.
[*Long silence.*] (WFG, 62–3)

Critics have compared Beckett's 'dead voices' to Dante's souls in Purgatory. This connection is, *pace* Beckett and his 'indifference' to erudite interpretations, valid and illuminating, for in Canto I of *Purgatory* we find the following exhortation: 'Here let death's poetry arise to life' (line 7). The 'dead voices' and the dead poetry, the *morta poesia*, refer both to the poetry of the *Inferno* and to the souls who in the *Inferno* are dead to God and His grace, yet the canto immediately goes on to invoke Calliope, the muse of heroic or epic poetry, who is asked to perform some act of resurrection. In other words, the allusion to Dante opens up an area of intertextual speculation on (the possibility of) hope. Furthermore, the references to ashes prefigure a central image and theme in *Endgame*. But what is most important here is the inability to find the right words to describe existence: the leaves may also be ashes. While only the signifiers change, the signified is the constant of nothingness, or, more precisely, of indifferentiation. Even if leaves here and the tree throughout the play are privileged, they must be perceived less as objects with an allegorical meaning than as signifiers in a complex web of textual play.

An analogous example is found in *Endgame* where a concrete detail of set design becomes an intratextual signifier. The initial stage directions tell us that there is 'Hanging near the door, its face to the wall, a picture' (*E*, 11). The position of the picture immediately implies a rejection of something in the past (perhaps the image of someone whom one wants to forget, perhaps a troubling scene), but half-way through the play it takes on a new and more powerful meaning when Hamm says:

I once knew a madman who though the end of the world had come. He was a painter – and engraver. I had a great fondness for him. I used to go and see him, in the asylum. I'd take him by the hand and drag him by the hand to the window. Look! There! All that rising corn! And there! Look! The sails of the herring fleet! [...] All that loveliness! [*Pause.*] He'd snatch away his hand and go back into his corner. Appalled. All he had seen was ashes. [*Pause.*] He alone had been spared. [*Pause.*] Forgotten. [*Pause.*] It appears the case is ... was not so ... so unusual.   (*E*, 32)

In his own writings on painters, Beckett insists on impotence and failure, as in his 'dialogues' on Tal-Coat, Masson and, especially, Bram van Velde collected in *Proust and Three dialogues* and later in *Disjecta*. In *Endgame*, he goes further and suggests that, for Hamm, the artist's vision of desolation leads to madness, for in all beauty he sees only ashes. However, we must remember that this is yet another of Hamm's stories and therefore cannot be wholly trusted. Perhaps there was indeed no 'loveliness' at all, perhaps the artist did see correctly, but had to be certified as mad because no society can allow its inhabitants (or its inmates!) to proclaim and represent the greyness, the entropy, the decaying of existence. Art as truth rather than as prettiness must consequently be refused, so the picture is turned to the wall.

This interpretation is consonant with the pessimism which is so often ascribed to Beckett. Yet the picture has a role in the play that goes beyond simple allegory. Clov later replaces the picture with the alarm-clock, while keeping its face to the wall (*E*, 46): the mechanical has replaced the artistic. As Clov says, 'Something is taking its course' (*E*, 17, 26); this implies that our lives are a series of passive repetitions and that we are merely cogs in a machine that is slowly running down. And then finally Clov places the alarm-clock on the lid of Nagg's bin (*E*, 50): the mechanical has been substituted for procreation as it is incarnated by Nagg who is 'Accursed progenitor' and 'Accursed fornicator' (*E*, 15–16).

The point is not the force of any individual idea but that idea follows idea; each proposes something different but also arises from and refers on to another. This form of intratextual reference may be seen as centripetal, as binding the text together, giving it formal coherence – which is not to say that such reference provides a security blanket for readers. Rather it reminds us that all and every text must be read as text and not as direct communication or as authority. Each symbol is not a specifically coded means of communicating, but a call for participation in meditation and speculation.

A further example reinforces this point. *Endgame* opens:

CLOV: [*Fixed gaze, tonelessly.*] Finished, it's finished, nearly finished, it must be nearly finished. [*Pause.*] Grain upon grain, one by one, and one day, suddenly, there's a heap, a little heap, the impossible heap.

                                                         (*E*, 12)

Hamm later takes up Clov's words: 'It's finished, we're finished. [*Pause.*] Nearly finished.' (*E*, 35). This is certainly a repetition, but it is significant that Hamm equates 'we' with the 'it' and the 'something' that dominate Clov's discourse; human beings are running down like an unwound clock, like the universe itself. Beginning with a preoccupation with ending, Clov's musing moves swiftly to the evocation of a paradox regarding the impossibility of genuine, logical progress. This philosophical challenge haunts the play, but most readers are unlikely to pick up the reference until Hamm rewrites Clov's speech: 'Moment upon moment, pattering down, like the millet grains of. . .[*he hesitates*]. . .that old Greek, and all life long you wait for that to mount up to a life' (*E*, 45). Most critics have assumed that these are both allusions to Zeno's millet-seed paradox: 'A grain of millet falling makes no sound; how can a bushel therefore make a sound?' In a sense, this paradox could be used to describe the central anxiety in Beckett's world: because $1 = 0$, then, mathematically, $1,000 = 0$ – and yet we do find 'impossible' heaps, so in what can we believe – in 'logic' or in empirical experience? As so often in Beckett's works, though, the reference is more complex than an amnesiac recollection of a text once read, for another paradox and another 'old Greek' are being evoked. One of Zeno's followers, Eubulides of Miletus, established the *sorites* (or heap) paradox in which he proposed that there can be no such thing as a heap of sand, since one grain does not make a heap and adding one grain is never enough to convert a non-heap into a heap. The problem of Beckett's dramatic use of the heap has exercised many critics. Hugh Kenner offers a challenging new avenue to be explored when he proposes another source: 'Sextus Empiricus the Pyrrhonist used just this example [the heap] to show that the simplest words – words like "heap" – were in fact empty of meaning. It is like asking when a play may be said to have had a "run"'.[24] Beckett's fascination with paradoxes is grounded in his conviction that we can (partially) know only ephemeral moments and that, in a world in which there is no God, we consequently seek for 'logical' explanations – which are themselves fictions and manipulations of reality; even the exact science of mathematics becomes another series of texts to be read with suspicion.

The prospect in *Godot* of becoming 'a little heap of bones' becomes a dominant, if problematic, concern in *Endgame*, and then recurs in concrete form in *Happy days* as the mound in which Winnie is embedded. Unlike her predecessors, Winnie would like to go on living and talking, so Zeno's paradox of Achilles and the tortoise would comfort her in that it suggests that she will never be completely covered. One must, of course, recognize that Beckett is *using* these paradoxes rather than proposing them as creeds or as models for existence. As with the St Augustine allusion, we shall never know whether his discourse is amnesiac or whether the con-fusion of Zeno, Eubulides and Sextus Empiricus is deliberate.

What is certain is that his writing is highly intertextual and that Beckett is constantly referring not only to ideas but to the ways in which these ideas have been formulated. The plays are saturated with references to the writings of others, as allusion is piled on allusion or parodic quotation. Many are obvious to 'literate' readers, such as Hamm's frenzied cry 'My kingdom for a nightman!' (E, 22) which echoes Richard's cry 'A horse! a horse! my kingdom for a horse!' (Richard III, V.iv.7). Others are obvious to enthusiasts of 'popular' culture, such as Hamm's angry response to Nagg's demands for his 'pap': 'The old folks at home!' (E, 15) which ironically evokes the nostalgia of the well-known American song Swanee River. Intertextual references are essentially centrifugal. They fragment the text and send readers off on chases for meaning, for explanation, for enlightenment. Some of these may be wild-goose chases, but in order to understand how Beckett's texts work, we must accept that there is always a *presupposition* of reference. Every Beckett text is built on the premise that whenever we speak or write, we are using someone else's thoughts and language. We are condemned or 'damned' to construct ourselves through the discourses of others, whether we like it or not. And each time we write, we are rewriting and therefore transforming (and deforming!) what we and others previously wrote.

Beckett consistently quotes and repeats himself mischievously throughout his work. He also constantly refers to the writings of thinkers whom he simultaneously admires and wants to challenge. His engagement with pre-Socratic and modern European philosophy is evident in all the plays, and he clearly expects his readers to know – or to be willing to find out about – much mythological figures as Flora, Pomona and Ceres (E, 30). The obsession with dying/ending may seem to be the thematic undertow of Beckett's plays; his characters, however, have no sufficient language of their own, and so their discourses are always dependent for meaningfulness on what has already been said – and on the creative intervention of readers.

What Beckett says in his plays is not totally new. However, what he *does* with his saying is radical and provocative; he uses his play-texts to remind (or tell) us that there can be no certainty, no definitive knowledge, and that we need to learn to read in a new way, in a way that gives us space to bring our contestations as well as our knowledge to our reception of the text. Brought up in a severely Protestant environment and having attempted an M.A. dissertation on Descartes, Beckett could not avoid referring to Christian texts and to canonical exegeses. The most obvious and recurring reference is to Descartes's Cogito ergo sum. In Whoroscope (1930), he aggressively rewrites this founding statement of modernity as *Fallor ergo sum* (I make mistakes, therefore I am). This is a clever and cynical comment on the culturally accepted authority of Descartes and, by extension, of all philosophers. Yet, as the Hamiltons remind us,[25] Descartes's *Cogito* itself echoes St Augustine's earlier refutation of scepticism *Si fallor, sum* (If I am deceived, I am), and is therefore already engaged in an intertextual manoeuvre. In his plays, Beckett moves from evident manipulative rewriting to indirect reference. In *Endgame*, Descartes's theory is evoked and parodied in terms of emotion when the decrepit Nagg is analysed:

> CLOV: He's crying.
> [*He closes the lid, straightens up.*]
> HAMM: Then he's living. (E, 41–2)

The explicit *ergo* ('therefore'/'then') of Cartesian thinking is as true and as false as the implicit 'so . . . maybe' of pre-Socratic philosophy; for Beckett's characters and for his readers, logic is the great 'proof', the great temptation, and above all the great lure. Somehow we must persuade ourselves that we exist, somehow we must find justification for our lives. In *Godot* and *Endgame*, as in many of the later plays, such proofs of existence as movement, thinking, dialogue and a relationship with God that have been proposed by philosophers are replaced by anxiety – by an anxiety which leads to the compulsion to repeat and, above all, to fictionalize.

It should be stressed that the fictions and dialogues created by the characters are often based on previous texts. After all, none of us can speak or write unless we have already heard and read. A fascinating feature of Beckett's plays, poems and novels is that, although one can detect a deeply serious meditation on ancient and modern philosophy, he often chooses to use and to parody statements that have become clichés of contemporary thought (Zeno's paradoxes, Descartes's *Cogito*, Berkeley's *Esse est percipi*, and so on). This strategy might seem patronizing, implying both that readers can be expected to recognize only well-known statements, and also that the author knows more and is merely playing a cynical game with his own (low) expectations of readers' knowledge. However, Beckett's intertextual referencing operates more positively. By alluding to, and rewriting, clichés, he is underlining the fact that many statements have become part of common parlance precisely because they say something that is relevant to our individual and communal lives. We are thus propelled into a re-evaluation of why these affirmations have become essential parts of modern thought. In other words, Beckett alerts us to the power of the past and asks that we re-read and reconsider it.

His characters are amnesiac and therefore unaware of what they are (mis-)quoting. Yet they all refer back to the Bible, perhaps because it is the text which both founds our society and poses challenging questions to atheists. On virtually every page of *Godot* and *Endgame*, we find allusions to the Bible and to Christian doxology. While many of these allusions will pass by the 'average' reader/spectator, it is useful to signal some of the ways in which Beckett's plays are informed, and indeed structured, by his Christian education.

We have already seen how, in the Beckettian world, the Gospels should not be trusted as authority. There is undoubtedly, nonetheless, an abiding concern with the Bible – as text and as culturally established authority. While both his parents were Protestants, it was his mother May Beckett who insisted that her children should know the Bible thoroughly. May's Protestantism was stern and canonical and she ensured that her children learned passages by heart. Beckett's adult writerly response, which is grounded in textual familiarity, is essentially atheistic, but it also consists in an exploration and exploitation of the Bible as text – as one text amongst many.

Pozzo describes human beings as 'Of the same species as myself [...] Made in God's image!', and goes on to speak of their likeness to him as 'imperfect' (*WFG*, 23–4). There is here a conscious exploitation by Beckett of the image–likeness opposition established by the writer(s) of Genesis, which sends us back to read the biblical text (Genesis, 1), especially since Estragon later names himself as Adam (*WFG*, 37). Conversely, Hamm says to Clov that humanity might start again from a flea or a crablouse (*E*, 27). Here he is arguing from a mock Darwinian, evolutionist position, but even he cannot refrain from a 'Catch him, for the love of God!' God is omnipresent in Beckett's work as a textual figure who can never be known (because He does not exist or is dead) and who is always present (because the Bible is the founding text of our civilization).

Beckett's plays are full of theological and philosophical questions, such as Estragon's 'Do you think God sees me?' (*WFG*, 76) and Clov's 'Why this farce, day after day?' (*E*, 26), which send us on an exploration of the history of ideas and to an interrogation of authority. It is essential to recognize, with Beckett, that we all remember only fragments of what we once read and that we cannot reconstruct the past: we have parts of the puzzle, but do not see how they could ever have fitted together. When Estragon decides to try Pozzo with other names, Pozzo responds both to Abel and to Cain, thereby representing victim and murderer or 'all humanity' (*WFG*, 83). Yet earlier we find a reference to another pair of brothers when the Boy speaks of his brother who minds the sheep whereas he minds the goats (*WFG*, 51). This might initially appear to be an innocent statement, but as the biblical references multiply, we are drawn back to it and recall that God 'shall set the sheep on his right hand, but the goats on the left' (Matthew, 25: 33). In heaven as on earth, there must always be division and difference; there is no unity, no harmony.

If many of the biblical allusions are semi-occulted, the reader nonetheless senses that there are connections to be made, just as one senses that Lucky's speech must have a logical argument hidden within the incoherence.[26] This sense, is, however, a product of the cultural history that has taught us to seek for meaning, for a cause-and-effect logic. One of the most pungent parodies is Hamm's 'Get out of here and love one another! Lick your neighbour as yourself' (E, 44). This patently rewrites Jesus's exhortation 'Thou shalt love thy neighbour as thyself' (Matthew, 19: 19) which is one of the cornerstones of His teaching, yet the phrase occurs also in Leviticus, one of the most censorious books of the Old Testament (Leviticus, 19: 18). If the same divine directive can be given both by the stern avenging God who spoke to Moses and by the compassionate, forgiving Son of God, Jesus, its universal authority is necessarily undermined. This is not to say that Beckett is attacking Christianity, merely that he is reminding us of the textual nature of the Bible and thereby suggesting that it does not have to be believed *in toto* or as dogma.

While the Bible has been used here as an example, the same can be said about all of the many philosophical and literary works to which repeated reference is made. Adorno argues persuasively that Beckett's work is creatively challenging because it can be seen as philosophical satire which uses references to canonical works in order to undermine their authority: he speaks crucially of 'the precariousness of what Beckett refuses to deal with, interpretation'.[27] This view is right, if somewhat unnerving. *Godot* and *Endgame* are powerful (and highly comic) pieces of theatre. They are also works of literature which need to be read as well as seen, which call into play all the knowledge that readers may have. Beckett's vision is frequently described as pessimistic. His works are also said to be élitist in their constant intertextual references: after all, as Estragon says: 'People are bloody ignorant apes' (WFG, 13). I would argue that what is crucial is that the *presupposition* of reference, however parodic it may be, is ultimately optimistic – and democratic. None of us needs to notice and follow up every single allusion, yet we cannot but realize that the text of each play is pointing outside itself. Whether our favoured field is the Bible, literature, philosophy or popular songs, we will each pick up some of the references and so accept that all is not even 'nearly finished' (E, 12). Our strongest defence against the absurdity and the entropy of existence is the necessity – and the joy – of co-creating the text by continually changing its shape as we connect different ideas and images, as we perceive it to be unauthoritative precisely because it is a *cento*, a patchwork of manipulated quotations.

Suspicious of all authority and especially of the authority of the founding texts of Western culture, Beckett studs *Godot* and *Endgame* with references to these very texts in order to make his readers think and speculate, to make them participate in his anxious oscillation between certainty about what is untrue and uncertainty about what may be true. This abdication of authorial power and this appeal to the creative intervention of readers mark Beckett out as one of the founding fathers of, and one of the major witnesses to, our Post-Modern condition.

Make sense who may (cf. *CSPL*, 316), for make sense we must...

NOTES

1 Quoted in Colin Duckworth (ed.), *En attendant Godot*, xxiv–xxv.
2 See Alan Schneider, 'Waiting for Beckett', in *Beckett at sixty*, 38.
3 Quoted in Duckworth (ed.), *En attendant Godot*, lix. Although Beckett's response here insists on his 'alienation' from erudite interpretations, it also prefigures the more generous interpretive stance he adopted in the 1980s.
4 Quoted in Alec Reid, *All I can manage*, 11.
5 Quoted in Deirdre Bair, *Samuel Beckett*, 495.
6 Ibid., 449.
7 Ibid., 544.
8 Quoted in Lawrence Graver and Raymond Federman (eds.), *Samuel Beckett: the critical heritage*, 10.
9 Quoted in McMillan and Fehsenfeld, *Beckett in the theatre*, 18.
10 For a particularly illuminating analysis of repetition, see Steven Connor, *Samuel Beckett*, 115–39.
11 See, for example, Hugh Kenner, *A reader's guide*, 36.
12 Letters from Beckett to Alan Schneider dated 12 April 1956 and 21 June 1956, quoted in McMillan and Fehsenfeld, *Beckett in the theatre*, 168.
13 Ibid., 59–60.
14 Quoted in Ruby Cohn, *Back to Beckett*, 152.
15 Although many critics have sought to distance Beckett's work from French Existentialism, Adorno begins his seminal essay on *Endgame* by insisting that 'Beckett's œuvre has several elements in common with Parisian existentialism' (119; I quote from Jones' translation in *New German Critique* which is both more accurate and more subtle than the Weber translation in Chevigny's *Twentieth-century interpretations of 'Endgame'*).
16 Sigmund Freud, *Beyond the pleasure principle*, in *The Pelican Freud library*, vol. XI, *On metapsychology: the theory of psychoanalysis* (Harmondsworth: Penguin, 1985), 283–7.
17 Samuel Taylor Coleridge, *Biographia literaria*, (London: J. M. Dent, 1905), 161.
18 Quoted in Tom F. Driver, 'Beckett by the Madeleine', *Columbia University Forum*, 4. 3 (1961), 23.
19 *Beckett at sixty*, 34.

20 See McMillan and Fehsenfeld, *Beckett in the theatre*, 59.
21 Alice and Kenneth Hamilton, *Condemned to life*, 35–6.
22 See McMillan and Fehsenfeld, *Beckett in the theatre*, 80.
23 J. P. Little, *Beckett*: *'En attendant Godot' and 'Fin de partie'*, 57–8.
24 Hugh Kenner, *A reader's guide*, 123.
25 Alice and Kenneth Hamilton, *Condemned to life*, 93.
26 See for instance Anselm Atkins, 'A note on the structure of Lucky's speech', 309.
27 Adorno, 'Trying to understand *Endgame*', 121.

RECOMMENDED READING

Adorno, Theodor W., (trans. Michael T. Jones), 'Trying to understand *Endgame*', *New German Critique*, 26 (Spring–Summer 1982), 119–50.
Alvarez, A., *Beckett*, Glasgow: Fontana/Collins, 1973 (especially chapter 4).
Atkins, Anselm, 'A note on the structure of Lucky's speech', *Modern Drama*, 9.3 (December 1966), 309.
   'Lucky's speech in Beckett's *Waiting for Godot*: a punctuated sense-line arrangement', *Educational Theatre Journal*, 19 (1967), 426–32.
Bair, Deirdre, *Samuel Beckett: a biography*, London: Vintage, 1990.
Beckett at sixty: a Festschrift, London: Calder and Boyars, 1967.
Bersani, Leo, *Balzac to Beckett*, New York: Oxford University Press, 1970.
Bishop, Tom and Raymond Federman (eds.), *Samuel Beckett*, Paris: Editions de l'Herne, 1976 (see especially the essays by Alan Schneider, Erika Ostrovsky, Julia Kristeva, Walter A. Strauss and Hélène Cixous).
Burkman, Katherine H. (ed.), *Myth and ritual in the plays of Samuel Beckett*, London and Toronto: Associated University Presses, 1987 (see especially the essays by Claudia Clausius, Susan Maughlin, Lois More Overbeck and Stephen Watt).
Chevigny, Bell Gale (ed.), *Twentieth-century interpretations of 'Endgame'*, Englewood Cliffs, N.J.: Prentice-Hall, 1969.
Cohn, Ruby, *Back to Beckett*, Princeton University Press, 1973.
   Just Play: Beckett's theater, Princeton University Press, 1980.
   (ed.), *Casebook on 'Waiting for Godot'*, New York: Grove Press 1967.
   (ed.), *'Waiting for Godot': a casebook*, London: Macmillan, 1987.
Connor, Steven, *Samuel Beckett: repetition, theory and text*, Oxford: Basil Blackwell, 1988.
Cousineau, Thomas, *'Waiting for Godot': form in movement*, Boston: Twayne, 1990.
Duckworth, Colin (ed.), *Samuel Beckett, En attendant Godot*, London: Harrap, 1966.
Esslin, Martin (ed.), *Samuel Beckett: a collection of critical essays*, Englewood Cliffs, N.J.: Prentice-Hall, 1965.
Fletcher, John (ed.), *Samuel Beckett, Fin de partie*, London: Methuen, 1970.
Friedman, Melvin J. (ed.), *Samuel Beckett now*, University of Chicago Press, 1970.
Graver, Lawrence, *Waiting for Godot*, Cambridge University Press, 1989.
Graver, Lawrence and Raymond Federman (eds.), *Samuel Beckett: The critical heritage*, London: Routledge and Kegan Paul, 1979.

Hamilton, Alice and Kenneth, *Condemned to life: the world of Samuel Beckett*, Grand Rapids, Mich.: William B. Eerdmans, 1976.

Henning, Sylvie Debevec, *Beckett's critical complicity: carnival, contestation, and tradition*, Lexington, Ky.: University Press of Kentucky, 1988.

Kalb, Jonathan, *Beckett in performance*, Cambridge University Press, 1989.

Kenner, Hugh, *A reader's guide to Samuel Beckett*, New York: Farrar, Strauss and Giroux, 1973.

Lawley, Paul, 'Symbolic structure and creative obligation in *Endgame*', *Journal of Beckett Studies*, 5 (1979), 45–68.

Little, J. P., *Beckett: 'En attendant Godot' and 'Fin de partie'*, (Critical guides to French texts, no. 6), London: Grant and Cutler, 1981.

McMillan, Dougald, and Martha Fehsenfeld, *Beckett in the theatre: the author as practical playwright and director*, vol. 1 From 'Waiting for Godot' to 'Krapp's last tape', London and New York: John Calder and Riverrun Press, 1988.

Murray, Patrick, *The tragic comedian: a study of Samuel Beckett*, Cork: The Mercier Press, 1970.

Noguchi, Rei, 'Style and strategy in *Endgame*', *Journal of Beckett Studies*, 9 (1984), 101–12.

Pountney, Rosemary, *Theatre of shadows: Samuel Beckett's drama 1956–76*, Gerrards Cross: Colin Smythe, 1988.

Reid, Alec, *All I can manage, more than I could: an approach to the plays of Samuel Beckett*, Dublin: Dolmen Press, 1968.

Simard, Rodney, *Postmodern drama: contemporary playwrights in America and Britain*, Lanham, New York and London: University Press of America, 1984.

States, Bert O., *The shape of paradox: an essay on 'Waiting for Godot'*, Berkeley and Los Angeles: University of California Press, 1978.

Velissariou, Aspasia, 'Language in *Waiting for Godot*', *Journal of Beckett Studies*, 8 (1982), 45–58.

Zurbrugg, Nicholas, *Beckett and Proust*, Gerrards Cross: Colin Smythe, 1988.

5

PAUL LAWLEY

Stages of identity: from *Krapp's last tape* to *Play*

Beckett's plays of the 1970s and 1980s form a well-defined grouping: we can refer to them as 'the late plays' with confidence. The pairing of *Waiting for Godot* and *Endgame* has generally proved a helpful critical move, even if these, the 'longer plays', cannot sensibly be referred to as a period grouping (they are hardly 'early'). But what of the major stage plays which come between these groupings: *Krapp's last tape* (1958), *Happy days* (1961) and *Play* (1963)? Are there critical rather than merely chronological reasons for regarding them as forming a micro-sequence? Is it helpful to group them together?

We can begin to answer these questions by observing the centrality to all three plays of monologue. *Waiting for Godot* and *Endgame* both contain monologues; but *Krapp's last tape*, *Happy days* and *Play*, different as they are, are all *essentially* monological. Even though none of the three consists entirely of a single voice speaking, the radical treatment in all of them of the isolated consciousness invites definition in terms of monologue. There is an interesting complication, however: monologue in Beckett tends, paradoxically, to yield more voices than one. Hamm in *Endgame* offers a model of the process: 'babble, babble, words, like the solitary child who turns himself into children, two, three, so as to be together, and whisper together, in the dark' (*E*, 45). Monologue is never single: Krapp has his tape recorder to multiply voices, Winnie her quotations and 'voices', and the inquisitor-light of *Play* interlaces no less than three monologues into a single brutal relay. If as a sequence these three plays make monologue central, they also render it problematic. Far from revealing and confirming individual identity, as we might expect the mode to do, monologue in these plays tends to destabilize and disperse it.

The process is readily recognizable in the earlier plays. Both Pozzo, in *Godot*, and his successor Hamm have monologues. Pozzo's is a speech about the twilight (*WFG*, 37–8), and Hamm's his 'chronicle'-story about the peasant who came crawling to him (*E*, 35–7). Each speech is developed in a comically self-reflexive manner, as a set-piece performance, and each generates different tones: Pozzo alternates between 'lyrical' and 'prosaic' tones, and Hamm between 'narrative' and 'normal' tones. In each case the act of performance itself has produced a dissociation of tones – performance-tone from commentary-tone. Both plays press the dissociation even further, for Pozzo and Hamm have servants who are required to utter: Pozzo orders Lucky's 'Think' (*WFG*, 42) and Hamm extracts a final speech from Clov (*E*, 50). In both cases the tonal dissociation has been displaced onto the relation between master and servant. It is as though the fission of tones has generated separate characters – separate, yet still vitally connected. The speaker/ performer is now a servant; his master a director, a commentator and a regulator of utterance.

Glancing forward to one of the last plays, *Ohio impromptu* (1981), we find that the dualism of performer and regulator now forms the basis of the dramatic mechanism. Two figures sit at a table. Their appearances are identical – they are two yet one. They differ only in function: one is a Reader, the other a Listener. In fact Listener is rather more than a listener; by a series of knocks on the table he regulates the Reader's delivery of a 'sad tale' (*CSPL*, 287) from a book which lies open at its last pages. *Ohio impromptu* is only the most explicit example of the dramatic interaction which forms the basis of the dramaturgy of the late plays. The pattern of dominance and subservience which was so notable in the earlier plays has become highly ambiguous. Nevertheless both Pozzo/Lucky and Hamm/Clov are still called to mind. Above all, Listener's last pages direct us back to *Krapp's last tape*, for it is there that Beckett first isolates the 'dual monologue' and explores the regulation of utterance which is intrinsic to it.

Krapp's last tape seems to need little preamble. Critics have often emphasized the accessibility of the play. Its setting, to begin with, is unproblematic. 'Unlike other Beckett stage characters,' observes Ruby Cohn, 'Krapp is rooted in a familiar world whose every detail is realistically plausible.'[1] The situation invites dramatic treatment: an old man reviews his life, ponders the decisions he once made and assesses his present predicament. The means of review is a tape recorder, and if the setting 'in the future' (*CSPL*, 55) seems at first odd, we quickly realize that it is there in the interests of chronological plausibility – Krapp in 1958 could not be made to listen to tapes from a time when such recording materials were not available.

We learn about Krapp's recording habits not from the sixty-nine-year-old man we see before us on the stage, but from the voice of his thirty-nine-year-old self on the tape he chooses for listening. On the 'awful occasion' (*CSPL*, 57) of his birthday, Krapp was then, and is now, in the habit of reviewing the past year and 'separating the grain from the husks' – that is, isolating the moments of value, of fertility and nourishment, to set against encroaching death ('when all *my* dust has settled'). But this process can hardly constitute a neutral record. 'I close my eyes,' says Krapp-at-thirty-nine, 'and try and *imagine* them' (my emphasis). Memory and imagination blur in the tapes, which thus annually record not a life, not even the 'grain' of a life, but the *imagining* of that grain. So when Krapp-at-sixty-nine begins his birthday task by listening to Krapp-at-thirty-nine tell how *he* began his birthday task by 'listening to an old year, . . . at least ten or twelve years ago' (*CSPL*, 58) – in which Krapp-at-twenty-nine or twenty-seven tells . . . – we are made intensely conscious of the *mediating* process which the tape recorder represents. As Andrew K. Kennedy remarks: 'It is like seeing a face endlessly reflected between two mirrors.'[2] Furthermore, the face can hardly recognize its own reflection. Beckett is careful, early in the play, to drive a wedge between the Krapp we see on the stage and the Krapp we hear on the tape. We *see* a short-sighted old man, who is bored, frustrated, cracked of voice and clownishly possessed of an autoerotic passion for bananas. We *hear* the 'strong [. . .], rather pompous' voice of one who proclaims himself physically 'sound as a bell' and intellectually at the 'crest of the wave – or thereabouts' (*CSPL*, 57). The two Krapps share a weakness for drink and bananas, and an ability to laugh at the aspirations of an even younger Krapp, though rather in the way that two entirely different persons might share something. The situation is both comic and strange, the result of the confrontation not simply of an arid present with a rich past, but of conflicting formations of the self emerging from a series of such formations.

Krapp, then, is inevitably split. His practice of recording commits him to that state. But then he is an habitual separator in every sphere. If *what* he does with the recorder is an attempt to separate the grain from the husks, *where* he does it is no less the product of separation: within his single room he has made his 'den', and within even that area is the pool of light with his table at its centre. Even the rhythm of the play's action could be said to be determined by Krapp's rage for separation. The actor Rick Cluchey describes Krapp as 'a notorious self-interrupter' and quotes Beckett, in his directorial capacity, as saying of the character: 'His whole life has been interruption.'[3] Krapp constantly interrupts both himself and his taped voice. The interruptions are made in the interests of his grain-from-husks separation. He switches off in order to look up a word or to brood, to go off for a drink, or simply to wind forward or back. To get what he wants, he plays, skips, plays again, winds back and repeats: in short, he *edits*. The physical act of this process is insisted upon in the stage directions, and in Beckett's own productions of the play close attention was always paid to the gross materiality of the recorder and the tapes – their weight, their noise, their bulk, their sheer awkwardness. These are the recalcitrant objects the editor must manipulate.

But Krapp is not only an editor. We infer from several details that he is by vocation a writer – he refers ironically to an 'opus ... magnum' (*CSPL*, 58) – and we may be puzzled that this is not emphasized by Beckett. Yet in a sense everything we see and hear Krapp doing is authorial: on the tape he (re)imagines his past, and on the stage he edits it into his present. It is here that *Ohio impromptu* becomes helpful, for it is as though the taped voice of Krapp-at-thirty-nine is the performer or creator, and Krapp-at-sixty-nine the listener/regulator. In both plays the text to be manipulated is fixed and the process of its delivery dual. 'Krapp's last tape' is not *only* the one we see him recording; it surely includes what he makes of the thirty-year-old tape he listens to. Old Krapp aims to regulate this 'last tape' just as Listener will regulate the last reading of the 'sad tale' in *Ohio impromptu*.

What, then, is the significance of the passages Krapp listens to on the tape? After listening to the tape's review of an even older tape, Krapp listens to the accounts of three episodes which are entered in his ledger as 'Mother at rest at last', 'Memorable equinox' and 'Farewell to love' (*CSPL*, 57). Not surprisingly, in view of Krapp's preoccupation with the activity of separation in the play, two of these episodes are narratives of separation. But all three are also concerned with the possibility of reunification.

The first episode, the narrative of Krapp's experience of his mother's death, hinges on an exclusion. He sits outside, on a bench by the weir, where he can see her window. Her death is signalled by the rolling down of a blind. A few moments later he gives a black rubber ball to a little white dog. This apparently trivial detail is narrated as a kind of renunciation: 'I shall feel it, in my hand, until my dying day. [*Pause.*] I might have kept it. [*Pause.*] But I gave it to the dog' (*CSPL*, 60). But this renunciation of something substantial (it is 'hard, solid') at the moment of his exclusion is, as Beckett points out in his production notebook,[4] also a gesture of mingling: the black ball goes to a white dog. Other details in the episode confirm the pattern. Whilst waiting at the weirside, Krapp is rejected (an exclusion of sorts) when he makes approaches to a nursemaid. As a '*dark* young beauty [...] all *white* and starch' (*CSPL*, 59, my emphases), who wheels a newly born child in 'a big black hooded perambulator, most funereal thing', she combines opposites. As a nurse, she is a surrogate mother, and when Krapp (at both thirty-nine and sixty-nine) remembers her eyes, 'Like ... [*hesitates*] ... chrysolite!', we relate this memory to the very next words we hear: 'the blind went down' (*CSPL*, 60). The window is a kind of eye, and the eye thus takes on a maternal association. With these eyes closed against him, Krapp is excluded from a longed-for unity. As he exclaims later: 'The eyes she had! [...] Everything there, everything' (*CSPL*, 62).

Yet when the taped voice offers the old Krapp a euphoric experience of the necessity for a reconciliation of opposites, he rejects it absolutely. The second episode is a perfervid evocation of a 'memorable night in March' when, in a howling wind, at the end of the jetty (the scene is again at a water's edge), the younger Krapp 'saw the whole thing. The vision at last' (*CSPL*, 60). Old Krapp winds through the 'vision' with mounting impatience, but we are still permitted to hear, through the rhetorical whirl, images of the light and darkness, and what they represent, in poise ('equinox') and even union. Ironically, this narrative of reconciliation reveals the split between Krapp and his younger self at its widest. The exultant rhythms of the vision are now absurd to him.

It is not that the rhetoric of the vision is too much for Krapp, but that it is of the wrong kind. Winding on, he finally fixes on its rhetorical opposite: the becalmed rhythmic poise of the lake-setting for his 'Farewell to love'. He plays the episode once, breaks off to record this year's tape, and then returns to it as if by compulsion. The ledger-entry suggests a general decision, but the taped voice recounts a particular case. As they drift in a punt on a lake, in the blazing sunshine, the young Krapp and his beloved agree that it is 'hopeless' and 'no good going on' (*CSPL*, 61) with their relationship. In what follows, the imagery recapitulates that of the first episode with great poignancy. Again it is a scene of separation, and again Krapp strives for union at the very moment of separation. As she lies on the floor of the punt, the girl's eyes are closed against the sun. 'I asked her to look at me and after a few moments -[*pause*] – after a few moments she did, but the eyes just slits, because of the glare. I bent over her to get them in the shadow and they opened. [*Pause. Low.*] Let me in' (*CSPL*, 61). His plea is not only – perhaps not at all – physical. The opening eyes, shadowed in the sun, recall for us the mother's blinds, the nursemaid's 'chrysolite' and the 'Incomparable' eyes of an even older girlfriend mentioned on the tape. 'Bianca in Kedar Street' (*CSPL*, 58; herself a mingling: Bianca means white in Italian and Kedar black in Hebrew). 'The eye', Beckett told Rick Cluchey, 'is the organ of interruption between light and dark'.[5] But by the same token it can also hold the promise of continuity, of union, as it does for Krapp, in the eyes of his women. 'Let me in' is a plea to heal separation and exclusion. The episode ends in rhythmic equipoise, balancing fluid and solid, movement and stillness (and, in the gently swinging overhead lamp of Beckett's own productions, light and shadow[6]): 'I lay down across her with my face in her breasts and my hand on her. We lay there without moving. But under us all moved, and moved us, gently, up and down, and from side to side' (*CSPL*, 61). The moment is, perhaps, less erotic than it is maternal–filial. The ideal which is touched is a complex of the Mother, the Eye, and the reconciliation of opposites. Rather than a memory, it is an imaginative reliving.

And this is where the irony lies. For as we listen to this taped moment, what we see amounts to a near-parody of the scene. 'Lie down across her' (*CSPL*, 63), Krapp instructs himself as he replays the episode, and in his pool of light he bends over the tape-machine, his hand on it. 'Become as much as possible one with the machine', Beckett advised the actor Pierre Chabert.[7] It is a poignant instruction. For the broken Krapp his machine, with its reassuring bulk and its twin revolving spools, has become a maternal–erotic substitute ('Spooool!' (*CSPL*, 56) coos Krapp early in the play, with a sucking infantile relish). It enables him, subjunctively, to 'be again' (*CSPL*, 63) and so escape momentarily 'The sour cud and the iron stool' (*CSPL*, 62) and the polarization of wild fantasy and sordid functional sex, that make up his life now. Yet at the end of the play the taped voice of his younger self seems almost to be mocking Krapp. We see the old man, 'drowned in dreams and burning to be gone', and we hear the voice from thirty years before: 'Perhaps my best years are gone. When there was a chance of happiness. But I wouldn't want them back. Not with the fire in me now. No, I wouldn't want them back' (*CSPL*, 63).

We have considered how Krapp's urge to separate is manifested not just in his editing and regulation of the tapes but in his life-decisions: at thirty-nine, he renounced his 'chance of happiness' in order to realize the energy of his creative fire. The irony of the play's ending depends upon our feeling that his decision to renounce mattered, that it really *was* the vital moment. Yet Beckett assured both Cluchey and Chabert that 'whichever decision he might have taken, he would have failed'; 'I thought of writing a play about the situation in reverse: Mrs Krapp, the girl in the boat, would be prowling around behind him, and his failure, and his solitude would be just the same.'[8] To believe unreservedly in the 'chance of happiness' would be to take Krapp at his own valuation. But it is precisely the sense of *mediation* established by the tapes and the recorder, the editing and the regulation, that should give us pause. We return to Krapp's 'grain' and 'husks'. The mother's death and the 'Farewell to love' were consciously *shaped* as turning-points by the younger Krapp and are accepted as such by old Krapp. The 'Memorable equinox' was likewise shaped, but that is now decisively rejected! We might 'wind' forward to *That time* (1976), and the sneer of one of the surrounding voices at the Listener: 'turning-point that was a great word with you before they dried up altogether always having turning-points

...' (*CSPL*, 230). So is Krapp. He constructs a scenario in which individual choice matters: he has shaped his life badly, but *he* has shaped it nonetheless, and that at least is reassuring. However, the dense mediation of the tape recorder ensures that the play is shadowed by a sense that the power to shape is itself a fiction: it can never be grounded because what is being shaped by the process of editing is itself always already shaped, edited. Krapp cannot shape his experience definitively because he has no unmediated access to the past. This is the real scene of exclusion ('Let me in'). The tape recorder is a necessity for him, but it serves ultimately to confirm precisely the split in identity which it was meant to close.

This reading of *Krapp's last tape* takes us some way from our initial idea of the play as showing an old man's review of his life and decisions. However, we can now recognize a significant continuity between *Krapp* and *Happy days*: both plays are concerned with the continuous *construction* of individual identity in the face of an encroaching threat. In *Krapp* the threat is Time, impalpable yet ubiquitous, not ever-present only because it eats away at every presence. In *Happy days* the threat is more immediately obvious; it is made visible.

The chief character of *Happy days*, Winnie, is being progressively swallowed, sucked down, by that 'old extinguisher' (*HD*, 50), the earth. The scenario is the most surreal in all of Beckett's drama, not just by virtue of its stage imagery – bizarre though that is – but because of the juxtaposition, at once grotesque and poignant, of Winnie's physical situation with her verbal and gestural manners. Buried first up to her waist and then up to her neck in a low mound in the 'Blazing light' of an 'unbroken' desert plain, she strives, desperately but unflaggingly, to project herself, in appearance and speech, as a well brought-up, decent, middle-aged married woman – not necessarily a housewife, but 'normal' nonetheless: 'About fifty, well-preserved, [...] plump, arms and shoulders bare, low bodice, big bosom, pearl necklace' (*HD*, 16). She is painfully aware of her physical situation, but not of its absurdity. It is her unawareness which makes her absurd; but, as Beckett told the actress Billie Whitelaw,[9] it is also her strength. It enables her to address herself to the task of self-construction with an extraordinary grace and tenacity, and to fend off the sense of hopelessness which mounts throughout the play just as surely as she sinks into her mound.

Winnie's resources for survival are twofold: words and her bag. In fact the status and function of her words are similar to those of the objects to be found in the 'capacious black bag, shopping variety', which lies beside her on the mound. In her situation, words are not just a means of self-expression but objects available for organization and manipulation in the task of survival. Thus they take on the status of *derived* materials. The famous words of others constitute her greatest bulwark; she is an inveterate alluder: 'That is what I find so wonderful, a part remains, of one's classics, to help one through the day' (*HD*, 74). This cultural memory is hardly infallible ('What is that unforgettable line?'; *HD*, 64, but she trusts it more than she does her personal memory. Indeed, personal memory has often to be surrounded by notional quotation-marks, qualified in a speech-act, before she will accept it: 'I used to think ... [*pause*] ... I say I used to think ...' (*HD*, 64). Accessible only by citation, her own past consciousness assumes the removed, quasi-fictional status of Krapp's tapes. Like her allusions to the 'classics', it is real only *as* language. Yet if this move makes it available as a resource – language being what she so badly needs – it threatens simultaneously to undermine her efforts in self-construction. Her wholesale derivation of verbal material from other sources, whether the classics, her quaintly artificial 'sweet old style' (*HD*, 32) or her own past consciousness regarded as other, has the effect of compromising Winnie's status as the *origin* of her own discourse. So too does the plurality of her voices, manifest in the text and, as Ruby Cohn reports, made explicit by Beckett in his instructions to the actress Eva-Katharina Schultz: 'She [Winnie] was to speak in three main voices – a neutral prattle, high articulation to Willie and childlike intimacy to herself.'[10] To these may be added the 'narrative' voice required for her stories.

The accumulation of these features puts us in doubt. Is Winnie dispersed among these voices? Are we indeed witnessing a character called Winnie, or the *performance* of 'Winnie' by a consciousness not fully constructed or 'centred'? Certainly what we hear and see in the theatre is a performance, but the distinguished actresses who have played the role of Winnie – among them Madeleine Renaud, Peggy Ashcroft and Billie Whitelaw – have been *playing* a performer. Winnie is, of necessity, a virtuoso of the inconsequential. She must improvise through her day, every day, with words and her bag as her only resources. Her situation harks back to *Endgame*, which is both more explicitly metatheatrical ('I'm warming up for my last soliloquy'; *E*, 49) and less urgently so. The sardonic play with the audience in *Endgame* ('I see ... a multitude ... in transports ... of joy', *E*, 25) has given way to an eerie sense of threat: 'Strange feeling that someone is looking at me' (*HD*, 52–3). Hamm and Clov are both double-act and audience to one another, but in *Happy days* that complementarity has almost disappeared. Winnie has a companion, but the results of her attempts to provoke a duet are mostly hilarious failures.

The companion is of course her husband Willie. He is only partly visible behind the mound in Act I – reading his paper, tending his wound, sheltering under the 'rakish angle' (*HD*, 24) of his boater – and completely invisible in Act II, until he emerges resplendent for the climax of the play. Winnie also provides a commentary on his other, unseen activities. He is a grotesquely comic figure, yet he is vital to Winnie's continuing effort of self-construction because he is her audience. More than that, he represents to her the very idea of audience. When she imagines even the possibility of his no longer listening she suffers what Beckett as director called 'crises of loquaciousness',[11] in which she gives way to a panicked gabble.

So the performer has her audience; she has the materials, many of them derived, out of which she will improvise her verbal script; she has her bag-full of homely props: toothbrush, mirror, spectacles, brush, lipstick, medicine, hat, comb, nail-file, musical-box, together with one distinctly unhomely one – a revolver. Unanticipated extras are provided by Things Happening: her parasol catches fire, and she spots 'a live emmet' with its eggs. It is rather unpromising material, but she must regulate her use of it to get through the day. Her regulation is in the form of self-exhortation: she instructs herself to begin her day, to put on (and off) her hat, to sing her song, to pray her prayer. In between she makes her toilette, polishes her spectacles, files her nails, tells her stories and comments on her own delivery. She frequently counsels herself against doing something too much or too soon, against squandering or saving her resources, and even ponders the problem of regulation itself. As with Krapp, interruption is an inevitable part of regulation. Beckett told Billie Whitelaw: 'One of the clues of the play is interruption. Something begins; something else begins. She begins but doesn't carry through with it. She's constantly being interrupted or interrupting herself. She's an interrupted being.'[12] If Winnie is, as Beckett described her, an 'organized mess',[13] we can recognize her self-interruptions as a vital part of the process of self-organization.

Winnie shares her need for regulation with Krapp – though without his degree of duality – and her metatheatricality with Hamm – though without his ironic explicitness. But her situation is defined by a condition which is apparent in neither of the earlier plays. Winnie is not just a regulator; she is herself regulated in a basic but increasingly harsh way by another metatheatrical feature: the bell which signals performance. 'It hurts like a knife', she says, 'A gouge' (*HD*, 70). Her 'day' is that period 'between the bell for waking and the bell for sleep' (*HD*, 32). The sound may not impinge upon our attention in Act I, where we hear it only at the beginning; but in the very different world of Act II, with Winnie now embedded up to her neck, her props unavailable and her words used to keep an increasingly eerie environment at bay, we hear it no less than five times. When she is awake it will not let her close her eyes, and (she tells us) when she is to sleep it will not let her open them. Beckett had at first thought of an alarm-clock to fulfil the timing-function which he needed for Winnie, but, as S. E. Gontarski points out,[14] the revision from a domestic device controlled by Winnie herself to a penetrating, impersonal theatre-device sounding from offstage was decisive. Regulation now comes to resemble a form of torture. Among Beckett's earlier stage-pieces, only the mimes – especially *Act without words II* (written in 1956), with its goad from offstage – have foreshadowed this.

Winnie defines her ontological situation with great imaginative precision in the two stories that she tells in the course of the play. She offers one of them as a memory, but both are metaphoric realizations of what Beckett referred to as her 'inextricable present'.[15] The stories occupy strong, if not climactic, positions in both acts. In the first of them, Winnie tells of her encounter with the 'last human kind – to stray this way', a Mr and Mrs 'Shower' or 'Cooker', who approach 'hand in hand' with 'in the other hands bags' (their linkage figures that of Winnie and Willie). The man, a 'coarse fellow', gazes at the embedded Winnie and asks 'What does it mean? . . . what's it meant to mean?' (*HD*, 56). The characteristic spectatorial question seems inevitable given the couple's alternative names, which are from the German *schauen*, to look, and *gucken*, to look or peep (a *Zuschauer* is a theatrical spectator). The wife's rebuff, though, is delivered with a sustained vehemence that carries Winnie's own passionate rejection of the question ('And you, she says . . . what are you meant to mean?'), and climaxes in the sudden violence of 'let go of my hand and drop for God's sake . . .!' (*HD*, 56).

Winnie's vehement act of narrative is a bid to define and control her situation, not least in terms of gender. Steven Connor puts it thus: 'As a woman, Winnie allows the dramatization of the gaze as both violation and necessity [. . .] Here, the female spectacle looks at itself, and watches the audience look at it.'[16] Although gender is different from sexuality, the two categories are brought into relation in Act II – firstly when Winnie retells the climax of the Shower/Cooker story. This time the man's questions are prurient ('Has she anything on underneath? he says') and his partner's sudden violence issues in explicit statement: 'Drop dead!' (*HD*, 76). The joined hands seem to represent for Winnie the sexualized link between female spectacle and male spectator. This reprise of the Shower/Cooker climax immediately precedes the climax of Winnie's other story, previously interrupted. This one, about a little girl four or five years old called Mildred, re-imagines the play's other theatrical relationship – that between Winnie and her enemy, the bell – in terms of a grotesque sexual violation. Milly and her 'Dolly' echo Winnie and her Willie: the 'big waxen dolly' has the 'China blue eyes' and the straw hat of Willie. But this is no simple parallelism. Even though Milly shares her gender with the narrator, her name rhymes with Willie's and her progress 'backwards on all fours' down the stairs of her home harks back to his Act I entrance into his offstage shelter-hole ('Not head first, I tell you!'; *HD*, 36). The postural specificity confirms that both are images of womb-retreat. Mildred, who 'will have memories, of the womb, before she dies' (*HD*, 70), tiptoes 'down the silent passage' (*HD*, 72) and creeps under the table to play with Dolly. The story is interrupted by 'Shower/Cooker', but its deferred climax comes, with appropriately sudden violence, in the void after Mrs Shower/Cooker's 'Drop dead!': 'Suddenly a mouse ran up her little thigh and Mildred, dropping Dolly in her fright, began to scream'. Winnie gives us the screams – which are *her* screams too. Milly's family gathers, but it is 'Too late' (*HD*, 76). The very silence over what actually happens, together with Winnie's own screams, works to indicate the experience that the story both dramatizes and displaces. When Winnie retreats in the only way she now can, the bell gouges her awake. She *must* perform. The Milly-story images the bell's sound, and all it stands for, as a sexual violation – a defloration. Together with the Shower/Cooker story, this one effects a disturbing sexualization of the medium in which Winnie constructs her being: the theatre.

There can be no resolution for Winnie. Willie finally makes his appearance, in ludicrous formal dress and with parody moustache, and as he crawls painfully up Winnie's mound (a peculiar echo of Milly and the mouse?), she sings, softly and solo, the *Merry widow* waltz duet from her musical-box: 'It's true, it's true,/You love me so!' (*HD*, 82). The revolver is 'conspicuous to her right on mound' (*HD*, 64), but we cannot know – *she* cannot know – if Willie is 'dressed to kill' (as the jokey stage direction has it; *HD*, 78) or to kiss. The bell stings her eyes open once more, 'They look at each other' (*HD*, 82), and the play ends in a unique harmonization of the pathetic and the grotesque.

An emphasis on the more grotesque elements of *Happy days* will enable us to recognize more easily the features it shares with *Play*. Indeed the continuity between these pieces is not difficult to notice. Tone, tempo and appearance are different, but in many respects the three unnamed figures in the later play (a man and two women) are in an extreme version of Winnie's situation. We register both difference and likeness. Where she undergoes gradual physical constriction, embedded up to her waist, and then up to her neck, they are held throughout set up to the neck in three 'identical grey urns', each 'neck held fast in the urn's mouth' (*CSPL*, 147). Where she articulates, with maximum variety of inflection, a text that she is free to invent moment by moment, they deliver the fixed text of a single banal story, narrated from their separate viewpoints, with toneless voices and in rapid tempo. Where she is highly expressive in physical and facial gesture, their faces are 'impassive throughout', pointing 'undeviatingly front' and 'so lost to age and aspect as to seem almost part of urns' (*CSPL*, 147). Where she is unprotected in the blazing 'holy light' (*HD*, 76) of an 'unbroken plain and sky' ('very pompier trompe-l'œil backcloth'; *HD*, 16), they are shades in 'almost complete darkness' (*CSPL*, 147), revealed only by the 'Hellish half-light' (*CSPL*, 152) of a tormenting spot, as if in some infernal afterlife. Where her play has two acts which are very different in mood and tone, theirs has the awful duality of a *da capo*. Finally, and most importantly, where Winnie has a bell which regulates her waking and sleeping and cuts into her when she is disobedient, the urn-bound shades of *Play* have as 'unique inquisitor' a spotlight, which alone, and immediately, provokes their speech, 'swivelling at maximum speed from one face to another' (*CSPL*, 158). The metatheatrical nature of the inquisition is now not audible and periodic but visible, constant and inescapable. The light extracts speech and illuminates the speakers: without it there could be no play. But its operation is a form of torture, and the 'characters' are victims. Our status as spectators necessarily places us in collusion with the light: the inquisitor is our agent. The theatrical contract itself is illuminated by the operation of the light.

The light prompts, interrupts (even in the middle of a word), closes; it seems to *play*. And then it requires a repeat of the whole text. Our readings of *Krapp* and *Happy days* encourage us to recognize the light as a regulator. Throughout this sequence of plays, the process of regulation has become increasingly impersonal. Krapp is a very fallible regulator in an obviously dualistic situation; he struggles with his machine to construct an acceptable scenario for himself. Winnie exhorts herself by name, interrupts herself, worries about her self-regulation, but by the second act of the play it is becoming apparent that the significant dualism is located outside her: she is herself regulated, and the bell, cruel yet impersonal, impresses that fact upon us. The mechanical nature of the regulator, and its operational centrality within the dualistic situation, is confirmed by the light in *Play*. Regulation is now torture. In fact the direction of regulation has reversed itself: in *Krapp* man humanizes machine as he manipulates it; in *Play* machine *de*-humanizes humans as it manipulates them.

The musicality of *Play* is a measure of the light's dehumanization of the characters in the urns. All Beckett's plays invite the musical analogy in their structure, rhythm and delivery, but *Play*, as the author's stage directions and notes indicate, positively requires it – there is even a carefully scored chorus at the beginning of the text. The heads speak not just in response to the light but in the attempt to get it off themselves, hence words for them are a defence-mechanism, a set of blocks necessary less for meaning than for their abstract function. And at the rapid tempo of the light's conducting, rhythmic patterns, both local and structural, readily emerge.

Yet if words are effectively emptied of meaning for the heads, it is not the same for the audience. In a competent production we hear the words, even at the rapid tempo, second time through if not first. And where the effect is bizarrely comic in the first run-through, any such response is drained from us in the repeat. What we hear is a text in two sections plus a chorus.[17] In the second section, called by Beckett the 'Meditation', the heads speak words which attempt to make sense of their position. Although their urns touch one another, none of them is aware of the others in any way. Yet their effort is as though concerted. W1 asks if it is 'the truth' she must tell, 'and then no more light at last [...] So it must be something I have to say' (CSPL, 153); W2 wonders if the light, if anyone, is listening or looking, or bothering at all; M asks 'Have I lost ... the thing you want?' (CSPL, 155) but he experiences the light as 'Mere eye. No mind' (CSPL, 157). The explanatory paradigm proposed by W1 is attractive, for us as for them, but ultimately unsatisfactory: 'Penitence, yes, at a pinch, atonement, one was resigned, but no, that does not seem to be the point either' (CSPL, 156). So perhaps 'all is falling [...] on empty air. Nothing being asked at all' (CSPL, 154). These explicit meditations on the light's possible demands are combined with evocations of their physical experience of it. Ruby Cohn notes that in an early draft of the play Beckett refers to the light as 'soliciting'.[18] The terms used by the heads are likewise sexual in their connotations: 'Or you will weary of me. Get off me' (Play, 1964 Faber edn, 15); 'some day you will tire of me [...]'; 'Go away and start poking and pecking at someone else' (CSPL, 152). Winnie's sense of spectacle as sexual violation is intensified in the perceptions of the heads, for this is a gross parody of love-play: 'Weary of playing with me. Get off me. Yes' (CSPL, 157).

The metaphorical linkage between the operation of the light and sexual activity hints at the significance of the story the three heads tell, each from its own viewpoint, in what Beckett termed the 'Narration' section of the text. The story is the old one of sexual infidelity involving the eternal triangle of Man (M), Wife (W1) and Other Woman (W2). Man takes up with Other Woman; Wife suspects and confronts Other Woman; Man at first denies the affair then confesses; Wife forgives and crows; Man takes up again with Other Woman; Wife begins to suspect again. But then, in this version, Man mysteriously disappears ... The story as told is dense with deliberate melodramatic cliché and gestures of a physical particularity and extravagance that contrast wildly with the extreme constriction we see on the stage. For example: 'Judge then of my astoundment when one fine morning, as I was sitting stricken in the morning room, he slunk in, fell on his knees before me, buried his face in my lap and . . . confessed' (*Play*, 1964 Faber edn, 11). The story is located firmly in the past; it seems that after death they tell of their triangular lives. But what we notice are those moments at which the past-tense story seems to be giving a displaced description of the *present* operation of the light which calls it forth. It is, after all, a story about a man *going back* to one woman, then to another, seemingly unable to *leave* either; the wife inevitably *makes a scene* and the man pretends to *make a new start*. The uncertain end of the story drama-tizes the heads' wish for the light: the man *stops coming* and disappears. The continual shifts, the metatheatre, the repeat, the inexplicable wished-for end – all are there in displaced, narrativized form. The detail is closely worked, and the resulting ironies savage. Not the least of these is the align-ment of the man's activity with that of the light. When W2 says 'Give me up' (*CSPL*, 152) to the light in the Meditation, she is replicating W1's command to the man in the Narration: 'Give her up [. . .] Give up that whore' (*CSPL*, 148). W1's description of the man's pursuit of the affair, 'there was no denying that he continued as . . . assiduous as ever', fits the light's activity too, and his questions to his wife (W1) reflect further on the parallel with the light's 'care' for each of its urn-bound victims: 'Have I been neglecting you? How could we be together in the way we are if there were someone else?' (*CSPL*, 148). M's outrage seals the connection: 'what do you take me for, a something machine?' (*CSPL*, 149). Ultimately, the counter-point of narrative and dramatic mechanism is played out in the very shifts of the light:

> W1: [. . .] What he could have found in her when he had me –
> *Spot from* W1 *to* W2.
> W2: When he came again we had it out. I felt like death [. . .] That meant he
> had gone back to her. Back to that!
> *Spot from* W2 *to* W1   (*CSPL*, 150)

The strange double application of the pronoun 'he' invites us to echo W2's question: 'Who he [. . .] and what it?' (*CSPL*, 150).

The association made by the dramatic counterpoint between the operation of the light and the activity of M is on the face of it an odd one. The point about M is that he is weak and indecisive: in the story he wavers between the two women, trying to convince himself that he loves and needs them both, yet momentarily considering all women 'vermin' (*CSPL*, 151). The counterpoint does not, it needs to be emphasized, *identify* M with the light, but the association is still disconcerting. Surely the 'unique inquisitor' is *absolutely* distinct from its victims? The particular kind of dualism characteristic of Beckett's work suggests otherwise. Consider a group of short radio plays he wrote between 1961 and 1963 – that is, between *Happy days* and *Play: Words and Music, Rough for radio I* and *II*, and *Cascando*. In each of these a detached, even brutal, master/regulator extracts a text from one or two servant/creators. By now this is recognizable territory for us. But each of these plays has a final *peripeteia* in which the detached master is revealed to be slavishly dependent upon his servants. It is the terminal relationship foreshadowed by Krapp and his recorder.

Articulation of the dramatic reversal is difficult. But it is there even in *Play*. The problem is that it is situated not at a particular point in the diegesis, but in the changing perception of the audience: it depends upon our coming to recognize that the light *shares* the predicament of the figures it tortures. And, like M in the story, it must be felt to waver and to come back and be unable to end. The key, in any production of the play, will be the nature and effect of the variations in tempo, delivery, order and intensity of light adopted for the repeat. Beckett's printed note (*CSPL*, 158), added only after the initial productions, contains his suggestions. In later years he became sceptical that they could ever make the necessary impact in production.[19] But if they can be made effective, then, in Beckett's own words: 'The inquirer (light) begins to emerge as no less a victim of his inquiry than they [the heads] and as needing to be free, within narrow limits, literally to act the part, i.e. to vary if only slightly his speeds and intensities' (*D*, 112). 'Mechanical' turns out to be not the right word for the 'unique inquisitor'; the repeat invites us to revalue the whole dramatic situation. The light depends upon the heads, and even though they are 'Dying for dark', they fear that 'the darker the worse' (*CSPL*, 157); so they *need* the light too. They are all there together. And we, the spectators, are there too. This is the Beckettian *anagnorisis*.

Steven Connor sees the *peripeteia* of *Play* in terms of power: 'the reversal of perceptual positions brings about a shift in the relations of appraiser and appraised. The effect is not to elide or abolish power. Rather, it is to point to power as centreless and unfixed, as consisting in exchange rather than in permanence'.[20] In the stage plays up to and including *Play*, the reversal of power-relations (Who requires What from Whom?) almost always involves the radical revaluation of something firmly established. After *Play*, in the late pieces, power-relations are often ill-defined, the instabilities everpresent and the reversals always imminent. This is not to say that *Play* is a turning-point ('that was a great word with you'; *That time*, *CSPL*, 230), but that it offers an illuminating standpoint for an overview of Beckett's plays. It enables us to look back on the territory of our own study because it develops the dualist pattern of monologue, which we identified in the earlier plays and examined in *Krapp* and *Happy days*, to a point where its intrinsic instability is made manifest. And it points forward to a study of the late plays by prefiguring the perceptual indeterminacies that surround the same pattern there. Read or viewed as a sequence, *Krapp*, *Happy days* and *Play* chart the increasingly sharp definition of what Beckett spoke of in 1949 as the artist's 'obligation to express' (*PTD*, 103). It is a definition which is articulated ever more explicitly in terms of the theatrical medium – and, specifically, in terms of the relations of power which structure that medium. Krapp editing the taped voice; Winnie compelled by the bell and held by the earth; the urn-figures tortured by the light: all strive to stage an adequate presence. When we reach *Play* we find that the force which obliges its victims to speak is also obliged *to* them for their response, because it is itself mysteriously obliged by some *other* force. As spectators in the theatre, we take our places, if only for a moment, in this continual staging of identity as spectacle.

NOTES

1 Ruby Cohn, *Back to Beckett*, 167.
2 Andrew K. Kennedy, *Samuel Beckett*, 69.
3 Rick Cluchey and Michael Haerdter, '"Krapp's last tape": production report', in Knowlson (ed.), *Theatre workbook*, 130.
4 Ibid., 27.
5 Ibid., 134.
6 Ibid., 106–7 (production with Chabert); also 137 (production with Cluchey).
7 Pierre Chabert, 'Samuel Beckett as director', in Knowlson (ed.), *Theatre workbook*, 105.
8 Ibid., 128; 87.
9 *The Beckett Circle* 2 (Summer 1979), 4.
10 Ruby Cohn, *Just Play*, 253.
11 James Knowlson (ed.), *'Happy days': the production notebook*, 177.
12 Ibid., 16.
13 S. E. Gontarski, *Intent of 'Undoing'*, 74.
14 Ibid., 77–9.
15 Knowlson (ed.), *'Happy days': the production notebook*, 150.
16 Steven Connor, *Repetition, theory and text*, 183–4.
17 See Martin Esslin, 'Samuel Beckett and the art of broadcasting', *Encounter*, 45 (September 1975), 44.
18 Cohn, *Back to Beckett*, 199.
19 See Maurice Blackman, 'The shaping of a Beckett text', 103; also see Rosemary Pountney, *Theatre of shadows*, 36.
20 Connor, *Repetition, theory and text*, 180.

RECOMMENDED READING

Abbott, H. Porter, 'Tyranny and theatricality: the example of Samuel Beckett', *Theatre Journal*, 40 (March 1988), 77–87.

Blackman, Maurice, 'The shaping of a Beckett text: *Play*', *Journal of Beckett Studies*, 10 (1985), 87–107.

Catanzaro, Mary F., 'The voice of absent love in *Krapp's last tape* and *Company*', *Modern Drama*, 32.3 (September 1989), 401–12.

Cohn, Ruby, *Back to Beckett*, Princeton University Press, 1973, chapter 4.

Just Play: Beckett's theater, Princeton University Press, 1980.

Connor, Steven, *Samuel Beckett: repetition, theory and text*, Oxford: Basil Blackwell, 1988, chapters 6 and 8.

Fehsenfeld, Martha, 'From the perspective of an actress/critic: ritual patterns in Beckett's *Happy days*', in *Myth and ritual in the plays of Samuel Beckett*, ed. Katherine H. Burkman, Rutherford, N.J.: Fairleigh Dickinson University Press, 1987, 50–5.

Gontarski, S. E., *Beckett's 'Happy days': a manuscript study*, Columbus: Ohio State University Libraries, 1977.

The intent of 'Undoing' in Samuel Beckett's dramatic texts, Bloomington: Indiana University Press, 1985, chapters 4 to 6.

Gordon, Lois, '*Krapp's last tape*: a new reading', *Journal of Dramatic Theory and Criticism*, 5 (1990), 327–40.

Henning, Sylvie Debevec, 'Narrative and textual doubles in the works of Samuel Beckett', *Sub-stance*, 29 (1981), 97–104.

Kennedy, Andrew K., *Samuel Beckett*, Cambridge University Press, 1989, part 1, iv–vi.

Knowlson, James, *Light and darkness in the theatre of Samuel Beckett*, London: Turret Books, 1972.

'Drama after *Endgame*', in James Knowlson and John Pilling, *Frescoes of the skull: the later prose and drama of Samuel Beckett*, London: John Calder, 1979, 81–120.

(ed.), '*Happy days*': the production notebook of Samuel Beckett*, London: Faber and Faber, 1985.

(ed.), *Samuel Beckett: 'Krapp's last tape'*, a theatre workbook*, London: Brutus Books, 1980.

(ed.), *The theatrical notebooks of Samuel Beckett*, vol. III: '*Krapp's last tape*', London: Faber and Faber, 1992.

Laughlin, Karen, 'Beckett's three dimensions: narration, dialogue, and the role of the reader in *Play*', *Modern Drama*, 28.3 (September 1985), 329–40.

Lawley, Paul, 'Beckett's dramatic counterpoint: a reading of *Play*', *Journal of Beckett Studies*, 9 (1984), 25–41.

McMillan, Dougald, and Fehsenfeld, Martha, *Beckett in the theatre: the author as practical playwright and director*, vol. 1. From '*Waiting for Godot*' to '*Krapp's last tape*', London: John Calder, 1988, chapter 5. (Vols. II and III forthcoming.)

Overbeck, Lois M., 'The metaphor of play in Samuel Beckett's *Play*', in *The many forms of drama*, ed. Karelisa V. Hartigan, Lanham, Md.: University Presses of America, 1985.

Worth, Katharine, '*Waiting for Godot' and 'Happy days': text and performance*, London: Macmillan, 1990.

'Past into future: *Krapp's last tape* to *Breath*', in *Beckett's later fiction and drama: texts for Company*, ed. James Acheson and Kateryna Arthur, London: Macmillan, 1987.

Worthen, W. B., 'Playing *Play*', *Theatre Journal*, 37 (1985), 405–14.

6

H. PORTER ABBOTT

Beginning again: the post-narrative art of *Texts for nothing* and *How it is*

'TEXTS FOR NOTHING'

Yes, I'd have a mother, I'd have a tomb, I wouldn't have come out of here, one doesn't come out of here, here are my tomb and mother, it's all here this evening, I'm dead and getting born, without having ended, helpless to begin, that's my life. (*CSP*, 101)

From the start, *Texts for nothing*, which Beckett wrote in 1950–1, has been one of the orphans in his *œuvre*. Few major critics have adopted it, and its individual texts are rarely anthologized.[1] This has come about not so much from its difficulty as from the location of that difficulty in the course of Beckett's development. The referential uncertainty and drift in the passage above is easily matched by passages in the book Beckett wrote just prior to the *Texts*:

I have no explanations to offer, none to demand, the comma will come where I'll drown for good, then the silence, I believe it this evening, still this evening, how it drags on, I've no objection [...] (*T*, 376)

But this prose, late in *The Unnamable*, culminates the steady, inexorable progress of the 'trilogy', a progress that contextualizes it and, in so doing, to a certain extent naturalizes it. If the trilogy is not impeccably linear, if it enacts a gradual progress of unravelling and disembodiment rather than the triumphant arrival at a goal, its progressive disembodiment nonetheless belongs to a narrative; and the narrative in its turn conforms to the oldest pattern of story-telling, the voyage or quest. As such it repeats a pattern deployed widely in Beckett's fiction up to this point in his career. Despite the rather wonderful incompetence of both his voyages and voyagers, Beckett has still collaborated with the linear orientation which the mind appears to crave in narrative.

Nothing shows the power of that appeal more than the abundance of linear, end-oriented, readings that have been laid over the Beckett *œuvre* since people began writing about him in the late fifties. In many of these readings, *Texts for nothing* marks a pause in the story of the *œuvre*. It has seemed a succession of misfires, marking the end of Beckett's 'great creative period' (1945–50) – the last splutterings from the trilogy, flung together in an aftertext.[2] This failure of linear continuity, temporarily disrupting the *œuvre* before its next major development, is matched by what appears to be the wilful shredding of narrative linearity within the *Texts*. Gone is the sense of trajectory with its increasingly frenetic crescendo that bound *The Unnamable* together. Instead, from page to page we find shards of scene and place, little suggestions of voyages that never go anywhere – 'To set out from Duggan's door, on a spring morning of rain and shine, not knowing if you'll ever get to evening, what's wrong with that?' (*CSP*, 81) – and only serve to draw attention to the absence of any overall pattern. Finally, to put the effect beyond all doubt, Beckett hacked the book into thirteen pieces with no very clear indication at all as to why one text should follow another.

There have been valiant efforts to restore narrative order to the *Texts*,[3] but like the effort to make a story of its author's *œuvre*, the enterprise is probably a mistake. Hugh Kenner aptly described the *Texts* as having, in the Beckett *œuvre*, its own original and originating integrity. After it, Kenner notes, 'the Text, the short work with no real subject but its own queer cohesion, is a recurrent mode for Beckett's imagination to explore'.[4] This not only seems truer to the work (honouring an artistic integrity that Beckett must have felt when he published the *Texts* as a complete work), but truer to the way Beckett's works succeed each other. Almost everything he wrote, including the individual books of the trilogy, has had the quality of a new undertaking and a new departure.

Like other new departures, perhaps even more radically so, the *Texts* came out of a different generic mix. Planning them, Beckett jumped almost entirely free from the predominating narrative tradition which he drew on in the trilogy. In the *Texts*, the inspiring genre is not the quest but the broad non-narrative category of the meditative personal essay. This is a genre which extends out of Montaigne's *Essais* and includes a rich Romantic tradition of associative lyrical meditations ranging from Rousseau's *Rêveries d'un promeneur solitaire* to Coleridge's Conversation poems. More particularly, one can extrapolate a good deal of the ambience and imagery of these texts from the meditations of the English 'Graveyard' poets, beginning with Beckett's arch allusion to Young's *Night thoughts* in Text 8: 'the hour of night's young thoughts' (*CSP*, 99). Note, especially, Young's language of twilight liminality:

> This is creation's melancholy vault,
> The vale funereal, the sad cypress gloom;
> The land of apparitions, empty shades!
> All, all on earth is shadow [...]
> > This is the bud of being, this dim dawn,
> The twilight of our day, the vestibule.   (Night I, 116–23)

One can put this (including its vaguely iambic dying fall) beside any number of twilight passages throughout the *Texts*:

> I hear the curlews, that means close of day, fall of night, for that's the way with curlews, silent all day, then crying when the darkness gathers, that's the way with those wild creatures and so short-lived, compared with me.
>
> (*CSP*, 72)

> Theirs all these voices, like a rattling of chains in my head. That's where the court sits this evening, in the depths of that vaulty night [...]   (*CSP*, 87)

> Those evenings then, but what is this evening made of, this evening now that never ends, in whose shadows I'm alone, that's where I am, where I was then, where I've always been [...]   (*CSP*, 109)

Again, like almost everything that Beckett wrote, the *Texts* not only carries on from its generic roots, but in doing so starts afresh. By appropriating the Romantic tradition of the associative, incondite meditation, Beckett accentuates his difference. In the Romantic tradition, the quality of being formally unreined is grounded in the confidence that the individual mind can generate, through the free exercise of its own powers, texts which would be at once beautiful and wise, coherent and deep. The very looseness of the form in this tradition was a promise of higher connectedness; its obscurity, an intimation of higher meaning. But in Beckett's hands, the 'looseness' of the text augments the anxiety of relatedness and the despair of meaning. In this way Beckett used the tradition to dismantle the structure of thought it rested in, a Romantic metaphysics that, in mid-century, was still thoroughly ingrained in Western cultural mythology.

> The graveyard, yes, it's there I'd return, this evening it's there, borne by my words, if I could get out of here, that is to say if I could say, There's a way out there, there's a way out somewhere, to know exactly where would be a mere matter of time, and patience, and sequency of thought, and felicity of expression. But the body, to get there with, where's the body?   (*CSP*, 103)

Here, as everywhere in this work, Beckett stands the Platonic structure of Western thought on its head. The very transcendence which his predecessors celebrated is, in these meditations, an inescapable plague, floating this voice in a kind of no-place. In such a context, the graveyard becomes a nostalgic locale where the price of admission was a body. For Young, the graveyard was a place one passed through, coming out on the other side refined of one's material being. In this text it seems instead a longed-for point of re-entry. Where those in the Romantic tradition could, if their powers served them, by-pass the graveyard and visit the transcendent realm, riding 'the viewless wings of poesy', here all is already 'borne by' words and one can only hope to hit upon that 'felicity of expression' which would land one in the brute materiality of the grave.

Such at least seem to be the predominating thematics. But one must be careful how one reads them. Here, for example, is how the above passage goes on to conclude Text 9:

> It's a minor point, a minor point. And I have no doubts, I'd get there somehow, to the way out, sooner or later, if I could say, There's a way out there, there's a way out somewhere, the rest would come, the other words, sooner or later, and the power to get there, and pass out, and see the beauties of the skies, and see the stars again. (CSP, 103)

The swerve in the last two clauses is superbly unexpected, its special impact prepared for by the succession of syntactical impedances that lead up to it. But what do these two clauses indicate? A nostalgia for life, not death? Is there conscious and self-deflating sentimentality in this calculated tremolo, these near clichés – 'beauties of the skies, and see the stars again' (the next text begins: 'Give up')? What does 'pass out' mean in the clause immediately preceding? (Can it mean pass out of 'here' where he is currently stuck if it follows 'to get there'?) Does it mean to pass on up out of the grave, to move backwards through death into life? This is a figure which Beckett has used before, yet in what non-literal sense can we interpret it? How does it fit?

All of which is to say that what is so difficult about *Texts for nothing*, what people have found so frustrating about it, is also what is rather wonderful about it: its capacity continually to sprout something new in its words, something that at once fits and does not fit, the 'same old murmur' yet still unexpected:

> I stay here, sitting, if I'm sitting, often I feel sitting, sometimes standing, it's one or the other, or lying down, there's another possibility, often I feel lying down, it's one of the three, or kneeling. (CSP, 83–4)

In the action of its sentences, *Texts for nothing* repeats in concentrated form the process of continuation and beginning again that I ascribed to the separate instalments in Beckett's *œuvre*. Looked at in this way, the *Texts*, far from being detritus from *The Unnamable*, cobbled together in a pseudo-text, is instead the first full and thoroughgoing deployment of what can be called an aesthetic of recommencement. The seeds of this aesthetic are scattered everywhere in the work before 1950, but what makes it show so clearly in the *Texts* is Beckett's deliberate abandonment of the very practice that had worked so well in the trilogy and given it so much of its power – its masterful deployment of the quest. To save his art, he had to dispose of what was perhaps the single most effective weapon in his arsenal. Beckett certainly must have felt the power of the quest structure while he was writing the trilogy, just as his public continues to celebrate its power. It is doubtless the resonance of that power which has given the trilogy much of its 'legitimacy' in the pantheon of great prose fiction – and, as noted above, thrown the *Texts* into the shade.

'[I]t's the end that gives meaning to words' (*CSP*, 96), says the voice in Text 8. Though the trilogy is technically endless, it defined a progression which made, in retrospect, an arrow of meaning. It organized what went before and gave the various parts in their turn a kind of belonging. It is this sense of direction that is missing in the *Texts* and that gives it its radical newness. In this new departure, the *un*-quest or absolute of non-narrative – the twelve gaps between these Texts – is as important as the Texts themselves. The importance of these gaps is at once ontological and metaphysical, for they represent that absence out of which something keeps miraculously coming: 'I'm the clerk, I'm the scribe, at the hearings of what cause I know not' (*CSP*, 85). The gaps give fresh emphasis, as here at the start of Text 5, to the way words erupt, ever the same, yet always with bizarre strokes of difference. There is no end to this, only new beginnings. 'Tender mercies', as Mouth says in *Not I*, 'new every morning' (*CSPL*, 221–3).

And how, the voice asks, 'are the intervals filled between these apparitions? Do my keepers snatch a little rest and sleep before setting about me fresh, how would that be?' (*CSP*, 89). And what, Moran asks in *Molloy*, 'was God doing with himself before the creation?' (*T*, 154). Augustine was asked the same question long ago and replied that God was busy preparing Hell for people who asked such questions. Augustine's joke papers over one of the great theological mysteries. Beckett's absurd hypothesis about the intervals between the Texts restores attention to the same mystery. Is there anything in that unthinkable space out of which all things come? How does one even begin to think about beginning?

'HOW IT IS'

others knowing nothing of my beginnings save what they could glean by hearsay or in public records nothing of my beginnings in life   (*HII*, 13)

The next major prose text Beckett published was written almost a decade after the *Texts*. First composed in French, *How it is* was published in 1961 as *Comment c'est* (which in English means, roughly, 'how it is'). As critics almost immediately noted, 'comment c'est' is a close homophonic pun on either 'commencer' ('to begin') or 'commencez' ('begin').[5] Since Beckett had published barely any prose at all since the *Texts*, the pun has given powerful encouragement to those who have wanted to see in it a declaration by the author that his creative powers had been reborn. A comparison of manu-scripts from before 1951 with those after shows that Beckett was truly strug-gling to get going again in the fifties. Works like *Molloy* fairly flowed while the later work is a mass of revisions. This view of the matter was partially confirmed by Beckett himself in an interview with Israel Shenker in 1956 when he said that the work from 1946 to 1950 came to him very quickly, but that after that there was nothing but disintegration: 'the very last thing I wrote – *Textes pour rien* – was an attempt to get out of the attitude of disintegration, but it failed'.[6] The view was still further reinforced by the publication of two short prose texts in the interim between these two long ones, the first entitled *From an abandoned work* (1956); the second, an advance segment of *Comment c'est*, entitled 'From an unabandoned work' (1960). Add to this the extraordinary difference in the prose of *How it is*, broken up into brief unpunctuated strophes, and the almost perfect and unprecedented symmetricality of its three-part structure ('before Pim with Pim after Pim'), and there is little cause for wonder that many (this writer included) have seen in it not only a major new departure but a turning-point in Beckett's art.

There are, however, problems with this argument. One problem is that, if prose production was difficult for Beckett during the fifties, those years saw nonetheless the vigorous creation of significant dramatic work, including *Endgame* (Beckett's favourite among his plays), *Krapp's last tape*, two mimes, and his first works in the genre of the radio play, beginning with his longest and to many his finest, *All that fall*, and including *Embers*.

Another important consideration is the timing of the Shenker interview referred to above. It caught Beckett shortly after the publication of the *Texts* (in 1955, in the volume *Nouvelles et textes pour rien*). It caught him, in other words, at a point of apparent completion. These points could be hard on Beckett. He had no gift for endings, which may have been what prolonged the prose project of the late forties, first to two books and then to a trilogy. It is important, then, to acknowledge how deeply inflected were his remarks to Shenker by this repetition of an old trauma. Moreover, though he was speaking gloomily of the *Texts* as the end of the line, they had been, as I have argued above, a more radical departure in their way than almost anything that had come before them.

Finally, what needs special acknowledgement is how carefully Beckett appears to have bound his new departure of 1960 to that of 1950.

> how it was I quote before Pim with Pim after Pim how it is three parts I say it as I hear it   (*HII*, 7)

To begin with, by 'quoting' – that is, by implying that the voice that transmits the text is somehow separate from the voice that originates it – these opening lines connect directly with a central theme of the trilogy and *Texts for nothing*: the bewildering multiplicity of the speaking subject ('who says this, saying it's me? Answer simply, someone answer simply'; *CSP*, 82). This is a riddle that moves like a ghost through almost everything Beckett wrote in the forties and is an integral feature of a larger mystery: where, finally, do the words come from? How do they get put together in the way they do?

More particularly, the opening lines of *How it is* pick up the device of quotation from the very last words of the *Texts*:

> [...] as soon now, when all will be ended, all said, it says, it murmurs.
> (*CSP*, 115)

In context, the last four words of the *Texts* are an exotic grammatical turnabout, suggesting a quotational hall of mirrors. Beckett not only picks up the device in *How it is* but adds an extra stitch at the end of his opening strophe by rephrasing 'I quote' in these words: 'I say it as I hear it' (to say it as one hears it is to quote). In doing so, Beckett exactly quotes his own words in Text 5: 'the things one has to listen to, I say it as I hear it' (*CSP*, 86).[7] It is, as it were, the quote quoted. It remained for Beckett to take the last word of the *Texts*, 'murmurs', and make it a seed-word quoted everywhere in *How it is*. In effect, all these deliberate strokes retroactively determinate *Texts for nothing*, cancelling that sense of an ending with which Beckett was trying hard to cope as he spoke with Israel Shenker.

From its first words, then, *Comment c'est* acknowledges the aesthetic of recommencement that Beckett had already developed with such compaction in *Texts*. Working together, these two projects carry out the wisdom of the pun: 'commencer' is 'comment c'est'. Beginning again, he returns again. Commencing, he quotes.[8] As I argued above, it was the insistence of this insight that had led Beckett in the *Texts* to the strategic deployment of the gap between texts. These twelve gaps were in their turn yet another seed for *How it is*. They grew into roughly eight-hundred-and-twenty-five gaps, each of which, as John Pilling has pointed out, enabled a formal reenactment of the book's inception.[9]

Setting out again, as he had a decade before in the *Texts*, Beckett bound his new work into yet another literary tradition, this time the epic, a form traditionally devoted to two subjects: *comment c'est* and *commencer*, how it is and how it all began. Just as the *Texts* alluded richly to the tradition of the personal meditation, so allusions to the epic tradition abound richly in *How it is*. The circularity of this world, the sense of endless torment, the fragmentary 'abandon hope' (*HII*, 52) all suggest Dante's *Inferno*.[10] The reference to 'life above in the light before I fell' (*HII*, 118) suggests the circumstance of Satan in *Paradise lost*, as the other falls (his wife's, his father's) suggest that of Adam. These and many other echoes have been amply detailed in the literature on *How it is*. Here I want to sketch the case that Beckett, in his reprocessing of the two epic subjects – how it is and how it began – abolishes the traditional structure and thematics of the former, subsuming the entire subject of 'how it is' into an ontology of new beginnings.

I Showing how it is

In the epic tradition, showing how it is has meant showing how things fit, how they work out. In the Bible and in epics coming out of the biblical tradition, this has meant in addition showing how the working-out of things is just: justifying, as Milton described his task in *Paradise lost*, 'God's ways to man'. It has meant showing how even pain and suffering have their place in the order of things, and how in the long run punishments fit crimes (as Dante sought to do with such exacting attention to detail in *The divine comedy*).

But in the world painstakingly elaborated by the epic bard of *How it is* – 'here where justice reigns' (*HII*, 146) – justice has been distilled to a final Newtonian essence as the perfection of order. The final object of 'our justice' is to show that 'we're regulated thus':

> to his eyes the spectacle on the one hand of a single one among us towards whom no one ever goes and on the other of a single other who never goes towards anyone it would be an injustice and that is above in the light
>
> (*HII*, 135)

In this recycling of the parable of the sheep (Matthew, 18:12–13), every Pim becomes a Bom, every victim a victimizer. The entire problem of accounting for the presence of evil is resolved in the symmetry of 'an eye for an eye'. Any minor disturbance in the system – as for example the problem of the distribution of sacks, on which so much of the book's late energy is expended – would bring the whole 'caravan' to a halt, leaving its participants 'frozen in injustice' (*HII*, 149).

Establishing the plausible exactitude of this symmetry is the epic challenge. In the third and last book of this epic, the drama becomes, increasingly, a drama of mathematics, as the creator strives against insuperable odds to work out in arithmetical terms the order he has been inspired to communicate. In desperation, he introduces radical changes at the eleventh hour in order to achieve some kind of fit:

> there he is then again last figures the inevitable number 777777 at the instant when he buries the opener in the arse of number 777778 and is rewarded by a feeble cry cut short as we have seen by the thump on skull who on being stimulated at the same instant and in the same way by number 777776 makes his own private moan which same fate
>
> something wrong there
>
> and who at the instant when clawed in the armpit by number 777776 he sings applies the same treatment to number 777778 with no less success
>
> so on and similarly all along the chain in both directions for all our joys and sorrows all we extort and endure from one another from the one to the other inconceivable end of this immeasurable wallow   (HII, 153–54)

'Something wrong there' is what prevails in the end. Proclaiming in the last pages that his construction is all wrong, this creator folds up and packs away the epic tradition and its dream of containment. Throughout, the scraps of memory from how it is 'above in the light' have anticipated this failure of the tradition by repeatedly piercing the fabric of his construction in random incisions.

With the failure of his authorship, comes the failure of the poet's authority. This failure of authority also goes to the heart of the epic mode. Of all the genres, the epic is the most authoritative. Anointed, visited in a dream, inspired by the highest muse, the epic poet is chosen and, through that choice, granted the power to speak in the declarative and prophetic modes. For this reason, the reader is encouraged to see *through* what Milton considered an accommodation to our intelligence – the mere discourse and design of the epic itself – to the absolute truth of which it has been the chosen vehicle. In Beckett's update of the tradition, our gaze is drawn relentlessly instead to the vehicle itself. We are never allowed to forget its constructedness. Over and over, we are notified that there is 'something wrong there', that things are not working out, that, finally, the whole thing is its own punishment, a terrible burden that its creator cannot wait to be rid of. It is indeed that punishment for the unbelieving, referred to in Augustine's cosmic joke and meted out in hyperspace: not an actual but a virtual Hell. Enduring it, we are taken a long way from Wordsworth who, at the conclusion of his own epic vision, sang in triumph of

The rapture of the Hallelujah sent
From all that breathes and is, was chasten'd, stemm'd
And balanced by a Reason which indeed
Is reason; duty and pathetic truth;
And God and Man divided, as they ought,
Between them the great system of the world
Where Man is sphered, and which God animates.
(Prelude (1805), XIII, 262–8)[11]

The abolition of justice and authority is part of the larger project of abolishing the deeply held Western proclivity to see 'how it is' as design. This point brings us back to the subject of narrative, for narrative is the pre-eminent way of representing time as an entity with shape, of seeing history in terms of design. Above, I argued that in the *Texts* Beckett for the first time freed himself fully in his prose work from the seductive power of narrative. In this regard, again, *How it is* is not a turning-point or brand-new beginning but a recommencement. Nothing so vividly manifests its status as post-narrative art than Beckett's travesty of the epic, world-girdling narrative that determines its structure. The function of this 'narra-tive' is not to enlighten but to stupefy: 'before Pim with Pim after Pim' or 'the journey the couple the abandon'. On every page we are reminded of the whole structure. Like the world in God's imagination, it is all a foregone conclusion – always present in all its parts without the faintest vestige of narrative suspense. So if we are to look for what is interesting in this book, we must look elsewhere. As some early reviewers testily pointed out, there is hardly anything of interest in the impoverished world of Pim and Bom. The only 'events' that surprise are those that come in at right angles to the text, fragments from 'life above in the light' which pierce it like meteors: 'I see a crocus in a pot in an area in a basement a saffron the sun creeps up the wall a hand keeps it in the sun this yellow flower with a string' (*HII*, 22). Like the fragments that litter *Texts for nothing*, these 'rags of life in the light' lack all semblance of that natural consecutiveness which is the life blood of narrative.

At the end of this text, when the voice packs up its construction, it does not eliminate everything. What goes is the order to which it aspired. Packing this structure away, it rejects not only the misrepresentation of design but its tyranny – and most notably the tyranny implicit in the artistic tradition which would command obeisance to design. In *How it is*, this tyranny is vividly represented in Part Two by the hand that carves its words in the back of its victim. All of this is rejected.[12] But the mud, the voice, the rush of words, and the curious and still unexplained being that lays claim to them remain: 'only me in any case yes alone yes in the mud [...] with my voice yes my murmur' (*HII*, 159). The book winds up, in other words, where it began.

2 How it began

The productivity of Beckett's aesthetic concentration, applied to what I have referred to as the wisdom of his pun on beginnings, does not stop where we left it above. Beyond the fused meanings which make up its content, this pun also bears freight as the trope for which it stands. 'In the beginning was the pun', Beckett wrote in *Murphy*, over twenty years earlier (*Mu*, 48). In doing so he played on ancient wisdom that what is derives from the *logos*, or, in the English biblical term, the Word of God: 'In the beginning was the Word.' To translate the biblical *fiat* into an all-generative pun was to invoke both the creative power of language and its problematic ambiguity, a semantic multiplicity which is with us in this text from its originating pun. Out of this slippery word of beginning comes the entire structure of *How it is*. Yet thanks, too, to the excessiveness of language, the structure produced is as fragile as it is elaborate, subject increasingly, as we have noted, to the doubts of its 'crawling creator' (*NO*, 43). If the structure is corrupt, if perfecting it is absolutely the wrong way to proceed, the linguistic energy that both built it up and took it down again is no less worthy of awed attention.

In the very proclamation that his cosmic project is 'all balls' (*HII*, 158), our discreator finishes off his handiwork with a pun as grand as the one with which it began, for the expression 'all balls' procreates while it cancels. By binding negation with both the male organs of generation and the spheres of the universe, we are told that, like it or not, understand it or not, nothing ends. To end is, as Beckett wrote elsewhere, to end yet again. That is, to begin. What is important in both of these puns is their relocation of the action. In place of narrative action and the traditional tyrannies of design, authority and containment, we have here the action of linguistic productivity.

Beckett accentuated this view of things when he recycled the biblical metaphysics of origin even further by fusing the creativity of the word with that of matter – the 'warmth of primeval mud' (*HII*, 12) in which the entire text is embedded. The repeated, unsettling image of 'mud in the mouth' or the crawler's tongue 'lolling' in the mud, recycles both the mud out of which God made Adam, and the Word by which God gave life to the mud. In similar fashion, Beckett's word-producer gives life to Pim:

> who but for me he would never Pim we're talking of Pim never be but for me anything but a dumb limp lump flat for ever in the mud but I'll quicken him you wait and see   (*HII*, 58)

and, it would appear, gives life even to himself: 'I hear me again murmur me in the mud and am again' (*HII*, 138).

The point to stress is the way in which, as Estragon said in *Waiting for Godot*, 'everything oozes' (*WFG*, 60). In this text, everything – imagery, mythology, language – is subject to the ooze of recyclement. The borderlessness of puns, the way they recycle meaning, matches the recycling of Christian mythology, matches the recycling of food and language:

> suddenly we are eating sandwiches alternate bites I mine she hers and exchanging endearments my sweet girl I bite she swallows my sweet boy she bites I swallow [. . .] (*HII*, 33)

Similarly the verbal background noise which he refers to as 'quaqua' – 'the voice quaqua from which I get my life these scraps of life in me when the panting stops' (*HII*, 22) – is a kind of pre-articulated verbal mud. If William Hutchings is right that quaqua is the latinate version of 'caca',[13] then here is yet another pun-abetted ooze of how things circulate. In this text, the concepts of expressing and excreting, like those of listening and eating, ooze each into each in a constancy of recyclement. This activity of recycling is also manifested in the abundance of repeated, yet subtly recontextualized, phrases that recur throughout the book ('I quote', 'above in the light', 'the panting stops', 'no knowing', 'vast tracts of time', 'something wrong there'), a device which was to become a salient feature of Beckett's late signature. It even shows up in the punctilious way in which no proper name is allowed to stand on its own in this book. All identity is, as it were, oozing from one term to the next: Pim to Bom to Bem, Pam to Prim, Kram to Krim, Skom to Skum.

It is in the continual originating power of the language of this work, then, the volatility of its conceptual interchange, that the interesting action takes place. Throughout the epic construction of an entirely fraudulent world and the tedious narrative it seeks to contain, this action continues to happen, always present, always intruding to remind us how it really is: that is, how the imagistic and conceptual flow keeps starting in surprising new ways, over and over again.

It remains to ask a final question: is language, then, in command? Is *How it is* a kind of Post-Structuralist manifestation of both language's indeterminacy (always gliding between signifieds) and language's dominion (making and unmaking worlds)? Is it a text in which the idea of extralinguistic agency and origination has evaporated, and the whole double issue of how things are and how they came to be can be accounted for in the processes of language?

To answer this question, we have first to answer the question: how is this text read? To do so, let's look closely at a fragment of its verbal action. Here is a strophe from late in Part Three:

> and later much later these aeons my God when it stops again ten more fifteen more in me a murmur scarce a breath then from mouth to mud brief kiss brush of lips faint kiss
>
> (*HII*, 148)

There are, I want to argue, three ways in which this strophe not only can be read, but is inevitably read. To begin with, it asks to be normalized, which is perhaps just another way of saying that this prose is not entirely strange. Within the first few pages, we are given enough information about the circumstances of the speaker to know that this text is gasped out with no time for the niceties of discourse which ordinarily help a reader comprehend. Later, it is characterized explicitly as 'unbroken no paragraphs no commas not a second for reflection' (*HII*, 78) and again as 'little blurts of midget grammar' (*HII*, 84). That information, together with the local coherences in every passage, makes the impulse to turn this prose into comprehensible discourse irresistible. Mentally, we seek to finish a job we understand to be incomplete. We may not do so successfully – more often than not, we cut our losses and move on – but something like the following happens as we read:

> And later, much later
>   (these aeons, my God!),
> when it [the panting] stops again,
> [with] ten more, [or] fifteen more [words] in me,
>   a murmur,
>   scarce a breath;
> then,
>   from mouth to mud [they go],
>   [a] brief kiss,
>   [a] brush of lips,
>   [a] faint kiss.

Worked out in this way, the strophe can be 'understood' as one more late variation on the interchange of mud and word out of which the text arises. We also see in the first exclamation a distant alignment of the nutritive pauses, during which breath (inspiration) is recovered and the words (of the muse?) are heard, with the 'aeons' out of which creation originally came. And in the last series of three phrases, we are reminded that the cycle of generation is powered by *eros*. In this way, we 'comprehend' this strophe. Most commentary on *How it is* is based implicitly on this kind of normalization (just as I have repeatedly normalized passages to make points in the course of this essay).[14]

But Beckett did not write this text as I have normalized it. He wrote instead,

and later much later these aeons my God when it stops again

So before normalization is achieved, and even after it, there is a more fluid experience of the hesitation between possible normalizations. In the line just cited, the exclamation 'my God' can apply to 'these aeons' (as I have it above) or to 'when it stops again' or even to 'ten more fifteen more in me' in the line immediately following (my God, think of it, ten more words in me!). Similarly, 'in me' can refer backward to 'fifteen more' or forward to 'a murmur': '[there are] fifteen more in me' or 'in me [there is] a murmur'. I feel reasonably confident about the normalization of the whole passage I have provided above. Yet going back to the text as printed, I find it hard, even with this master-normalization in mind, to resist the subtle encroachment of these other normalizations. And not only these, but strange ones, too – abnormalizations like 'murmur scarce', 'mouth to mud brief', and 'lips faint'.

There are, then, these two kinds of reading that play off each other as the text proceeds, the one asserting control as the other entertains the relinquishment of control. But there is also a third reading that happens. I know of no way adequately to represent it, but this gets at what I mean:

and later much later
these aeons my God
when it stops again ten
more fifteen more in me a murmur
scarce a breath then
from mouth to mud
brief kiss brush of lips faint kiss

What I want to represent here is the way in which the sound effects become so insistent in this prose that they seem to take over from the meaning. I have organized these lines roughly according to the domination of internal rhyming patterns. But to my ear it is the simple fascination of unusual aural effects that generates this third reader-relationship, one that adds its resistant counterpoint to the play of normalization discussed above. Coming on a line like this:

brief kiss brush of lips faint kiss

one feels the desire to let go of sense altogether and simply to enjoy the extraordinary sensory effect the contriver of this text has, once again, managed to achieve. As he notes, elsewhere, 'first the sound then the sense' (*HII*, 104); or to put it in context:

so many words
so many lost
one every three
two every five
first the sound
then the sense

If one hears Swinburne here, it is not inappropriate. Like so much of Swinburne, like Poe, like Tennyson, like Hopkins, Beckett writes a poetry in which sound seems to want to come into the ascendant, arrogating to itself the place traditionally held by meaning.

My stress, however, falls not on this last effect, but on the extraordinarily rich interplay of effects that comes about through the co-existence of the three modes of reading that the text demands. In this elegant interplay of meaning and sound lies the answer to the other question left hanging above. If this text breeds in the fertile ooze of language, submitting to the rule of deferred meaning, the signs of artifice are nonetheless everywhere in abundance. Bringing to ruin the epic of containment and radiant design, Beckett concentrated attention on the wonders of origination. Combining the rhetorical strategies I have just enumerated, he trebled his capacity to surprise us with ever new and striking inventions from the same old material. The counter-tropes of reduction, negation, cancellation and despair – always parts of the Beckett signature – invariably set off the vigour of that productivity. As Shira Wolosky recently argued in an essay on the *Texts*, Beckett's 'gestures toward reduction inevitably give way to reproductive and inventive energy'.[15] I think he is right. My own object has been to show how these two texts, which critics have so often held widely apart from each other, can be seen as a joint project in which Beckett distilled his art. Abandoning narrative – the remaining structural implement of an art of containment – enabled him to concentrate his power with full efficiency on an art of recommencement.

NOTES

1 Pilling, in *Frescoes of the skull*, 41–60, is one of the few who have promoted the *Texts*, devoting a full chapter specifically to make up for this neglect. His is the only text-by-text analysis of this work that I know of. Among the rare republications are those of Texts 4, 8, and 13 in *Monologues de minuit* ed. Ruby Cohn and Lily Parker (New York: Macmillan, 1965), 117–32.

2 Michael Robinson's early characterization can stand for many: 'The thirteen *Textes pour rien* ... which Beckett himself considers a failure, clearly prolong the inquiry of *The Unnamable*', *The long sonata of the dead* (New York: Grove Press, 1969), 209. The phrase 'great creative period' is quoted in Raymond

Federman and John Fletcher (eds.), *Samuel Beckett: his works and his critics* (Berkeley and Los Angeles: University of California Press, 1970), 63.

3 The very lack of sequence has been a challenge to some. The most ingenious reading of the structure of this work is by Paul West, who proposed that its thirteen instalments correspond to the thirteen last days Beckett spent in the womb before his birth on Good Friday, 13 April. See 'Deciphering a Beckett fiction on his birthday'.

4 Kenner, *A reader's guide*, 119.

5 Others almost as quickly noted, and also resonant, are *commençais, commençait* and *comme on sait.*

6 Israel Shenker, 'An interview with Beckett', *New York Times*, 5 May 1956, section II, 1,3. Cited in Lawrence Graver and Raymond Federman (eds.), *Samuel Beckett: the critical heritage* (London: Routledge and Kegan Paul, 1979), 148.

7 The same point holds for the two French texts: 'je le dis comme je l'entends' (163). This is not the only quotation of the *Texts* in *How it is*; see Knowlson and Pilling, *Frescoes of the skull*, 43.

8 In the same way, *Texts for nothing*, for all the brilliance of its departure from the trilogy, engaged frequently in alluding to it, often quite explicitly: as for example to *Molloy* and *Malone dies* (83), to *Godot* (85), to 'The calmative' (73), and to 'The end' (86). The best close analysis of Beckett's way of beginning by returning in *How it is* is Victor Sage's 'Innovation and continuity in *How it is*'.

9 Knowlson and Pilling, *Frescoes of the skull*, 63.

10 As many have noted, there is strongly suggestive language in Canto VII of the *Inferno* where Dante depicts the punishment of the sullen and slothful. See Robinson, *The long sonata of the dead*, 216; Kenner, *A reader's guide*, 138; Hutchings, '"Shat into Grace"', 69.

> che coi sospiri sui,
> L'auqua i fa brombolar stando là drento,
> Come vede per tuto i ochi tui.
> Piantai nel fango i grami dise a stento:
> Bruta vita, d'acidia nu impastai,
> Passà avemo là sora al sol, al vento;
> E in fango adesso semo qua impiantai.
> Nel gosso ghe vien rota sta canzon,
> Che drio man tuta no i pol dirla mai.   (VII:118–26)

> with their gasps
> [They] Send bubbles to the surface of this ooze
> As glancing roundabouts you may observe.
> Fixed in the slime they say: 'Sullen we were
> In the sweet air cheered by the brightening sun
> Because of sulky vapors in our hearts;
> Now here in this black mud we curse our luck.'
> This burden, though they cannot form in words,
> They gurgle in their gullets
>   (Dante Alighieri, *The divine comedy*, trans. Thomas G. Bergin
>   (New York: Grossman, 1969), 52)

11 One of the three or four greatest twentieth-century contributions to the tradition of epic mastery is Joyce's *Ulysses*, a text Beckett may well have had in mind in devising the fanfare of 'yesses' in which the book culminates, affirming the

completeness of its failure, and playing off, as John Pilling suggests, against the 'yesses' of Molly Bloom that punctuate Joyce's epic (John Pilling, *Samuel Beckett* (London: Routledge and Kegan Paul, 1976), 45). Beckett made a similarly inverse allusion to Joyce's other epic when he wrote John Calder in 1960 that the project under construction was 'work in regress' (cited in Smith, 'Fiction as composing process', 118).

12 The connections between art and tyranny is a theme that Beckett would develop more fully in his last radio play, *Rough for radio II*, almost immediately after completing *Comment c'est*. He would return to it with the same kind of near explicitness late in his career in the stage plays *Catastrophe* (1982) and *What where* (1983).

13 Hutchings, '"Shat into grace"', 87n.

14 Some have even consistently added normalizing aids in their citations from *How it is*, as for example Susan Brienza in her nonetheless helpful reading: ' if he talks to himself / no / thinks / believes in God / yes / every day / no ' (*Samuel Beckett's new worlds*, 98).

15 Wolosky, 'Negative Way', 227; Victor Sage said the same thing with the emphasis reversed when he wrote of *How it is* that Beckett's 'wit is a machine for making possibilities look like poverties' (Sage, 'Innovation and continuity in *How it is*', 102).

RECOMMENDED READING

On 'Texts for nothing'

Brienza, Susan, '*Texts for nothing*: "Going on" through stylistic devices', in *Samuel Beckett's new worlds: style in metafiction*, Norman, Okla.: University of Oklahoma Press, 1987, 20–47.

Caws, Mary Ann, 'A rereading of the traces', *L'Esprit créateur*, 11.3 (Fall 1971), 14–20.

Dearlove, J. E., *Accommodating the chaos: Samuel Beckett's nonrelational art*, Durham, N.C.: Duke University Press, 1982, 74–84.

Hill, Leslie, *Beckett's fiction: in different words*, Cambridge University Press, 1990, 133–40.

O'Donovan, Patrick, 'Beckett's happy few', *Zeitschrift fur Französische Sprache und Literatur*, 100 (1990), 168–79.

O'Reilly, Magessa, '*Textes pour rien* XIII de Samuel Beckett: édition critique et étude de variantes', *Revue d'histoire littéraire de la France*, 90.2 (March–April 1990), 227–37.

Pilling, John, '*Texts for nothing*' in: James Knowlson and John Pilling, *Frescoes of the skull: the later prose and drama of Samuel Beckett*, London: John Calder, 1979, 41–60.

Rose, Marilyn Gaddis, 'The lyrical structure of Beckett's *Texts for nothing*', *Novel*, 4.3 (Spring 1971), 223–30.

West, Paul, 'Deciphering a Beckett fiction on his birthday', *Parnassus*, 7.2 (1983–4), 319–22.

Wolosky, Shira, 'The negative way negated: Samuel Beckett's *Texts for nothing*'. *New Literary History*, 22.1 (Winter 1991), 213–30.

On 'How it is'

Brienza, Susan, 'From an abandoned work: "Breaking up I am"', in *Samuel Beckett's new worlds*, Norman, Okla.: University of Oklahoma Press, 1987, 48–70.

Carey, Phyllis, 'Beckett's Pim and Joyce's Shem', *James Joyce Quarterly*, 26.3 (Spring 1989), 435–9.

Dearlove, J. E., 'The voice and its words', in *Accommodating the chaos: Samuel Beckett's nonrelational art*, Durham, N.C.: Duke University Press, 1982, 85–106.

Hutchings, William, '"Shat into grace" or a Tale of a Turd: why it is how it is in Samuel Beckett's *How it is*', *Papers on Language and Literature*, 21.1 (Winter 1985), 64–89.

Kenner, Hugh, *A reader's guide to Samuel Beckett*, London: Thames and Hudson, 1973, 136–46.

Pilling, John, '*How it is*', in James Knowlson and John Pilling, *Frescoes of the skull: the later prose and drama of Samuel Beckett*, London: John Calder, 1979, 61–78.

Sage, Victor, 'Innovation and continuity in *How it is*', in *Beckett the shape changer*, ed. Katharine Worth, London: Routledge and Kegan Paul, 1975, 85–103.

Singer, Alan, 'The need of the present: *How it is* with the subject in Beckett's novel', *A metaphorics of fiction: discontinuity and discourse in the modern novel*, Tallahassee, Fla: University Presses of Florida, 1983, 115–56.

Smith, Frederik N., 'Fiction as composing process: *How it is*', in *Samuel Beckett: humanistic perspectives*, Pierre Astier, Morris Beja and S. E. Gontarski (eds.), Columbus: Ohio State University Press, 1983, 107–21.

St-Pierre, Paul, '*Comment c'est* de Beckett: production et déception du sens', *La Revue de lettres modernes*, 605–10 (1981), 89–113.

7

JONATHAN KALB

The mediated Quixote: the radio and television plays, and *Film*

No epoch-making artist simply accepts his or her means of art-making as handed down from previous artists. From Aristophanes to Michelangelo to Shakespeare to Molière to Picasso to Beckett, all can be seen (sometimes only in retrospect) to have engaged in lifelong critiques of their working media. This is never in itself a reliable indicator of greatness, and in twentieth-century art – which, high and low, good and bad, has been pre-occupied with reflexivity – it is an especially poor one. Sometimes, however, an artist's critique is so confident, thoroughgoing and persuasive that it causes significant change in the public's idea of what a particular medium is, or can be. As critics have frequently pointed out, Beckett's stage plays actually changed many people's notions of what can happen, or is supposed to happen, when they enter a theatre.

Due to a number of factors, the same claim cannot be made about his works for radio, film and television, which have had far less influence than the theatre works. First, Beckett's media plays (as these are now irrevocably called; why and when theatre ceased being a medium is a mystery) have had far less circulation. Rarely produced or re-broadcast after their premières, they are largely inaccessible except as published scripts, which are in many cases coldly schematic guides to creating artworks rather than completed artworks themselves. Second and more fundamental, all three media are too young to have had much experience of significant change, their brief histories being dominated by distrust of alternatives to commercial programming, though this is less true in radio, and still less so in film. For an artist of Beckett's uncompromising temperament to turn his attention to any of them – especially television, in the second decade of its global domination – is for him virtually to ensure that his efforts will be marginal.

If one happens to be Samuel Beckett, however, marginalism isn't necessarily pernicious. 'Success and failure on the public level never mattered much to me', he wrote to Alan Schneider, his American director, in 1956; 'in fact I feel much more at home with the latter, having breathed deep of its vivifying air all my writing life' (D, 106). In 1949, Beckett had argued in *Three dialogues* that a certain kind of creative failure had moral value: 'to be an artist is to fail, as no other dare fail [. . .] failure is his world and the shrink from it desertion' (D, 145). In other words, he seemed to say, lack of notoriety and influence mean nothing if they stem from monastic dedication, or from quixotic straining after some inner image of perfection. The novelist Robert Coover, comparing Beckett with the character Don Quixote, once described the enduring fascination commanded by 'the impotent old clown caught up in the mad toils of earnestness'[1] – implying that, even in those arenas where Beckett won worldly success, it might be more appropriate and fruitful to speak of his field of impotence, not influence.

The point is, despite its relative lack of influence, Beckett's gaze at radio, film and television was just as piercing as it was at theatre; in fact, in some ways these media suited him better. In his perpetual search for purer and purer distillations of expression, the professional theatre, with its endless ego-battles, financial hassles and publicity pressures, was never an ideal working environment. Now and then he would put up with the public eye, in an effort to see his works realized according to his original vision, but it caused him much discomfort; the experience of travelling to New York for a film shoot in 1964, for instance, was so hard on him that he never again considered working in film or returning to the United States. Two other points are probably of more crucial importance, though: first, a perfectionist is better served by recordable media than by live media because the former offer the chance to freeze and preserve (nearly) perfect performances for posterity; and second, the distinctive formal issues associated with these media – questions of subjective versus objective point of view, the benevolence or malevolence of the camera eye, and so on – coincide surprisingly well with many lifelong preoccupations of Beckett's, such as the agonistic themes of darkness and light, sound and silence, and the problems of veracity and subjective identity in fictional narrative.

Moreover, the progression from radio to film to television in his career also involves a movement toward increasingly pure distillation. To borrow a phrase from *Footfalls*, Beckett seems to have spent years 'revolving it all' (CSPL, 243) imperfectly in various genres and media – 'it' being that totalized or essentialized artistic statement usually achieved once, if ever, in an artist's lifetime – until finding, in his seventh decade, a means of getting 'it' right (or, again, nearly) once and forever. In what follows, my emphasis will be on what appear to be Beckett's general aims, the 'it' or 'its' he was reaching toward both in each medium and in the three media as a progressive sequence.

THE RADIO PLAYS

The story of Beckett's introduction to radio drama has been told by numerous commentators, notably Martin Esslin and Clas Zilliacus, who provide valuable information about the circumstances of Beckett's first contracts with the BBC in the early 1950s and his subsequent 'commission' to write *All that fall* in 1956. Between the lines in these accounts is the implication that Beckett's motivation for working in radio, and perhaps some aspects of his first radio play, were already clear in his mind when the BBC suggested he contribute something to its Third Programme. Disembodied voices, particularly the sort that act as goads to the imagination, had been an important feature in his prose fiction for years, and in retrospect it seems only natural that he would eventually make use of a medium in which dramas could be peopled entirely with invisible characters. The invisible as persistent prod to the visible, absence and silence as indispensable integuments for what is present and audible: these were trademark formal features in his work by the time he set about writing *All that fall*.

'Whenever he makes the test of a new medium, Beckett always seems to take a few steps backward [toward naturalism]', wrote John Spurling in 1972.[2] At first it may seem strange to apply to radio a concept so bound up with stage pictorialism as naturalism, but anyone comparing *All that fall* with the radio plays that followed it would understand at once what was meant. Unlike the later plays, *All that fall* could be seen as a quaint aural picture of provincial Ireland around the turn of the century. To see it exclusively that way would be superficial, of course, but Beckett's free use of Irishisms (the play marks his return to English after a decade of writing in French) and the considerable trouble he took over details of local atmosphere cannot be ignored.

Also, as Esslin notes, in the prodigious literature of radio drama it would be difficult to find a work more concerned with visual textures than *All that fall*. The play, which tells a relatively straightforward story set in a fictional but recognizably Irish town called Boghill, is dense with tactile references: 'let me just flop down flat on the road like a big fat jelly out of a bowl'; 'As if I were a bale'; 'You are quivering like a blancmange' – all of these, incidentally, references to the central character, Maddy Rooney (*CSPL*, 14, 18, 29). The story follows old Maddy through various encounters with local residents as she goes to meet her blind husband Dan at the railway station, dwells for a while at the station as Dan's train is delayed, and then follows the Rooneys on their way home. The reason for the delay is the plot's one suspense element, and in the last line, when a subsidiary character reveals that an accident occurred involving a child who fell on to the tracks, the suspicion arises (due to scattered hints earlier) that Dan was in some way responsible for it.

Zilliacus has called this work 'Beckett's *To Damascus*, a station drama portraying the passion of Maddy Rooney', and that description is helpful as long as one also understands that the 'passion' is fraught with satire and accompanied by several other, peculiarly Beckettian, structuring devices.[3] (The train-station/station-of-the-cross pun would certainly be typical of Beckett.) The play's first half is quite as much preoccupied with filling time and remarking on language as with revealing Maddy's personality – or soul, to continue the passion allusion – while she moves through her chance meetings-cum-stations, whereas the second half is a drama of delay on the model of *Waiting for Godot*: Beckett premises the action on a mystery and then makes it impossible for us to confirm or deny our suspicions about it. The play is constantly *not* satisfying the desire for information it generates and ultimately leaves us to discover for ourselves that the ambiguities and uncertainties surrounding the planted hints – such detective-fiction questions as whether or not the ball in Dan's hand belonged to the accident victim – are left intentionally open.

Informational considerations quickly become secondary, in any case, when one listens to *All that fall*. The primary experience of the play in performance is of a sound-world that does not attempt to convince us of its veracity except as a product of Maddy's (and Beckett's) imagination. The 'rural sounds' at the opening, for instance ('Sheep, bird, cow, cock, severally, then together' *CSPL*, 12), which return later, are not only flagrantly artificial in themselves – they were radio drama clichés even in 1956 – but are also continually used in ways that remind us of their radiophonic origin; animals and objects greet Maddy's mention of them with absurd efficiency and dispatch. Zilliacus writes that Beckett intends to contrast 'the imperturbability of the animal sound systems' with the myriad anxieties associated with human language;[4] 'Do you find anything...bizarre about my way of speaking?' asks Maddy of Christy, her first conversation partner (*CSPL*, 13). In any case, Beckett also clearly intends to suggest that the entire action may take place in Maddy's mind.

The quality of Maddy's voice in the first BBC production, directed by Donald McWhinnie, supports this. The actress Mary O'Farrell speaks closer to the microphone than the other actors, as if in confidence to the listener, and she often talks over the beginnings and ends of others' lines, delivering Maddy's numerous *non sequiturs* in a way that implies that others (including Dan) have no reality for her except insofar as they further her ongoing mental composition. As Esslin writes, Maddy's journal 'has a nightmare quality; it might indeed be a bad dream';[5] we are never entirely sure, however, whether it is her dream or ours. (It should also be mentioned that her nightmarish isolated condition is often said to be emblematic of the biblical fallen state. '"The Lord upholdeth all that fall and raiseth up all those that be bowed down,"' she says late in the action, after which she and Dan join in 'wild laughter' (CSPL, 38). The play's sundry references to falling mostly deflate the biblical conceit, reducing fateful misfortunes to clownish pratfalls, and death-and-damnation imagery to sexual innuendo.)

Maddy's conversations with her neighbours (and their dialogue exchanges with each other) notwithstanding, the action of All that fall is propelled by her monologuing. As with many other Beckett works, the idea that the central speaker may really be alone generates a network of underlying questions and themes related to the notion of 'company': can the imagination provide sufficient company to alleviate loneliness, especially the writer's special brand of that malady? When the artist is truly honest with himself, what can he say he knows for certain, or presume to depict outside the interior landscape of his skull? The subtext and formal features of All that fall convey the substantial content, through means similar to what Pierre Chabert has identified in Endgame: 'Words emanate from silence and return to it; movement emanates from immobility and returns to it. All movements, all gestures move, so to speak, within immobility, are a victory over immobility and have value only in the tension they maintain in relationship to immobility.'[6] All that fall, which begins and ends with the image of an old woman alone in a house, playing Schubert's 'Death and the maiden', emanates from lonely silence and returns to it, achieving forward movement as a victory over a sort of fundamental paralysis. Maddy is constantly on the verge of stasis, inanition, not going on, the local cause of which is fits of sadness associated with memories of 'little Minnie' (apparently her dead daughter), the chronic cause of which is much more general and profound. 'Oh to be in atoms, in atoms!' she says 'frenziedly' at one point (CSPL, 17), as if her problems were traceable somehow to her existence as a coherently assembled human.

The play keeps on being detoured, 'derailed', by quasi-philosophical discourses that ultimately have to do with Maddy's fears, and the greatest of her fears is, apparently, of disappearance. Each time she feels ignored in a conversation she interrupts petulantly after a moment and asserts her existence: 'Do not imagine, because I am silent, that I am not present' (CSPL, 25). Anthropomorphically speaking, even language itself ignores her as it goes about its business, forming expressions that become common to others' ears but remain strange to hers. Like O in Film, however, Maddy also has a conflicting fear of 'perceivedness', of being seen; confronted with a hinny that won't stop gazing at her, for instance, she suggests moving out of its 'field of vision' (*CSPL*, 13).

Beckett's primary focus in this uncharacteristically populous play, in other words, is a strange condition of precarious suspension between existence and non-existence, which radio is ideally suited to explore. 'Only the present speaker's presence is certain [in radio],' writes Zilliacus; 'the primary condition of existence for a radio character is that he talk.'[7] Hence the author's famous objection to the idea of presenting *All that fall* on stage: 'Whatever quality it may have [. . .] depends on the whole thing's *coming out of the dark*', he wrote in a 1957 letter to his American publisher.[8] Artistic constructions based on the solipsistic notion of people and things jumping willy-nilly in and out of existence simply cannot function in fleshy, concrete media.

Embers, Beckett's next radio play, is a transitional work in which conventional plotting and recognizability of place have been sacrificed even though a strong interest in tactile pictorialism is still apparent. Unlike *All that fall*, in which a modest interpretative effort is necessary to see beyond the surface narrative about a nattering old woman, *Embers* has no surface narrative other than that of a haunted man talking about talking to himself, telling stories that he never finishes, and sometimes aurally experiencing (along with us) the ghostly people and things in his stories. Written in 1959, *Embers* opens with the sound of a man's boots 'on shingle' and the sound of the sea, at first 'scarcely audible', then incrementally louder (*CSPL*, 93). Henry, the man, is wrestling with his imagination – a spectacle we witness in the form of sound-effect commands barked out as if to obedient radio technicians: 'Hooves! [*Sound of hooves walking on hard road. They die rapidly away. Pause.*] Again! [*Hooves as before.*]'

Henry, who may or may not be walking by the sea with his daughter Addie nearby, addresses his dead father, who may or may not have committed suicide in the sea. The father fails to respond – the text implies that he occasionally does respond at other times – and Henry tells a story about a man named Bolton (perhaps a father-surrogate) who has called for his doctor Holloway one winter night, for obscure reasons that may have to do with wanting to die. Henry then speaks to a woman, also apparently dead, named Ada, his former companion and mother of Addie, who speaks sympathetically but distractedly back to him. For most of the remainder of the action Ada and Henry reminisce about old times, some of which are dramatized as auditory flashbacks involving other characters. Henry complains several times of not being able to rid himself of the sound of the sea, and Ada suggests that he consult Holloway about both that and his incessant talking to himself. When Ada no longer answers him, Henry tries unsuccessfully to command the sound effects again, returns briefly to the Bolton story, and then ends by seeming to make a note in his diary: 'Nothing, all day nothing. [*Pause.*] All day all night nothing. [*Pause.*] Not a sound' (*CSPL*, 104).

It is probably safe to say that the word 'nothing' in Beckett's work must never be taken literally. 'Nothing' is invariably his way of referring to not quite nothing – his favourite designation for something depleted, waning, but still there, or else for that enormous, ineffable something always left to express after the artist's 'power to express' has been exhausted. ('*Nothing is more real than nothing,*' says Malone; *T*, 177.) The words 'not a sound' are both a lie (after all, we listeners have heard a great deal and so has Henry) and the truth (the play ends at that point, and whatever Henry heard was something other than sound if it occurred in his head). In *Embers*, as elsewhere, Beckett employs linguistic duplicity as an example of, and metaphor for, all that is ephemeral and unverifiable in life. Like the hearthfire burnt down to embers behind Bolton – the word 'embers', repeated several times in the play, is usually accompanied by the phrase 'not a sound' – Henry's imaginative stratagems for fending off the looming maw of nothingness, symbolized by the omnipresent sound of the sea, are always growing thin but never exhausted.

Embers is also transitional in that it contains in embryo many of the reflexive formal games that Beckett would later focus on obsessively in the radio plays (the exception being *Rough for radio II*), the television plays, and the middle and late prose fiction. Both Henry's closing lines and his opening line, 'On', for instance, are as much simple technical references to the play's beginning and ending as they are orders to his mind or descriptions of its activities. In Everett Frost's 1988 production, actress Billie Whitelaw's sing-songy, confidently feeble, self-consciously spectral voice made especially clear that Henry switched Ada on and off, and removed all possibility of her being understood as a physically present conversation partner independent of Henry.

The switching word, 'open', which later plays an important part in *Cascando*, also appears in *Embers* and again recalls the issue of 'company' mentioned above: after seeing Holloway through the window, Bolton 'goes down and opens' (*CSPL*, 94). To open one's house or mind, either to someone or to the memory of someone, is to interrupt the bliss of solitude and silence that the Beckett hero always longs for but never quite possesses (and never finds to be bliss after stealing a taste of it – e.g., after death). Like *Krapp's last tape*, in which a sixty-nine-year-old switches back and forth over the same bit of audiotape, listening to himself whispering 'Let me in' to the memory of an old lover's eyes (*CSPL*, 61); like *...but the clouds...*, whose climactic moment is a man blurting out 'Look at me' to the remembered image of a woman (*CSPL*, 261); like *What where*, in which the main character punctuates the dialogue with the phrases 'I switch on' and 'I switch off' and, after obscure interactions with other characters who look conspicuously like him, says, 'I am alone' (*CSPL*, 311) – like these and many other Beckett works, *Embers* poses an irresolvable dilemma concerning the relative values of solitude and companionship. The protagonist wants his imagined creations to exist as concretely and satisfyingly as corporeal companions but then to go away, to switch off, at less than a moment's notice.

The explicit association of mechanistic switching with the engagement of the imagination, which would become one of the most fruitful metaphors of Beckett's later career, is one of two salient distinguishing features of the last three radio plays, *Words and Music*, *Cascando* and *Rough for radio I* (the latter an early study for *Cascando* whose performance Beckett discouraged). The other feature is the introduction of music as an autonomous character, which also anticipates another important later development, primarily in the media work: collapse of faith in verbal language. The author himself drew attention on several occasions to musical structures in his plays (*Endgame* as 'a string quartet', *Play* as 'a score for five pitches', for instance),[9] and even if he had written nothing but novels and stories it would be clear from the cadences and phrasings of his prose that he possessed a highly developed musical sensibility. In the final radio plays, however, he does not so much embrace music as an overarching structural concept that subsumes writing as rather pit music against language in a dramatic showdown over their relative merits.

Written in 1961 as a collaboration with a specific composer, the author's cousin John Beckett, *Words and Music* begins with the sound of a small orchestra tuning up and a man's voice competing for air space as he too 'tunes up', reciting sentences by rote describing the passion of 'sloth' (*CSPL*, 127). A crotchety man named Croak shuffles on, refers to Words as 'Joe', to Music as 'Bob', and enjoins them: 'My comforts! Be friends!' Croak turns out to be an impresario of sorts who thumps a club on the ground and barks orders to Words and Music, alternately and together, to entertain him by illustrating first the concept of love, and then that of age. The two 'comforts' or 'balms' compete to satisfy him, Music playing love- and age-themes, Words reciting more rote formulations, poems and nostalgic descriptions of a woman's face, which causes the impresario to groan and cry out 'Lily!' at one point (*CSPL*, 132). In the end he shuffles off as if unable to bear the memories which the descriptions awaken, and Words and Music are left alone, Words sighing, Music repeating one of its last phrases (an illustration of 'that wellhead' deep within Lily's eyes).

Unlike Dan or Ada, Words and Music prove to be at least partly independent of the central imagining agent in their play, Croak. They do not always
obey him, they are heard before he enters and after he leaves, and it is
possible in the end to read them as muses, creative forces in their own right
living their own noumenal lives. This work, then, fits the general trend of
the radio dramas toward focusing on communicative means, which muses
(among other things) incontestably are. *Words and Music* also presents a
special problem, however: its action consists of a relatively conventional
dialogic exchange, but the dialogue is missing half its lines – lines that the
play implies should match, sentence for sentence, in musical terms, the
specificity and subtlety of Beckett's language.

It is hardly surprising that neither his cousin nor subsequent composers
have been up to the task. In one case (John Beckett's score) the music
proved unable to communicate ideas specific enough to qualify as rational
lines, much less repartee, and in another (Morton Feldman's score for
Frost's 1988 production) the composer came to feel constrained by the text's
requirements. In the director's words, Feldman struggled 'in the face of the
imposed concisions'. Frost adds: 'I do not mean to imply that I am in any
way regretful [...] Such is emphatically not the case. But with this play
more than the others, it will take several productions with a variety of
musics before we can feel reliably that we have begun to get to the bottom
of its complex and interesting possibilities.'[10] But the play's production
difficulties run far deeper than questions of agreement in style; unless
Music convinces us that it has at least held its own in the strange mimetic
competition with Words, the action of the play lacks dramatic tension.
Beckett once reportedly said to Theodor Adorno that *Words and Music*
'ends unequivocally with the victory of the music'.[11] Yet far from proving
the superiority of music as pure sound, liberated from rational ideas and
references, the play confines it to a function very similar to that of a filmic
signature score. *Cascando*, written in French a month or so later, seems
planned explicitly to overcome this mimetic limitation.

Cascando is also a collaborative work for which Beckett did not write the
necessary music. This time his first collaborator was the Romanian-born
Marcel Mihalovici (who had previously written an opera based on *Krapp's
last tape*) and the original *Cascando* on French radio (RTF) was consider-
ably more 'operatic' (meaning more extensively orchestrated) than any
other Beckett radio production before or since. With this play, however,
even a seemingly weighty matter like extent of orchestration *can* remain a
question of style, because Beckett's text does not require music to function
as a conventional conversation partner. In fact, the characters Voice and
Music operate virtually independently of each other.

Like *Words and Music*, *Cascando* has a central imaging agent, named Opener, but he takes a much softer approach with his muses than Croak does. Instead of barking specific orders, Opener calmly speaks the generalized phrases 'I open' and 'I close', and the action that follows is more like tandem or parallel monologues than dialogue. Sometimes Voice and Music start and stop without Opener's explicit sanction, and some of Opener's lines imply that Voice and Music occasionally work together to a common purpose – 'as though they had linked their arms' – although this is unverifiable in the text (*CSPL*, 143). Music's part is indicated only by dots extending across the page like a long ellipsis, and Voice's consists of a frequently interrupted story which he cannot finish and which he is not sure is 'the right one' (like the narrators in the novels) about a man named Woburn, one of those quintessential, stumbling Beckett figures walking by the sea in a greatcoat. Opener speaks haughtily between the story sections, scoffing at the notion that he and Voice might really be the same character ('They say, He opens nothing, he has nothing to open, it's in his head'; *CSPL*, 140), and, of course, the more he insists that there is 'No resemblance' the more we listeners suspect that there is (*CSPL*, 142).

From the outset, the central question in *Cascando* is not 'who may speak?' but rather 'when may *I* speak and with which voice?' In contrast to *Words and Music*, the characters do not begin by tuning or warming up, practising for some future performance that will be more authentic or significant than this one. Co-operatively, they plunge straight into a concerted, multiform effort to finish a story, giving the present-tense action a greater urgency and forward momentum than any of the previous radio plays had – primarily because listeners do not spend time wondering about plot questions, such as why Words and Music don't co-operate. Like *Embers*, *Cascando* contains Beckett's first rethinking for performance of formal techniques originally cultivated in his stories and novels. Voice's relationship to his subject (read: surrogate self), for instance, is the same as Jacques Moran's in *Molloy*, E's in *Film*, and the spotlight's in *Play*, one of pursuit; Woburn is as much chased as described. Also, Opener's repeated denial that he is the storyteller (or, by extension, the story's subject) and Voice's constant self-interruption – each two- to four-word phrase is followed by an ellipsis – prefigure the self-denying, fragmentary character Mouth in *Not I* and Beckett's habit through the 1970s and 1980s of using the fragmentary as a metaphor for a damaged whole.

Most important, though, *Cascando* contains Beckett's purest distillation of the essence of the radio medium. The stage direction *Silence* appears twenty times in the eight-page play (more than in any other radio play except *All that fall*, which is over three times longer), and a significant part of listening to a production is the experience of being returned again and again to one's own sound-space. With only the thinnest of fictional conceits – actors pretending to be characters, actors and characters pretending to be in places and times other than here and now – the author transports the ephemeral products of his imagination by the most ephemeral means (electronic waves and sound impulses) and makes them oscillate in a sort of minimalist dance between presence and absence, between 'going on' (the 'obligation to express') and what professionals call, usually without Beckettian irony, 'dead air time'. Of all media, radio offered Beckett – to use his own wry description of his writerly efforts – the purest opportunity to put a 'blot on silence'.[12]

'FILM'

Like *All that fall*, Beckett's one work for cinema has been frequently described as a 'commission'. In 1963 Barney Rosset, his American publisher, decided to expand into film producing and invited Beckett (as well as Harold Pinter and Eugène Ionesco) to write something for the medium. As with radio, however, it is unthinkable that Beckett would have turned his attention to film solely because an opportunity arose for immediate production. The text of *Film* shows that he had given the medium hard thought for some time; indeed, according to Deirdre Bair, his fascination with it dates back to 1935 when, as a young man searching for professional direction, he wrote to Sergei Eisenstein in Moscow asking to be hired as an apprentice.[13]

Film is, as Linda Ben-Zvi writes, 'a film about film'.[14] Its very title is generic, like that of *Play*, indicating that the work will deal with fundamental qualities or principles of its medium rather than simply use film as an unobtrusive story-telling vehicle. Unlike *Play*, however, *Film* was the first and only work Beckett wrote for the medium, and unlike *All that fall* and *Eh Joe* (his first work for television), it was not originally produced under state-of-the-art studio conditions. To be sure, the published text contains wisdom about the medium, but technical naïvety on both Beckett's and director Alan Schneider's part prevented some of it from surfacing in the completed first version. (Schneider had never directed a film before.)[15] Yet *Film* is also a work of its time, displaying many of the same formal obsessions as the French New Wave, just burgeoning in the early 1960s: a reflexive concern with the staring camera eye, an invocation of Hollywood icons such as Buster Keaton along with a general consciousness of film history, and a resistance to montage in the Bazinian tradition (surprising considering Beckett's early interest in Eisenstein, but not surprising considering the absence of montage and cross-fading techniques in the radio plays).[16]

The deceptively simple action of *Film* consists of a cat-and-mouse game played by a single protagonist 'sundered into object (O) and eye (E), the former in flight, the latter in pursuit'. E is the camera, O the character on-screen, and E pursues O from behind, trying not to exceed a 45-degree angle beyond which O 'experiences anguish of perceivedness' (*CSPL*, 163). It is 'a variation on the old Keystone Kops chase',[17] writes Ben-Zvi, which Beckett says should have a 'comic and unreal' climate. Comedy aside, much in the film depends on establishing two different visual 'qualities' clearly distinguishing between O's point of view and E's – one of many details that proved far more technically complicated than either the author or the director realized. Only in the end do we see O's face (Keaton with a patch over one eye), after which a quick cut to E (another view of Keaton, with the opposite 'quality') reveals that 'pursuing perceiver is not extraneous, but self' (*CSPL*, 163).

The three-part, silent, black-and-white action moves from a public to a private milieu, with most of part one omitted in Schneider's production because the footage turned out to be unusable and re-shooting prohibitively expensive. The printed text of part one ('The street') calls for O to come into view 'hastening blindly' along a wall, dressed ponderously in a 'long dark overcoat,' as surrealistic couples in summery costumes rush by in the opposite direction. A woman he jostles 'checks him' with a firm 'sssh!' – the film's only sound – which communicates humorously that the work is silent by conscious choice, perhaps even out of homage, not for want of resources. (Beckett rarely uses a technical means simply because it is available; in fact, he is likely to reject as a 'gimmick' any technique that lends an air of adroitness or ingenuity to his terra *in*firma.) The woman and her companion then express horror upon looking straight at the camera, establishing the convention of 'agony of perceivedness' (*CSPL*, 165).

Part two ('The stairs') consists of another brief encounter leading to horror of the perceiving camera, this time by an old woman carrying flowers. Finally, part three ('The room') deals with O's fate when he relaxes in an 'illusory sanctuary'. After an extended, comic section in which he covers a window and mirror and ejects or covers anything with eyes or resembling eyes (dog, cat, goldfish, an envelope with round fasteners – an early title for the work was *The eye*), O sits in a rocking chair and inspects seven photographs of himself at various points throughout his life – as compact a biography as the one told when Krapp listens to his taped self describe an earlier taped self. O destroys the photos, as well as a print of 'God the Father' hanging nearby, before falling asleep, and then E creeps round along the wall and ends up in position to stare O in the face. 'Search of non-being in flight from extraneous perception breaking down in inescapability of self-perception' is Beckett's summary of the action (*CSPL*, 163).

Much critical commentary on *Film* has centred on the work's Latin epigraph – '*Esse est percipi*', to be is to be perceived – from the philosopher George Berkeley (1685–1753), who believed that the material world had no independent existence outside sentient minds, which in turn exist only because God perceives them. Two lines after this quote, however, Beckett, in typical fashion, backs off from fully endorsing it: 'No truth value attaches to above, regarded as of merely structural and dramatic convenience.' Anyone familiar with his language games, or with his famous statement that 'it is the shape that matters', understands that issues of 'structural and dramatic convenience' are invariably metaphysical concerns for him, and questions about the pertinence of Berkeley's dictum are inevitable for those studying the work.

Some, recalling that Berkeley was an Anglican bishop, suggest that Beckett intends to give a religious maxim an atheistic twist. Vincent Murphy, for example, regrets that 'E becomes a kind of surrogate of God in a world in which God no longer perceives'[18] – a desolate view that overlooks, among other things, the degree to which Beckett's humour undercuts all definite, and therefore over-serious, identifications, such as E with God. Others point out that O and E are partly blind and therefore imperfect perceivers (recall the eye patch), suggesting that Beckett is well aware of the devalued sort of being conferred by terrestrial perception such as E's, and that his intention is to underscore that fallen state; Sylvie Debevec Henning, for instance, writes that 'there can never be full unity of the self, nor any perfect self-identity – not, at least, that we would ever be aware of'.[19]

Still another reading might focus on the eye/I pun (later made central in *Not I*) and on the way Beckett again pursues a metaphysical meditation through critiquing his working medium. The pun hangs on the notion that E may or may not be ultimately equivalent to O and that the seeing 'eye' is primarily occupied with acquiring self-knowledge, the problem of clearly seeing an 'I'. In contrast to Bishop Berkeley, who would say that such clarity is impossible without the perceiving light of God, Beckett wonders about the validity of all neat subject–object distinctions, divine or human (that notion of 'company' again). A contemporary theorist might add that neither a film's characters nor its narrator-surrogate (the camera-eye as subjective 'I') really *exists* until a machine shines incandescent light through celluloid, generating sharp, ephemeral images that fool viewers into believing that the camera-eye is perceiving in the present and that perceivedness is necessarily desirable. Decades before the word 'scopophilia' became fashionable, driven partly perhaps by his abhorrence of publicity and bloodhoundish critics, Beckett was asking essential questions about the invasiveness of the camera and the use of it as an ontological validator.

THE TELEVISION PLAYS

That Beckett wanted to write for a medium like television at all is as interesting as any of the works he made for it. As mentioned above, television has been dominated by the narrowly circumscribed formats of commercial programming since its birth, and those formats have contributed to egregious, worldwide psychological changes: shrinking attention spans, discouraging reading and encouraging passive, narcotized habits of viewing art of all kinds. Unlike radio and film, television has not (yet) been through anything like a Golden Age in which individual artists could exploit it for idiosyncratic purposes. Apart from the efforts of a few quixotic souls like Beckett, whose art always distinguished itself by demanding a greater than usual level of viewer/reader concentration, the medium's high-art potential remains untested. 'In being popular culture's *raison d'être*, television is [...] identical with power', writes Alan M. Olson.[20] Beckett, the inveterate outsider, used it to consider his lifelong issues of powerlessness: 'I'm working with impotence, ignorance [...] I think anyone nowadays who pays the slightest attention to his own experience finds it the experience of a non-knower, a non-can-er.'[21]

Some academic critics, wishing to protect these works' canonical position by treating them exclusively as 'video art' (i.e. for privileged viewers in gallery and museum contexts), may bristle at this way of introducing them; and it must be conceded that, though Beckett did own a television set, there is no proof he was reacting against any specific object. The five works he created for television (six counting *Was wo*, his adaptation of *What where*) contravene common preconceptions mainly by answering to standards of compositional precision that we have come to expect only in other media, such as painting. From the vaudeville gags in *Godot* to the casting of Keaton in *Film*, however, Beckett has a long history of mixing high- and low-culture (one reason why he so often figures in debates about Post-Modernism), and the subtitles and original production circumstances of these works make clear that he thought of them specifically as 'television plays' for mass broadcast.

Predating his next work for the televisual medium by a decade, *Eh Joe* (1965) is a transitional piece in which Beckett is still using the camera as an antagonistic pursuer, as in *Film*, but the setting has become entirely interior and sound has returned, literally with a vengeance. Generally, the main difference between a film image and a television image is that the latter is fluorescently back-lit, cruder in resolution and confined to a small box; taking this into account, Beckett now poses ontological questions not by 'sundering' a highly mobile protagonist on a big screen but by setting up ambiguities about the relation of a spoken text to a relatively still visual picture. These plays contain very little physical movement – and certainly no chase scenes, except perhaps *Quad*, in which the figures seem driven by some inner demon. Unlike *Film*, *Eh Joe* is an insular, inward-referring work designed for a medium typically watched by supine viewers isolated in intimate spaces.

The play begins with a man sitting on a bed, seen from behind, who peremptorily inspects three rectangular openings – window, door and cupboard – locking each afterwards and drawing a curtain over it, as if to ensure he is alone. He returns to the bed and the camera approaches within a yard of his face, stopping when a woman's voice begins speaking: 'Joe . . . Joe'. For approximately twenty minutes this Voice – which insists that it is not coming from his mind and identifies itself as one of his discarded lovers – harangues him about his past womanizing and other personal failings, and we watch the reactions of his face, which Beckett says is 'impassive except insofar as it reflects mounting tension of *listening*' (CSPL, 202). (From *All that fall* to *Ohio impromptu*, Beckett worked from the premise that the act of listening holds inherent dramatic value.) The words stop only for a few seconds at nine specified points, during which the camera pulls in closer to his face, so that by the final section only a fragment, from brow to lower lip, is visible as Voice finally fades out.

Eh Joe has never been a favourite of Beckett's critics, some of whom dismiss it outright as melodramatic and obvious: a lecherous man haunted by guilt in the form of a torturous voice from his past. As I have explained at length elsewhere, however, such analyses neglect formal features and ambiguities beneath the clichéd surface that prefigure fundamental aspects of his subsequent, admittedly richer, television works.[22] Added to the standing uncertainty over whether Voice really comes from Joe's mind is an uncertainty over the relation between Voice and the camera: are they equivalent, allied? The camera never moves while Voice speaks, and it sometimes seems like a separate, perhaps subordinate, entity. After twenty minutes, the close-up of the man's face (the play was written for and originally produced with Jack MacGowran) becomes far more eloquent than Voice's monotonous verbal assault. Among other things, her loquacity may act as a smokescreen, designed to distract viewers temporarily from the complex depths of a portrait, making those depths all the more impactful when they are noticed later, and this effect is only heightened by the portrait becoming fragmentary in the end. Beckett's aesthetic of wholeness-in-fragmentariness is pursued on television by means of rectangular framing.

Ten years later, when he began *Ghost trio* (1975), the author had already made the transition to his later stage dramas, and there is a complex mutual influence, which may never be fully teased out, between those dramas and his mature television work. The later stage dramas generally dispense with the provisional naturalism used in the plays up to *Happy days* (as well as in *Eh Joe* and *Film*, for that matter), presenting rather meticulously sculpted tableaux at which the audience stares while a musical flow of words with some enigmatic relationship to the tableau emanates from the stage. They are also populated with characters who are not only ephemeral (Maddy-as-sound impulse, O-as-light image, Joe-as-collection of fluorescing dots) but downright ghostly, possibly dead – 'not quite there', Beckett once said about May in *Footfalls*. The television plays from *Ghost trio* on also fit this pattern, the difference being that the visual images become more and more finely wrought, the texts increasingly sparing with speech.

Ghost trio takes its name and mysterious, ethereal atmosphere from a Beethoven piano trio (op. 70, no. 1) entitled *The ghost* (written for an opera based on *Macbeth*), parts of which Beckett specifies should be heard at various points in the action. In the first of three sections ('Pre-action') we see a seated male figure (F) bent over a cassette player, 'clutching hands, head bowed, face hidden', and hear a female voice (V) describe the environment in tones that range from neutral to sardonic:

> Good evening. Mine is a faint voice. Kindly tune accordingly. [*Pause.*] Good evening. Mine is a faint voice. Kindly tune accordingly. [*Pause.*] It will not be raised, nor lowered, whatever happens. [*Pause.*] Look. [*Long pause.*] The familiar chamber. [*Pause.*] At the far end a window. [*Pause.*] On the right the indispensable door. [*Pause.*] On the left, against the wall, some kind of pallet. [*Pause.*] The light: faint, omnipresent. No visible source. As if all luminous. Faintly luminous. No shadow.   (*CSPL*, 248)

The room, of course, is not at all familiar, to us or (apparently) to F, and as Ben-Zvi points out, the more V describes it the stranger it seems.[23] V instructs us to 'look closer' at 'the kind of wall [...] the kind of floor', and the camera responds (sometimes) by showing different grey rectangles, so plain we would take them for simple geometric cut-outs if V did not name them. 'Look again,' she says. 'Knowing all this, the kind of pallet [...] the kind of window [...] the kind of door [...] Look again' (*CSPL*, 249).

Part two begins with V's statement 'He will now think he hears her', which reveals that F is waiting for some woman (an early title for the piece was *Tryst*), though it also reveals, in the light of the author's previous uses of waiting, that the woman is unlikely to arrive and introduces questions about the identity of V. Is she the awaited woman? F's reluctant muse? Death, 'who will not come to release him from a life to which he barely clings?' (James Knowlson's suggestion).[24] As V narrates – 'Now to door [...] No one [...] Now to window' (*CSPL*, 250) – F rises and, moving soundlessly in an almost puppet-like manner, inspects the room's various openings, including a dark, grave-like corridor outside the knobless door, then returns to his seat and music. In part three V does not narrate and F goes through similar but not identical activities (examining his face in a mirror, for example), eventually opening the door to find a boy in a glistening black oilskin, who 'shakes head faintly', then 'turns and goes' (*CSPL*, 253–4).

The imperative 'look again' in part one applies not only to the rectangles but also to the rest of the play and, by extension, to the other television plays, all of which (except *Eh Joe*) employ cyclical repetition: 'look again', Beckett seems to say, not only at the picture at hand but at the way you looked the first time, at how that may have been inadequate. This might be called the model of the 'double-take' – contrasting distant and near views of the same scene – and it is another example of Beckett incorporating the viewer's process of viewing into his drama. Like many other Beckett works, *Ghost trio* is partly about the failure of a central agent to perceive clearly. F seems to have been in this 'familiar room' for some time, yet he moves soundlessly about the space, looking distractedly at his own face, as if everything were foreign; only at the end, after the boy has left and the Beethoven piece finishes, does he raise his head and smile, as if finally freed from anticipation. Similarly, viewers are distracted by the rectangles and the playfulness of the voice, which seems to say little that is vital for understanding the action, although, as Ben-Zvi writes, that distraction turns out to be vital:

> Each rectangular shape is seen against a still larger rectangle: the window against the wall, the door against the wall [...] All these rectangles, of course, are subsumed in the framing rectangle of the television screen, possibly being viewed in the rectangle of 'the familiar room' of the viewer [...][25]

Beckett's play, in other words, is partly about the fact that television itself has grown too familiar.

...but the clouds... (1976) was first broadcast by the BBC together with *Ghost trio* and an adaptation of *Not I* in a programme entitled *Shades*, but its elegiac, rueful tone recalls *Nacht und Träume* (1982) more than the earlier television plays. The title is a phrase from the closing stanza of W. B. Yeats' poem 'The tower', which Beckett could recite from memory and which concerns reconciliation with the decrepitude of old age and death:

girding himself for a final bout of plying his 'sedentary trade' in a tower sanctuary, the indomitable poet half convinces us that, there, 'the death of friends' and similar losses can 'Seem but the clouds of the sky/When the horizon fades/Or a bird's sleepy cry/Among the deepening shades'. Beckett never completely relinquishes his sardonic tones, but there is a greater than usual level of earnestness in ...*but the clouds*... and *Nacht und Träume*, as if whatever mental censor had previously prevented his works from becoming saturated with emotion had suddenly disappeared.

...*but the clouds*... begins with a brief, obscure view of a man (M) bowed over an invisible table, a view the camera subsequently returns to fifteen times. As his voice (V) narrates, M is repeatedly seen moving in and out of a lighted circle surrounded by darkness, V explaining that the movement is his daily routine: arrival from 'having walked the roads since break of day' (entrance at left of circle), change into his nightclothes (exit and re-entrance at right of circle), and exit to his 'little sanctum' (top of circle), where he crouches in the dark and 'beg[s], of her, to appear' (*CSPL*, 260). This 'her' is a woman (W), presumably a lost loved one, whose face appears briefly on the screen whenever he speaks of summoning her. Pedantically distinguishing among four cases – W not appearing, appearing, appearing and lingering, appearing and speaking – V becomes emotional near the end and addresses her directly ('Look at me [...] Speak to me'; *CSPL*, 261) before reciting Yeats' closing lines in synch with her inaudible lips.

Nacht und Träume also begins with a view of a man (Dreamer) seated at a table, 'right profile, head bowed, grey hair' (*CSPL*, 305), only this time there is no narrator; the story is told entirely in pictures (as were the stories that seemed most reliable in *Eh Joe*, *Ghost trio* and ...*but the clouds*...). The only speech is a barely intelligible line from a Schubert *Lied* – 'Hölde Träume, kehret wieder' ('Lovely dreams, come again') – sung by a male voice, which lulls the Dreamer to sleep. In a square cloud above him we see his dream: himself seated in the other direction, being visited by dis-embodied hands that touch him gently, offer him a chalice, wipe his brow, then join with his hands to form a cushion for his head. This sequence is then repeated, except that the second time the camera pulls in close so that the dream cloud fills the screen, revealing details not perceivable before: among them, a distinct religious flavour and a congeries of references to classical painting. 'Look again', the work seems to say, not only at its particular action but at all secular and art-historical assumptions about this author.

Along with *Quad*, a compelling work completely without language, these two plays mark a great wordsmith's break with words near the end of his life, instances of him working more as a composer or painter than a traditional playwright. Indeed, Beckett took a painterly, 'hands on' attitude toward all his television plays, directing them himself and refining them at Süddeutscher Rundfunk in Stuttgart after assisting with the original BBC productions, ensuring that the images, sound and pacing would be preserved on tape exactly as he had imagined them. ...*but the clouds*... and *Nacht und Träume* are also particularly significant in his *œuvre*, however, because they use his real emotions about death unashamedly as artistic grist. Beckett was known for being tactically old his entire career, preoccupied with creating narrative personae who joked about death and half seriously praised the glory of ending. Where his personae exist in worlds peopled only by ghosts, and may in fact be ghosts themselves, the mental distance necessary for irony is harder to achieve.

There is a gem-like, iconic quality to all the television plays, particularly Beckett's own productions, which stands as a tacit criticism of all art that is made less painstakingly, with less monastic obsessiveness. Acts of formal originality such as the model of the 'double-take' are the closest Beckett ever came to explicit political critique, but, as with so much he said quietly and subtly, the power of the acts is extraordinary once they are understood. Beckett takes a medium famous for destroying the capacity of humans to think rigorously and perceive clearly and uses it to make plays about the infinitude of the soul and the grandeur of the smallest mortal memory. As a painter of miniatures employs a magnifying glass to achieve an impression of perfection, Beckett uses technical instrumentation to augment human perception and, by implication, dignify it, sending his ghostly emissaries from the humanist 'heap' through the air waves into people's living rooms.

NOTES

1 Robert Coover, 'The last Quixote', 139.
2 John Fletcher and John Spurling, *Beckett the playwright*, 44.
3 Clas Zilliacus, *Beckett and broadcasting*, 37.
4 Ibid., 50.
5 Martin Esslin, 'The art of broadcasting', 131.
6 Pierre Chabert, 'The body in Beckett's theatre', 25.
7 Zilliacus, *Beckett and broadcasting*, 56.
8 Quoted in Zilliacus, ibid., 3.
9 Ibid., 103.
10 Everett Frost, 'Fundamental sounds', 374–5.
11 Quoted in Zilliacus, *Beckett and broadcasting*, 114.
12 Quoted in Kalb, *Beckett in performance*, 233.
13 Deirdre Bair, *Samuel Beckett: a biography* (London: Jonathan Cape, 1978), 204.
14 Linda Ben-Zvi, 'Samuel Beckett's media plays', 31.

15 See Schneider's apologia, 'On directing *Film*', in Samuel Beckett, *Film* (New York: Grove Press, 1969), 63–94.
16 See Zilliacus, *Beckett and broadcasting*, 60.
17 Ben-Zvi, 'Samuel Beckett's media plays', 30.
18 Vincent J. Murphy, 'Being and perception', 47.
19 Henning, '*Film:* a dialogue between Beckett and Berkeley', 99.
20 Olson, 'Video icons and values', 2.
21 Beckett to Israel Shenker in 1956, in Lawrence Graver and Raymond Federman (eds.), *Samuel Beckett: the critical heritage*, 148.
22 See Kalb, *Beckett in performance*, 95–116.
23 Ben-Zvi, 'Samuel Beckett's media plays', 36.
24 Knowlson, '*Ghost trio/Geister trio*', 199.
25 Ben-Zvi, 'Samuel Beckett's media plays', 35.

RECOMMENDED READING

Avila, Wanda, 'The poem within the play in Beckett's *Embers*', *Language and Style*, 17.3 (1984), 193–205.
Ben-Zvi, Linda, 'Samuel Beckett's media plays', *Modern Drama*, 28.1 (March 1985), 22–37.
Brater, Enoch, *Beyond minimalism: Beckett's late style in the theater*, New York and Oxford: Oxford University Press, 1987.
Chabert, Pierre, 'The body in Beckett's theatre', *Journal of Beckett Studies*, 8 (Autumn 1982), 23–8.
Coover, Robert, 'The last Quixote', *New American Review*, 11 (1971), 132–43.
Dodsworth, Martin, '*Film* and the religion of art', in *Beckett the shape changer*, ed. Katharine Worth, London and Boston: Routledge and Kegan Paul, 1975, 161–82.
Elam, Keir, '*Not I*: Beckett's mouth and the ars(e) rhetorica', in *Beckett at 80/ Beckett in context*, ed. Enoch Brater, New York and Oxford: Oxford University Press, 1986, 124–48.
Esslin, Martin, 'A poetry of moving images', in *Beckett Translating/Translating Beckett*, ed. Alan Warren Friedman, Charles Rossman and Dina Sherzer, University Park: Pennsylvania State University Press, 1987, 65–76.
'Samuel Beckett and the art of broadcasting' in *Mediations: essays on Brecht, Beckett and the media*, New York: Grove Press, 1982, 125–54.
Fletcher, Beryl S., John Fletcher, Barry Smith and Walter Bachem, (eds.), *A student's guide to the plays of Samuel Beckett*, London and Boston: Faber and Faber, 1978.
Fletcher, John and John Spurling, *Beckett the playwright*, revised edition, New York: Hill and Wang, 1985.
Frost, Everett, 'Fundamental sounds: recording Samuel Beckett's radio plays', *Theatre Journal*, 43.3 (October 1991), 361–76.
Gontarski, S. E., 'The anatomy of Beckett's *Eh Joe*', *Modern Drama*, 26.4 (1983), 425–34.
Henning, Sylvie Debevec, '*Film:* a dialogue between Beckett and Berkeley', *Journal of Beckett Studies*, 7 (Spring 1982), 89–99.

Kalb, Jonathan, *Beckett in performance*, Cambridge University Press, 1989, chapter 6.

Knowlson, James, '*Ghost trio/Geister trio*', in *Beckett at 80/Beckett in context*, ed. Enoch Brater, New York and Oxford: Oxford University Press, 1986, 193–207.

Lawley, Paul, '*Embers*: an interpretation', *Journal of Beckett Studies*, 6 (1981), 9–36.

Marculescu, Ileana, 'Beckett and the temptation of solipsism', *Journal of Beckett Studies*, 11/12 (1989), 53–64.

McWhinnie, Donald, *The art of radio*, London: Faber and Faber, 1959.

Murphy, Vincent, J., 'Being and perception: Beckett's *Film*', *Modern Drama*, 18.1 (March 1975), 43–8.

Olson, Alan M., 'Video icons and values: an overview', in *Video icons and values*, ed. Alan M. Olson, Christopher Parr, and Debra Parr, Albany: State University of New York Press, 1991, 1–16.

Pilling, John, *Samuel Beckett*, London: Routledge and Kegan Paul, 1976, chapter 4.

Russell, Catherine, 'The figure in the monitor: Beckett, Lacan, and video', *Cinema Journal*, 28.4 (Summer 1989), 20–37.

Schneider, Alan, 'On directing *Film*', in Samuel Beckett, *Film*, New York: Grove Press, 1969, 63–94.

Van Laan, Thomas F., '*All that fall* as "a play for radio"', *Modern Drama*, 28.1 (March 1985), 38–47.

Worth, Katharine, 'Beckett and the radio medium', in John Drakakis (ed.), *British radio drama*, Cambridge University Press, 1981, 191–217.

Zilliacus, Clas, *Beckett and broadcasting*, Abo: Abo Akademi, 1976.

8

KEIR ELAM

Dead heads: damnation-narration in the 'dramaticules'

E un ch'avea perduti ambo li orecchi
per la freddura, pur col viso in giùe
disse 'Perché cotanto in noi ti specchi?'[1]

Dante, *Inferno*, Canto XXXII

BECKETT'S 'DRAMATICULES': THE DYING AND THE GOING

When, in 1978, the actor David Warrilow asked Samuel Beckett to write him a play about death,[2] he would appear to have been guilty of a fortunate tautology. Fortunate, because the playwright's generous response to the request was the beautiful miniature *A piece of monologue* (1979), whose opening is surely his most chillingly paradoxical statement of the chosen theme: 'Birth was the death of him' (CSPL, 265). But a tautology nonetheless, at least according to the play's protagonist, Speaker, who – as if in reply to the actor – denies that any other topic is even thinkable, or speakable: 'Never but the one matter. The dead and gone. The dying and the going.' Or to put it another way, to ask Beckett for a play on death was like asking, say, Petrarch for a sonnet on love: as if he might have written one that was *not*. All of Beckett's drama, especially his later drama, insofar as it is 'about' anything, is essentially 'about death'.

Despite Speaker's categorical response, however, the request for a play on death is not necessarily ingenuous: it questions, on the contrary, the very possibilities and limits of dramatic representation. In what sense can the drama, dedicated from its beginnings to showing forth action, and thus forms of life, claim to show forth the form of non-life? How can the theatre present or re-present what Speaker himself can define only in terms of absence ('gone', 'the going')? What, indeed, does it mean to posit a semantics (Speaker's 'matter') of that which, in all senses, cancels matter? If, for

145

Beckett's Speaker, death alone is speakable, this does not guarantee that it is in any significant way tellable or showable.

Which is not to say that death has never been successfully put on stage. The history of the drama is full of celebrated deaths and of the famous dead, of 'the going' and 'the gone'. Insofar as 'the going', the business of dying, constitutes a decisive if residual form of action, it has always enjoyed a privileged place in drama, from Oedipus' murder of his father onwards. But to show a killing, or even an expiring (the death of Lear), is still to stage an ultimate form of life, and does not really address the problem posed by Warrilow's commission. As for the 'gone', the companions of Hamlet's father, they have likewise crossed the boards in great numbers. Almost invariably, however, the dramatic dead have been figured in terms of the living: as ghosts intervening in the affairs of this world (*Hamlet*), or occupying the space of living memory (Alving in Ibsen's *Ghosts*), or (Banquo at the banquet) haunting the border between external space (the banqueting hall) and psychic space (Macbeth's feverish imagination). Death appears inevitably to demand embodiment on stage as life, absence as presence.

If it is true that *A piece of monologue*, together with Beckett's other later plays, is indeed dedicated as Speaker claims to the 'going' and the 'gone' – and this remains to be demonstrated – the question arises as to what these plays add to, or subtract from, the traditional dramatic poetics of deathly presence in staging the 'one matter'.

An immediate answer is that, in quantitative terms, Beckett has subtracted decidedly more than he has added. *A piece of monologue* itself occupies a mere five printed pages in the *Collected shorter plays*, and appears to be, on first reading, more a textual fragment than a drama in any canonical form.[3] This is an initial clue to Beckett's later poetics: the relationship between semantic configuration (the 'matter') and textual fragmentation is presumably not casual, even if not necessarily causal. That the play's extreme brevity is indeed strategic is strongly suggested by the analogous minuteness of the other late dramatic texts from *Come and go* (1965) onwards; none of them takes up more than eight pages of printed text or more than thirty minutes of performance time.

A piece of monologue, then, belongs to a group of brief or fragmentary texts that are best defined by a term that Beckett himself first coined in the subtitle to *Come and go*: 'dramaticule' (literally 'playlet').[4] There is evidence that Beckett conceived the minuscule play as an idiosyncratic genre of its (and of his) own,[5] which he cultivated to an extraordinary pitch of expressive economy. Taken together, these formidably condensed late 'textlet's constitute what is surely the most intense and disquieting body of texts conceived for the twentieth-century stage.

THE WOMEN COME AND GO TALKING OF ...

Come and go inaugurates the series of dramaticules by experimenting with various modes or reduction and omission.[6] The stage, according to Beckett's production notes, is reduced to a small softly lit playing area, empty of set or props and surrounded by darkness. The bodies of the three actresses are hidden by 'dull' and 'nondescript' costumes, and their faces partially covered by their hats. The characters they represent are given abbreviated names (Flo, Vi, Ru) and use speech that is lexically sparing (the entire dialogue comprises one hundred and twenty-seven words), monosyllabic ('Ru: How do you find Flo? Vi: She seems much the same') and semantically elliptical, not to say reticent ('Ru: Let us not speak [*Silence*]'; *CSPL*, 194).

It is undoubtedly this latter form of omission, namely, leaving things unspoken, that most troubles the audience, as it struggles[7] to make a plot out of the comings and goings of the three dramatic graces (or perhaps witches: 'Vi: When did we three last meet?'[8]). It is symptomatic of the play's referential reticence that its central speech event is the repeated act of whispering, an action which blatantly excludes the theatrical auditor. At the centre of *Come and go* is some unmentionable subject or object, around which the abbreviated women conduct their abbreviated verbal business:

FLO: What do you think of Vi?
RU: I see little change [*Flo moves to centre seat, whispers in Ru's ear. Appalled*] Oh! [*They look at each other. Flo puts her finger to her lips.*] Does she not realize?
RU: God grant not.

The unnamable object of Flo's discourse, foregrounded by her very evasiveness, is, we are left to infer, the imminent death of the third party, the absent Vi. The same pattern of whispered revelation and appalled reaction is repeated twice, with each of the women playing in turn the parts of revealer, listener and doomed third person. By means of these symmetrical variations, Beckett succeeds in creating, in eighteen minimal speaking (or better, non-speaking) turns, a triple dramatic irony worthy of Greek tragedy, whereby each character knows the fate of the other two, but not her own. Death, the ineffable, is Other, or at least Others'.

Come and go, then, is in the first instance 'about' death to the extent that its doomed women talk and walk *around* the topic, which comes to constitute literally the absent centre of the play; only when each figure in turn leaves centre stage can her impending doom be whispered by one of the others. There is a ritual quality to their movement,[9] which culminates in their holding hands to form a ring at the end, just as they had at the beginning. 'I can feel the rings', says Flo in the closing line (*CSPL*, 195): a sign, perhaps, that they are all married or engaged, but also a possible pun, as if to say that they have formed analogous and still-remembered rings in the past. This is confirmed by Ru's earlier allusion to 'Holding hands . . . that way', and by Vi's invitation to 'hold hands in the old way'. There is more than a suggestion, then, that the present situation is itself a repetition of similar past meetings, and indeed that the women's hand-holding has been taking place over a period of years and perhaps decades ('Flo: Just sit as we used to, in the playground at Miss Wade's'). In this sense 'ring' becomes the key term in the dramaticule, standing for the circularity of the grouping on stage, the circularity of their talk around an empty centre, but also the circular or cyclical nature of their progress through time, their habitual ringing of changes on their way towards their shared doom.

The ring thus becomes an emblem of *Come and go*'s own theatrical and semantic 'aboutness', its wilful leading of its audience in an interpretative round dance ('What is it *about*?'). The play's annular quality is reinforced by its apparent referential self-closure: not only does the drama turn about itself in space and time, it also speaks about itself, from its title on: 'come and go' at once succinctly describes the main stage business and cruelly synthesizes the main dramatic action, stating the irreducible *fabula* of the women's shadowy lives, from birth ('come'), through possible copulation (again 'come'[10]) to death ('go', which here, as in *A piece of monologue*, becomes synonymous with 'die'). Birth is the death of them.

What we appear to have, then, is a drama whose unspeakable 'matter' is the empty middle of a rigidly closed hermeneutic circle which fatally traps the struggling spectator, since his inevitable question 'What is it *about*?' is precisely what the play is primarily 'about', that is the very difficulty of naming its object. If this is so, then the novelty of the audience's experience is that of a strategically frustrating poetics of evasion, a novelty that has more to do with the play's sleight-of-hand adroitness (now we tell you, now we don't) than with any radical reworking of the conventions of dramatic representation. For all its absent and deadly centre, the dramaticule still seems to present a liminal form of life and a marginal mode of presence. The women have come but are not yet gone; each relates the other's death as a potential, not an actual (or as it were on-going) event. We are still, it would appear, within the dramatic tradition whereby death can only be told, or avoided, from the vantage-point of the living.

And yet this may not be the whole dramaturgic story of *Come and go*. Audience response to the dramaticule seems to involve a degree of disquiet that is quite beyond the emotional reach of evasive self-reference. This suggests that the ring-like semantics of the play may be less hermetically and hermeneutically sealed than they appear. To discover why, we need to look beyond what is done and (un)said by the women in the drama and consider the very condition of their doing and being on stage. The disturbing seductiveness of the play in performance resides at least partly in the immediate visual image of hidden bodies and truncated faces gliding with choreographic repetitiveness in the half-light, an image that initially creates perceptual, as opposed to conceptual, difficulties: 'One sees little in this light,' says Flo, as if on behalf of the spectator. This literally obscure iconography sets off its own semantic resonances, however. The women's semi-visible and semi-corporeal indefiniteness suggests that the crepuscular space they inhabit may not be entirely of this (the audience's) world. Their problems with light recalls the stage play immediately preceding theirs, *Play* (1963), whose three talking heads are suspended in the dark, outside time and space, in keeping with the iconographic convention that associates darkness with death. Could it be that Flo, Vi and Ru, each of whom believes the others to be going, are in fact all already gone? Has their unspeakable whispered doom already taken place, or is it indeed still taking place in some infinitely suspended *now*?

Such a reading radically modifies our perspective on the referentiality of the dramaticule. The unspoken 'matter', missing centre of the closed circle of verbal reference, is perturbingly shown on stage by means of a different form of absence, namely the absence of light. Death reveals itself through omission, as 'non-matter'. This reading also radically modifies our perspective on the women's own perspectives. The terrible triple irony of each character's ignorance of her own fate is multiplied exponentially by their being collectively 'gone'; none of them knows the destiny that awaits her in an imminent future that has already taken place. In this reading, it is the darkness that paradoxically illuminates the play's elusive 'aboutness', forcing open the semantic circle. And once opened up, the circle is not easily resealed. Other implications ensue. If the women have met their doom, what kind of space is it that they now inhabit? The darkness, again, irresistibly suggests a Dantean beyond, one of the obscurer zones of the Purgatory, or still more of the Inferno, made iconographically familiar to our own culture above all through the illustrations of Gustave Doré.

The implications of this further referential opening-up are even more wide-ranging, bringing us to re-think, among other things, the play's sparing speech acts. Flo, Vi and Ru's ritualistic and repetitive act of whispering becomes less a futile game of hide-and-speak than the actual purgatorial, or even infernal, punishment to which they are condemned. If so, this is the cruellest irony of all: the women are doomed for eternity to whisper each other's doom, and their very whispering constitutes their damnation.

At this point, the play's key lexical item takes on a new and troubling referential force. In the gloomy perspective of a Dantean and Doréan iconography, the 'rings' are no longer merely what Flo, Vi and Ru (possibly) wear, nor the stage configurations that they form, nor even their punitive repetitions in time: the rings are above all the dismal landscape within which they are situated, namely the closed and impenetrable circles of Dante's Hell.[11]

Where does this quite different, infernal mode of circularity leave us? Apparently at the opposite semantic pole from the poetics of self-reference, that is to say within a transcendental dramatic eschatology in which being 'gone' is not simple absence but terrible present-ness, in the form of an eternal and agonizing instant.

GODFORSAKEN HOLE

ANIMATOR: Have you read the Purgatory, miss, of the divine Flor-
              entine?
STENOGRAPHER: Alas no, sir. I have merely flipped through the Inferno.
                                    Rough for radio II (CSPL, 118)

Truncation, darkness, repetition, concealment, evasion, circularity: the dramaturgic strategies established in *Come and go* are taken to their outer limit in Beckett's second dramaticule, *Not I* (1972), justly considered one of his finest texts. Truncation in *Not I* takes the most extreme iconic form imaginable or representable: the half-hidden and dimly lit bodies and faces of Flo, Vi and Ru give way to the faintly illuminated and disembodied mouth of Mouth, suspended eight feet up in the dark air above upstage right. Darkness likewise surrounds the second barely perceptible figure, the black-djellaba-shrouded downstage Auditor. Repetition finds emphatic verbal expression in Mouth's refrain-like discourse fragments ('tiny little thing...'), and gestural expression in the four slow wing-flap movements of Auditor's arms, punctuating Mouth's oral flow. Concealment from the audience, which in *Come and go* has the overt but circumscribed form of whispering, takes over the second dramaticule altogether in the almost total incomprehensibility of Mouth's rapid and disjointed speech. 'Mouth's voice unintelligible behind curtain', reads the opening stage direction, signalling the intention to make the spectators' Herculean perceptual and cognitive labours the primary ingredient of their experience of the play.

Evasion is announced in the title of *Not I* as its principal theme or event. Mouth's chief endeavour throughout the play is, according to Beckett's uncharacteristically explicit note to the text, her 'vehement refusal to relinquish third person'. Mouth's desperate struggle to avoid saying 'I' is marked by four moments of crisis in which her monologue becomes a dia-logic question-and-answer with an inner voice inaudible to the theatre audi-ence: 'what?... who?... no!... she!'. Mouth's emphatic 'she!' is an implicit response to and rejection of the first person singular pronoun that threatens to invade her resolute 'she'-narration and to transform her into a reluctant 'I'-narrator. In resisting the encroaching 'I', Mouth rejects a double subject-ivity, both as subject of the *énonciation*, the act of telling, and as subject of the *énoncé*, the told events themselves.[12] Which is to say that she refuses identification both with the narrative present and with the narrated past, the wretched life that her fragmented story elliptically relates, beginning from the beginning: '... out ... into this world ... this world ... tiny little thing ...' (*CSPL*, 216). If Flo, Vi and Ru can speak of death only as belonging to others, Mouth can speak of life – 'her' life – only as lived by another, else-where, in the past.[13]

As for circularity in *Not I*, once again it is in the first instance corporeal: no longer the hand-holding rings formed by the women in *Come and go*, but the hypnotic, mobile and polymorphous ring of Mouth's narrating mouth. The spasmodic movements of this disconcertingly disembodied organ sus-pended in the dark re-enact the elementary events referred to in Mouth's narration: her conception ('no sooner buttoned up his breeches'; 217), her birth ('out ... into this world [...] godforsaken hole called ...'; 216), an apparently isolated experience of copulation ('just as the odd time ... in her life ... when clearly intended to be having pleasure'; 217), defecation ('nearest lavatory ... start pouring it out'; 222), speech ('... words were coming ...'; 219), weeping ('or that time she cried'; 220), visual perception ('she fixing with her eye'; 218), auditory perception ('all the time the buzzing ... so-called ... in the ears'; 217). Thus the mouth, detached from its bodily context and so from its codified meaning (as 'mouth'), becomes a corporeal and semantic (black) hole onto or into which the spectator may project any number of literally organic senses: it takes on in turn the roles of vagina, uterus, anus, mouth proper, eye and ear.[14] Mouth refuses life, but her mouth mimes its decisive aspects.

In *Not I*, then, the 'godforsaken hole' on stage shows forth a fractured existence in the very attempt to deny its own pronominal, bodily and onto-logical bond with that existence. As in *Come and go*, the poetics of negation here becomes theatrically self-referential; ironically, the more Mouth defends her non-subjectivity, the more she betrays her reluctant self-awareness as stage subject–object, narrating the discovery of her own act of narrating ('sudden urge to ... tell'; 222), the discovery of her own vocali-zation ('certain vowel sounds'; 219), the discovery of a light ('the beam') that corresponds to the faint spot illuminating her and, above all, the discovery of the spectators' watching eyes, located in an unflattering public space ('nearest lavatory ... [...] till she saw the stare she was getting'; compare Estragon's scornful 'that bog' with reference to the audience in *Godot*; *WFG*, 15). Unwilling subject of the monologue, Mouth finds herself an even more unwilling object of audience perception. Her attempted private evasion of self turns into a cruel public self-exhibition.

What leads us out of this auto-referential circle is once again the sheer potency of Beckett's stage image. The negated and fragmented floating body, reduced literally to its speaking part, evokes not only the psychological experience of splitting (whereby Mouth may be seen as a limit-case schizoid personality) but also the eschatological experience of afterlife torment.

The frame of reference is once again Dantean. If Beckett's narratives, especially the early narratives, are predominantly purgatorial (the figure of Belacqua in *More pricks than kicks*, for example, is taken from the *Purgatorio*[15]), his drama seems to be dominated by the *Inferno*: first by Upper Hell with its gluttons and adulterers (the adulterous M of *Play*, condemned to relive forever his banal amorous triangle), but increasingly by the deeper and darker Nether Hell, to which Dan Rooney refers in *All that fall*: 'Like Dante's damned, with their faces arsy-versy. Our tears will water our bottoms' – an allusion to the sorcerers whose tears 'travelled down the cleft of their backs, wetting their buttocks' (Canto XX, 21–2).[16] It may be that Beckett's literary and dramatic career represents a gradual descent into the regions of the underworld (the opposite journey from Dante, who passes from Hell through Purgatory to Paradise). Thus of all the circles of the Nether Hell, the one that comes to dominate Beckett's later theatrical imagination is the final and terrible Circle IX, peopled by the lost souls of traitors in the ultimate state of sin. Here, in the extreme gloom of the abyss – 'less than night and less than day, so that I could barely see ahead of me' (Canto XXXI, 10–11) – Dante encounters the talking heads of the traitors emerging from the frozen lake of Cocytus, their bodies invisible beneath the ice: 'I heard it say, "watch how you go – take care that your feet do not trample on the heads of the wretched and weary brotherhood"' (Canto XXXII, 19–24). The bodiless heads, moreover, have suffered further physical loss, causing the poet to stare in shocked fascination: 'And one who had lost both ears for the cold, still keeping his face down, said: "Why do you stare at us so hard, as if in a mirror?"' (Canto XXXII, 52–4; cf. my epigraph).

This sight of a floating and earless face, irresistibly captivating to the eye of the spectator, is strikingly close to the reluctant theatrical exhibition offered by Mouth in *Not I*. The Dantean genealogy of the play is even more precise, however. Moving on, the poet tramples the face of a traitor, and then demands to know his name. The sinner refuses to reveal his identity, provoking Dante to an act of physical violence against the helpless head: 'At that I seized him by the scruff of the neck, saying "You'd better tell me your name, or you won't have a single hair left here on your head," to which he replied: "Pluck out all my hair, I will not tell you who I am, nor show you my face, even if the whole weight of your body were to crush my head a thousand times"' (Canto XXXII, 97–102). At this point the poet learns the traitor's identity, not directly from him but from a neighbouring sinner: 'I already had his hair twisted in my hand, and I had torn out a tuft or two, as he howled, eyes lowered, when another cried out "What's wrong with you, Bocca? Aren't you content to play music with your jaws, but now have to start howling like a dog? What the devil's come over you?"' (103–8). The head belongs, then, to Bocca, literally 'Mouth', a Florentine traitor of the Ghibellines at the Battle of Montaperti. Dante's Bocca, reduced virtually to a garrulous '*bocca*', attempts to conceal his own identity, and only the insistence of the pitiless spectatorial poet causes his secret to be discovered.

It seems more than feasible, therefore, that Beckett's Mouth has her genesis in Dante's 'Mouth', and that like the traitor Bocca she is doomed to the endless concealment of her identity through logorrhoeic speech. Her damnation lies in her very she-narration, which ends with the self-invitation, or condemnation, to start again – 'pick it up' – as much as to say that she can never escape the eternal return of her telling in the abysmal circle ('godforsaken hole called. . .') in which she is trapped.

Why Mouth should be comparable to a medieval Florentine traitor is another matter. It may be that her very evasion of identity constitutes, as Hélène L. Baldwin suggests, her sin, as it were a form of self-betrayal: 'On the basis of *Not I*, it seems that Beckett has presented the drama of the *Purgatorio* or perhaps even the *Inferno* pared down to a twelve-minute recital of sin by a single mouth which refuses to admit personal guilt and responsibility.'[17]

A more interesting question raised by Mouth's Dantean allegiances involves the position of the theatrical spectator with regard to her infernal pains. Dante's Bocca has two spectator–auditors, the poet himself and his spiritual guide, Virgil. In Doré's celebrated representation of the scene in which the poets observe the damned heads of Cocytus, both are draped in dark robes (see fig. 1). In *Not I*, the one internal Auditor, present on stage, is similarly robed in black, and is thus iconically comparable either to Virgil or to Dante. The attitude of the Auditor is expressed, in Beckett's own words, through a 'gesture of helpless compassion' (prefatory note; *CSPL*, 215). It might be noted that Dante is severely upbraided for his own compassion towards the sorcerers mentioned by Dan Rooney: 'If God lets you, oh reader, profit from reading my poem, ask yourself how I could remain

Figure 1   Gustave Doré: Cocytus

dry-eyed when I saw, close up, our human image so distorted [...] Yes, I wept, [...] until my guide said to me: "Are you too like the other fools? Here pity lives only when it is dead: who is more wicked than he who is moved to compassion at God's punishments?"' (Canto xx, 19–30[18]). Dante learns the Virgilian lesson, so much so that he is able to maltreat Bocca in Canto xxx without any such scruple ('I already had his hair twisted in my hand [...]'; see fig. 2).

If the Auditor shares the early compassion of Dante, there is some suggestion that Beckett attributes the pitilessness of Virgil and of the later Dante to the audience. The second auditor–spectator present, in the playhouse, not only remains immobile before the spectacle, but continues to transfix the sinner with his relentless gaze ('till she saw the stare she was getting'). It is, indeed, this very stare that provokes Mouth's current suffering, causing her to 'die of shame'. The invasive presence of the spectatorial eye compels Mouth to 'die' again and again, and to make a shameful spectacle of her death.

The equation of the watching eye with infernal or purgatorial torment is already implicit in *Play*, in the reactions to the spot/eye ('mere eye', 'get off me'). In the earlier play, however, the punishment comes from the stage, from some divine or directorial or authorial watcher who plays with his imprisoned characters. In *Not I* the responsibility for protracting Mouth's suffering rests decidedly with the external spectator. It is the audience's unforgiving eye/ear that, like the spot in *Play*, forces Mouth to speak, compelling her to undergo her damnation-narration performance after performance. Mouth's hell is her very condition of having to exhibit herself to us, this being the defining role of a *dramatis persona*. If she manages to evade the 'I', she cannot equally avoid the eye: 'Not eye' is an impossible condition for a stage figure to achieve. Indeed, Mouth's own mouth, as we have seen, becomes, among other organic objects, an eye, mirroring back the spectator's cruel gaze. '"Why do you stare at us so hard, as if in a mirror?"' asks the damned head of Cocytus.[19]

THE R.I.P. WORD

Of the seven dramaticules published after *Not I*, six share its dominant 'infernal' dramaturgic and iconographic modes.[20] First, the dimly perceived *tête-morte*,[21] which reappears with obsessive regularity: *That time* (1976) presents Listener's 'old white face, long flaring white hair as if seen from

Figure 2   Gustave Doré: Bocca degli Abati

above out-spread' (*CSPL*, 228; as if seen, one might ask, by *whom* 'from above'?); *Footfalls* (1976) gives us the analogously ancient head of May with her 'disshevelled grey hair' (*CSPL*, 239); *A piece of monologue* (1979) has the icon of Speaker's 'White hair, white nightgown, white socks' (*CSPL*, 265); W in *Rockaby* (1981) is described as 'Prematurely old. Unkempt grey hair. Huge eyes in white expressionless face' (*CSPL*, 273); the image is doubled in *Ohio impromptu* (1981), where Listener's 'Bowed head propped on right hand. Face hidden [. . .] Long white hair' is mirrored in the almost identical appearance of Reader, 'As like in appearance as possible' (*CSPL*, 273); and this multiplication of identical aged heads is extended further in *What where* (1983), in which all four players are 'as alike as possible', with 'same long grey gown' and 'same long grey hair' (*CSPL*, 310). Death, or Hell, cancels difference.[22]

Second, the darkness visible in which the dead heads float. The obscuration sequence is as follows: '[. . .] stage in darkness. Fade up to LISTENER'S FACE' (*That time*); 'Lighting: dim, strongest at floor level, less on body, least on head' (*Footfalls*); 'SPEAKER [. . .] barely visible in diffuse light' (*A piece of monologue*); '*Light*: Subdued on chair. Rest of stage dark. Subdued spot on face constant throughout' (*Rockaby*); 'Light on table midstage. Rest of stage in darkness' (*Ohio impromptu*); 'Playing area [. . .] dimly lit, surrounded by shadow' (*What where*). These plays are all haunted, in more senses than one, by shades.

Invariably, moreover, the dim heads are theatrically eccentric. In all of these miniature 'brothers to *Not I*,[23] the hellishly look-alike faces are strategically marginalized on stage, and thereby estranged from the customary position of protagonist–subject of the action. They have literally lost their centrality. If Mouth is suspended 'about 8 feet above stage level' and relegated 'upstage audience right' (*CSPL*, 216), the face of Listener in *That time* is elevated 'about 10 feet above stage level' and placed 'midstage off centre (*CSPL*, 228), analogously the 'strip' along which May walks in *Footfalls* is situated 'downstage ... a little off centre audience right' (*CSPL*, 239); Speaker in *A piece of monologue* is found 'well off centre downstage audience left' (*CSPL*, 265); W's chair in *Rockaby* rocks 'facing front downstage slightly off centre audience left' (*CSPL*, 275); V in *What where* is discovered 'downstage left' (*CSPL*, 310). Each of these *dramatis* (im)*personae* is geometrically tangential to his/her own residual existence.

The actions performed by these shadowy no-bodies are almost always manically or mechanically repetitive.[24] Rather than moving they are moved. May in *Footfalls* is forced to pace unhaltingly up and down her strip, forever tracing the same parabolic trajectory; W in *Rockaby* is rocked with slow regularity, the see-sawing of her rocker being 'controlled mechanically' by some external force (*CSPL*, 275). Even the imperative *'Pause.Knock'* pattern with which Listener punctuates the reading in *Ohio impromptu* seems, in its fixated frequency, to control him as much as it does the interrupted Reader. And so it is with these dramatic residues' self-haunting speech acts, made up of fragmented and ritualistic phrasal refrains, from Speaker's 'no such thing. . .' (*CSPL*, 265) to W's 'all eyes/all sides' (*CSPL*, 275) to Reader's '. . .left to tell' (*CSPL*, 285). Far from governing their own speech, Beckett's late Speakers are fatally bespoke.

Beckett develops, then, a powerfully post-subjective rhetoric specific to the dramaticule as sub-genre, in which a limited repertory of constrictive bodily, scenic and discursive 'figures' produces an extraordinary series of combinational variables. A crucial figural constant of this rhetoric is the two-edged strategy of reticence that we encountered in the earlier plays. The 'ineffability' strategy, is expressed through the *Come and go* mode of ellipsis: 'M: though scarcely a girl any more . . . [*brokenly.*] . . . dreadfully — [. . .]' (*Footfalls*; *CSPL*, 242); 'No sudden fit of . . . no word' (*A piece of monologue*; *CSPL*, 266); 'I have been sent by – and here he named the dear name' (*Ohio impromptu*; *CSPL*, 287). The 'negated subjectivity' strategy operates through the 'Not I' evasion of the first-person pronoun; Mouth's desperate 'she' reappears less dramatically in *Rockaby*, and is varied as 'he' in *A piece of monologue* and *Ohio impromptu*, as an unstable and indeterminate 'I/ you/she/he/it' in *Footfalls*: 'A little later, when as though she had never been, it never been [. . .]' (*CSPL*, 242); and as a self-addressed 'you' in *That time*, where the problem of saying 'I' is explicitly lexicalized by C, who asks his alter ego – or rather, later ego – Listener: 'Did you ever say I to yourself in your life come on now [*Eyes close*]' (*CSPL*, 230). It is the very endeavour never to 'say I to yourself' that constitutes the final trace of 'your life' in these dramas.

Repetition and (self-)denial converge. Increasingly, the vocabulary of the dramaticules becomes the lexis of reiterated negation. Their dominant lexical items are the unforgiving 'N' words, from the melancholy 'no time gone in no time' that closes *That time* (*CSPL*, 235), to the anguished 'Not there? Amy: Not there' that marks the sense of loss in *Footfalls* (*CSPL*, 243), to the emphatic and apparently definitive ending N of *Ohio impromptu*: 'Nothing is left to tell' (*CSPL*, 288). The increasing sway exercised over Beckett's lexicon by 'No's knife'[25] is best exemplified by the nth-power negatives of *A piece of monologue*, which proceeds through a vertiginous logic of progressive self-undoing, and undoing of its own undoing, so that even the N words are negated, as if they were excessively affirmative: 'None from window. No. Next to none. No such thing as none' (*CSPL*, 265).

But for all the 'Nothing left to tell' topos, there still remains in most of the dramaticules the absolute *necessity* to tell. Beckett's biographical relics, or biological relicts, are driven by an ineluctable narration compulsion that keeps them going in spite of everything (which is to say in spite of 'Nothing').[26] A, B and C, the past voices of Listener in *That time*, recount to him in tireless alternation those moments in his past which constituted him as 'I'–'you'. May and her offstage Mother both relate the lifelong Lady Macbeth-like pacing of May/Amy ('you'/'she'/'I') in a narration that appears already written, and indeed already read: '. . . Amy – the daughter's given name, as the reader will remember – ' (*CSPL*, 243). Speaker summarizes ('Words are few') the grotesquely schematic womb/tomb *curriculum vitae/curriculum mortis* of the absent, or possibly present, 'him': 'Birth was the death of him. Ghastly grinning ever since. Up at the lid to come. In cradle and crib. At suck first fiasco. With the first totters. From mammy to nanny and back. All the way. Bandied back and forth. So ghastly grinning on. From funeral to funeral. To now' (*A piece of monologue*; *CSPL*, 265). Reader is obliged by the insistent knocking of Listener to repeat, re-start or cut what he optimistically calls 'The sad tale a last time told' (*Ohio impromptu*; *CSPL*, 288). A last time until the next time.

One of the voices in *That time*, B, suggests to his listening 'self' that his life story, itself a mere fiction, is really only a form of protection against the invading dark: 'just one of those things you kept making up to keep the void out just another of those old tales to keep the void from pouring in on top of you the shroud' (*CSPL*, 230). Life, as Macbeth puts it, is but a walking shadow, a tale told by an idiot, and the purpose of its telling is, according to B, to keep death at bay. But this is surely – like Reader's 'last time' – a consolatory illusion, since the tellers' telling turns out once again to be essentially 'about' death rather than 'against' death. In addition to the frequent references in the narratives to the grave, to the dark, to the night – see for example, Speaker's syntactically ambiguous 'Born dead of night' which can be read as 'Born, dead of night' or 'Born dead, of night' (*CSPL*, 265); to the closing of the day, to the void, to the winter, to the end, to being 'deep asleep' (*Footfalls*; *CSPL*, 239), and the explicit invocation of ghosts, those on stage as well as off – 'Ghost light. Ghost nights. Ghost rooms. Ghost graves. Ghost . . . he all but said ghost loved ones' (*A piece of monologue*; *CSPL*, 269) – the later dramaticules are sown with Beckettian code-language for dying or for death. The most prominent code item is the verb 'go' and its derivatives, in the *Come and go* sense of the word: 'A: all gone long ago [. . .] C: come and gone come and gone no one come and gone in no time gone in no time' (*That time*; *CSPL*, 228, 235); 'Speaker: All gone so long. Gone. Ripped off and torn to shreds' (*A Piece of monologue*; *CSPL*, 266); 'going to and fro' (*Rockaby*, passim).

'Gone. Ripped off': Kristin Morrison observes that the word 'rip' in *A piece of monologue* – (see 'Ripped from the wall', 'Ripped off and torn to shreds', and in particular the phrase 'Waiting on the rip word' [*CSPL*, 269]) – is another key term in the play, expressing the primary meaning of 'violent slashing', as in 'rip-tide', and thus 'a break in the surface of the drama which reveals the truth of motives, feelings, themes.[27] 'The rip word in *A piece of monologue*', claims Morrison, 'is "begone", that word by which the speaker dismisses from his life that which he has always really wanted'.[28] Thus 'rip' becomes a second code word synonymous with the first, 'go' and its derivatives, and thus with 'die' and its cognates. Indeed, this sense is encoded acronymically in the 'rip' word itself, whose referentiality is disclosed in its own graphemic make-up – /R/ /I/ /P/, *Requiescat In Pace*. The language of Beckett's dramaticules is all a cipher for the R.I.P. word.

TO HELL OUT OF THERE

The fear that their narration compulsion, their enforced telling and re-telling of the rip word, may in fact constitute a form of (narration-) damnation, does dawn on Beckett's last stage creatures, albeit occasionally and subliminally. *Ohio impromptu*'s Reader, describing 'his' sinking into his unconscious, the hell of his own mind, evokes the landscape of the lightless and petrifying regions of Circle IX: 'Buried in who knows what profounds of mind. Of mindlessness. Whither no light can reach. No sound. So sat on as though turned to stone' (*CSPL*, 288), just as V's disenchanted self-description, in *What where*, as solitary and immobile object of time in a 'still' present, recalls Virgil's explanation of the lost soul's individual re-discovery of its own eternal doom (Canto VI, 98–100):

> I am alone.
> In the present as were I still.
> It is winter.
> Without journey.
> Time passes.
> That is all. (*CSPL*, 316)

If these plays are brothers to *Not I*, their narrating heads are neighbours to the doomed Mouth of Cocytus. Speaker describes the Mouth-like depri-vation of body and light that reduces 'him' to a 'dark whole' (*CSPL*, 268), or rather to a dark part, a dark hole, since that is 'No such thing as whole' (269): 'Into dark whole again . . . Hands gone. Light gone. Gone. Again and again. Again and again gone' (268). And the dark hole delivers the dark word – the rip word that 'parts the dark' – in an eternal (still)birth that associates mouth with womb with tomb with the dark parts of hell: 'Waits for first word always the same. It gathers in his mouth. Parts lips and thrusts tongue forward. Birth. Parts the dark [...] Gone. Again and again. Again and again gone. Mouth agape. A cry. Stifled by nasal. Dark parts. Grey light' (268).

The most direct infernal allusions in the later dramaticules, however, are those disseminated in *That time*, all three of whose narrative voices refer to hell ambiguously as somewhere either to get to or to get out of: 'and on to hell out of there when was that' says C (228), who later describes 'your' solitary attempts at self-comforting, again on the way to, or already in, hell: 'with your arms around you whose else hugging you for a bit of warmth to dry off and on to hell out of there and on to the next not a living soul in the place only yourself' (229). C's perception of a 'place' without 'a living soul' is confirmed by B: 'all still no sign of life not a soul abroad no sound' (228). And the uncertainty as to whether the addressed 'you' is going to, or already in, the desolate 'place' is stronger still in the exhortations of A: 'time to get on the night ferry and out to hell out of there' (232), and again, 'only get back on board and away to hell out of it and never come back' (235). The ferry takes 'you' out to hell but also (hopefully) out *of* there.

A's 'ferry' becomes one of the play's most frequently reiterated terms, and thus presumably one of its allusive theme (or 'rip') words: 'straight off the ferry and up with the nightbag' (228); 'just the one night in any case off the ferry one morning and back on her the next' (229); 'that last time straight off the ferry' (231). The image of a ferry going busily to and fro cannot but evoke, in the context of an explicitly named 'hell', the figure of Charon transporting the damned souls to the underworld. Here again Beckett's iconography is emblematic. In Canto III, Dante first sees the fearful ferryman coming his way from the opposite 'sad shore' of the Acheron or Styx: 'Then, with my eyes lowered for shame, I stopped speaking, lest my talk should vex him [Virgil], and went to the riverside. And lo, towards us in his boat came a white-haired old man [...]' (79–83). Beckett's initial stage direction, it will be recalled, describes Listener's head as comprising an 'Old white face' with 'long flaring white hair'. Listener, the putative 'you' of the interwoven narratives, may thus be a ferried lost soul or himself a white-haired Stygian transporter, coming and going but always staying where he is: 'only get back on board and away to hell out of it'. Or he may be, like Mouth's Auditor, a silent Dantean observer ('I stopped speaking') who 'mirrors' the object of his perceptions. In any event, A's 'and never come back' is surely not a promise of escape ('out of it') but a condemnation never to return to *this* side of the river. '"Never hope to see the sky again"', warns Dante's Charon, '"I come to ferry you to the other side, to eternal darkness, fire and ice"' (84–7).

Being on the 'other side' means, above all, being on the stage half of the theatre–audience divide. The identification of the hopeless 'place' of the speakers' suffering with the *lieu scènique* itself is powerfully encoded in several plays. B in *That time* describes 'your' situation as being 'alone in the same the same scenes making it up that way to keep it going keep it out on the stone' (233), and again 'you back in the old scene wherever it might be might have been the same scene' (233). B's 'scene' bears the semantic traces of the French *scène*, stage, the same old stage representing the same old scene of sorrow. And to be in a scene, on the *scène*, means above all to be *seen*, as C (See?) becomes progressively aware in the course of his narration: 'look round for once at your fellow bastards thanking God for once bad and all as you were you were not as they till it dawned that for all the loathing you were getting you might as well not have been there at all the eyes passing over you' (234).

The stare of their fellow bastards, the eyes passing over them, is the acutest source of unease for all the *têtes-mortes*. There are recurrent references, in several texts, to the act of looking through, or being looked at through, a window, perhaps equivalent to the spatial frame of the stage: 'From its single window he could see [...] Unfamiliar room. Unfamiliar scene' (*Ohio impromptu*; CSPL, 285); 'facing only windows/other only windows/all eyes/all sides [...] at her window/to see/be seen' (*Rockaby*; CSPL, 277, 281); 'As at window. Eyes glued to pane staring out' (*A piece of monologue*; CSPL, 268). The implicit accusation directed towards the gaping bastards in the audience is that of indifference to, if not a form of sadistic pleasure in, the speaker's distress: eyes glued to pain staring out.

Altogether, the spectator is not well treated in Beckett's last plays. The Protagonist's brave final act of political dissidence in *Catastrophe* seems to be a form of rebellion against the tyranny of the Director, but its actual object is the public, whom P dares to stare back at, to the audience's audible disapproval:

[*Pause. Distant storm of applause. P raises his head, fixes the audience. The applause falters, dies. Long pause. Fade-out of light on face.*]

Not only is the spectator made to struggle for meaning, but when he thinks he has found it he discovers that it is a finger, or an eye, or perhaps a mirror, pointed towards him.

But even the unflattering reference to it as heartless voyeur of the pains of hell is more than the audience can take home with satisfying certainty. Beckett's otherworldly allusions are in no sense consolatory, even to the extent of offering definite, and thus consoling, condemnation. There is nothing final, still less resolutive, in his dramaturgy of death or in his iconography of hell. As in all his drama, from *Godot* and *Krapp* onwards, Beckett plays the game of the transcendental – ontological, theological, eschatological – signified, ensnaring the audience in the absolute illusion of the Absolute, only to undo these revelations by refracting the spectator's enquiring gaze onto himself. Thus the 'Make sense who may' gauntlet thrown down explicitly in *What where* (*CSPL*, 316) is not a challenge to try making something out of nothing (there is no such thing as 'hole', pure emptiness waiting to be arbitrarily filled), but a sort of *caveat spectator*, an admonition to take responsibility for one's own hermeneutic reworkings of the dangerously alluring referential traces the dramatist has planted for us. Watcher watch thyself.

In the dramaticules, Beckett's particular dramatic and iconic strategy is continually to invoke an afterworld elsewhere and, as it were, an afterlife elsewhen – 'or was that another place another time' [*That time*; *CSPL*, 234] – thereby opening up the prospect of a structured Dantean universe, made up, in the best medieval exegetical tradition, of analogical meanings (the iconic 'similarity', for example, with the *Inferno*), anagogical meanings (life as an anticipation of death, death as a re-enacting of life) and allegorical meanings (drama itself as a mode of damnation). Such meanings, though they prove in the end to be a kind of metaphysical *trompe-l'œil* for the interpretative eye, do not disappear altogether, remaining suspended like dimly perceptible forms in the dark. Beckett's poetics of the 'one matter' offers his spectator *ignis fatuus* glimpses of the fire and ice on the other side, but, unlike the ferryboat on the Acheron, returns him to the hell of his own making on *this* side of the divide.

NOTES

1 'And one who had lost both ears for the cold, still keeping his face down, said: "Why do you stare at us so hard, as if in a mirror?"'; all translations from Dante are mine.
2 See Charles Lyons, *Samuel Beckett*, 169.
3 The writing of *A piece of monologue* actually begun in 1977, prior to Warrilow's 'commission', overlaps with the composition of *Company*; in manuscript the two works have passages in common.
4 *Come and go: a dramaticule* (London: Calder and Boyars, 1967).
5 Beckett collected a number of the later dramatic texts in their French version under the title *Catastrophe et autres dramaticules* (Paris: Editions de Minuit, 1986).
6 On the process of reduction in Beckett's composition of the play, see Rosemary Pountney, 'Less = more', 11–19.
7 Karen Laughlin analyses the audience's hermeneutical labours with regard to this play in 'Looking for sense . . .', 137–46. Audience response to Beckett's late plays in general is discussed by the same author in 'Seeing is perceiving: Beckett's later

plays and the theory of audience response', in Robin J. Davis and Lance St J. Butler (eds.), *'Make sense who may': essays on Beckett's later works* (Gerrards Cross: Colin Smythe, 1988), 20–9.

8 The play's frequent Shakespearean references are examined by Hersh Zeifman, '*Come and go*: a criticule', 137–44.

9 On the ritualistic aspects of Beckett's drama, including the late plays, see Katherine H. Burkman's introduction to her 1987 collection.

10 An earlier version of the play contains explicit references to sexuality, and in fact begins with the reading of excerpts from a pornographic narrative. See Pountney 'Less = more', and Kristin Morrison, *Canters and chronicles*, 114–16.

11 Karen L. Laughlin, 'Looking for sense . . .', 141, reports one audience member's immediate association of the 'rings' with Dante's *Inferno*.

12 For the *énoncé/énonciation* distinction, see Roman Jakobson, *Selected writings. II: word and language* (The Hague: Mouton, 1971), 133; the implications of this distinction for the drama are examined in my *The semiotics of theatre and drama*, 144–8.

13 The question of subjectivity in *Not I* is analysed by Enoch Brater, 'The "I" in Beckett's *Not I*'; Hersh Zeifman, 'Being and non-being'; Lois Oppenheim, 'Anonymity and individuation'; Mary Catanzaro, 'Recontextualizing the self'; John H. Lutterbie, '"Tender mercies": subjectivity and subjection in Samuel Beckett's *Not I*'.

14 For the multiple bodily reference in the play, see my essay on *Not I* in Brater (ed.), *Beckett at 80/Beckett in context*.

15 Michael Robinson rightly affirmed, in 1969, that 'Beckett's heroes are not in Hell but Purgatory: a Purgatory of waiting on the verge of timelessness' (*The long sonata of the dead*, 69–70). On the Beckett–Dante relationship, see also Hélène L. Baldwin, *Samuel Beckett's real silence*; Neal Oxenhandler, 'Seeing and believing in Dante and Beckett'; Wallace Fowlie, 'Dante and Beckett'; Martha Fehsenfeld, 'Beckett's late works: an appraisal'.

16 All quotations and line numbers from *La divina commedia* refer to the edition edited by Daniele Mattalia (Milan: Biblioteca Universale Rizzoli, 1988).

17 Hélène L. Baldwin, *Samuel Beckett's real silence*, 142.

18 Virgil goes on to explain to Dante that 'pity (*pietà*) lives here only when it is dead' (28), distinguishing between *pietà* (pity) towards men (*pietas erga homines*), and *pietà* (piety) towards God (*pietas erga Deum*). Pity is allowed only if compatible with piety. Compare the dialogue between Belacqua and the Ottolenghi at the end of Beckett's short story 'Dante and the lobster' (*MPTK*, 18). Beckett's friend Thomas MacGreevy uses Dante's line as the epigraph to his poem 'Fragment'.

19 Compare Beckett's *Film*, in which the eye is at once persecuting offscreen presence (the camera) and internal object of focalization.

20 The seventh is *Catastrophe* which, partly because of its political theme, does not altogether conform to the 'dead heads' mode of the other late plays.

21 *Têtes-mortes* (literally 'dead-heads') is the title Beckett gave to a collection of his short fictions in French (Paris: Editions de Minuit, 1967).

22 Enoch Brater(*Beyond minimalism*, 134) observes that the similiarity of the faces in these plays is itself a feature of the Dantean Hell: 'Simile qui con simile è sepolto' ('Like to like is buried here', *Inferno*, Canto XI, 130).

23 Beckett described *That time* as 'brother to *Not I*' (Knowlson and Pilling, *Frescoes of the skull*, 206).

24 Repetition in the late plays is examined by Steven Connor, in *Samuel Beckett: repetition, theory and text* (chapter 6: 'Presence and repetition in Beckett's theatre', 115–39), and by Carla Locatelli in *Unwording the world* (chapter 3: 'Beckett's theater since the 1970s', 112–53).

25 See the collection of short fictions entitled *No's knife* (London: Calder and Boyars, 1967). Beckett's ways of 'undoing' are explored in depth by Carla Locatelli in *Unwording the world*, and by S. E. Gontarski in *The intent of 'Undoing'* (Bloomington: Indiana University Press, 1984).

26 See Charles Lyons, 'Beckett's fundamental theatre', 87: 'The recitation of the narratives in these plays reveals both the characters' need to speak the text and their desire to be free of that obsession.'

27 Kristin Morrison, 'The rip word in *A piece of monologue*', 349.

28 Ibid., 349. The first manuscript version of the play is in fact entitled 'Gone'.

RECOMMENDED READING

Acheson, James, 'The shape of ideas: *That time* and *Footfalls*', in James Acheson and Kateryna Arthur (eds.), *Beckett's later fiction and drama: texts for Company*, London: Macmillan, 1987, 115–35.

Baldwin, Hélène L., *Samuel Beckett's real silence*, University Park and London: Pennsylvania State University Press, 1981. (See in particular chapter 9: 'The April morning. The purgatorial quest in *Not I*', 136–42).

Ben-Zvi, Linda, *Not I*: through a tube starkly', in Linda Ben-Zvi (ed.), *Women in Beckett: performance and critical perspectives*, Urbana: University of Chicago Press, 1990, 243–8.

Brater, Enoch, 'The "I" in Beckett's *Not I*', *Twentieth Century Literature*, 20.3 (July 1974), 189–200.

Beyond minimalism: Beckett's late style in the theatre, New York and Oxford: Oxford University Press, 1987.

Burkman, Katherine H. (ed.), *Myth and ritual in the plays of Samuel Beckett*, Rutherford, N.J.: Fairleigh Dickinson University Press, 1987.

Catanzaro, Mary, 'Recontextualizing the self: the voice as subject in Beckett's *Not I*', *South Central Review: The Journal of the South Central Modern Language Association*, 7.1 (Spring 1990), 36–49.

Connor, Steven, *Samuel Beckett: repetition, theory and text*, Oxford: Basil Blackwell, 1988, chapters 6 and 7.

Davis, Robin J. and Lance St J. Butler (eds.) *'Make sense who may': essays on Beckett's later works*, Gerrard's Gross: Colin Smythe, 1988.

Doll, Mary A., 'Rites of story: the old man at play', in Katherine H. Burkman (ed.), *Myth and ritual in the plays of Samuel Beckett*, 73–85.

Duckworth, Colin, 'Performance and interpretation of two recent Beckett plays: *Rockaby* and *Ohio impromptu*', *Australasian Drama Studies*, 2 (October 1983), 35–41.

Elam, Keir, *The semiotics of theatre and drama*, London and New York: Routledge, 1980.

'*Not I*': Beckett's Mouth and the ars(e) rhetorica', in Enoch Brater (ed.), *Beckett at 80/Beckett in context*, New York: Oxford University Press, 1986, 124–48.

Fehsenfeld, Martha, 'Beckett's late works: an appraisal', *Modern Drama*, 25.3 (September 1982), 355–62.

Fletcher, Beryl S., John Fletcher, *A student's guide to the plays of Samuel Beckett*, London: Faber and Faber, 1985.

Fowlie, Wallace, 'Dante and Beckett', in Stuart Y. McDougal, (ed.), *Dante among the moderns*, Chapel Hill: University of North Carolina Press, 1985, 128–52.

Gontarski, S. E., '"Making yourself all up again": the composition of Samuel Beckett's, *That time*', *Modern Drama*, 23.2 (June 1980), 112–20.

'Text and pre-texts of Samuel Beckett's *Footfalls*', *Papers of the Bibliographical Society of America*, 77 (1983), 191–5.

Kalb, Jonathan, '*Rockaby* and the art of inadvertent interpretation', in *Beckett in performance*, Cambridge University Press, 1989, 9–23.

Kennedy, Andrew K., 'Mutations of the soliloquy: *Not I* to *Rockaby*', in Davis and Butler (eds.), '*Make sense who may*', 30–6.

Knowlson, James, and John Pilling, *Frescoes of the skull: the later prose and drama of Samuel Beckett*, London: John Calder, 1979.

Laughlin, Karen, '"Looking for sense …": the spectator's response to Beckett's *Come and go*', *Modern Drama*, 30.2 (June 1987), pp. 137–46.

Lawley, Paul, 'Counterpoint, absence and the medium in Beckett's *Not I*', *Modern Drama*, 26.4 (December 1983), 407–14.

Levy, Shimon, *Samuel Beckett's self-referential drama: the three I's*, London: St Martin's Press, 1990.

Libera, Antoni, 'Beckett's *Catastrophe*', *Modern Drama*, 28.3 (September 1985), 341–7.

'Reading *That time*', in Davis and Butler (eds.), '*Make sense who may*', 91–107.

Locatelli, Carla, *Unwording the world: Samuel Beckett's prose works after the Nobel Prize*, Philadelphia: University of Pennsylvania Press, 1990, chapter 3: 'Beckett's theater since the 1970s', 112–53.

Lutterbie, John H., '"Tender mercies", subjectivity and subjection in Samuel Beckett's *Not I*', in Joseph H. Smith (ed.), *The world of Samuel Beckett*, Baltimore: Johns Hopkins University Press, 1991, 86–106.

Lyons, Charles, *Samuel Beckett*, London: Macmillan, 1983.

'Beckett's fundamental theater: the plays from *Not I* to *What where*', in Acheson and Arthur (eds.), *Beckett's later fiction and drama*, 80–97.

'Male or female voice: the significance of the gender of the speaker in Beckett's late fiction and drama', in Ben-Zvi, (ed.), *Women in Beckett*, 150–61.

McCarthy, Gerry, 'On the meaning of performance in Samuel Beckett's *Not I*', *Modern Drama*, 33.4 (December 1990), 455–69.

McMillan, Dougald, 'Human reality and dramatic method: *Catastrophe*, *Not I* and the unpublished plays', in Acheson and Arthur (eds.), *Beckett's later fiction and drama*, 98–114.

McMullan, Anna, 'Samuel Beckett's *Cette fois*: between time(s) and space(s)' *French Studies: A Quarterly Review*, 44.4 (October 1990), 424–39.

'The space of play in *L'impromptu d'Ohio*', *Modern Drama* 30.1 (March 1987), 23–34.

Morrison, Kristin, 'The rip word in *A piece of monologue*', *Modern Drama*, 25.3 (September 1982), 349–54.

Canters and chronicles: the use of narrative in the plays of Samuel Beckett and Harold Pinter, Chicago and London: University of Chicago Press, 1983.

O'Gorman, Kathleen, 'The speech act in Beckett's *Ohio impromptu*', in Davis and Butler (eds.), *'Make sense who may'*, 108–21.

Oppenheim, Lois, 'Anonymity and individuation: the interrelation of two linguistic functions in *Not I* and *Rockaby*', in Davis and Butler (eds.), *'Make sense who may'*, 36–45.

Oxenhandler, Neal, 'Seeing and believing in Dante and Beckett', in Mary Ann Caws (ed.), *Writing in a modern temper: essays on French literature and thought in honor of Henri Peyre*, Saratoga, Calif.: Anima Libri, 1984, 214–23.

Pountney, Rosemary, 'Less = more: developing ambiguity in the drafts of *Come and go*', in Davis and Butler (eds.), *'Make sense who may'*, 11–19.

Robinson, Michael, *The long sonata of the dead: a study of Samuel Beckett*, London: Hart-Davis, 1969.

Sherzer, Dina, 'Portrait of a woman: the experience of marginality in *Not I*', in Ben-Zvi (ed.), *Women in Beckett*, 201–7.

Simone, R. Thomas, '"Faint though by no means invisible": a commentary on Beckett's *Footfalls*', *Modern Drama*, 26.4 (December 1983), 435–46.

'Beckett's other trilogy: *Not I*, *Footfalls* and *Rockaby*', in Davis and Butler (eds.), *'Make sense who may'*, 56–65.

Sportelli, Annamaria, '"Make sense who may": a study of *Catastrophe* and *What where*', in Davis and Butler (eds.), *'Make sense who may'*, 1988, 120–8.

States, Bert O., 'Catastophe: Beckett's laboratory/theatre', *Modern Drama*, 30.1 (March 1987), 14–22.

Wilson, Ann, '"Her lips moving": the castrated voice of *Not I*', in Ben-Zvi (ed.), *Women in Beckett*, 190–200.

Zeifman, Hersh, 'Being and non-being: Samuel Beckett's *Not I*', *Modern Drama*, 19.1 (March 1976), 35–46.

'*Come and go*: a criticule', in Pierre Astier, Morris Beja and S. E. Gontarski (eds.), *Samuel Beckett: humanistic perspectives*, Columbus: Ohio State University Press, 1983, 137–44.

'*Catastrophe* and dramatic setting', in Davis and Butler (eds.), *'Make sense who may'*, 129–37.

9

ANDREW RENTON

Disabled figures: from the *Residua* to *Stirrings still*

Beyond *How it is* Samuel Beckett's prose fiction is marked by a series of techniques or strategies brought to bear upon the work in order to perpetuate it. That is, the processes of self-reduction which are formally evident in the late prose texts become the very subject of the texts themselves. This reductionist tendency is not, however, simply a condensing of stylistic detail, but may be observed within the motivation of the prose's content.

The late prose texts become increasingly interconnected and self-referential. One text literally generates another. A text may 'defeat' another, in the manner of *Enough*'s opening exhortation, '[a]ll that goes before forget' (*CSP*, 139), or the torn sheet of writing in *As the story was told* (*AST*, 196). Conversely (but amounting to much the same thing) the text may compulsively repeat what has already been written. One might suggest, for example, that *Imagination dead imagine* evolved, or devolved, from *All strange away*. Resorting to manuscript materials may support this, but the evidence lies embedded within the texts themselves. The latter text even opens with the title of the former. Again, it is important to emphasize that this is not simply a stylistic resonance, but a re-negotiation of something altogether more solid. It is as if the *written* has become three-dimensional, and must be assimilated from all sides. A return to the text, therefore, will always be a complex repetition, taken at tangents to the original narrative.

In this way, *Imagination dead imagine*'s closing tableau of 'that white speck lost in whiteness' (*CSP*, 147) provides the starting point for the situation of *Ping*, which transposes that image into '*All known* all white bare white body' (*CSP*, 149 – italics mine). It is as though the superficial *content* of the work is very much a given, but the *subject* of the work – which operates at a deeper level – is something else again.[1] That subject is the text itself, or rather how to keep rewriting that text. If the earlier prose, particularly the first 'trilogy', was marked by a constant exhortation to 'go on', in the later prose, although Beckett is still obliged to confront 'the problems that beset continuance',[2] there is a realization that continuance means reiteration of the subject-of-continuance.

Much criticism dealing with Beckett's work has elaborated upon his late-Modernist position where language is seen to struggle against silence. Yet the discourse of Beckett's work, in drama and in prose, as it was received during his lifetime, was a continuous narrative construed from the obligation towards speech and, consequently, writing. This, of course, would always be tempered by the repeated Beckettian paradigm of impotence. Beckett's was an art of impending silence, coupled with the obligation to overcome that silence. This reading gives Beckett and Beckett's work something of a stoic dignity, as it survives against all odds.

Yet what has been rarely noted, despite the persistent return by Beckett's readers to early critical works as supposed manifestoes of intent, is that these odds have been deliberately weighted against Beckett, by Beckett himself. Where obligation and impotence work together, as Beckett first sets out in the *Three dialogues with Georges Duthuit*, we may perceive not only a struggle towards expression, but also one, equally powerful, *against* expression:

> The expression that there is nothing to express, nothing with which to express, nothing from which to express, no power to express, no desire to express, together with the obligation to express. (D, 139)

Of course, there is always something to express. Beckett's difficulty with writing, in fact, is that expression occurs despite itself. He cannot stop it. The work, therefore, does not merely rhetoricize the aporia generated within itself, but in acknowledging that process, struggles against the solidification, or reification, of metaphor.

It would be impossible to construct a text without metaphor or, indeed, without figuration of any kind. Perhaps in Beckett we witness the closest anyone has come within a literary language to eradicating the figural, but we know that the language retains its charge precisely because it figures despite itself. In addition to that ultimate obligation to express (or to figuration), there is an obligation to resist that expression throughout the work, disfiguring, as it were, the self-troping of the text. This anti-figuration is a figuration in itself. The anxiety of starting a narrative which is always about to end, even before it has begun, produces these virtual figures. In *For to end yet again*, for example, there is a sense of something figured, or described, in order to stand *in the place of something else*:

> Place of remains where once used to gleam in the dark on and off used to glimmer a remain. Remains of the days of the light of day never light so faint as theirs so pale. Thus then the skull makes to glimmer in lieu of going out. (CSP, 179)

A few lines into the text, the narrative collapses upon itself.[3] The word 'lieu' (carried over from the French text) manages to suggest place where time would perhaps be more appropriate. It solidifies the ostensibly transitional passage from one state of being to another.

Beckett's activity as a writer, from the early 1960s until his death in 1989, was an exploration of various means of treating this inevitable figuration. Yet if Beckett's work appears formally *sui generis*, and there is a recogniz- able 'Beckettian' style, it is necessary to look at each of the late *Residua*[4] as individual critical moments, where Beckett will turn against himself, and recommence his enterprise from a wholly different strategic position on each successive occasion. One such example is the 'trilogy' of novels which were brought together as the last book published during Beckett's lifetime, under his own title of *Nohow on*. Each presented Beckett with entirely different obligations and difficulties, but, more importantly, even the simplest observation renders visible the very different conception and execu- tion of the three works. *Company*, for example, was first written in English, translated into French, and thereafter the English text was revised in the light of the French. Conversely, *Ill seen ill said* was first composed in French. *Worstward Ho* was written in a style so different from anything Beckett had attempted previously that he was unable to effect a translation of the work into French at all.[5] The translation history of these texts represents just one of the ways in which strategic inversions take place in between works, as if to undo the prior (and, indeed, prioritized) work. This becomes a rhetorical turn in itself, generating new substance out of opposition made of resist- ance, where the tools of resistance became the thing itself. Yet Beckett's position has not remained stable since his declaration in 'Dante. . .Bruno. Vico. .Joyce' regarding Joyce's *Finnegans wake* in 1929, where form and content were wholly unified:

> Here form *is* content, content *is* form. You complain that this stuff is not written in English. It is not written at all. It is not to be read – or rather it is not only to be read. It is to be looked at and listened to. His writing is not *about* something; *it is that something itself.* (D, 27)

This passage has often been cited as some kind of prefiguring for Beckett's own work. Yet it is worth looking at the passage again for traces within it of something which Beckett is not yet completely able to achieve in writing. We may now read the passage as an agenda which successfully resists Beckett. The agenda which Beckett is setting here is less concerned with the conflation of form and content, but rather with a sentence he does not quite say: 'It is not *to be* written at all.' This suggests that, for Beckett, the text does not want to be written, it cannot be written, just as it cannot ever be read. Thus the failure which is such a recurring theme within Beckett's work, and criticism of his work, is not merely the impending blank page or the disintegrating pencil, but also a failure of the author (and his reader) to perceive his own work. The writing renders itself unreadable.

By extension, it is possible to see Beckett's later work as a constantly reiterated strategy against content, which in itself may generate the convolutions of form. In dramatic pieces such as *That time* there is a perceivable attempt at the dissolution of form and content, a struggle against the obscurely termed 'solution of continuity' (*CSPL*, 227). Similarly, the doggedly anti-mimetic presentation of *A piece of monologue* attempts *not* to con-fuse action and narrated action. It is a trait common to much of Beckett's late drama, and a similar strategy occurs within the prose. In a way, the prose dramatizes this attempted dissolution, yet it is always unstable, since it carries indissolubility at its centre. What may be hoped for, at best, would be a temporary disfiguring or, to use a highly Beckettian term, a voiding of an elemental procedure.

Accordingly, Beckett works himself into the unenviable position of having to reify this void. This is a project that will always seek virtuality. It deals with imponderables, whilst seeking to formulate not an objectivity of language, but what might be more clearly understood as an objecthood of language. The text is always on its way towards becoming something of a sculptural object. What we read as a published text is a temporary solidification. Sometimes, indeed, the solidification is so successful that the text may not be 'turned' (re- or dis-figured) any further, as in the case of the 'untranslatable' *Worstward Ho*.

Even a comparatively expansive text such as *The lost ones* was not without its self-imposed narratological closure. The text was left incomplete for several years, until Beckett appended its final paragraph. This purgatorial scene (revealing Beckett at his most indebted to Dante) is a complex cross-current of narrative actions involving some two hundred figures 'each searching for its lost one' (*CSP*, 159). Unusually for Beckett, these narrative strands offer a synchronic presentation of the various stages of suffering that the individual will undergo on his or her search until 'vanquished'. Perhaps this discrepancy in Beckett's writing practice made *The lost ones* unable to be completed for some time. Indeed, it is possible to see a trace of the difficulty which overcame Beckett just before the end of the penultimate paragraph and the start of the later addition:

> Like a single body the whole queue falls on the offender. Of all the scenes of violence the cylinder has to offer none approaches this.

> So on infinitely until towards the unthinkable end if this notion is main-
> tained a last body of all by feeble fits and starts is searching still. There is
> nothing at first sight to distinguish him from the others dead still where they
> stand or sit in abandonment beyond recall.   (*CSP*, 177)

What Beckett must do to achieve closure (and continuance) for his text is to
focus the field of vision on the individual as he resumes writing. The previous paragraph ends with the multitude figured as a unified mass (if only
one of dead weight), and an extreme of the suffering available within the
cylinder. This de-individuation and summation of suffering is itself a logical
determinant for the text's abrupt ending. It appears to be unable to reach a
more extreme position within its narrative. Beckett's strategy upon resump-
tion is to speed up 'infinitely' the process he has previously established in a
movement towards a 'last state' (*CSP*, 178).

This so-called last state is paradigmatic of Beckett's subsequent narrative
structures. The three *Still* texts (*Still*, *Sounds* and *Still 3*) explore precisely
this moment before absolute stasis, where the text has to resort to another
kind of discourse to perpetuate itself. For this is a narrative of non-events
and tendencies *towards* actions, rather than the actions themselves.
Inevitably, the narrative may not be sustained indefinitely, but in order to
evade an absolute stasis of writing (in imitating the stasis prescribed) the
text will recast itself, again and again, attempting to reiterate the scene, and
complete a description. Completion or closure here is the possibility of
leaving the subject as that subject has been fully annotated. In these texts it
is as though Beckett has set up a rhythm, echoing in the verbal repetitions
from text to text, and in the sounds which are more crucial, perhaps, than
the visual tableau.

After a text such as *The lost ones*, which proves difficult to continue, here
it is as though Beckett's text refuses to close itself down. *Still* and *Sounds*
end in parallel with intentions of 'Leave it so all quite still [. . .]' (*CSP*, 185)
and 'Leave it so then this stillest night till now of all quite still [. . .]'[6] *Still 3*
ends with 'still so long then out',[7] after a 'sudden white black', where
opposing shades become equivalent, and signal a visual end to the tableau
and, therefore, an end to the text which sustains it in the imagination. In this
way, Beckett seals off the text, giving it a finitude that 'achieves' the piece in
the act of completion, but rendering continuance thereafter all the more
problematic.

This creative, or 'decreative', process, to use Beckett's term, reverses
normative procedures, even including Beckett's own. During the last years
of Beckett's life, his work became less concerned with the act of writing
than the act of reading. For the most part, this was a self-reading: an

anxious realization that there was nowhere else to turn except towards the earlier, already petrified, Beckett. This was never a satisfactory reading for Beckett, but it does allow for the suppression of what *Film* calls '[a]ll extraneous perception' (*CSPL*, 163). In other words, stylistically at least, Beckett becomes self-consciously Beckettian.

Perhaps the most self-consciously, if not actually self-referential, self-reading text of Beckett's later work is the last text published during his lifetime, *Stirrings still*. The *Stirrings still* texts are almost entirely composed of echoes and reiterations of his previous work. It is perhaps useful to think of *Stirrings still* as less a continuous text – although the published version very much gives that impression – and more a series of texts which attempt to rewrite each other in turn, much in the manner of the *Still* series. They do offer a progression, but they may be usefully read concurrently as well as consecutively, as vain attempts at self-erasure combined with the vain struggle for self-disclosure. *Stirrings still* is an elaboration upon the scene of instruction and comfort offered in the play *Nacht und Träume*, as both protagonists are to be found in the same position and situation:

> One night as he sat at his table head on hands he saw himself rise and go. One night or day. For when his own light went out he was not left in the dark. Light of a kind came then from the one window. (*AST*, 113)

This is a recurring scene within Beckett's work, where some form of devised figment of the self becomes a provider of intellectual company and self-defining significance. As a process of creating the other, it could also be seen as a retrograde iteration, after the fact, of how the scene of *Ohio impromptu* came into being. The *Stirrings still* texts might be folded into the narrated discourse of *Ohio impromptu* immediately before the turning-point in that text where the stranger appears:

> One night as he sat trembling head in hands from head to foot a man appeared to him. (*CSPL*, 287)

The parallel phrasing between the two works is remarkable and can hardly be fortuitous. The text is full of verbal echoes of this kind. Indeed, the density of allusion to Beckett's own work forms the greater substance of the text. Beneath the window, for example, there is 'still the stool on which till he could or would no more he used to mount to see the sky' (*AST*, 113–14). The word 'still' in particular is a reminder of the complex continuum of time between one text by Samuel Beckett and another. This scenario is close to that of *Endgame*, where Clov would mount his steps to view the world beyond the window(s) of the room. The protagonist in *Stirrings still*, like Clov whose 'light [is] dying' (*E*, 17), must witness his own physical and 'metaphorical' light being extinguished. Through the window the room is illuminated by 'that strange light' of *The end* (*CSP*, 53) which accompanies the 'emptied cloudless sky', in turn recalling the 'birdless cloudless colourless skies' of 'Sedendo et quiescendo' (*Dream*, 71)[8] and becoming the 'sunless cloudless light' of *Company* (*NO*, 20). Perhaps more specifically, this recurring Beckettian figure becomes the glow of night ('Moonless starless night') in *Company* and *A piece of monologue*, where there is 'no such thing as no light' but one which, ever diminishing, 'dies/died on till dawn and never dies/died' (*Company*, NO, 44; *A piece of monologue*, CSPL, 26).

The recurrence of the featureless sky image in Beckett's work is significant because it suggests a deliberate impulse towards exclusion. What is more exceptional about the image, however, is that it actively seeks *not* to evoke a sensory response by way of materials which will always engender a highly charged, sensory, emotional response. Beckett's tendency to comment on the 'emptied' sky, rather than a featured one, seems to represent some kind of formal and metaphorical ideal for him. He always seeks to determine this state of absence. It is a virtual figure, a disfigured figure, one where figuration is highly disruptive.

Figuration is not only disruptive; it is also extremely unstable. Beckett's prose has to respond to the elusiveness by constantly reconstructing itself from first principles. The second paragraph of *Stirrings still* rewrites its first paragraph, barely introducing new material to be worked through:

> One night or day then as he sat at his table head on hands he saw himself rise and go. First rise and stand clinging to the table. Then sit again. Then rise again and stand clinging to the table again. Then go. Start to go. On unseen feet start to go. So slow that only change of place to show he went. As when he disappeared only to reappear later at another place. Then disappeared again only to reappear again later at another place again. So again and again disappeared again only to reappear again at another place again.
>
> (*AST*, 115)

Here the 'disappearings' and 'reappearings' are like those in *Ohio impromptu* and *Nacht und Träume*, and yet the language starts to mime the activity it seeks to describe. Indeed, momentarily, the language seems to fold upon itself. The sentence beginning 'As when he disappeared ...' has either forced a false jump in the narrative, or is slightly ungrammatical. Given the bare details which Beckett has set down, the sentence should begin, 'As *if* he disappeared ...'. Beckett, it would appear, is making assumptions about a past in a way which he would not characteristically seek to do. The text, here, gives the impression of determining its writer, and is seeking evidential finitude, whereas Beckett knows there is no such thing, only conditionality.

Indeed, endings are strongly asserted in Beckett's texts, but it appears that the definition of an ending will always fall just beyond the confines of the text, as for example in *For to end yet again*:

> Through it who knows yet another end beneath a cloudless sky same dark it earth and sky of a last end if there had to be another absolutely had to be.
>
> (*CSP*, 182)

The cloudless sky returns again, as some harbinger of closure, but this is an unachievable closure. The text seeks a definite ending, but syntactically is unresolved at the end of the sentence. Both of these tendencies are carried forward at once, to achieve this moment when, after an entire narrative of ending, an ending occurs which simulates the ending prescribed within the narrative. But Beckett also knows that confirmation of that ending will only occur with the blank space after the final full stop, in a space beyond his jurisdiction, as it were.

Beckett negotiates this idea in other ways, too. For example, in *Lessness*, he produces an unending, unendable, text. *Lessness* consists of one hundred and twenty sentences, or rather sixty, each employed twice. These sixty sentences subdivide into six 'families', each of which is, according to Beckett, 'formally differentiated and the ten sentences composing it "signed" by certain elements common to them all'.[9] The system is not immediately apparent within a reading of the text, although the formal similarity between sentences of the same 'family' is self-evident. What is important is the 'internal' structure which enables the text to be composed at all. *Lessness* certainly develops from *Ping* in its subject matter, but it also develops out of *Ping*'s intractability. A renewed strategy comes into effect after one text has been subjected to extensive reductive techniques. This process of reduction disrupts the syntax of the prose to such a degree that it appears to offer no potential for flexibility, or variability. It is in this climate that Beckett succeeds in developing a system whereby there is a suggestion, and potential, for infinite regeneration of the text. Yet this system is a closed one, and the resultant narrative both ironizes and reinforces itself through repetition. There can be no extraneous detail appended to this system, but the permutations are, for our purposes at least, all but infinite, and we might assume the subsequent sentence series to have a cumulative semantic effect.

Within its prescribed range of discourse *Stirrings still* follows an exhaustive process of linear optional selection, like the voice in *Company*, or *Worstward Ho*, rather than the prescribed elements of *Lessness*. The Beckettian narrative, therefore, does not consist of a progression from point A to point B, but rather mimes that progression, and offers itself as a tangible parenthesis within the 'aspired' ends of that narrative. We assume that a narrative always *intends* to take us from A to B, yet Beckett cannot even assume so relatively minimal a stability in his own constructs. Beckett situates his narrative in no place at all. His cursory scenic descriptions only play at situation. The simple movement described in *Stirrings still* is the move to '[a]nother place in the place [. . .]' (*AST*, 115). It is as though place cannot help suggesting itself within a narrative, once that narrative becomes vaguely peopled or motivated. In *Worstward Ho*, Beckett hypothesizes 'A place. Where none [. . .] Thenceless thitherless there' (*NO*, 104). Removing the possibility of movement attempts to exclude any suggestion of place, since place can only be defined by movements towards or from. Yet *Worstward Ho* generates an extended text from this refusal to progress, and in its way becomes an eminently linear narrative about this impossibility. Even at this achieved stasis, non-figuration is quite impossible:

> Dim whence unknown. At all costs unknown. Unchanging. Say now unchanging. Far and wide. High and low. Say a pipe in that void. A tube. Sealed. Then in that pipe or tube that selfsame dim. (*NO*, 113)

An absolute void is inconceivable, and the text resorts to this extraordinary figuration to accommodate the void somehow. Or rather, in this case, the void accommodates an inner 'sealed' vacuum. A void within a void is a paradox since, obviously enough, the presence of something within the void (even if it is a similarly defined void) clearly negates all qualities pertaining to the void. But the narrative leaves us with a residual charge of what the void is, or is not. It is as though the text can only retain a series of signifiers which have strayed from conventional usage. These terms themselves have been voided, in place of the unavoidable scene described. In other words, this text's attempt to describe nothing generates, in spite of its primary intention, precisely this text.

Narrative here is generated by the overt suppression of intent. In Beckett's later plays, such as *Ohio impromptu* and, more particularly, *A piece of monologue*, where the action prescribed in the spoken text is categorically not pursued in the stage directions, the discrepancy between the text and the stage presence forms the greater part of the dramatic tension. We can only make sense of the performance by reading for difference, or by seeking an anti-mimesis between the key elements of the performance. The distancing devices of the voice speaking in the third person cannot hide the physical similarities of Reader in *Ohio impromptu* and Speaker in *A piece of monologue* to their respective recounted counterparts. We can only perceive Reader or Speaker according to how they do not, and cannot, conform to the narrative to which they are obliged. The play can only be written, perhaps, if it aspires not to resemble a play at all.

As intent is suppressed within the text so, too, events become, to use *Ill seen ill said*'s term, 'occulted'. Indeed, *Ill seen ill said* hides events well beneath its surface. The world, for all we are given, is '[a]t the inexistent centre of a formless place' (*NO*, 58), like the voids in *Worstward Ho*. Time is posited as the semblance of a present, 'as were we still', as the voice of Bam declares in positioning the scenario of *What where* (*CSPL*, 310). *Ill seen ill said* stands at the centre of the *Nohow on* trilogy, representing a real space more closely than the other two texts. *Company* posits a place through the imagination. Yet it deliberately lacks detail; it is dark, to allow the freer flow of the imagined. *Worstward Ho* provides a negative image of this, where time, space and bodily mass are all virtual representations. The perceived reality of *Ill seen ill said* is 'figment', but the constructions seem to be left behind as 'traces', or discarded vessels of the complete lived sign.[10] *Ill seen ill said* comes into play after the event, 'tracing' the kind of auto-biographical (or what H. Porter Abbott calls 'autographical'[11]) events which feature so extensively in *Company*. In this way, *Company* offers the event without its consequence, and *Ill seen ill said* presents the consequence without the event. These traces in both *Ill seen ill said* and *Worstward Ho* are concerned with the 'ill said' and the 'missaid' respectively. *Ill seen ill said* is doubly enriched in its deferred reality, however, by paradoxically resort-ing to the only reality it can exhume from itself as writing-machine. This writer has three psychological strategies available to him. The first is the ability to intervene editorially. The second is memory, acquired knowledge, here taking the form of old words, old books. The third is the use of imagination.

The editorial participation, ever-present in all acts of writing, becomes more significant here, because there is a sense that it is already-written. Neither Beckett nor his authorial voice wishes the reader to forget the opacity of the constructed text. The illusion is always to be dispelled. Indeed, it seems that, for most of the work, the opacity is specifically con-structed to be broken down again into its illusory components. 'On' pro-motes flow, whilst 'Enough' denies it. 'Careful' and 'Gently gently' are self-administered admonitions, warning the narrator not to give too much away too soon. They also double as markers for the reader's experience of the text, ironically enough alerting him or her to the very detail that the writer wishes dissimulated. Irksome doubts regarding the efficiency of words arrest the description in every paragraph. Not only does the narrator have to contend with the construction (or assumed discovery) of a series of unresol-vable enigmas, but also the words fail to extricate him from difficulty.

There is an inability to speak out the event, and this informs *Ill seen ill said* stylistically, not only within these intra-textual devices, but insofar as the text is itself, perhaps paradoxically, a tribute to the art of misdirected meaning. The narrator is always drawing the attention to the words themselves as ever more inadequate. Between the eye and the word there is always a double deferral of meaning. We receive 'the wrong word' (*NO*, 65) or '[t]oo weak a word' (*NO*, 95), and that itself comes only after a misperception of the scene. The deferral works in reverse as the words become animate, almost corporeal: '[a] few drops' (*NO*, 91). Perhaps in creating *Ill seen ill said* Beckett also created the obligation to start afresh, since the text was too communicative despite all his efforts. The product of this secondary necessity must be untranslatable and unable to be deferred any further. Beckett's solution proved to be *Worstward Ho*, the skeleton of *Ill seen ill said*, with all the detail of a motivated narrative of action suppressed: words with the intent of signifying nothing.

This systematic programme of exclusion is reflected both within the structure of Beckett's work, and within the narrative content. *Stirrings still* deals with the progressive loss of what *A piece of monologue* calls 'loved ones' (*CSPL*, 265). One by one, loved ones are excluded, up to, and including, the self. Perhaps the ultimate aim is the disabling of the self, and the forced closure that would consequently be applied to the narrative, since closure itself implies completion, the end of *something*. There is, for example, Bam in *What where* who, acting upon instructions from his alternative self, Voice, is condemned ultimately to his solitary physical presence and the dictations of his voice. There is a similar tension in *Stirrings still* between the protagonist and his own ghost. Like Bam, he is unable to help himself. Whereas in *Ohio impromptu* 'he had once half hoped some measure of relief might flow' (*CSPL*, 285) from this exclusive tendency, in *Stirrings still* the phrase is echoed, confirming that half-hope for a return to another, whilst now also half-fearing it and wishing it never to happen.

Beckett's texts establish a series of lexical and syntactical dynamics that develop and distil themselves into quite definite moments of ending. There is also the renewal that comes from the text being read and re-read. These chains of self-interpretation do not typically follow a simple linear progression (or, for that matter, regression) but rather diverge in many temporal directions, creating complex patterns of influence. If the first section of *Stirrings still* positions itself along a path from *Ohio impromptu* towards *Nacht und Träume*, so it, too, is reviewed in three further texts, two of which Beckett incorporates into *Stirrings still*. Each rewrites the first and all seem to work internally with the others, only becoming distinct units of text after much compositional deliberation.[12]

Creating a text for Beckett seems to be a compulsive, repetitive act, where the divergence sublimated from the source text is the new text that is created. The second section of *Stirrings still* is close in structure and content to its predecessor. In the manner of the first section it revolves, even improvises around, the strokes of the clock and the cries heard from afar. It is as though this section has 'found' these elements in the first section and has appropriated them in an almost abstract way. Yet manuscript evidence seems to support the individuation of each text. Rather than continuations of the one theme, they are anxious repetitions, each trying to establish (or possibly, for the writer at least, diminish) a representation of the self. In this second attempt, however, the protagonist is no longer ambivalent towards the cessation of the sounds, but is distressed by 'unknowing and no end in sight' (*AST*, 125). The text frames, or simulates, a mental internalization, as the Beckettian mode of verification is questioned in another way:

> As one in his right mind when at last out again he knew not how he was not long out again when he began to wonder if he was in his right mind. For could one not in his right mind be reasonably said to wonder if he was in his right mind and bring what is more his remains of reason to bear on this perplexity in the way he must be said to do if he is to be said at all?   (*AST*, 120–1)

This opening strategy operates within the same mode as the closing moments of the narrative in *Ohio impromptu*:

> Or was it that buried in who knows what thoughts they paid no heed? To light of day. To sound of reawakening. What thoughts who knows. Thoughts, no, not thoughts. Profounds of mind. Buried in who knows what profounds of mind. Of mindlessness.   (*CSPL*, 287–8)

Both *Ohio impromptu* and *Stirrings still* deny the external world at key moments within their discourse. *Ohio impromptu* more specifically denies it by this exclusive act of concentration. The text performs another *volte face*, and seeks to emerge from the closed space, only not at a moment of mental emptiness, but rather as a result of a complex sequence of thinking about thinking. This activity lies at the heart of the suppressive instinct in Beckett's creative enterprise. The Cartesian *cogito* is ever-present but corrupted: *I think therefore I am* becomes *I think I am not in my right mind therefore I am*. This axiom has evolved from the compressed instructions of *Worstward Ho*:

> Say for be said. Missaid. From now say for be missaid.   (*NO*, 101)

In this way, Beckett signals a diachronic structure, which he operates within time and place and within text. Beckett is not only conjuring the 'more or less reasonable being' just 'to be' but, perhaps more importantly, to 'be said'. The writer, therefore, comes to the new text with an awareness that it has always already been said. This is not only to suggest that the new text is a repetition of prior texts, but that the very text emerges in a state of having been always already written. The problem that the writer faces is that the text has already been empowered and, ironically, control over the text would necessitate disabling it in some way.

This saying is, of course, a resaying, a missaying, and Beckett's disabling device is an external vision presented in contrast to the scene of the room. It is a simple inverted figure, suggesting the outside from within. Yet despite its attempts at difference it, too, is a much-sublimated revision of another Beckett text, *That time*. Not only are the internal settings of the three narratives evident, but also they combine with a verbal reconstitution, sometimes reinstated in a quite dissimilar context, but carrying rhythms and echoes of the earlier piece:

> To this end for want of a stone on which to sit like Walther and cross his legs the best he could do was stop dead and stand stock still which after a moment of hesitation he did and of course sink his head as one deep in meditation which after another moment of hesitation he did also. But soon weary of vainly delving in those remains he moved on through the long hoar grass resigned to not knowing where he was or how he got there or where he was going or how to get back to whence he knew not how he came. So on unknowing and no end in sight. (*AST*, 124–5)

The reference to 'Walther' must surely be to Walther von der Vogelweide, whose poetry Beckett admired and adapted in *Echo's bones*. We find Walther's stone in all three narratives of *That time*. In *Stirrings still* the lack of the stone, making sitting technically (that is, within the prescribed rules of the text) impossible, suggests a standing position like the 'stock still' paragraphs of *That time*. The second of these is especially revelatory:

> stock still side by side in the sun then sink and vanish [...] (*CSPL*, 232)

Here the 'stock still' phrase is placed in the context of the sinking sun, the phrase 'sink and vanish' hereinafter taking over as an echoic device. We hear the phrasing being imitated with the word 'sink', but here it is the head rather than the sun which is active. Intentionality gives way to a rather abstract, musical thematics. In the second sentence the 'remains' could be 'Foley's folly', that 'ruin' where he 'hid as a child'. It, too, is overgrown, not with 'hoar grass' but 'nettles'. The long grass, however, might recall 'the ears or the bent or the reeds', where the B-narrative of *That time* searches itself for the right turn of phrase. The A-narrative of *That time* deals with the child running away from his home environment in parallel with his ancient self seeking to get 'away to hell out of it all and never come back', like the new protagonist 'resigned to not knowing how [...] to get back'. The drastic gesture of the child, itself a simultaneous assertion and a denial of the self, causes a revelation when 'the truth began to dawn' that all options had been closed down for himself, that there was 'no getting out to it that way so what next [...]':

> none ever came but the child on the stone among the giant nettles with the light coming in where the wall had crumbled away poring on his book well on into the night some moods the moonlight and they all out on the roads looking for him or making up talk breaking up two or more talking to himself being together that way where none ever came   (CSPL, 233)[13]

The isolation of the 'ruin' where 'none ever came' is developed into the text's 'remains' where 'he knew not how he came'. This 'not knowing' repeats A's 'not knowing where you were or when you were or what for'. There is no worldly or personal interaction, and so a scale of self-defining values is not plausible.

The briefest and final text of *Stirrings still* also echoes *That time*:

> There then all this time where never till then and so far as he could see in every direction when he raised his head and opened his eyes no danger or hope as the case might be of his ever getting out of it   (AST, 127)

The phrasing is uncannily similar to the earlier play: B – 'as far as eye could see [...]' (CSPL, 229), C – 'till you hoisted your head and there before your eyes when they opened [...]' (CSPL, 229), B – 'as the case might be [...]' (CSPL, 232), A – 'no getting out to it that way [...]' (CSPL, 231).

Even in this brief text Beckett seems both obligated by and obligated to his previous efforts at 'getting out of it', despite the categorical desire to bring the narrative to an end. To end is to say for it to end, in the same way that, for example, *A piece of monologue* brings itself into being by the utterance of the word 'birth' and is closed by the word 'gone'. Here the completion of a phrase is elusive due to an essential missing word that 'he could not catch': 'oh how [*word*] it were to end' (AST, 126). Beckett posits 'sad or bad' as possibilities, in circumstances wishing 'to warn' (AST, 128), for example. Yet the very offer of these words is a deliberate evasion by the narrative voice. The word that is intended is the word that cannot be said. These examples are merely false trails, simulated emotional colours. There is no word except the notion of one missing, around which the text is constructed. This practice finds form in Beckett's posthumously published text, *what is the word*. In this case the text is brought into being by the word 'folly' and is an exercise in extending the text into a sentence from there. It completes itself only insofar as it becomes another echo of the familiar themes, one stage removed:

> folly for to need to seem to glimpse afaint afar away over there what –
>
>   (AST, 134)

This really is a self-defeating text. It is the one Beckett sought for most of his working life. It cannot adhere to narrative principles, becoming rather a series of axioms on the way towards or from a narrative. It is not even a set of instructions on how to construct a text, but something more deliberately frustrating: a seductive metatext, which only offers a hypothesis of what it paradoxically cannot offer.

The most active play, of course, in *what is the word* is the possibility that 'what' is indeed the word, despite any better intentions. Contrary to the outward signs offered by the text, Beckett is actively seeking failure in finding the elusive word. This process will, in the end, produce a word in the absence of the word sought. Writing obliges itself to make its mark, even if it is a semantic erasure. 'What', with or without a question mark at the end of the phrase, is the mark. Beckett has disabled the mechanism of writing to disallow completion, offering something to stand in its place, a parenthetical statement, almost, in permanent attendance and expectation.

NOTES

1 John Pilling also notes that *Ping* is 'a reduction of material from the drafts of *The lost ones*'. *Samuel Beckett* (London: Routledge and Kegan Paul, 1976), 50.

2 'Avigdor Arikha', in Richard Channin, André Fermigier, Robert Hughes et al., *Arikha* (Paris: Hermann, 1985), 9.

3 Indeed, an earlier variant on the French version of this text, *Abandonné*, does actually stop at this point. Published as *Abandonné*, in collaboration with Geneviève Asse (Paris: Editions Georges Visat, 1972).

4 The term is Beckett's own, coined for a collection of shorter prose of that title (London: John Calder, 1978). The volume contains: *From an abandoned work, Enough, Imagination dead imagine, Ping, Lessness* and *The lost ones*. The genericization of the term thereafter belongs more to his critics than to Beckett himself.

5 A translation into French has been effected, entitled *Cap au pire* (Paris: Editions de Minuit, 1991). One other book by Beckett – his book on Proust – was first published in English in 1931 (London: Chatto and Windus), and was not translated into French during his lifetime. (Both translations by Edith Fournier.) One might speculate, perhaps, that Beckett found returning *Proust* to Proust's mother tongue problematic.

6 *Essays in Criticism*, 28.2 (April 1978), 156.

7 Ibid., 157.

8 'Sedendo et quiescendo', *transition* 21 (1932), 17.

9 Unpublished manuscript lodged in Beinecke Rare Book and Manuscript Library, Yale University. Cited in Rosemary Pountney, *Theatre of shadows: Samuel Beckett's drama 1956–1976* (Gerrards Cross: Colin Smythe, 1988), 154.

10 'TRACES' appears to have been a possibility for the text's title, as it is inscribed on a final publisher's typescript (probably not in Beckett's hand), to be crossed

out and replaced by 'MAL VU MAL DIT'. Manuscript lodged at Reading University Library, MS. 2207.

11 H. Porter Abbott, 'Narratricide: Samuel Beckett as autographer', passim.

12 The unpublished text in this series indicates Beckett's return to prior texts most strongly by going so far as to make a direct reference to the opening lines of *Watt*, written some forty years previously. It is, in fact, a slight misquotation, but clearly demonstrates that Beckett's self-reading is potentially quite literal. (Reading University Library, MS. 2933.)

13 This paragraph is of additional consequence as it stands within *That time* as something of an anomaly, since it is the only paragrapah to use the third person instead of the second.

RECOMMENDED READING

Abbott, H. Porter, 'Narratricide: Samuel Beckett as autographer', *Romance Studies* 11 (Winter 1987), 35–46.

Arthur, Kateryna, 'Texts for *Company*', in James Acheson and Kateryna Arthur (eds.), *Beckett's later fiction and drama: texts for Company*, London: Macmillan, 1987, 136–44.

Ben-Zvi, Linda, *Samuel Beckett*, Boston: G. K. Hall, 1986, chapter 5.

Brienza, Susan D., *Samuel Beckett's new worlds: style in metafiction*, Norman, Okla.: University of Oklahoma Press, 1987, chapters 6 to 12.

Cohn, Ruby, *Back to Beckett*, Princeton University Press, 1973, chapter 5.

Davies, Paul, 'Twilight and universal vision: Samuel Beckett's *Ill seen ill said*', *Temenos*, 11 (1990), 88–103.

'*Stirrings still*: the disembodiment of Western tradition', in John Pilling and Mary Bryden (eds.), *The ideal core of the onion*, Reading: Beckett International Foundation, 1992, 136–51.

Finney, Brian, '*Still* to *Worstward Ho*: Beckett's prose fiction since *The lost ones*', in Acheson and Arthur, *Beckett's later fiction and drama*, 65–79.

Fitch, Brian T., 'The relationship between *Compagnie* and *Company*: one work, two texts, two fictive universes', in Alan Warren Friedman, Charles Rossman and Dina Sherzer (eds.), *Beckett Translating/Translating Beckett*, University Park: Pennsylvania State University Press, 1987, 25–35.

Fournier, Edith, '*Sans*: cantate et fugue pour une réfuge', *Lettres nouvelles* (September–October 1970), 149–60.

Hansford, James, '*Imagination dead imagine*: the imagination and its context', *Journal of Beckett Studies*, 7 (Spring 1982), 49–70.

'Seeing and saying in *As the story was told*', *Journal of Beckett Studies*, 8 (Autumn 1982), 75–93.

Hill, Leslie, *Beckett's fiction: in different words*, Cambridge University Press, 1990, chapter 8.

Janvier, Ludovic, 'Le Lieu du retrait de la blancheur de l'écho', *Critique*, 237 (February 1967), 215–38.

Krance, Charles, '*Worstward Ho* and *on*-words: writing to(wards) the point', in

Lance St John Butler and Robin J. Davis (eds.), *Rethinking Beckett: a collection of critical essays*, London: Macmillan, 1990, 124–40.

Lawley, Paul, 'Samuel Beckett's "art and craft": a reading of *Enough*', *Modern Fiction Studies*, 29.1 (1983), 25–42.

Levy, Eric P., '*Company*: the mirror of Beckettian mimesis', *Journal of Beckett Studies*, 8 (Autumn 1982), 95–104.

Mood, John J., '"Silence within": a study of the *Residua* of Samuel Beckett', *Studies in Short Fiction*, 7 (1969), 385–401.

Murphy, P. J., *Reconstructing Beckett: language for being in Samuel Beckett's fiction*, University of Toronto Press, 1990, chapters 5 to 12.

Pilling, John, '*Company*', *Journal of Beckett Studies*, 7 (Spring 1982), 127–31.

'The significance of Beckett's *Still*', *Essays in Criticism*, 28.2 (April 1978), 143–57.

'Ends and odds in prose', in James Knowlson and John Pilling, *Frescoes of the skull: the later prose and drama of Samuel Beckett*, London: John Calder, 1979, 131–91.

'A criticism of indigence: *Ill seen ill said*', in Patrick A. McCarthy (ed.), *Critical essays on Samuel Beckett*, Boston: G. K. Hall, 1986, 136–44.

Read, David, 'Beckett's search for the unseeable and unmakeable: *Company* and *Ill seen ill said*', *Modern Fiction Studies*, 29.1 (Spring 1983), 111–25.

Renton, Andrew, 'Texts for performance/performing texts: Samuel Beckett's anxiety of self-regeneration', *Performance*, 60 (Spring 1990), 15–29.

'*Worstward Ho* and the end(s) of representation', in Pilling and Bryden (eds.), *The ideal core of the onion*, 99–135.

Segrè, Elizabeth Bregman, 'Style and structure in Beckett's *Ping*: "that something itself"', *Journal of Modern Literature*, 6.1 (February 1970), 124–47.

Smith, Frederik N, '*Ill seen ill said*: Beckett's pastoral elegy', *Postscript*, 9 (1992), 31–40.

Solomon, Philip H., 'Purgatory unpurged: time, space and language in *Lessness*', *Journal of Beckett Studies*, 6 (Autumn 1980), 63–72.

Trieloff, Barbara, '"Babel of silence": Beckett's post-trilogy prose articulated', in Butler and Davis, *Rethinking Beckett*, 89–104.

Watson, David, *Paradox and desire in the fiction of Samuel Beckett*, London: Macmillan, 1991, chapters 5 to 7.

Zurbrugg, Nicholas, '*Ill seen ill said* and the sense of an ending', in Acheson and Arthur, *Beckett's later fiction and drama*, 145–59.

'Seven types of postmodernity: several types of Samuel Beckett', in Joseph H. Smith, (ed.) *The world of Samuel Beckett*, Baltimore: Johns Hopkins University Press, 1991, 30–52.

10

ROGER LITTLE

Beckett's poems and verse translations or: Beckett and the limits of poetry

and Dante and the Logos and all strata and mysteries

('Alba')

That fierce endeavour to bring the intellectual and the emotional into focus which characterizes Beckett's work is reflected in his poetry as much as in his theatre and prose. The differences are partly generic, though to a lesser extent than might at first appear, and partly chronological. On the one hand, the generic continuum of preoccupation and manner means that not only must all of Beckett's writings be considered as directly relevant to the understanding of the poetry but also that all Beckett criticism is potentially so. On the other hand, the poetry was produced predominantly in the 1930s, with a further substantial foray in the late 1940s but only occasional ones thereafter, notably in the mid-1970s. Novels and drama made demands on Beckett's creative energies and relegated the forms of verse while simultaneously diverting the essential poetic thrust into other channels. In investigating Beckett's poems, the reader is drawn to explore the limits of poetry.

In a profound way, the opening of Beckett's 1929 essay, 'Dante...Bruno. Vico..Joyce' (D, 19), alerts us to the fact that 'the danger is in the neatness of identifications'. More pragmatically, it is worth reflecting on what constitutes the corpus covered by the title of the present essay. The English reader has at his or her disposal the *Collected poems 1930–1978* most recently published by Calder in 1984. For present purposes, since a promised volume comprising the previously uncollected poems had not materialized in time for this study to take account of it, this is our point of reference. As the English reader discovers when reaching Part Two of the volume, proficiency in French is taken for granted, for the section contains poems written in French by Beckett, sometimes, but not always, accompanied by his English versions of the texts. The question of Beckett's self-translations will require further consideration. His translations from French writers – Eluard,

Rimbaud, Apollinaire, Chamfort – constitute Part Three, with a brief but telling 'Tailpiece' drawn from *Watt*.

It is understandable that Beckett's translations from the French should be excluded from the French edition of his *Poèmes*, most recently reprinted by Editions de Minuit in 1988. It is less comprehensible that none of his English poems should figure there either in the original or in translation. A couple of extra pithy jingles among the *mirlitonnades* scarcely compensate for this loss. It means that the French reader will perceive Beckett's poems as an even slighter proportion of his total output than the English reader, and this perhaps explains why so little attention has been paid to them by French critics. It is curious that Beckett, who controlled closely the selection of texts that he considered worthy of inclusion in his *Collected Poems*, should have denied the French reader direct access to those English-language poems which form the bulk of his verse production. The consequent view of what constitutes the corpus of Beckett's poetry depends arbitrarily on the reader's language of departure. The author's will on the matter may have changed according to the readership envisaged, but for reasons which remain unclear.

It is convenient then, but again not lacking in arbitrariness, to take the more complete volume as a starting-point. A dozen or so early poems, published in various magazines or collections, are excluded; they are made available, with commentary, in the one book so far devoted to Beckett's poetry, Lawrence Harvey's 1970 study.[1] One may reasonably surmise that an unknown number of unpublished poems was no less purposely kept under wraps. A similar range of exclusions applies to the material translated from other authors. Not only did Beckett translate more Eluard texts than appear in the *Collected poems*, he also published elsewhere substantial translations from other French writers, a handful of Italian poems and a whole anthology of Mexican poetry.[2] Some of this material, such as the translations done for Nancy Cunard's 1934 *Negro anthology* and the Mexican volume, was to generate income and, in retrospect, disparaging remarks by the translator. But the precise degree to which uncollected items, whether original or translated (a distinction which itself begs questions) should be categorized with unpublished items as unworthy of attention because they fall outside the acknowledged *œuvre* is open to debate. It is legitimate to recognize at one and the same time the double corpus, one the totality of Beckett's production, the other what, at a given time, he was prepared to stand over. The former may well, in various ways, throw interesting light on the latter, most obviously in helping to determine the very criteria by which the selection was made. Here too are fascinating limits to explore.

It is probably the critical compulsion to classify by genre, however, which impinges most insidiously and most nefariously on our understanding of what constitutes Beckett's poetry. It is manifestly not restricted to his poems, yet old habits die hard (and Beckett panders to them wittily in his *mirlitonnades*). A century and a half has gone by since the prose poems of Aloysius Bertrand, *Gaspard de la nuit*, were published, marking the essential separation of poetry and verse, the former an attribute or quality, the latter a technique. With the recognizable separation of the two came the freedom to explore, in whatever style seemed most appropriate, the potentialities of poetry. That these were inalienably realized through words remained axiomatic in the definition of the art. But words are not merely tokens of meaning and communication; their physical and phonic qualities, their history and connotative texture, can be exploited to produce effects greater than the sum of their component parts. It is therefore not so much that the semantic thrust is reduced – indeed it may well be increased – as that attention is shifted proportionately in favour of verbal texture. Narrative and discursive elements are held in check and balance by phonetic patterning or the rhythms created by particular strategies of syntax. More broadly, the very conception of overall structure may be determined by an image rather than by a story-line to which all else is subservient.

To anyone familiar with Beckett's work, it will be apparent that these last observations, however brief and general, are intended to bring to mind his writings in prose and for the stage. That it was possible for a wit to observe of *Waiting for Godot* that 'Nothing happens. Twice.' bespeaks the relative unimportance of narrative in the play. Whether words flow in cascading torrents, as in Lucky's speech, or snowball into the breathless staccato of *The Unnamable* or *Not I*, or are set as minimal utterances between stops and silences, our attention is drawn to the rhythm as much as to the meaning. Phonetic clusters form round key words, such that in *Ill seen ill said*, for example, that favourite word of Beckett's late years, the untranslatable 'On', generates a network of echoes and reverberations: 'one', 'no', 'know' ...[3] Such instances, which could be multiplied indefinitely across Beckett's work, serve here simply to underline the lack of coincidence between his poetry and his poems. The two concepts are absolutely not coterminous, and the limits imposed on the present study are therefore those of expediency rather than anything else.

Even the status of what is covered by the title '*Collected poems*' is not without its ambiguities, however. Are the translations of Part Three, those from various French writers, to be accorded the same importance as Beckett's original poems, whether in French or English? We are probably disinclined to think so, yet they figure as poems wittingly *collected* by

Beckett and incorporated into his canon. They furthermore form the longest and what might be considered the culminating section of the book. (Their absence from the French edition is, as we have seen, matched by the absence of all of the English poems.) We clearly cannot afford to be dismissive of them when the second part also contains translations, in this case self-translations, representing a transition from the English poems of Part One to the translations of Part Three. The likelihood that the process of translation impinged on those of creativity becomes a certainty not simply by the double meaning of 'making one's own' but also by the general evidence of creative self-translation in Beckett and, ostensibly – even ostentatiously – as regards the early poems, by their multilingual, multicultural nature. The brilliant student of languages, who was trying to come to terms with his Protestant ethic in relation to his sexuality as well as with the problems of writing, there leads his reader a merry dance.

The complex details of the steps have been exhaustively traced, notably by Harvey. Present circumstances make it more appropriate at this juncture to reflect on the techniques and forms apparent in the poems and on the attitudes they suggest. The fact that so many of the poems predate Beckett's ventures into other genres and so bear witness to his literary apprenticeship means that they can be revealing of his attitudes as it were in the raw. Even if our judgment of the quality of the product has to contain reservations, our awareness of the processes of production is likely to be enhanced. We always have to bear in mind, however, that it is a *process* and that it will necessarily evolve, greater maturity bringing greater mastery and with it a battery of new techniques for self-expression, self-revelation and self-veiling.

The exhibitionism of such an early poem as 'Whoroscope' (*CP*, 1–6), the competition-winning bravura piece from 1930, is a clear instance of an *embarras d'intelligence*: it is too clever for its own good. Yet it is equally clear that Beckett was clever enough to be fully aware of this and that the ironies contained within the text, as well as the parodic archness of the notes, mimicking those of Eliot's *The waste land*, are integral to his strategy. The pun of the title and wordplay elsewhere (such as the Joycean 'prosti-sciutto' in line 13) are signs of that cleverness which both masks and reveals the author's shyness, a mode of overcompensation potentially irritating in its flashiness as a diversionary tactic and yet prompting a smile of connivance and consequent interest in the depths it half-conceals. Where does the exfoliation of the onion stop? Who has the last laugh, the author or the critic? It can only be the former, and this being so we must tread warily in the steps of those for whom the highest achievement can be no better, according to Beckett, than hysterectomies performed with a trowel.[4] Our best motto has to be Beckett's words from *Worstward Ho*: 'Fail again. Fail better' (*NO*, 101).

Somewhere in that nexus of contradictory intensities evident in the early poems must lie the quintessential Beckett. He himself had to tussle with them before finding an accommodation with and for the mess.[5] Only for the purposes of analysis must one tease out the tangled strands and see, for example, how the more or less overt eroticism vies with the puritanical morality of a 'four percenter' (as the Anglo-Irish Protestants in the Free State were called), how a passionate relish for making words his own has to come to terms not just with their previous existence but with their very sociability as exchange, how a fierce sense of self goes hand in hand with an urgent need to share, how that self is both protected and projected by adopting personae, how, to use Brendan Kennelly's less formal terms, 'piss-taking and freedom-giving' are facets of the same syndrome.[6] It is a sense of obligation that brings these multidirectional forces into focus, an obligation to self, to art, to society, nurtured by Protestantism and fostered by Geulincx, among others, in a sensitive mind certain of its powers but far from certain of their best orientation.

The neatly-turned 'Gnome' (*CP*, 7) eschews and seemingly condemns the parade of knowledge embodied in 'Whoroscope'. The inescapable circularity it describes and embodies nonetheless involves learning as one of the points it passes through, seen first in a positive light through the eyes of tradition by way of a cliché: 'the years of learning'. That cliché is set within another which defines a condemnatory attitude on the part of adult society *vis-à-vis* young people's education: 'Spend the years of learning squandering'. The apostrophe to youth seems almost to be a recommendation, however resigned, and so condemnation is leavened by paternal(istic) forgiveness. The clichés anchor the opening firmly in traditional social attitudes and prepare the terrain for other points of view to use that base as a foil for their emergence. The unexpected object of 'squandering' is not time or money, but 'Courage'. Following the line-break, it disrupts the cliché and introduces a value determined rather from within the young person addressed than by the society around him. Courage is summoned, what is more, not for purposes generally valued by adults but 'for the years of wandering', a phrase directly derived from the German *Wanderjahre*, which cannot help but evoke the tradition of Goethe's young Werther. The interplay of positive and negative valuations ascribed to the succeeding components continues through the whole unpunctuated *perpetuum mobile* of the poem. Ostensibly the last two lines declare society's disdain for youth's antisocial preoccupations, and we witness 'a world politely turning / From the loutishness of learning'. For Beckett to project into a mind capable of rejecting learning as loutishness is a considerable feat of self-distancing. But 'turning / From' means more than 'turning away from'; it can also be interpreted as 'turning thanks to' or 'turning under the influence of'. Instead of reading 'a world' as society, and in this case 'polite society', it would then mean 'the earth' and it would be Galileo's learning, condemned by the Church as 'loutish', that, on behalf of all scholarship, ironically triumphs over staid conventionalism.

The appearance of Galileo is no surprise after his role in 'Whoroscope' (lines 5–10), where the notes specify the conservative Descartes's 'contempt' for Galileo's 'expedient sophistry concerning the movement of the earth'. The heavy irony applied to Galileo's revolutionary theories is part of Beckett's strategy in that poem and is re-applied in 'Gnome', where assimilation is the key feature in its re-enactment of perpetual motion, in its insistent rhyming of present participles emblematic of continuity, in its brevity and lack of cultural display and learned annotations. To have placed it immediately after 'Whoroscope' (and notably out of chronological order) is to assert both the affinity of subject-matter despite appearances and the absolute difference of manner. To explicate 'Gnome' solely in terms of Beckett recording his father's voice is a gross oversimplification and distortion. The recently silenced voice – Beckett's father had died in the summer of 1933 and 'Gnome' is dated 1934 – may well haunt the son but the latter affirms his independence from it (as well as from Joyce's) and asserts a more comprehensive set of values.

Insofar as those values encompass *inter alia* the notion of 'years of wandering', apparent aimlessness having its own virtues and rewards, it is pertinent to turn next to what I think of as the 'peripatetic' poems which make up most of the 1935 collection *Echo's bones*. Together, indeed, in terms of the number of lines, the 'Enueg', 'Sanies' and 'Serena' series form the bulk of Beckett's poems in English. They are bounded parenthetically by short poems, 'The vulture' and 'Echo's bones', which, pointedly unpunctuated again, adumbrate themes to become familiar: life as derisory, fed on by lower life, reduced to essentials which are in turn called into question. More generally the use of the journey, a traditional metaphor for life, prefigures much of Beckett's writing.

The collection opens with a present participle and ends in a timeless continuous present, and it is against this flux that art strives to make something memorable. Revitalization of clichés, reuse of quotations, re-application of old models: these are weapons in the poet's armoury. Beckett's tactics alter according to the occasion, but the 'Enueg', 'Sanies' and 'Serena' poems all derive from medieval Provençal models, and the stylization of courtly love informs the sexual code echoed not only there but also in the lesser or the greater deaths of 'Alba' and 'Da tagte es' (*CP*, 15, 27).

'Enueg I' (*CP*, 10–12) retraces geographically a walk of a few miles from south to west of Dublin, from Portobello along the canal and via the Fox and Geese near Kilmainham to Chapelizod and the River Liffey. Local topography is not, however, Beckett's main concern, but the selective microcosm of his mind marking the stations of his cross. 'So on, / derelict' anticipates so many of Beckett's later characters that we are not surprised to encounter an enigmatic child for whom 'want' and do' are as irreconcilable as for Beckett are 'can't' and 'must'. Nor at this stage of Beckett's development is it surprising to find his fullest exploitation of phonetic resources, appropriated by the powerful anti-Romantic line 'a slush of vigilant gulls in the grey spew of the sewer', capped by an unacknowledged quotation, this time translated from Rimbaud, to end the poem. Even the slight shift from what in the French is an adjective, '*saignante*', to the verbal participle 'bleeding' is a small index of Beckett's preference for continuity. But the function of the quotation seems to be to raise the inevitably inconclusive conclusion to a plane poetically higher than Beckett feels himself capable of achieving at this stage, while making a gesture both towards the sea that lies downstream and encompasses the world and towards non-being which, to the suffering protagonist, seems a desirable ideal. The fact that, in the process of declaring 'the sea's arctic flowers' non-existent, poetry brings them into existence in the mind, is merely one of its beneficial ironies.

The journeys around Dublin, on foot or bicycle ('Enueg I', 'Enueg II', 'Sanies I' and 'Serena III'), in the west of Ireland ('Serena II'), or across London ('Serena I') or Paris ('Sanies II'), are not ends in themselves but explorations in a poetic manner. Crucial to that manner are arresting juxtapositions which interrupt and subvert any narrative progress. Languages are juxtaposed without the apology of italics: 'Exeo in a spasm' opens 'Enueg I' (*CP*, 10); English, German, Englished Greek and Latin tumble over one another in 'her dazzling oven strom of peristalsis / limae labor' in 'Serena I' (*CP*, 21) and so forth. The rationale and consequent meaning and fulfilment of allusions and conniving quotations are withheld in an intellectual equivalent of the prick-teasing which recurs so insistently in the poems. The unspeakable words of sex and the congenitally private parts are diverted from vulgarity on occasion by a single letter: we find the goat in 'Enueg I' 'remotely pucking the gate of his field', follow the narrator of 'Sanies II' 'slouching up to Puvis', and note later, in 'Ooftish', the 'bullock's scrotum' (*CP*, 12; 19; 31). On each occasion the meaning as stated is valid; these tiny, potent acts of shy self-censorship embody an acknowledgment of social codes in the very process of cocking a schoolboy snook. The sleight of word which is to be a Beckett hallmark is present from the start.[7] Thus when he writes 'I have dismounted to love' in 'Sanies I' (*CP*, 18), the simplest reading makes good sense: he has got off his bike to have sex. But if he dismounts only to mount, it is not foolish also to understand that conscience makes a coward of him in the sexual act and that he has to withdraw from it in order to feel his love more fully. Puritanism and lustiness make uneasy bedfellows. Ambivalence of expression, in which both A and not-A are true, is a direct reflection in Beckett of the complexity of his being.

So too with cultural references and more or less veiled quotations. Once we have teased out their individual significance, it is their juxtaposition that bewilders and perhaps dissatisfies, so brief is the fizzle of fireworks between preparation and burnt-out cases. Such a display occurs when the lyric 'I' of 'Sanies I', desperately close to Samuel Beckett, cycles through the north Dublin countryside,

> pounding along in three ratios like a sonata
> like a Ritter with pommelled scrotum atra cura on the step
> Botticelli from the fork down [...] (*CP*, 17)

We understand the description of the cyclist on his steed with its three Sturmey-Archer gears (giving 'Stürmers' later in the poem), clad in quasi-Renaissance manner as if with cod-piece and what would now be called tights (the 'poor forked animal' of *King Lear* being a more likely candidate for attention than the fork of the bicycle frame), his mood determined by the quotation from Horace. But do we not remain uneasy at the sudden shifts from the reference to sonata form to the German knight, to Latin and on to the Italian painter? Is the allusive something elusive to be tracked down, or something illusive, shimmering alluringly but mocking pretensions? Do the successive Little-Jack-Hornerisms not distract rather than illumine? Or could a hint of self-satisfaction in a poem of self-exploration be a mark of honesty? Does the poet not have his tongue firmly in his cheek? Insofar as we might be inclined to reply to all these questions in the affirmative, accepting the inherent contradictions and tensions, we might be getting close to Beckett's essential manner. For the very awkwardness at this juncture is integral to his honesty as he strives to be true both to his emotions and to his intellectualism. The profound obligation to self has not yet found projections and a manner which simultaneously recognize his obligation to the reader. The words which protect his vulnerability while probing it for its complex sensitivities have yet to come into sharp and sustained focus.

If there is evidence in 'Cascando' (*CP*, 29), dated 1936, of beneficial simplicity of utterance with no loss of sensitivity or subtlety, it is the group of poems written in French between 1937 and 1939 which first provides evidence of mastery of worth, world and word. Most hints of posturing and exhibitionism have gone, and the use of French may well be significant in this process of purification. Since French would become the language of creation for so many of Beckett's major works, including the trilogy and the earliest published plays, it is worth reflecting that his first public foray into French was through these poems. His formal studies had been followed by years in Paris. In the 1930s he plunged into translation from French into English, and Eluard's manner leaves its unostentatious imprint. But a writer does not lightly choose to abandon his mother tongue. The intellectual challenge represented by the mastery of a foreign language seems to a large extent to have replaced in Beckett the urge to parade his cleverness (reflecting the intellectual challenge of learning), which is subsumed in and assimilated by his use of French. From the reader's point of view, the more acceptable mask replaces the less; from the writer's, a crucial creative as well as psychological step has been taken.

Disjunctive techniques remain, of course, whether of referential juxta-position, the writer's Modernist self-awareness (as in 'et on attend / adverbe', rather as 'Sanies I' has 'I see main verb at last' (CP, 43; 17)) or the conniving letter which suggestively hides another (as in 'formicante'). In the poem from which these examples are taken, 'être là sans mâchoires sans dents' (CP, 43), a learned reference to Roscelin stands out like a thumb sore from pulling out plums. Does the poet expect his reader to be familiar with the name? Or to reach for an encyclopaedia? Or to muzzle ignorance, mutter envy and move on? Is it helpful to know something of Roscelin de Compiègne's nominalist doctrine dating from the late eleventh and early twelfth centuries? Or is this a fragment shored against the ruins to uncertain effect? The answers do not seem to arise naturally from the overall economy of the poem, in contrast to the fully integrated 'loque de chanson' which would not only be familiar to a French reader from folklore but which also encapsulates transparently in its first line as quoted (in italics as line 8 of the poem) the love-making episode which forms the bulk of Beckett's poem. Does the implicit reference to Roscelin's idea that only the individual is real help us to understand the poet's difficulty in coming to terms with his sense of isolation, even of solipsism? Or to sympathize more fully with his frustrated inability to lose himself in someone else? Can medieval doubt as to the nature of the Trinity be other than disproportionately brought to bear on the two-in-one of having sex? The learning is at least more lightly worn in these poems than in the earlier ones, and is largely restricted to general knowledge as it was then understood: the Greek myths, as in 'jusque dans la caverne ciel et sol' (*CP*, 53), or Kant and the Lisbon earthquake in 'ainsi a-t-on beau' (*CP*, 48). When Gabriel de Mortillet is evoked, he is, appropriately, no more than a stone statue in the 'Arènes de Lutèce' (*CP*, 52). Knowledge petrifies. It is the hardest lesson to learn.

To exemplify its complete assimilation and show how, without change of preoccupation, limpidity probes the notion of self and other to telling effect just as in the novels and plays, one might look at two poems using the voice as a key feature, one from the 1937–9, the other from the 1947–9 group of poems, likewise written in French. In 'musique de l'indifférence' (*CP*, 46) the general (not to be confused with the abstract) replaces the particular. The opening series of nouns in enumerative apposition produces uncertainties in their relationships which the reader can tease out, a process continued throughout thanks in part to the lack of punctuation. The core statement 'du silence [...] / couvre leurs voix' is a paradox co-ordinated with the second one, which ends the poem: 'que / je n'entende plus / me taire'. The paradoxes remain unresolved, but tellingly explore identity and relationships through notions of sound and silence. The lyric 'I' allows a projection which nonetheless remains more directly identified with the poet than do his characters in play or novel while, through the similarity of preoccupation, confirming the proximity of Beckett's characters to his inner being.

Those voices are heard again in 'que ferais-je sans ce monde sans visage sans questions' (*CP*, 60), where a 'gouffre de murmures' is linked, again in apposition, with both silence and self, the lack of punctuation again allowing both readings. The narrator, 'regardant par mon hublot si je ne suis pas seul', has years of philosophical reflection behind him but now eschews erudite references and thereby gives his isolation a keener edge because, paradoxically, it is more fully shared. As he ends 'sans voix parmi les voix / enfermées avec moi', he expresses the impossibility of adequate expression, internalizes the other voices with which he might have communicated had they remained other, yet engages in the dialogue which becomes possible only when the individual is *by* himself, the *Doppelgänger* stalking the 'Arènes de Lutèce', the converter of sterile loneliness into creative solitude. The absolute lack of cultural exhibitionism makes of the poem a masterpiece of penetration, its simplicity of expression allowing the reader to unravel the complexities of its thought.

Not a single proper name interrupts the flow of the 1947–9 poems. The initials in the title 'Mort de A. D.' (*CP*, 56) seem merely discreet towards a dead colleague and yet are more likely chosen to represent the universality of death by combining the French and English words for it, the latter being conjured from the letters 'de A D'. Beckett's preoccupation with death and with the myriad pathetic ways in which man prepares for it from the cradle or before is directed, in the novels and plays, into more sustained metaphors of the eternal triangle of Eros (rampant in the early poems, disguised and diverted thereafter), Thanatos and Logos. There too the jokiness and jerkiness find fuller outlets, and from 1950 verse becomes an occasional rather than a dominant medium. Specifically, in the 1970s, the most blatant form of generally short-lined rhyming verse is adopted in its very contradistinction from prose to translate Chamfort's maxims and turn the sardonic pirouettes of the *mirlitonnades*. Recognizably lightweight *vers de mirliton*, these nevertheless contain the paradoxes and perspicacities of epigram and proverb, the profound sense of nonsense rhymes.

Beckett made no sustained attempt to translate the *mirlitonnades*, whereas he Englished several poems from the 1930s and 1940s. It is difficult to see a clear principle of selection behind what was and what was not translated, just as what he translated from others seems to derive from a mixture of his own purposes, both creative and money-making, commission and friendship. It is easier to observe an honest, straightforward translator at work in all the verse translations, however, with the interesting exception of the transposition of the 1976 poem 'hors crâne seul dedans' into 'Something there' (CP, 65–6). Elsewhere, the occasional omission or distortion is fully compensated by originality, the latter well represented by the re-activation as adjective of the word 'thoroughfare' ('In a most thoroughfare', 'In a so thoroughfare') in the version of Eluard's 'La vue' (CP, 106–7).

The underlying importance of Beckett's work as translator is its role in his coming to terms with himself through the distancing that French allowed him. The poems reveal that process with all its awkwardnesses, the very rawness of the early ones being a guarantee of authenticity. Perhaps at least until *Dream of fair to middling women* and a full correspondence are published, they are the best guide to Beckett's psyche in the crucial formative years.[8] The major writings of his maturity absorbed and redeployed the energies generated by that apprenticeship. French as a medium was first used for the 1937–9 poems; they are therefore an important staging-post on the road whose representation would be refined from the peripatetic poems into that familiar, quintessentially Beckettian metaphor. No less central an image, the solitary figure in the bare room desperately trying to reconcile himself to himself, to the Other, to life, to death, is equally tested in the poems and found eminently capable of further development. The ambivalent protections of the mask become the ambivalent projections of the masque. The difficult adjustments to self and society are made through words which belong to the community and yet must be juxtaposed in singular ways by the writer if he is to make his individual mark. The multiplicity of interactive obligations creates pressures on a vision which must enact that knot of contradictions. Beckett's bleak hilarities reverberate in the mind. The poems prepare and reflect his vision. The challenge and the joy is that there are no limits. Except in us.

NOTES

1 Lawrence E. Harvey, *Samuel Beckett: poet and critic* (Princeton University Press, 1970). See chapter 7, 'The jettisoned poems', 272–314.
2 For full details of Beckett's published translations, see chapter 3, 'Translations, manifestos and miscellaneous', in Raymond Federman and John Fletcher, *Samuel Beckett: his works and his critics* (Berkeley and Los Angeles: University of California Press, 1970).
3 Marjorie Perloff makes other interesting points on this text in 'Between verse and prose', 415–33.
4 'Les peintures des van Velde', *Cahiers d'art* (1945–6), 349–56, cited by Harvey, 437–8.
5 I echo here Beckett's comment: 'To find a form that accommodates the mess, that is the task of the artist now.' Cited by J. P. Little, *Beckett: 'En attendant Godot' and 'Fin de partie'*, Critical guides to French texts 6 (London: Grant and Cutler, 1981), 78.
6 See Brendan Kennelly, 'The four percenter', in *Beckett in Dublin*, ed. S. E. Wilmer (Dublin: Lilliput Press, 1992), 130.
7 Freud's study of the *mot d'esprit* might suggest a psychoanalytical reading of Beckett's fondness for the creative punning of paronomasia. See Sigmund Freud, *Jokes and their relation to the unconscious*, vol. VIII of *The standard edition of the complete psychological works of Sigmund Freud*, ed. James Strachey, (London: Hogarth Press, 1960).
8 Since this essay was written, *Dream of fair to middling women* has been published. Its readers will find many an episode which echoes, or has an echo in, the poems.

RECOMMENDED READING

Esslin, Martin, 'Samuel Beckett's poems', in *Beckett at sixty*, London: Calder and Boyars, 1967, 55–60.
Fletcher, John, 'The art of the poet', in *Samuel Beckett's art*, London: Chatto and Windus, 1967, 24–40.
Harvey, Lawrence E., *Samuel Beckett: poet and critic*, Princeton University Press, 1970.
Perloff, Marjorie, 'Between verse and prose: Beckett and the new poetry', *Critical Inquiry*, 9.2 (December 1982), 415–33.
Pilling, John, 'Beckett's poetry', in *Samuel Beckett*, London: Routledge and Kegan Paul, 1976, 159–83.

11

ANNA McMULLAN

Samuel Beckett as director: the art of mastering failure

Samuel Beckett's resistance to productions of his plays which depart from the precise stage directions indicated in the texts has attracted public and critical attention through a number of legal disputes between Beckett and a director or company who has flouted the author's directions.[1] The best documented of these is JoAnne Akalaitis' production of *Endgame* in Cambridge, Massachusetts in 1984, for the American Repertory Theater. The dispute was settled out of court, but both sides presented their case in statements to the audience. Robert Brustein of the American Repertory Theatre argued that

> Like all works of theatre, productions of *Endgame* depend upon the collective contributions of directors, actors, and designers to realize them effectively, and normal rights of interpretation are essential in order to free the full energy and meaning of the play [...] Mr Beckett's agents do no service either to theatrical art or to the great artist they represent by pursuing such rigorous controls.[2]

Beckett's statement, however, insisted that

> Any production of *Endgame* which ignores my stage directions is completely unacceptable to me. My play requires an empty room and two small windows. The American Repertory Theater production which dismisses my directions is a complete parody of the play as conceived by me.[3]

I do not intend here to evaluate the respective rights of author and director, but to explore the paradox which these disputes uncover at the heart of Beckett's dramatic practice as author–director. On the one hand, the increasingly precise stage directions of Beckett's later dramatic work, as well as the decision to prosecute in individual cases, indicates a desire to exercise almost absolute control over the execution of his plays. On the other, the failure or parody of attempts to impose authorial meaning and control is a predominant feature of Beckett's drama. In *Play*, for example, the Light at first seems to control the appearance and speech of the three heads, as if

196

trying to create a coherent narrative out of their fragmented utterances, but the repetition of the text suggests that it is as trapped in the theatrical mechanism as the heads. In this essay, I intend to place Beckett's strategies as director in the context of the struggle between power and powerlessness, mastery and failure, which recurs throughout the text and texture of Beckett's plays.

The first production to bear Beckett's name as director was a staging of Robert Pinget's *L'Hypothèse* in 1965, at the Musée d'Art Moderne in Paris.[4] This was the only time Beckett directed a play which he had not written, and he became director as a result of having been taken by Robert Pinget to an early stage of rehearsals with the actor Pierre Chabert. This production was then repeated the next year in a Beckett–Pinget–Ionesco bill, for which Beckett also directed *Va et vient* (*Come and go*). From 1966 to 1984, Beckett directed productions of his major plays in London, Paris and Berlin, using scripts and making notes in English, French and German.

However, Beckett had been involved in the production of his own plays right from the world première of *En attendant Godot* (*Waiting for Godot*) at the Théâtre de Babylone in Paris in 1953, directed by Roger Blin. Blin consulted Beckett during rehearsals, and Beckett's prompt-script from this production indicates textual changes and notes on staging.[5] While Beckett's role in this first *Godot* was more one of approving Blin's staging than initiating decisions concerning the *mise-en-scène*, available documentation indicates that Beckett had quite precise ideas for the style of performance he wanted for the play; many of the notes and additions in Beckett's prompt-script for the original production of *En attendant Godot* are stage directions for a formalized style of acting similar to that he called for when he directed *Godot* in Berlin twenty-two years later. The principle of separation of speech and movement, a hallmark of his later direction, is instituted at the very beginning. The stage direction for Vladimir's first line, 'approaching with little steps', is marked out and replaced by specific indications of when Vladimir 'advances' between phrases throughout the text.[6]

This evidence suggests that Beckett's experience of the rehearsal process of this first production of *Godot* led him to envisage a visual system of patterns complementing or counterpointing the themes and patterns of the text: an approach that he developed in his later productions. In relation to the 1975 Schiller Theater production of *Godot*, Walter Asmus reports that Beckett wanted to 'give confusion a shape through visual repetition of themes. Not only themes in the dialogue, but also visual themes of the body'.[7] Beckett's production notebook for this Schiller Theater *Godot* describes the patterns of the characters' movements. Estragon and Vladimir constantly separate and come together 'in alternating images of union and separation, stasis and activity'.[8] He also devised a pattern of arcs and chords, incomplete circles which suggest that 'although this world is circular and repetitious, it is also divided and incomplete'.[9]

In Beckett's later work, this attention to precise patterning of movement is incorporated into the text:

> In 1962 he had told Jean Reavey that with *Godot* and partially with *Fin de partie* he had just written dialogue without seeing the stage movement in strict detail. In the later plays he had been aware of every movement of the actors even before he wrote the dialogue, and he knew which direction his actors would face before they spoke because what he made them say depended upon it.[10]

In *Footfalls*, for example, the number of steps paced by May, the pattern of her pacing, and the moments in the text when she moves or when she is still, are prescribed by the stage directions, and are referred to in the text:

> v: But let us watch her move in silence. [*May paces. Towards end of second length.*] Watch how feat she wheels. [*M. turns, paces. Synchronous with steps third length.*] Seven, eight, nine, wheel.   (CSPL, 241)

Beckett's control of direction could ensure that this tight rhythmic structure was realized in performance.

The later plays also incorporate the separation between speech and movement, which became a major principle of Beckett's directorial practice. May is still as she speaks, and only paces in silence, or during the Voice's monologue. Indeed, Beckett's director's notebook for *Footfalls*[11] also emphasizes the sounds of May's performance, including May's turns, her trailing wrap, and her footfalls. There seems to be an explicit focus on the relationship or opposition between the verbal text and the non-verbal elements or patterns of performance.

The tension between meaning and pattern or performance emerges as a major preoccupation in the textual stages of the later plays. The stages of composition of the plays (which can be traced through the available manuscript sequences) reveal a process whereby meaning becomes increasingly suggestive and open, while the text is shaped into ever more precise semantic and sonorous patterns. The emphasis on rhythm and pattern has led some critics to describe the structure of Beckett's plays as musical. In his study of the manuscripts of the drama S. E. Gontarski argues that Beckett 'moves the drama closer to the spirit of music and away from its mimetic, referential level'.[12] Beckett encouraged such an approach when he remarked to Charles Marowitz that 'Producers don't seem to have any sense of form in movement. The kind of form one finds in music, for instance, where themes keep recurring.'[13]

However, these references to music fail to take account of the agonistic relationship between music and meaning in Beckett's drama. Alvin Epstein, who has acted in numerous American productions of Beckett's work, insists that 'No matter how abstract and disconnected you want to keep yourself from the meaning of the text, it still has meaning; it's not notes in music, where you can keep your distance. These are specific words, they say things, they have referential meaning.'[14] The characters, too, are constantly struggling with the meaning of their words. Indeed, failed authorship is at the centre of Beckett's approach to character, as his dramatic creatures attempt to tell 'how it was', to author a life or at least a story (never mind a 'character' in the traditional dramatic sense). Most of the plays from *Endgame* on focus on the telling of a life-story (though the distinction between history and fiction is subverted), resulting in a dramatic form which relies heavily on monologue. However, these narratives are disrupted and fragmented in the process of performance. This can be seen through the compositional process of *Play* and *That time*, where, in both cases, any narrative structure is countered by the fragmentation and re-ordering of the text into an abstract pattern for three voices. In *Footfalls*, the attempts to describe the life or absence of life of a shadowy figure in grey tatters, whether May or her own textual creation, Amy, is juxtaposed with the repetitive motion of the footfalls. The juxtaposition of meaning and pattern is therefore a major concern of Beckett the author (evident already in *Godot*, and intensified in the later plays), and one whose realization in performance Beckett as director was able to supervise in precise detail.

Beckett's separation of speech and movement creates what Karen Laughlin describes as 'a tension between the supposedly off-stage world evoked in the Speaker's narrative and the on-stage world visible to the audience'.[15] Laughlin goes on to argue that Beckett's theatre therefore sets up an opposition between the concept, what is imagined or interpreted, and the percept: 'Our Western philosophical tradition has tended to value the concept much more highly than the percept or sensation. Beckett's theatre appears to work against this valuation [...] Beckett's theatre inundates us with percepts.'[16]

Beckett's objections to certain productions of his work seem to be rooted in their disregard for his intense focus on the mechanics of conceptualization and perception. The minimalism of his dramatic material forces the audience to concentrate intently on the few perceptual elements offered. The creation of a more elaborate set tends to disrupt the perceptual intensity of the performance and overload it with 'concepts'. Cobi Bordewijk notes that '[Beckett] did not like the Dublin production [of *Godot*] of 1955 because of its back cloths in black, green and brown, suggesting the Irish bogland and the gloomy sky. Neither did he like the London production by Peter Hall with its cluttered stage and pauses which were not long enough and which were, to make matters worse, filled with heavenly music. He was against Svoboda's Salzburg production of 1970 with its baroque set implying bourgeois decadence.'[17]

Indeed, Beckett's theatre focuses on a dialectic between formal structure and interpretation, establishing a dynamic tensional relation between the two. His remarks on form in an interview in 1956 are particularly relevant to his dramatic work as author and as director:

> In my work, there is consternation behind the form, not in the form [...] the form and the chaos remain separate. The latter is not reduced to the former. That is why the form itself becomes a preoccupation, because it exists as a problem separate from the material it accommodates.[18]

Beckett's concern with form as author and as director can be related to his preoccupation with a crisis of knowledge in post-Renaissance epistemological history. During rehearsals of the 1975 Berlin *Godot* Beckett raised this issue with Michael Haerdter, who later recorded Beckett's views in a rehearsal diary:

> The crisis started with the end of the seventeenth century, after Galileo. The eighteenth century has been called the century of reason [...] I've never understood that: they're all mad! [...] They give reason a responsibility which it simply can't bear, it's too weak. The Encyclopedists wanted to know everything ... But that direct relation between the self and – as the Italians say – *lo scibile*, the knowable, was already broken ... Leonardo da Vinci still had everything in his head, still knew everything. But now! ... Now it's no longer possible to know everything, the tie between the self and things no longer exists ... one must make a world of one's own in order to satisfy one's need to know, to understand, one's need for order.[19]

Analyses of the Enlightenment project have revealed its association of knowledge with the rise of modern science, and the will to control and dominate nature, woman and truth:

> The dominating attitude toward both nature and women [...] is a product not of the inherent nature of men, but, rather, of Enlightenment thought and the rise of modern science [...] Paving the way for the appearance of the mechanical conception of nature was a change in the organic conception of nature that occurred in the early modern era: the disorderly side of mother nature began to be emphasized over her nurturing side. The emphasis on disorderliness carried with it the desire on the part of men to tame that disorder, to control nature.[20]

Beckett's relation to this legacy is ambiguous, as his authorial and directorial practice suggests. While exposing and parodying the will to domination and control through such figures as Pozzo, Hamm or the Director in *Catastrophe*, his own dramatic aesthetic relies on the extremely disciplined control of the body of the actor, and the establishment of a tight rhythmic order or pattern to which both the technical and the human resources of the theatre are subject. Beckett's aesthetic therefore exposes and parodies the continuing conceptual constraints of the dualisms which the Enlightenment project relied upon: in particular, the opposition between power and powerlessness, and between form and chaos. According to this epistemology, truth, knowledge and personhood are dependent upon a will to discipline, abstraction and authority. All areas of mystery and the unknown are relegated to areas beyond the laws and codes of dominant models of knowledge and representation, and can only be referred to in terms of absence and lack. In order to present powerlessness, and indeed to give it a shape, Beckett recreates a framework of entrapment or authority, however much he proceeds to parody or erode it.

Beckett's drama focuses on the sense of a universe controlled by mechanistic laws, imposed by the author–director: ' ... one must make a world of one's own in order to satisfy one's need to know, to understand, one's need for order [...] There for me, lies the value of the theatre. One turns out a small world with its own laws, conducts the action as if upon a chessboard ... Yes, even the game of chess is still too complex.'[21] On the other hand, his drama also evokes undefined spaces which escape or are excluded from the laws of the dramatic world – the area beyond the shelter in *Endgame*, for example. In all of the later plays, the illuminated acting area, where every movement of the actor is choreographed with the text, is juxtaposed with an area of darkness impossible to comprehend intellectually or perceptually. Beckett therefore establishes a central tension between the need to control through knowledge and perception, and the foregrounding of the limits of that control.

In particular, the narrowing down or minimalism of Beckett's *mises-en-scène* encourages an intense concentration on whatever signs are given, heightened by the speed or incoherence of some of the spoken texts and the lack of definition of the visual image. The play of mastery and failure is enacted both onstage and between stage and audience, as the audience attempt but fail to perceive and make sense of the stage world.

The reduction of the *mise-en-scène* in the later plays virtually to the body or head/lips and voice of the performer draws attention to the formal symmetry of the movement, where there is any, to the technological framework which the performer works within (the fade-ups and fade-outs of the light, and the sound of the chime in *Footfalls* for example), and to the discipline and discomfort endured by characters and actors to produce it. The body, or its absence, becomes a major focus of Beckett's dramaturgical and directorial practice: in particular, the body's ambiguous position at the intersection of concept, percept and performance.

Accounts of Beckett's procedure as a director emphasize that he never approached work with the actors through discussion of character or motivation. The emphasis was almost entirely on the shape, position and movement of the body and on the sound, rhythm or inflection of the voice. Kalb notes that Beckett encouraged performances which 'develop, as it were, backwards – beginning with external physical techniques and working inward toward psychological centres'.[22] Interviews with actors and actresses always stress the discipline required of the Beckettian actor. Brenda Bynum, interviewed by Lois Overbeck, describes her experience: 'Beckett puts you in a strait jacket as he does with the text. He makes your body and your senses cut off; whether it's your legs or eyes, physically he takes things away from you and puts you in an impossible situation and yet you must go on [. . .] The rules give you the freedom. In the most restricted circumstance, if you accept those restrictions, it is like a world in a grain of sand.'[23] The actress who has been most closely associated with Beckett's drama, Billie Whitelaw, has similar convictions:

> By the time you've gone through the process of learning [the text], which is no mean feat, of getting the words out so they're articulate, so that all the notes and 't's and vowel sounds are actually there, you don't have to do anything because he's done it. Something weird and extraordinary does happen, as long as you the actor don't get in the way. But in order not to get in the way, you have to be incredibly disciplined.[24]

Wladimir Krysinski argues that in theatre which privileges text and psychology, a theatre of communications, 'it is the word or the dramatic situation which conveys and constitutes the body'.[25] In more experimental forms of theatre, however, the body itself becomes a sign, as in Mime, where 'the primacy of the body, as machine and as technique, is the prime referent in the structure of manifestation, which is the prime function of the performance [. . .] In the evolutionary context of modern theatre, the body would seem to be situated at the intersection of mimesis and pure performative manifestation.'[26]

In Beckett's drama, while the body may be semantically invested through the narrative, the *mise-en-scène* often contradicts the textual narrativizing of the body, as in *That time* or *Not I*, where the body described in motion or in stasis in the text is conspicuously absent on stage. In *Rockaby* and *Ohio impromptu* the relation between the narrated body and the body on stage is the major focus of the ambiguous endings of both plays. In *Ohio impromptu* the figures in the text are described as '*Buried in who knows what profounds of mind. Of mindlessness*', yet the figures on stage raise their heads and gaze into each other's eyes. In *Rockaby*, the description of the mother's body in the text prefigures the final image of the old woman on stage:

in her best black
head fallen
and the rocker rocking   (*CSPL*, 280)

Yet we are also aware that what we are watching on stage is only a representation of death, or possibly a rehearsal. The dynamic relation between text and performance, between the 'eye of the mind' and that of the flesh challenges both the authority of the narrative and the knowledge gained through visual perception, by playing each against the other.

Beckett's interest in perception and particularly the mechanics of vision as a form of control, can be seen in the television plays (and in *Film*), where the camera relentlessly interrogates and holds the protagonist in frame. In Foucault's analysis of prisons, the observation and spatial manipulation of inmates in order to ensure greater visibility are major techniques in the exercise of power: 'the techniques that make it possible to see induce effects of power and [...] conversely, the means of coercion make those on whom they are applied, clearly visible'.[27]

However, perception is also distorted by technology in the television plays, notably in Beckett's adaptation of his last stage play *What where* for television, where the bodies of the players become shadowy images on the synthetic screen, poised between being and nothingness. In the stage plays he specifies dim lighting, or presents the body (or body parts) in motion, as in *Not I*, *Footfalls*, or *Rockaby*. The performer's body is therefore at the intersection of resistance and subjection of the will to authority and control which Beckett both parodies and enacts.

One of Beckett's late stage plays, *Catastrophe*, explicitly dramatizes the relations of authority within the processes of theatre, focusing on the relation between the Director and the performer's body. *Catastrophe* presents the figures of a Director, an Assistant and a Protagonist, with an offstage lighting technician, Luke. The play's action consists of a rehearsal of the spectacle of 'catastrophe' being prepared by the Director. The Director is presented unambiguously as an authoritarian figure, both within the theatre and beyond it – he leaves the rehearsal in order to attend a 'caucus'. The play is dedicated to Vaclav Havel, at the time imprisoned for his subversive writings. At the opposite pole, the (apparently) powerless victim is the

Protagonist. Placed on a plinth, his body is manipulated into an image by the Director, his Assistant, and the technician, Luke. As various critics have noted, this hierarchical paradigm of power relations admits of a plurality of readings.[28] However, the play focuses more on the framework of power and on the body within the frame, than on the interpretations it is capable of producing.

In its attention to the manipulation of the performer's body, *Catastrophe* is particularly self-reflexive, recalling other suffering images from Beckett's dramatic canon. The detailed control over the Protagonist's pose recalls the discipline to which Beckett subjects his actors and actresses, and the physical discomfort they endure in the process of rehearsal and performance. The manipulation of the technical resources of lighting recalls Beckett's own strategies as director, in particular, the focusing in of the spotlight on the mouth, head or body of the actor, as in *Not I*, *That time* and *Rockaby*.

The body of the Protagonist is wholly at the disposal of the Director and the Assistant; it is shaped, manipulated, whitened, and appropriated by the Director in order to realize his aesthetic/political aim – the displaying of this subjected body (the emphasis is again on the spectacle of the Protagonist's body, rather than on the intended interpretation by the fictional audience). The Protagonist has apparently no role to play except that of offering his body as dramatic material – his subjectivity is taken so little account of that a gag is considered unnecessary. The body becomes wholly exteriorized, divorced from the subjectivity 'within', which, utterly powerless, is denied representation. The whitening of the Protagonist's flesh emphasizes a process of denaturalization that also occurs in most of Beckett's later plays (e.g. *Footfalls*, *A piece of monologue*). This reinforces an Enlightenment view of nature as mechanistic; the body is not a mystery or a source of pleasure, but an object operating according to certain laws, which can therefore be subdued and controlled for economic/administrative/aesthetic use:

> the historical moment of the disciplines was the moment when an art of the human body was born [...] What was then being formed was a policy of the coercions that act upon the body, a calculated manipulation of its elements, its gestures, its behaviour. The human body was entering a machinery of power that explores it, breaks it down, and rearranges it.[29]

In *Catastrophe*, Beckett focuses particularly on the nature of spectacle as a form of subjection. This foregrounds the role of the audience in the play. We are aware of the potential and actual presence of spectators from the opening moments:

D: Why the plinth?
A: To let the stalls see the feet. (*CSPL*, 297)

The audience are manipulated by the Director into a position of consuming the image of the Protagonist, and therefore collaborate in his subjection. This seems to be an indictment of the audience as predator – consuming the spectacle of catastrophe for their entertainment, edification or aesthetic appreciation. The idea is reinforced as the taped applause at the end of the play provides the audience with a reflection (albeit an aural one) of their role as it has been constructed by the Director. The mechanics of spectacle therefore places the audience in confrontation with the Protagonist, even though the actual audience are likely to resist that role as it has been exposed to them, and position themselves in sympathy with the Protagonist.

Indeed, at the end of the play, a surprising reversal takes place.[30] As the recorded applause plays, the actor slowly raises his head and stills the audience's applause, overpowering their gaze by his own powerless one. In the end therefore, he asserts his subjectivity and his very powerlessness is seen as the source of his power – an authority of a very different order from that of the Director.

As in Beckett's own plays, the confinements and constraints placed on the actor produce the intense concentration which has become the hallmark of the best known Beckett actors, and particularly those who worked with Beckett. Powerlessness leads to a mastery closer to the mystics – more mastery of self than mastery over others (although the dignity of the Protagonist's gesture has the power to subdue the audience without physical coercion). It is the disempowerment of Beckett's protagonists, removed from the sphere of active engagement in the world, which guarantees their integrity. If on one level *Catastrophe* is an ironic portrayal of the discipline of theatrical production, and perhaps even Beckett's own practices as director, it is also a defence of the play/writer/actor who, due to his/her subjection to (and therefore non-exercise of) political or actantial power, has access to an inner force, which, within the moral order of the play, wins out. Ironically, however, and *Catastrophe* focuses precisely on this paradox, the privileging of transcendence as the highest moral state, as 'the mark of true humanity',[31] is rooted in the privileging of discipline, abstraction and mastery over the material elements of existence, which is also the foundation of the exercise of power which subjects the Protagonist in the first place.

This paradox also produces the characteristic quality of Beckett performers – the dual focus on discipline and 'human depth'. Irena Jun refers to the requirements of 'maximum concentration and absolute control of one's body and voice. Rehearsing and playing Beckett gives an actor the opportunity to master his own body and turn it into a perfect instrument'.[32] Through this process of discipline, the actor conveys Beckett's 'profound and deeply human message'. Brenda Bynum suggests: 'Yes, the visual images are overwhelming [. . .] absolute purity, not a syllable that wasn't essential. It seemed almost mathematical, a certain number of required syllables. Yet the emotions are in the spaces between.'[33]

The musical pattern of Beckett's drama therefore operates as both restraint and release. It subjects the body upon which it is imposed, yet it releases or articulates a poetics of impotence. However, *Catastrophe* emphasizes that the instrument of that music is the human body, and the process of producing it is painfully physical. Although the performer is 'obliterated' in Beckett's plays, especially as directed by him, the traces and trials of that obliteration show through in performance.

It is Beckett's paradoxical relationship to notions of authority and failure which underlies his most characteristic strategies as director, in particular, his use of the most rigorous systems of theatrical and juridical authority in order to safeguard his carefully crafted patterns of failure.

NOTES

1 Beckett's resistance to productions of *Waiting for Godot* with which he dis-agreed is discussed in Cobi Bordewijk's article, 'The integrity of the playtext: disputed performances of *Waiting for Godot*'. The article considers George Tabori's production of the play for the Münchener Kammerspiele in 1978, and gives details of Beckett's unsuccessful attempt to sue the production of *Waiting for Godot* with an all-female cast by De Haarlemse Toneelschuur, a theatre in the city of Haarlem, in 1988. Jonathan Kalb also discusses controversial pro-ductions of Beckett's plays in chapter 5 ('Underground staging in perspective'), in *Beckett in performance*.
2 Kalb, *Beckett in performance*, 79.
3 Ibid., 79.
4 See Ruby Cohn, 'Beckett directs', in *Just Play*, for more details.
5 See Dougald McMillan and Martha Fehsenfeld, *Beckett in the theatre*, chapter two ('*Waiting for Godot*'), for details of this production and Beckett's prompt-script, as well as Beckett's production notebooks for later productions of *Godot*, *Endgame* and *Krapp's last tape*.
6 Ibid., 79.
7 Ibid., 139.
8 Ibid., 177.
9 Ibid., 103.
10 Ibid., 90–1.

11 This notebook is held in the Beckett International Foundation in the University of Reading Library, MS 1976.
12 S. E. Gontarski, *The intent of 'Undoing'*, 184.
13 *Encore* 9, March–April, (1962), 44, quoted in *Beckett in the theatre*, 16.
14 Kalb, *Beckett in performance*, 194.
15 Karen Laughlin, 'Seeing is perceiving', 24.
16 Ibid., 27.
17 Cobi Bordewijk, 'The integrity of the playtext', 145.
18 McMillan and Fehsenfeld, *Beckett in the theatre*, 14.
19 Michael Haerdter, '*Endgame*: a rehearsal diary', in *Beckett in the theatre*, 231.
20 Susan J. Hekman, *Gender and knowledge*, 113–14.
21 McMillan and Fehsenfeld, *Beckett in the theatre*, 231.
22 Kalb, *Beckett in performance*, 39.
23 In Linda Ben-Zvi (ed.), *Women in Beckett*, 53.
24 Kalb, *Beckett in performance*, 238.
25 Wladimir Krysinski, 'Semiotic modalities of the body in modern theatre', 26.
26 Ibid., 149–50.
27 Michel Foucault, *Discipline and punish*, 170–1.
28 See for example Antoni Libera's allegorical reading in 'Beckett's *Catastrophe*', *Modern Drama*, 28.3 (1985), 341–7, and Robert Santag's 'A political perspective on *Catastrophe*' in Robin J. Davis and Lance St John Butler (eds.), '*Make sense who may*' (Gerrards Cross: Colin Smythe, 1988), 137–44.
29 Foucault, *Discipline and punish*, 137–8.
30 This underlines another meaning of the title catastrophe as a 'sudden reversal'.
31 Hekman, *Gender and power*, 74.
32 Ben-Zvi (ed.), *Women in Beckett*, 48.
33 Ibid., 52.

RECOMMENDED READING

Abbott, H. Porter, 'Tyranny and theatricality: the example of Samuel Beckett', *Theatre Journal*, 40 (March 1988), 77–87.

Ben-Zvi, Linda (ed.), *Women in Beckett: performance and critical perspectives*, Urbana: University of Illinois Press, 1990.

Bordewijk, Cobi, 'The integrity of the playtext: disputed performances of *Waiting for Godot*', in *Samuel Beckett today/Samuel Beckett aujourd'hui*, vol. 1: *Samuel Beckett 1970–1989*, Rodopi, Amsterdam–Atlanta, (1992), 143–53.

Chabert, Pierre, 'Beckett as director', *Gambit*, 28 (1976), 41–64.
'The body in Beckett's theatre', *Journal of Beckett Studies*, 8 (Autumn 1982), 23–8.

Cohn, Ruby, *Just Play: Beckett's theater*, Princeton University Press, 1980, chapter 12.

Feinberg-Jütte, Anat, '"The task is not to reproduce the external form, but to find the subtext": George Tabori's productions of Samuel Beckett's texts', *Journal of Beckett Studies* (n.s.) 1/2, (1992), 95–115.

Foucault, Michel, *Discipline and punish: the birth of the prisons*, trans. Alan Sheridan, London: Penguin, 1977.

Gontarski, S. E., *The intent of 'Undoing' in Samuel Beckett's dramatic texts*, Bloomington: Indiana University Press, 1985.

Hekman, Susan, *Gender and knowledge: elements of a postmodern feminism*, Cambridge: Polity Press, 1990.

Kalb, Jonathan, *Beckett in performance*, Cambridge University Press, 1989.

Krysinski, Wladimir, 'Semiotic modalities of the body in modern theatre', *Poetics Today*, 2.3 (1981), 141–61.

Laughlin, Karen, 'Seeing is perceiving: Beckett's later plays and the theory of audience response', in Robin J. Davis and Lance St John Butler (eds.), '*Make sense who may*', Gerrards Cross: Colin Smythe, 1988, 20–9.

McMillan, Dougald and Martha Fehsenfeld, *Beckett in the theatre*, London: John Calder, 1988.

12

ANN BEER

Beckett's bilingualism

'Heavenly father, the creature was bilingual!' (*MPTK*, 182). So exclaimed
Belacqua, in Beckett's first collection of stories. The throwaway remark,
directed towards a briefly appearing Scottish nurse, seems at first glance
unimportant. Yet it stands as a prophetic exclamation about the creature's
creator, Beckett himself. It also marks the only time in more than sixty years
of publication that the word 'bilingual' appears in his writing. The creature
was bilingual, like Belacqua, who dreamed in French, and Beckett made
them so. Bilingualism does much to distinguish this most distinct of artists.
To have two tongues, two modes of speech, two ways of responding to the
world, is to be necessarily outside the security of a unified single viewpoint.
The more bilingual he became, the less he spoke or wrote of it openly; the
less he drew attention to it, the more it shaped his mature vision. Far from
being a mere curiosity, bilingualism works at the heart of Beckett's aesthetic
activity, releasing waves of innovative energy decade after decade.

The casual reader could be forgiven, however, for missing Beckett's
bilingualism entirely. His texts, published in English and French, often bear
only the most discreet of labels: 'translated by the author/traduit par
l'auteur', when they are the second, not original, version. In the theatre,
translation details may not be provided at all. Moreover, Beckett, by accident or design, found himself in his maturity writing texts that he *knew*
would have to be self-translated. As a result, a sense of double existence
began to be inherent even in the first of the two versions. So successfully did
he create these linguistic twins that readers and audiences in either language
can move from work to work, from *Fin de partie (Endgame)* to *Happy days
(Oh les beaux jours)*, or from *Company (Compagnie)* to *Mal vu mal dit (Ill
seen ill said)* without the slightest awareness that in each pair one is an
original in their own language, the other a translation.

Stranger, though, is the extent to which many Beckett critics, at least until
the late 1980s, have written as though Beckett 'belongs' in their own language. Even the most careful of interpreters sometimes fail to mention that

the works they discuss came into being in the context of another culture. Yet many of these interpreters are highly conscious of issues of language in Beckett's work – philosophical, linguistic, psychological, aesthetic. Clearly their confidence rests on the secure knowledge that Beckett himself is the author of what they read, that in some sense these 'authored' versions are not translations at all. Such commentators have made a leap of faith, judgment or necessity, that has curious consequences both for the reading(s) of Beckett now possible, and for broader issues of theoretical debate. Major publications of the late 1980s on Beckett's bilingualism, such as *Beckett and Babel* and the first part of *Beckett Translating/Translating Beckett*, show how central to Beckett criticism this once marginalized characteristic of his work has become. It can be welcomed, now, into a new climate of ideas, through theoretical perspectives that celebrate internationalism, the subverting of certainties and the breaking of canonical traditions.

The pages that follow provide one brief view of the centrality and complexity of Beckett's bilingualism. Exploring its development demands some concentration on Beckett's earlier decades as an artist, since this is where the impulse towards bilingualism must be found. Such a focus suggests that bilingualism functioned as a medium for artistic self-renewal, was driven by both aesthetic and personal need, and allowed Beckett, even after his fame was established, a kind of privacy. His bilingual activity provokes questions for any serious reader. What view of the author emerges? What is the status of the doubled Beckett text? Do the works themselves insist on a certain kind of implied reader, to use Wolfgang Iser's term, and is that reader bilingual? As Beckett passes into literary history, his admirers may wonder where, if anywhere, this Parisian Irishman and his work belong.

The earliest roots of Beckett's bilingualism can be seen in the context of his linguistically divided homeland. Language has for many centuries been an issue in Ireland, especially in the context of nationalist struggle; it could not be taken for granted as it could in the other two countries where Beckett lived, England and France. As a privileged Dublin Protestant, Beckett was born into an English-speaking élite whose social dominance seemed secure but was soon to be threatened. In the years of unrest, the ancient Celtic tongue could be felt as both a symbolic and a real presence. Irish had the effect of making English visible *as* a language.

Decades later, in his radio play *All that fall*, Beckett would gently mock what had come of the Irish language movement. Dan Rooney discusses the Irish for 'the men's' at the station: 'Fir as they call it now, from Vir Viris I suppose, the V becoming F, in accordance with Grimm's Law' (*CSPL*, 35). It is a 'Grimm' law indeed that condemns some languages to inevitable decline. In the same play Beckett portrays that cultural oddity, the Church of Ireland Dubliner, with the Rooneys and the strange Miss Fitt. Misfits they are, in a country whose history and dominant religion have led in quite a different direction.

Never drawn to Celtic Ireland,[1] and repelled by what he saw as the Catholic church's repressive tendencies, Beckett was the offspring of a family for whom French was the obvious first foreign language, a civilizing European tongue. But for Beckett it quickly became far more, so that during his years as a student at Trinity College, he developed exceptional abilities as a French scholar. A cycling tour in the Loire in 1926, and then two years as Lecturer at the Ecole Normale Supérieure in Paris (1928–30), were enough to confirm the love-affair with a language that lasted throughout Beckett's life. In both critical and imaginative writing, he seemed to grasp that the 'old ego', both 'minister of dullness' and 'agent of security' (*PTD*, 21), could be left behind, and the new ego welcomed, through the shifts of consciousness and expression that an acquired language made possible. His major effort to become an academic, the critical monograph *Proust* from which these telling phrases come, can be seen as a catalyst of crucial importance. It catapulted him *into* the other language, at least for a preliminary skirmish, in the hilarious and slightly mawkish critique-cum-narrative *Le concentrisme*. Phrases from *Proust* reappear there hardly modified, and Marcel Proust's own style is blatantly parodied. For *Proust*'s 'an art that is perfectly intelligible and perfectly inexplicable' (*PTD*, 92), *Le concentrisme* has: 'cet art qui, semblable à une résolution de Mozart, est parfaitement intelligible et parfaitement inexplicable' (*D*, 42). For *Proust*'s 'Swann is the cornerstone of the entire structure' (*PTD*, 34), *Le concentrisme* had '"Le concierge", a-t-il écrit dans un de ses cahiers, "est la pierre angulaire de mon édifice entier"' (*D*, 36). The verbal links are almost exact but the mood has changed dramatically; the genre is narrative, not critical analysis, and the mood one of comedy.

Dream of fair to middling women, Beckett's long-unpublished novel, and *More pricks than kicks* reveal only too clearly the youthful writer's fascination with French. At one point in *Dream* the text actually switches into French, to quote a letter describing a homosexual encounter between two of Belacqua's Parisian friends (*Dream*, 19–22). There are innumerable references to French writers, and French stands as the path of bohemian freedom, good taste and new possibilities of expression. In one passage of *Dream* Beckett writes of his delight in verbal 'sparkles' or 'margaritas' that arise out of the 'ashes' or 'ready-made' aspects of style. He goes on:

> The writing of, say, Racine or Malherbe, perpendicular, diamanté, is pitted, is it not, and sprigged with sparkles; the flints and pebbles are there, no end of

humble tags and commonplaces [. . .] they give you the phrase, the sparkle, the precious margaret. Perhaps only the French can do it. Perhaps only the French language can give you the thing you want. *(Dream,* 48)

There is a somewhat precious quality to these lines, yet they reveal both Beckett's eagerness to assess this language of personal adoption, and his fascination with its literary possibilities. 'Perhaps only the French language can give *you* the thing *you* want' (my emphasis) is a telling phrase: personal need, as a writer, is the motivating force.

There can be no doubt, however, that in the 1930s Beckett's immediate literary ambitions continued to be in English publishing. His French, though good, was not at a level for serious invention. *Murphy,* occasional short stories, and the doomed playscript *Human wishes* all show Beckett seeking an audience in his dominant and mother tongue. His explanation for the failure of *Human wishes* is illuminating: frustrations with language caused its abandonment.[2] Equally revealing is his comment to Axel Kaun, a German correspondent, in a letter written in German. Discussing the possible success of a translation, Beckett said:

In dieser Beziehung aber bin ich vollkommen unfähig, ein Urteil zu fällen, da mir die Reaktionen des kleinen wie des grossen Publikums immer rätselhafter werden, und, was noch schlimmer ist, von weniger Bedeutung. *(D,* 51)

But in this respect I am totally incapable of arriving at a judgement, as the reactions of the small as well as the large public are becoming more and more enigmatic to me, and, what is worse, of less significance.

(D, 171, trans. Martin Esslin)

Frustration with the English literary community comes through this letter with force: Beckett neither understands it, nor cares very much that he does not. Meanwhile *Murphy* was greeted with widespread rejection before finally being published in 1938, and did not receive much attention even then. This experience presumably confirmed the restless writer's feeling that some link between speaker and audience was missing or distorted; his inner world and the taste and language of the larger world were simply not in tune.

Through a series of curious blocks and turns, bilingualism, the result of a scholarly obsession with French, and then of long visits to Paris, became a ticket to a full life in that other culture. Beckett's permanent move to Paris in 1937 marked the beginning of fifty-two years based mainly in that city or in the Marne countryside nearby – a much longer period than he spent in Ireland. The strength of Beckett's loyalty to his new community can be shown by several changes: he began to write poems and art criticism in French; with the encouragement of his friend Alfred Péron he began to translate *Murphy*; and most revealingly, he preferred to stay in Paris at the outbreak of war even when, as an Irish neutral, he could have gone 'home' to safety.

Written in English, but in France and in exceptionally dangerous circumstances between 1941 and 1945, *Watt* marks a point of extreme bilingual tension in Beckett's writing. It begins an exploration of English which continues, hidden and exposed, right through to *Worstward Ho*. Full of language games, puzzles, inversions and puns, sequences and lists, *Watt* has an almost mad comic energy. As the manuscript shows, Beckett had, by the latter stages of the novel, begun to think in French about his own work; his marginal comments are written in that language beside the English text.[3]

The liberation of France from foreign dominance and the liberation of Beckett's own imagination seem to have happened together, and in French. Immediately after the war, Beckett's writing was indeed like a 'flood' of French; he produced four novellas, four novels, two plays, four critical articles and seven poems within six years. He was also doing occasional commercial translation between his two languages in order to survive. As if symbolically, the central character of *Watt* makes a brief reappearance in the next work of long fiction, *Mercier et Camier*, having passed from English to French. For six years English, as a language of literary production, lies hidden like the dark side of the moon, its presence concealed in veils of metalinguistic reference.

Many of Beckett's protagonists at this period are both verbally adept and yet nervous, linguistically on edge, culminating in that extraordinary outpouring of language-consciousness, *L'Innommable/The Unnamable*. From almost any page, the sense of a doubled or alienated language springs forth with a kind of terror:

> Jamais que moi, qu'une parcelle de moi, reprise, perdue, manquée, des mots, je suis tous ces mots, tous ces étrangers, cette poussière de verbe [...][4]

> nothing ever but me, a particle of me, retrieved, lost, gone astray, I'm all these words, all these strangers, this dust of words [...]   (*T*, 354)

The dissociating from a stable identity and the flood of language have come together in a vortex: 'I'm all these words, all these strangers.'

During this period, though, a move back towards English became inevitable, given the relentless advance of Beckett's fame after the staging of *En attendant Godot*. The English-speaking audience that had eluded him in the 1930s was coming into existence. He began to experiment with collaborative translation into English. Richard Seaver, Patrick Bowles and others have described Beckett's meticulousness during these activities; he soon decided that collaboration did not decrease but added to the difficulties self-translation raised. With very few exceptions, he committed himself to completing all later self-translating without assistance.

In the early 1950s he began to write in English again, but in *From an abandoned work*, as the title suggests, saw the attempt as premature. Yet *From an abandoned work* revels in its linguistic medium. Its narrator exclaims, of a German word, 'Schimmel, nice word, for an English speaker!' (*CSP*, 130), savouring phonetic pleasure like Krapp with his 'Spool' four years later (*CSPL*, 56). The speaker also explains that he has a mind 'always on the alert against itself' (*CSP*, 131), and sums up: 'awful English this' (*CSP*, 137). He could hardly be more frank in sharing with readers the sense of surprise at the qualities of the mother tongue.

From the 1950s, the links between writing, self-translation and directing in the two languages became increasingly significant. Anyone interested in the genesis of Beckett's works needs to consider not only how his texts develop sequentially as originals, but also how the activity of translating an earlier text at a certain period can trigger images, ideas and forms in new works. With Beckett's gradual branching out into more and more genres and media – mime, radio, film, television – the kinds of translation and transformation become almost dizzyingly complex. The most intriguing of these cross-fertilizations include the translation of *Malone meurt* in the same year as the writing of *Fin de partie*, the writing of *Happy days* during the translating of *Comment c'est*, and the collaborative translation of *Watt* into French, after more than twenty years, at a time of intense theatre activity in 1966–8.

In the context of this linguistic to-and-fro movement, some of the issues inherent in Beckett's mature bilingualism become apparent. But the person whose special interest lies in a particular period of Beckett's work needs to be cautious about discussing what his self-translation 'proves', since, as should now be clear, his bilingualism is never static. Any generalization from one period can be misleading.

This development highlights the fact that, unlike almost all other major bilingual writers of the twentieth century, Beckett's bilingualism was entirely voluntary. He was not persecuted, for political, economic or religious reasons, as many exiled artists have been. Nor was he born into a minority language like many African and Asian writers and thus led towards the use of a dominant colonial tongue. Beckett's need for French can be seen as driven partly by aesthetic and partly by psychological needs. He made himself bilingual, and would have been a quite different artist if, like Joyce, he had continued to write in his mother tongue after moving abroad.

Beckett did provide some brief comments about his use of French. These range from the facetious 'Pour faire remarquer moi'[5] in 1948 to 'Parce qu'en français c'est plus facile d'écrire sans style.'[6] In 1956 he said that it was 'more exciting'[7] writing in French, and in 1957 that what he disliked in the English was 'a lack of brakes'.[8] Yet in the 1960s, he acknowledged English as a good theatre language because of 'its concreteness, its close relationship between thing and vocable'.[9] While illuminating something of his conscious aesthetic program at certain periods, these comments have the effect of concealing deeper reasons for a self-initiated bilingual art. Beckett's scholarly training in European literatures must be one significant element. His artistic sympathy with the contemporary scene in Paris is equally important; and it is also possible that his practical work as a linguist, studying grammar, style, language development, and the intricacies of translation, aroused a fascination with language which bilingualism allowed him to pursue. But beyond all this, Beckett's reluctance to discuss bilingualism in depth suggests that it worked at a profound level of his psyche, a level that he neither wanted to, nor perhaps could, expose.

Central to his bilingual art is a characteristic that for many other artists, including Edward Albee and Harold Pinter, helps to explain Beckett's influence on their own work: his constant ability to see artistic forms afresh. Beckett could come to the novel, the short story, the one- or two-act play with an astounding freedom. He could undo and remake them in full knowledge of a literary tradition but with the detachment of one who is not controlled by it. He renewed forms, often to vociferous protest, in ways that were previously unthinkable and have since come to seem 'natural'. *Godot* is the supreme example.

Bilingualism and biculturalism are surely central to this self-renewal. When acquired after early childhood, new languages involve a shift of focus, as Eva Hoffmann has illustrated powerfully in her memoir *Lost in translation*. Compelled to travel from Poland to Canada in 1959 because of renewed discrimination against Jews in her native country, she reacted to the shift of language with a hugely increased sense of linguistic consciousness:

> The problem is that the signifier has become severed from the signified. The words I learn now don't stand for things in the same unquestioned way they did in my native tongue. 'River' in Polish was a vital sound, energized with the essence of riverhood, of my rivers, of my being immersed in rivers. 'River' in English is cold – a word without an aura. It has no accumulated associations for me, and it does not give off the radiating haze of connotation.[10]

Initially alienated, since the exile was not of her choice, Hoffmann went on to revel in, and finally write in, this language which, for her, had been without 'accumulated associations'. Although there are, of course, many differences in their situations, Hoffmann's insight confirms what Beckett said about *his* native language. Perhaps, in the years of intense innovative activity, it had too much of that 'radiating haze of connotation' of which Eva Hoffmann speaks. Both in the works themselves and in Beckett's comments it is possible to see a powerful urge to break the hold of habit. Shifts of language are an enormous help in this enterprise. The avant-garde artist needs to be able to throw off the demands of conventional realism, needs to find a new syntax and new forms.

The discoveries of psychology allow another intriguing approach to Beckett's bilingualism, by way of personal motivation. Lawrence Graver has pointed out how feminism and psychoanalysis offer opportunities to look at Beckett in new ways; for example, by probing his childhood and later relationship with his mother as a major and yet often hidden theme in his writing.[11] An article by a psychoanalyst, Patrick Casement, raised these questions in 1982.[12] Psychological restlessness, extreme unease and a sense of separateness from the world he was born to pervade Beckett's work. In the 1920s and 1930s he was fascinated by madness and the sciences of the brain; his interest in brain research continued throughout his life. His own psychoanalysis and reading of Jungian material in London in 1934–5 may have been an influence on the crucial decision in 1937 to make Paris his home, even though he was still persevering with fiction in English. During the war, he spoke of *Watt* as a way of preserving his sanity;[13] it is also a *tour de force* of comic revenge on the Ireland he had abandoned to its peacetime neutrality. Yet, as Casement suggests, the unleashing of energy that produced the 'trilogy' and *En attendant Godot* could probably not have happened in the mother tongue – while that immensely influential mother still lived. Beckett began to attempt translations of these texts just at the period of his mother's dying. Only some years later did he return to English freely.

Where, if it is not secure in French or English, is the imaginative site to which Beckett's mature voice moves? This site is, undoubtedly, a place of great privacy. It has a monastic austerity, a feel of being deliberately apart from the anchored, detailed, material world of either culture – or any other. Slipping from world to world, the author maintains a voice that inhabits margins, thresholds and anonymous quiet spaces, often in transit or in solitude. With increasing attention to the 'vaguening'[14] of realist detail, Beckett purifies and intensifies the special space he has created, a space which, in its refined state, becomes simply human. 'L'artiste qui joue son être est de nulle part' Beckett wrote of Jack B. Yeats; 'The artist who stakes his being is from nowhere' (*D*, 148–9). Both parts of this statement are important: the risk – Beckett does not see art coming out of safety – and the lack of national, or local, identity. Bilingualism is a strikingly original way of preserving freedom and anonymity, and of resisting the assumptions and expectations of a specific culture.

To trace the development and variety of views about Beckett's bilingualism is a valuable lesson in cultural differences. For French Structuralists and Post-Structuralists, as well as some inheritors of the New Critical tradition, one central problem is the curious status of bilingualism itself. It does not appear in the individual text, and can therefore only be discussed in some larger, and extra-textual, framework that examines the author or the *œuvre* as a whole. If the author is 'dead' or a mere construct, then only textual reality is available; how does bilingualism fit within such constraints? For Brian Fitch, working within the context of French critical theory, the need to stay with close analysis of the text raises huge problems, so that he must develop a complex poetics drawing widely on philosophy and translation theory. He is almost obliged to apologize when, in a late chapter, he resorts to speculative discussions of Beckett's bilingual world:

> It is the Tower of Babel itself that furnishes the only adequate symbol for the predicament we now confront. It is as though Beckett's whole life's work, the process of its realization and indeed of its very conception, were a direct assault on the mythical tower itself and the latter had assumed the form of a windmill for this latter-day would-be Don Quixote. Such extravagant imagery, coming after the sober analyses of the preceding chapters, will perhaps come as something of a shock to my reader.[15]

Fitch, though of English birth and resident in English Canada, is a scholar in the French tradition. His emphasis is always on textual evidence itself. The American Raymond Federman speaks more freely of authorial intention and is perhaps one of those most qualified to do so, since he is himself a bilingual novelist in French and English:

> This is what it means to be a *writer as self-translator*. It means a total displacement of language from one culture to another. And yet, at the same time, especially in the case of Beckett, it means never stepping outside language. In other words, Beckett, in his bilingual work, allows us to listen to the dialogue which he entertains with himself in two languages [...].[16]

Many critics of the English-language tradition have no trouble with a 'common-sense' solution, imagining a transcendent author who has intentions, conscious or intuitive, and who is the central locus of the bilingual process. This is the approach that this essay has largely followed. Richard Fallis moves beyond the kind of dilemma of the more textually based critics when he sees Beckett as the creator of a transcendent space: his 'imaginative landscape is in some desolate place inside ourselves, neither French nor English nor Irish'.[17] So does a London reviewer, George Craig:

> Even if French speakers could read him only in French and English speakers only in English, there would still be one person inescapably aware of his double venture: Samuel Beckett. And it is a double venture, since the primary reality – that which can subsequently be translated – may be either English or French [. . .] The signs are that he is exploring a verbal no-man's-land where neither French nor English holds sway.[18]

In these comments, bilingualism leads inescapably back to the author. It becomes visible only when the reader has some sense of 'Beckett', even as a creation of the texts rather than a person of flesh and blood.

Whatever the view of the bilingual artist, the status of the double texts is indeed a conundrum, and a most unusual one. There is no doubt, for example, that Beckett's pre-1945 works were far more difficult to translate, from a referential point of view, because of their wealth of realist detail, than many of the later ones. The translation of *Murphy* is full of presumably accidental inconsistencies. The place in London called the 'Victoria Gate' at one point in the French text is also called 'la Porte Victoria' on another page.[19] 'Le Baron Fiel d'Absinthe' slips back, confusingly, into his English identity, 'Lord Gall'.[20] In *Molloy* and *Malone meurt*, on the other hand, cross-lingual jokes such as Lousse's parrot (who swears in both languages)[21] and the Englishman in the asylum[22] potentially allow for a mirroring humour in translation. Beckett does not always comply, preferring at times to change the passage altogether. He also allows himself, in the *Malone meurt*/*Malone dies* translation, a private joke. The 'Louis' family who entertain Sapo become the 'Lamberts' in translation. Together these names give *Louis Lambert*, the title of one of Balzac's novels about a young man who later goes mad. Only when the two texts are set side by side can this reference be found. Such cross-lingual connections add a special dimension to readings of Beckett; they also raise important questions about the nature and authority of a single text.

Each reader of Beckett comes to his words with a personal set of cultural and linguistic co-ordinates that may be alerted and exposed. There can be no neutral reading, nor any reading in any country or literary tradition that can claim primacy. Reader-response theory, now familiar from the work of Iser, Fish and others, shows why Beckett's work has the effect of a Rorschach test, reflecting back preoccupations and identity as each act of reading, unique and unrepeatable, takes place. Beckett creates his readers, his audience, with each text or script, working with minute levels of sensitivity in whichever language he is using. Nor does this happen only in the translations on paper; in one of his own rôles as theatre director in 1980 he carefully changed 'Connaught' to the more precise 'Kerry' for a production of *Krapp's last tape* that was to go to Ireland.

If bilingual awareness is so important, should the unilingual reader have to feel excluded from Beckett's world? Obviously, the answer is no. Only in a few countries (such as parts of eastern Canada and Cameroon) are English and French spoken by large numbers of a single community on a daily basis. Individuals and the intelligentsia of many other countries may speak both, but they are far outnumbered by readers and spectators of Beckett who do not. And, partly as a result of Beckett's own move toward elemental human themes and texts freed from much mimetic detail, he has been translated into an ever-growing number of other languages. The paradox of this most language-conscious of artists is the way his art triumphs over language-barriers altogether.

'Placing' Beckett in terms of national context is consequently an almost impossible task. He may be seen in many ways as a European, working in his late years in the era of Derrida, Foucault and Barthes. Yet he can be claimed with equal force as a master of the Irish tradition, inheritor of the mantle of Joyce, Yeats and Synge, as the successful Dublin festival in 1991 illustrated. *En attendant Godot* plays at the Comédie Française, that bastion of high French culture, while Dubliners flock to celebrate him as their own, revelling in the Irishness of his rhythms and his humour.

In his last productive years, Beckett made four quite different statements about language and languages, language and silence. In the brief, exquisite television play *Quad* he removed words altogether, removed with them any anchoring detail, even removed the definition of the players as male or female, creating a graceful ballet of silent human movement. In *Company* he wrote a text in English but revised it into French even during the writing; neither version was born independently. In *Mal vu mal dit* he used his French in a text of astounding beauty that draws deeply on the tradition of Racine and of Mallarmé. In *Worstward Ho* he explored the English language with affectionate humour; his many coined words, the stripping away of syntax, the grammatically perfect but unconventional affixations show delight in the language he had once abandoned. After so many years of self-translation, he told his English publisher and old friend John Calder that this work was 'untranslatable'.[23]

These four creative acts, all as surprising and original as anything earlier, prove Beckett's mastery of language and of form. 'Heavenly father, the creature was bilingual!', he had once written. The young man responsible for those words could hardly have suspected how loyally his languages would keep him company to the end.

NOTES

1 As is clear from 'Recent Irish poetry' and 'Hommage à Jack B. Yeats' (*D*, 70–6 and 148–9).

2 As reported by Deirdre Bair, *Samuel Beckett: a biography* (New York and London: Harcourt Brace Jovanovich, 1978), 255 and note, 673.

3 See my '*Watt*, Knott and Beckett's bilingualism', 51.

4 Beckett, *L'Innommable* (Paris: Editions de Minuit, 1953), 204.

5 'Notes about contributors', *transition 48*, 2 (June 1948), 147.

6 Niklaus Gessner, *Die Unzulänglichkeit der Sprache: eine Untersuchung über Formzufall und Beziehungslosigkeit bei Samuel Beckett* (Zurich: Junis Verlag, 1957), 32.

7 Quoted by Leonard Forster, *The poet's tongues*, 87.

8 Quoted in Clas Zilliacus, *Beckett and broadcasting: a study of the works of Samuel Beckett for and in radio and television* (Abo: Abo Akademi, 1976), 149. Cf. Beckett in a letter of 23 June 1983, quoted by Alan Astro in *Understanding Beckett* (Columbia, S.C.: University of Southern Carolina Press, 1990), 49: 'he said that in writing *Watt* language was "running away" with him'.

9 Zilliacus, 30.

10 Eva Hoffmann, *Lost in translation: a life in a new language* (New York: Penguin, 1989), 106.

11 Lawrence Graver, 'Homage to the Dark Lady: *Ill seen ill said*', in Linda Ben-Zvi (ed.), *Women in Beckett: performance and critical perspectives* (Urbana: University of Illinois Press, 1990), 148.

12 Patrick Casement, 'Samuel Beckett's relationship to his mother tongue', 33.

13 See Rubin Rabinovitz, *The development of Samuel Beckett's fiction* (Urbana: University of Illinois Press, 1984), 1 and note, 4.

14 S. E. Gontarski, *The intent of 'Undoing' in Samuel Beckett's dramatic texts* (Bloomington: Indiana University Press, 1985), 76.

15 Brian T. Fitch, *Beckett and Babel*, 180.

16 Raymond Federman, 'The writer as self-translator', 16.

17 Richard Fallis, *The Irish renaissance* (Dublin: Gill and Macmillan, 1978), 217.

18 George Craig, 'The voice of childhood and great age', *Times Literary Supplement*, 27 August 1982, 921.

19 Beckett, *Murphy* (French, first published 1947), (Paris: Editions de Minuit, 1965), 78 and 111.

20 Ibid., 75 and 198.

21 Beckett, *Molloy* (French), (Paris: Editions de Minuit, 1951), 55.

22 Beckett, *Malone meurt* (Paris: Editions de Minuit, 1951), 205.

23 Letter of 10 September 1985 from John Calder to Ann Beer. In fact, *Worstward Ho* was subsequently to be translated by Edith Fournier into French and by Erika Tophoven into German.

RECOMMMENDED READING

Adams, Robert, *Proteus, his lies, his truth: discussions of literary translation*, New York: Norton, 1973.

Beer, Ann, '*Watt*, Knott and Beckett's bilingualism', *Journal of Beckett Studies*, 10 (1985), 37–75.

'Beckett's "Autography" and the company of languages', *Southern Review*, 27.4 (Autumn 1991), 771–91.

Bowles, Patrick, Introduction to Friedrich Dürrenmatt, *The visit (Der Besuch der alten Dame)*, London: Jonathan Cape, 1962.

Casement, Patrick, 'Samuel Beckett's relationship to his mother-tongue', *International Review of Psycho-analysis*, 9 (1982), 33–44.

Cockerham, Harry, 'Bilingual playwright', in Katharine Worth (ed.), *Beckett the shape changer*, London: Routledge and Kegan Paul, 1975.

Cohn, Ruby, 'Samuel Beckett self-translator', *PMLA*, 65 (December 1961), 613–21.

Connor, Steven, *Samuel Beckett: repetition, theory and text*, Oxford: Basil Blackwell, 1988, especially chapter 5.

Federman, Raymond, 'The writer as self-translator', in Alan Warren Friedman et al. (eds.), *Beckett Translating/Translating Beckett*, University Park: Pennsylvania State University Press, 1987 .

Fitch, Brian T. *Beckett and Babel*, Toronto University Press, 1988.

Forster, Leonard, *The poet's tongues: multilingualism in literature*, New Zealand: University of Otago Press and Cambridge University Press, 1970.

Jones, A. R., 'The French *Murphy*: from rare bird to *cancre*', *Journal of Beckett Studies*, 6 (Autumn 1980), 37–50.

Kaelin, Eugene, *The unhappy consciousness: the poetic plight of Samuel Beckett*, Dordrecht, Boston and London: D. Reidel, 1981.

Mercier, Vivian, *Beckett/Beckett*, Oxford University Press, 1977.

Miller, Jane, 'Writing in a second language', *Raritan*, 2.1 (Summer 1982), 115–32.

Seaver, Richard, Introduction to '*I can't go on, I'll go on': a selection from Samuel Beckett's work*, New York: Grove Press, 1976, xxiii–xxvi.

Simpson, Ekundayo, *Samuel Beckett: traducteur de lui-même*, Quebec: International Center for Research on Bilingualism, 1978.

13

P. J. MURPHY

Beckett and the philosophers

Beckett studies, despite a phenomenal growth over the last three decades or so, has only just begun to articulate clearly and fully the essential 'differences' – in the traditional as well as more specialized meanings of the word – with which it is engaged, particularly with reference to the vexed but fundamental question of Beckett's relationship to the philosophers. Is Descartes, with or without the Baroque Rationalism of the Occasionalists Geulincx and Malebranche, critical in dealing with this issue, as the early period of criticism in English affirmed? Or is the 'Cartesian' question basically irrelevant, as is implied by those who chose to focus on Logical Positivism or Existentialism? Or are both of these approaches hopelessly *passé* in the context of Post-Structuralist critical theory? The whole question of Beckett's relationship to the philosophers is pretty obviously in need of a major critical reassessment.

In the first period of serious Beckett criticism, there was a consensus of sorts, with Martin Esslin expressing a condensed version of these views. Esslin praises Beckett for the 'purity of his approach to literature' and for 'seeking ultimate truths' which make 'his writings invaluable documents of human experience'; his works are thus 'important contributions to existential philosophical thought'.[1] But how can the 'purity of his approach to literature' (whatever that may be) be reconciled with existential experience? There simply can be no *direct* equation between Beckett's literary worlds and existential reality, when the question of their reference to our world is the very problematic to be explored. Esslin's statements epitomize a common tendency to circumvent the full implications of the problem by, at key critical junctures, identifying Beckett's characters as somehow real or human, when it is the rigorous investigation of their very status as bestowed by language that is at the heart of the Beckettian enterprise. For the writer expression necessarily precedes existence.

It is hardly surprising, then, that critics of the Post-Structural persuasion have begun to mount a serious challenge to these underlying assumptions.

Thomas Trezise has for example recently urged, against the whole ideology of existential humanism which he regards as the foundation of 'virtually the entire corpus of Beckett criticism', that this relies 'on an unexamined notion of the human subject'.[2] But this challenge is much less dramatic than it appears, since Beckett criticism, in spite of its bias towards existential humanism, has always been proto-deconstructionist in its general thrust, hence its fascination with the art of failure of Beckett's *Three dialogues*, with self-cancelling structures and, generally, with the various 'nothings' which undermine the very modes of expression. Granted, these elements were obliged to exist in an uneasy and finally unworkable alliance with phenomenology and existentialism; but this was still a potentially creative confusion for a student of Beckett able to work through its *non sequiturs*. To argue in a Derridean fashion, as Trezise proceeds to do, that the Beckettian world cannot be defined by negation as separation, 'a universe in which therefore the separation *from* exteriority precedes, founds, and conditions any and every relation *to* exteriority',[3] may have some theoretical coherence, and perhaps even a certain elegance; but then to throw the baby out with the bathwater entails some philosophical consolations – look how neat and tidy the bath is.

Any prospective student of Beckett, and particularly those interested in Beckett and philosophy, will find these approaches exposed in Iain Wright's very lucid and insightful account of Beckett and contemporary critical theory. Wright seeks a 'middle way' between the 'hyperbolic antinomies' of old-fashioned humanist readings which enshrine the author and the currently fashionable 'death of the author' school of Post-Structuralism which rejects the central philosophical notion of a constituting subject. Acknowledging that the language of the New Criticism can be very helpful, Wright nevertheless points out that a 'rather complicated irony' is at work in such readings:

> Beckett's narrators [of the 'trilogy'] are ceaselessly at work in a deconstructionist activity – foregrounding their own textuality, decentring the texts they inhabit, subverting subject positions, denaturalizing language – the issue is misery and meaninglessness, and that activity is what they seek continually, but unsuccessfully to escape *from*, back into a world of solid foundations, solid signifiers [. . .] the trilogy continually asks us to *frame* all these discourses and slowly to construct a mechanism for situating (*situating*, not closing) them – that is, another discourse, one that nowhere speaks in the texts but which it would be perverse to call anything but an *authorial* discourse [. . .] Beckett, as putative authorial presence, cares very much who's speaking; and the whole strategy of these later fictions is to get us to address ourselves to that question: the problematic of the subject.[4]

As the opening sentences of *Assumption* (1929) testify, Beckett began his literary career with these very questions: 'He could have shouted and could not. The buffoon in the loft swung steadily on his stick and the organist sat dreaming with his hands in his pockets.' This immediately raises the question of what the 'problematic of the subject' entails for a 'putative author', an author who has to find a means of accommodating the creature of the imagination ('the buffoon in the loft') and its agent ('the organist') even when the expression of the one threatens to deny the existence of the other. Even this early Beckett is the most philosophical of writers because he is the most literary of writers, that is, he has persistently sought for a clarification of the essential co-ordinates of the creative act: who is speaking? with what authority? how do the words of literature have reference to the world outside the text-in-itself? His famous trilogy is a critical juncture in this investigation; the post-trilogy works reveal Beckett's creation of other worlds in which the antinomies of existentialist and Post-Structuralist approaches are subsumed by a larger synthesis whereby Beckett forges new languages for being which afford unprecedented insights into the ontology of the world of fiction. But the groundwork for these later breakthroughs was laid in Beckett's first two novels, *Murphy* and *Watt*, where his very extensive and thorough reading of the philosophers is most in evidence and where, in ways as yet hardly recognized, Beckett formulated his own versions of the self and the boundary lines of its knowledge which would enable him to 'go on' after the celebrated impasse of *The Unnamable*.

Various well-known disclaimers aside, Beckett actually encouraged critics to adopt a philosophical perspective on his work, observing to Lawrence Harvey that 'if he were a critic setting out to write on the works of Beckett (and he thanked heaven he was not), he would start with two quotations, one by Geulincx: "Ubi nihil vales, ibi nihil velis", and one by Democritus: "Nothing is more real than nothing"'.[5] Beckett then drew particular attention to *Murphy*, where both these statements are prominently displayed. 'Where you are worth nothing, there you should want nothing': the influence of the Occasionalist doctrine of the Belgian Cartesian Arnold Geulincx, with its emphasis upon how in the mind alone man can be free, has long been recognized. The influence of Democritus on *Murphy* is a focus of more recent scholarship. Michael Mooney, for example, has written: 'while readers recognize that atomism supplies Beckett's work with elements of its philosophic substructure and that details from Democritus clarify particulars in his corpus, they fail to see how closely Murphy's third, "dark" zone approximates the Democritean void or how completely Democritean and Anaxagorean epistemology informs the novel'.[6] Yet for all its virtues this essay cannot resolve what Mooney calls 'the most puzzling question in

Beckett scholarship [...] the provenance of the three zones of Murphy's mind', and therefore cannot help us much with what Beckett referred to as 'the couple of pages of thinking which, in his view then (1937), justified the rest of the book and the "fireworks" it contained'.[7]

Many critics have noted the more obvious philosophical references in chapter 6 of *Murphy*. John Fletcher sees these pages as 'a riotous pot-pourri of many metaphysical systems'; Ruby Cohn sees them as a 'comic gamut' of ironically inappropriate erudition. More recently, Sylvie Debevec Henning, using Bakhtinian terminology, has viewed *Murphy* as an instance of a 'carnivalesque irony' in which 'unruly difference' presents a dynamic interplay of conflicting elements: the novel 'does not so much embody a specific philosophy as satirize what is perhaps the dominant strain of the Western tradition: a general faith in the reality, or possibility, of ultimate identity or totality'.[8] Yet *Murphy*, and chapter 6 in particular, does in fact 'embody a specific philosophy', namely, that of Benedict (Baruch) Spinoza, a philosophy which is evident in a number of detailed and decisive ways, from the epigraph through to the concluding discussion of the third zone of Murphy's mind.

The epigraph to chapter 6, '*Amor intellectualis quo Murphy se ipsum amat*' ('The intellectual love with which Murphy loved himself'), combines Propositions XXXV and XXXVI of the Fifth Part of the *Ethics*, 'Of the power of the intellect, or of human liberty', in which Spinoza describes the culminating points in the third level of knowledge that has led the way to the beatitudes. Spinoza's God as eternal cause of His own infinite perfections can bestow upon himself an 'intellectual love'. By substituting Murphy for God in this version, Beckett is not simply mocking his hero's self-love; he is, in fact, being faithful to Spinoza's principles, even if in this instance it is a *reductio ad absurdum*, since Spinoza proposes that as the enlightened individual approaches the intellectual love of God he, through reason, is joined to the timeless order of the universe and has become infinite. Interestingly, chapter 6 of *Murphy*, as a whole, resonates with the famous chapter 6 of the *Tractatus theologico-politicus* in which Spinoza affirms that 'reason is the basis of God, not God of reason, for if reason in the broad sense cannot be trusted, then nothing can be trusted, and we may as well not think'.[9] For Beckett's Murphy reason 'in the broad sense' cannot be trusted. Yet Murphy avoids the rigorously logical conclusion of the *Tractatus* by way of Spinoza's own three levels of knowledge in his 'parody of rational behaviour' (*Mu*, 78). The strategy is a kind of '*Quod erat extorquendum*' to adapt the witticism of *Murphy* (*Mu*, 127).

Spinoza's complete system (as expounded in the *Ethics*) is a series of interlocked deductions which, as they strive to set forth the character of the universe, take on a specifically self-enclosed character; within this system the search is for a good which could so fill the mind that all dependence on contingent circumstance would end and the perpetual transition from one object of desire to another would be transcended (a search which sounds remarkably similar to the plot of *Murphy*). 'Murphy's mind pictured itself as a large hollow sphere, hermetically closed to the universe without' (*Mu*, 76). Since this is only a 'picture' (openly scorned by the narrator) and not a Spinozist deduction in which God and Reason sanction the system, the self-enclosed nature of Murphy's mind is riddled with certain perplexities, uppermost amongst which is, at least initially, his 'fidgets' (*D*, 67) over the body–mind division. In the first four pages of chapter 6 of *Murphy*, Beckett adapts one of Spinoza's characteristic manoeuvres on this strategic issue; he plays Aristotelian and Cartesian notions off against each other.[10] Hence we have in *Murphy* fundamentally Aristotelian distinctions between substance and essential property, and 'between the actual and the virtual of his mind' (*Mu*, 76), but formulated within (and in opposition to) the Cartesian dualism of body and mind ('Murphy felt himself split in two', *Mu*, 77). Throughout chapter 6 the body–mind relationship is progressively drawn more and more towards Spinozist formulations. The discussion of how 'motion in this world depended on rest in the outside world' (*Mu*, 78) is a variant, however ironically twisted, of the infinite and eternal mode of extension which Spinoza calls 'motion-and-rest'.[11] Similarly, the discussion of 'forms with parallel' and of correspondences in various 'modes' is shaped by the distinctively Spinozist vocabulary of the *res extensae*, of the universe at large.

As the narrator comments in expatiating upon Murphy's mind as a closed system: 'of infinitely more interest than how that came to be so was the manner in which it might be exploited' (*Mu*, 78). The 'manner' and exploitation of these three zones of Murphy's mind are specifically indebted to Spinoza. Progression to the third level of knowledge, the *amor intellectualis* of blessedness, is first of all via the realm of the imagination and then the realm of science (or *ratio*). At the first level of knowledge, that of the imagination, there is, says Spinoza, a certain 'privation of knowledge' because of the disturbing presence of certain 'mutilated and confused ideas'.[12] In other words, the imagination combines in an abstract and haphazard way pictures which are only irrationally connected. Similar images blur together to form 'universals' of, say, the universal dog or man (Spinoza's examples).[13] Murphy's first zone ('the light') is specifically termed 'a radiant abstract of the dog's life, the elements of physical experience available for a new arrangement' (*Mu*, 78), such as the grotesque coupling of Miss Carridge with Ticklepenny. At the second level of knowledge there is freedom from finite individuality and things are seen under a certain form of eternity afforded by the exercise of *ratio*. In the second zone of Murphy's mind ('the half light') there are 'forms without parallel' and the mode of contemplation is pictured in scientific terms as a 'system' with 'others scarcely less precise' (*Mu*, 79).

It is in the third zone of Murphy's mind, the 'dark' with its 'flux of forms', that Beckett, while still following Spinoza in a number of important particulars, makes his most significant alterations. For Spinoza the third stage of knowledge, *scientia intuitiva*, is a synthethis of the first two stages and affords a comprehensive sense of the universals which the first two do not possess. It is a higher world and the individual is viewed in the light of the whole of reality. At this stage 'it is the task of philosophy to make knowledge conscious not only of the outside world but of itself, to bring back science to the common life, to infuse science with the light of concrete intuition'.[14] Hence here there is not a merging or losing of oneself in the absolute, but an enhanced comprehension of one's intricate interrelationships with reality, and of the concomitant obligations, as well as pleasures. Ethics and aesthetics come together: the philosopher now understands as the artist does. Murphy is, alas, neither an artist nor a philosopher; he 'exploits' his own revisions of Spinoza's ways to blessedness solely for his own pleasure and for his own selfish reasons.

Spinoza's God 'loves no one and hates no one';[15] Murphy revels in 'forms becoming and crumbling into the fragments of a new becoming, without love or hate *or any intelligible principle of change*' (*Mu*, 79; italics mine). The qualifying phrase here is vital. Without God and Reason Spinoza's metaphysics would naturally collapse; to then substitute Murphy, the 'surd', for God in the *amor intellectualis* is truly double Dutch. Beckett nevertheless goes out of his way to develop further correspondences with Spinoza. In chapter 6 a major and repeated point is that Murphy's movement between the three zones does not entangle him in the 'ethical yoyo'; there are not 'right forms and wrong forms' (*Mu*, 76), only a 'need' at various times to be in one of the zones. Now whilst Spinoza's philosophy is fundamentally an ethical and religious system, it also does not entangle itself in an allegorical 'yoyo' of good and bad. The pleasure for which man strives and the pain which he tries to alleviate are the key terms, just as they are in *Murphy*, with, of course, the decisive difference that Spinoza sees the ultimate pleasure as an identification with the intellectual love of God. Instead, Murphy, as Mooney points out, is pictured as a Democritean 'mote in the dark of absolute freedom' (*Mu*, 79). The pleasure which Murphy experiences at this point is 'So pleasant that pleasant was not the word' (*Mu*, 79), a direct echo of Spinoza at the point where the goal of blessedness has been reached: mere 'pleasure' becomes 'felicity' (*beatitudo*).[16] Murphy's 'pleasure' is indeed of a lower order, even when tarted up with these philosophical embezzlements; no wonder the narrator is 'relieved' to rid himself of this 'painful duty' to which his role makes him 'privy'. Since Murphy is in a perpetual state of 'becoming', he, too, is relieved, if in quite a different way, from the duties which go with Spinoza's system, the system to which he is so thoroughly indebted. *Quod erat extorquendum*, indeed.

These contradictions between the ethical and aesthetic aspects become painfully obvious in the encounter at the mental asylum between Murphy and little Mr Endon (Greek for 'within'). Here Murphy's pleasure in being a 'mote' in the 'flux of forms' turns into the horrible realisation that he is only 'a speck in Mr Endon's unseen' (*Mu*, 171). It is precisely in this passage that Beckett refers explicitly to Democritus and where Mooney's comments are most valuable. The Democritean elements blended in zone three of Murphy's mind are now shown to be incompatible with the Spinozist controlling framework. Instead of Spinoza's rhapsodic *facies totius universi* ('the face of the whole universe'), there is in the cornea of Mr Endon Murphy's 'own image,' but 'horribly reduced, obscured and distorted' (*Mu*, 170). Beckett's critical slant towards his central character here becomes clearer if we recognize that Beckett, always fascinated by the lives of philosophers in relation to their theories,[17] is alluding to an episode of very different import in the life of Spinoza. To advance his free-thinking, Spinoza sought instruction from Francis van den Enden who helped him with the classics, the physical sciences and the philosophy of Descartes. Such a community of intellects, in which pupils can see eye to eye with their teacher, is the direct antithesis of the Murphy–Endon impasse. Furthermore, throughout the novel there are references to a mysterious Mr Quigley, a Dutch uncle, his only 'next-of-kin' (*Mu*, 182) with whom Murphy 'strove to correspond' (*Mu*, 16), who 'spent his time between Amsterdam and Scheveningen' (*Mu*, 80), shuttling between the birth place and death place of Spinoza. After the fateful encounter with Mr Endon, the last 'picture' which Murphy tries and fails to raise is that of Mr Quigley.

Is nothing then left of the Spinozist system upon which Beckett drew so heavily in chapter 6? Not quite nothing. What is left is arguably the most important ingredient in Spinoza's philosophy, and certainly the most important for a twentieth-century writer such as Beckett: *conatus in suo esse perseverandi*, the drive towards self-preservation and expression of one's being. The sense of striving and trying are key aspects of *conation* (cf. *WFG*, 43), and these are the very words which figure in the first and last references to Mr Quigley, Spinoza's latter-day reincarnation in the novel.[18] Murphy is hungry in mind as he strives to recreate pictures of the outside world and the people within it; his 'small but implacable appetite' (*Mu*, 59) needs something more fundamental than the counterfeit version of Spinoza's third level of knowledge. It is at just this point that Beckett loses patience with his character and blows him up, *deus ex machina* fashion; these are the 'fireworks' which justify, as Beckett said, the rest of the novel, and they are primarily indebted to Beckett's very close reading of Spinoza, which underlies all the other more superficial philosophical references in the novel (Geulincx, Descartes and Democritus included). Beckett's concept of *conatus* is crucial throughout all the following works; it is at the core of Beckett's own striving to make sense of man's place in the world and his concomitant sense that – for the writer – this must also involve the accommodation of his fictional 'characters'' drive towards their own being.

Vivian Mercier speaks for most critics when he frankly admits 'it is impossible – for me at least – to find the same philosophic unity in *Watt* as there is in *Murphy*, nor is Watt's way of life the product of a conscious choice, as Murphy's at least *seems* to be'.[19] Discussing Jacqueline Hoefer's influential reading of *Watt* as a philosophical farce on Logical Positivism, John Fletcher also sensibly expresses certain reservations, and concludes that it 'seems safer to attribute these notions to a general influence emanating from the skeptical tradition of empiricism'.[20] Yet this influence can, in fact, be treated not only generally, but specifically. *Watt* is a Kantian novel; its conception, characterization, a number of crucial scenes, and its tantalizing last words, 'no symbols where none intended' (W, 255), cannot be fully appreciated without recognizing how Beckett read Kant.

Kant's influence on Beckett has been almost totally underestimated; until very recently significant references were relegated to a few footnotes.[21] This is in part due to the fact that most critics were not aware that Beckett went back to Kant throughout the formative decade of the 1930s. Brian Coffey reports that 'in 1938 Beckett wrote to Germany to order the *Complete works of Kant* and he asked the bookseller to send him what he termed "an antediluvian edition". When the volumes arrived Beckett spent much time with them'.[22] This is obvious in *Watt*, which Beckett began work on a few years later, even in terms of the characters' names. 'In the beginning was the pun', said *Murphy* (*Mu*, 48); Kant/Knott is a double negative from which will stem some unexpected affirmations, as Beckett sorts 'can't' from 'cant'. The Kantian negatives concerning what man could and could not know are dramatized in the journey of Watt to the house of Mr Knott. *Watt* is perhaps the decisive work for reappraising Beckett's relationship to the philosophical tradition in that it precedes Beckett's statements to the effect that he no longer read philosophers and that he conceived *Molloy* and all

that followed when he admitted his own ignorance.[23] Beckett's later acceptance of the limitations on what 'can' or 'can't' be known was essentially
worked out in *Watt*.

Watt's journey from the realm of everyday reality to the house of Mr
Knott is structured around Kant's metaphor of the two houses; there can be
no communication, Kant says, between the house of reason and the house of
supersensible reality. Watt, an 'experienced traveller' (W, 20), shows great
reluctance at having to make this impossible journey. Watt enters Mr
Knott's house by the back door and never does discover how it happened to
be open. When Watt arrives, he is greeted with a 'short statement' (W, 39)
by his predecessor of which he understands not a word. This is hardly surprising since Arsene, in a necessarily confused, if highly rhetorical, manner
is trying to recount his experience of a noumenal reality in which he was
able to enjoy a God-like identification with all creation: 'the sensations, the
premonitions of harmony are irrefragable, of imminent harmony, when all
outside him will be he'; (W, 40). Kant's philosophy offers the difficult and
paradoxical situation of man as phenomenally determined but noumenally
free, as determined and free at the same time, though under different
aspects.

There are key statements near the beginning and ending of Arsene's
monologue which are explicitly Kantian and which make it clear just how
important Kant was for Beckett in this novel. In the first, Arsene says that,
with reference to his 'personal system', 'the distinction between what was
inside it and what was outside it was not at all easy to draw'. He draws the
distinction in specifically Kantian terms: 'I perceived it with a perception so
sensuous that in comparison the impressions of a man buried alive in Lisbon
on Lisbon's great day seem a frigid and artificial construction of the understanding' (W, 43). This is a recondite reference to Kant's pre-critical *De Igne*
which commented on the Lisbon earthquake and which Beckett referred to
in his poem 'ainsi a-t-on beau' (CP, 46) where Kant is depicted as dis-
passionately viewing the spectacle of destruction: 'sur Lisbonne fumante
Kant froidement penché'.[24] The critique of Kant is not, however, simply an
ironic dismissal, for Arsene notably cannot sustain his 'existence off the
ladder' and so falls back into the 'old thing where it always was, back again'
(W, 44), in other words back again to the world in which the Kantian
distinctions and boundaries between the noumenal and phenomenal do
apply.

The second reference to Kant is more obvious, echoing his well-known
dictum in the *Critique of judgment* to the effect that '*Beauty* is an object's
form of purposiveness insofar as it is perceived in the object *without the
precondition of a purpose*'.[25] Arsene is no aesthetician, however, being con-

cerned rather with a number of excruciating questions of an existential nature as he tries to determine whether in all our comings and goings there might not be some larger pattern of meaning:

> For what is this shadow of the going in which we come, this shadow of the coming in which we go, this shadow of the coming and going in which we walk, if not the shadow of a purpose, of the purpose that budding withers, that withering buds, whose blooming is a budding withering? [...] And though in purposelessness I may seem now to go, yet I do not, any more than in purposelessness then I came, for I go now with my purpose as with it then I came, the only difference being this, that then it was living and now it is dead [...]   (W, 58).

In a footnote example of this 'Beauty', Kant says that, when 'we are judging the flower, we do not refer to any purpose whatever'. But Arsene does refer to a purpose, or at least the shadow of a purpose: man's coming and going is a budding and a withering, not an aesthetic stasis, and how do we make sense of that?

In any event, it is Watt who is ineluctably drawn towards questions of 'aesthetic judgment' (W, 165). At the centre of the novel, for example, Watt's encounter with the picture in Erskine's room is structured around the Kantian distinction between the beautiful and the sublime. The picture of a circle 'broken at its lowest point' (with 'in the eastern background' a point that might be its centre) has an untoward effect on Watt who has struggled thus far to keep his mind only on the surface of phenomena: 'at the thought that it was perhaps this, a circle and a centre not its centre in search of a centre and its circle respectively, in boundless space, in endless time, then Watt's eyes filled with tears that he could not stem [...]' (W, 127). Kant maintains that the beautiful nature concerns the form of the object, which consists in its being bounded; but the sublime can be located in a formless object, 'Insofar as *unboundedness* is presented, either in the object or because the object prompts us to present it, while we add to this un- boundedness the thought of the totality'. The sublime is a pleasure that arises only 'indirectly': 'it is produced by the feeling of a momentary inhi- bition of vital forces followed immediately by an outpouring of them that is all the stronger'.[26] Watt weeps: a 'negative pleasure' indeed.

The most important Kantian references come at the very end of the novel and set up a complex interaction between the final scene and the enigmatic last entry in the Addenda, 'no symbols where none intended'. The conclu- sion of Beckett's novel is patterned very closely on Kant's conclusion to 'Part I. Critique of aesthetic judgment', in the *Critique of judgment*: 'On beauty as the symbol of morality'. This is followed by an appendix ('On methodology concerning taste'), just as the 'end' of *Watt* is followed by an

Addenda, though the 'precious and illuminating material' contained there lacks anything so grand as a 'methodology'. Kant, in his appendix, distinguishes between schematic and symbolic ways of making a concept sensible: 'Schemata contain direct, symbols indirect, exhibitions of the concept'.[27] The promoting of the value of the symbol at the same time as its role is downgraded when compared to that of 'pure reason' is even clearer as Kant connects 'symbol' with 'morality': 'all of our cognition of God is merely symbolic'.[28] Kant maintains that the beautiful is the symbol of the morally good because we 'naturally' refer the former to the latter and hence require others to assent to it as a 'duty'. Speaking 'practically', Kant emphasized that the elevated thoughts which nature affords us have application in the everyday world: 'The common understanding also habitually bears this analogy in mind, and beautiful objects of nature or art are often called by names that seem to presuppose that we are judging [these objects] morally. We call buildings or trees majestic and magnificent, or landscapes cheerful and gay [...]'[29] This can be applied directly to the ending(s) of *Watt*: the 'common understanding' of the locals who watch Watt taking his leave of Mr Knott for good have no doubts about the Kantian equation of 'beauty', nature's symbols and God's morality:

> The trembling sea could not but be admired. The leaves quivered, or gave the impression of doing so, and the grasses also, beneath the drops, or beads, of gaily expiring dew. [...] [Mr Gorman] raised high his hands and spread them out, in a gesture of worship.   (W, 245).

They can make no sense of Watt, who does not fit into their scheme of things, their pretty picture. Beckett's parody of Kantian aesthetics and morality in these closing words is, however, critically focused in the very last words of the novel in its second ending, the Addenda: 'no symbols where none intended'. The conventional symbolism of Mr Gorman and his ilk are obviously not 'intended' as any resolution to Watt's dilemmas. He saw his picture, and it was not pretty or charming, nor could its 'unboundedness' be domesticated by a convenient and trite symbol system.

There is, however, a way out for Watt and his successors in Beckett's world: to become a writer, an artist of the real whose vision can incorporate 'somethings' and 'nothings' without becoming entangled with symbols (intended or not), a figure who can create viable 'as if'[30] propositions or fictions that will make his own predicaments more significant. Knott is indeed a good master; he compels his servants to leave him and to return to the way of life. Indeed, the last glimpse of Mr Knott at the beginning of Part IV depicts him in terms strikingly similar to those Kant used at the end of the *Critique of practical reason*, 'the starry skies above and the moral law within' (which served as Kant's own epitaph).[31] Mr Knott moves within a room lit by a 'large number of stars' and Watt, by the open window, watches 'the first night lights, human and celestial' (W, 215). Once he has left Knott's, Watt does seem to have escaped the crippling antinomies so rife there: 'Now I am at liberty, said Watt, I am free to come and go as I please' (W, 238).

Beckett broached the key question of how he had imaginatively appropriated the philosophical tradition for his own creative purposes in one of the most forthright and expansive interviews he ever gave. Discussing his need to create a world of his own by 'pure force of the imagination', Beckett supplied the historical context for such an endeavour:

> The crisis started with the end of the seventeenth century, after Galileo. The eighteenth century has been called the century of reason, *le siècle de la raison*. I've never understood that; they're all mad, *ils sont tous fous, ils déraisonnent!* They give reason a responsibility which it simply can't bear, it's too weak. The Encyclopedists wanted to know everything ... But that direct relation between the self and − as the Italians say − *lo scibile*, the knowable, was already broken.[32]

It should, however, be clear by now that Beckett's own writing grew out of a detailed critique of Enlightenment philosophers; no matter how 'mad' their 'systems' might be, Beckett salvaged key concepts from them and reworked them to make them his own. Beckett's own 'reasonings' with the 'pure imagination' notably owe a great deal (as will be seen) to Kant's *Critique of pure reason*, a work which stakes out the boundaries of knowledge. When the Unnamable, for example, mockingly appropriates Kant's Baconian motto for the *Critique of pure reason* (second edn), '*De nobis ipsis silemus*' ('As concerns ourselves we remain silent'), a great deal of irony accumulates around the 'motto' (T, 302). The Unnamable tries vainly to remain silent about himself because he cannot find a language − freed from various 'discourses of method' − which could do justice to what he regards as his authentic self. But it is from the 'remains of reason' (AST, 121), from the impasses of the philosophical tradition itself, that Beckett forges his own remarkable series of literary and philosophical investigations. The last lines of the trilogy, 'I can't go on, I'll go on' (T, 382), succinctly and powerfully capture, particularly in English, his fundamental indebtedness both to Kant and to Spinoza.

Beckett went to a great deal of trouble to mask these fundamental allegiances and perhaps this is one way of distinguishing their importance for him from other more secondary and slighting references.[33] The question of 'Cartesian' influences has been brilliantly summarized and laid to rest by Edouard Morot-Sir.[34] Hegelian influence, suspected by several critics, particularly with reference to the Absolute and the dialectic in the trilogy,[35] seems finally beside the point when Beckett could have come across the dialectic on his own or in a host of other sources. Beckett seems to have referred to Hegel essentially for ironic counterpoint. A case in point is the famous conclusion of *Molloy* – 'It is midnight. The rain is beating on the windows. It was not midnight. It was not raining' (*T*, 162). Hegel wrote to Schelling that *The phenomenology of mind* 'was concluded at midnight before the battle of Jena' (13 October 1806); as commentators have pointed out, 'this sounds rather fanciful. "On the night before the battle" there could have been no serious cannonade [raining down?] to disturb Hegel's meditations'.[36] It would appear that even philosophers of history can alter the dates and atmosphere in order to give a poetic and dramatic aura to their composition of fictions. In a similar vein, the witticism of *Murphy* – '"Perhaps you hadn't heard", said Wylie, "Hegel arrested his development"' (*Mu*, 152) – takes a chiastic twist in *The lost ones* where the refrain 'if this notion is maintained' echoes Hegel's central concept of the very medium in which philosophy works. For Hegel 'the world is a process that is self-contained, and so as a whole is at rest with itself'.[37] *The lost ones* as a comic inversion of the Hegelian Absolute, a self-contained and self-complete whole, speaks for itself. Beckett has, as it were, arrested Hegel's development.

A much more interesting and difficult case is Arthur Schopenhauer, of whom Beckett always spoke highly and whose style he praised. Beckett's study *Proust* shows a great deal of Schopenhauerian influence: it is as if Beckett had just put down *The world as will and representation* as he began to write it. But a brief assessment of Schopenhauer's influence on Beckett's later work will show how it was overshadowed by Kant, whose thought had a greater and more lasting impact. In the preface to the first edition of *The world as will and representation*, Schopenhauer declares that he starts from 'what was achieved by the great Kant'. He even advises his readers to look first at his special appendix 'Criticism of the Kantian philosophy'; while Schopenhauer found 'grave errors' in Kant he fully admitted Kant's crucial importance for him. Their basic differences emerge perhaps most clearly on the solution of Kant's third antinomy (freedom). Schopenhauer writes:

> it is very remarkable that Kant is obliged precisely here, in connection with the *Idea of Freedom* to speak in greater detail about the *thing-in-itself*, hitherto seen only in the background. This is very easy for us to understand after we have recognized the *thing-in-itself* as the will. In general this is the point where Kant's philosophy leads to mind, as mine springs from his as its parent stem.[38]

On this key distinction, Beckett, however much he may admire Schopen-hauer and find other aspects of his philosophy congenial, sides with Kant. Schopenhauer's identification of the thing-in-itself with the will is 'concretiz-ing Kant's thing-in-itself' which Beckett spoke so strongly against in the last sentence of *Le concentrisme* (1930) (*D*, 42). Arthur is, after all, only a servant at the house of Mr Knott, and Arthur grows tired of the 'fixities' and 'mysteries' of Knott's establishment, an apt summary of Schopenhauer's own critique of Kant. In an Addenda entry, Arthur is even mistaken in the garden for Mr Knott (his 'parent stem'?); but he is not Knott. In working out his own highly original responses to a number of linguistic, existential, and ethical issues, Beckett found Kant to be the indispensable philosopher, the thinker who more than any other supplied him with a philosophical grammar, or better yet, a Kantian syntax for realigning the proliferation of negatives encountered at the boundary lines of word and world.

The 'proper syntax of weakness' which Beckett stated was necessary in order to 'let being into literature'[39] could be regarded as a consequence of Beckett's radical revision of the cornerstone of the whole Kantian archi-tectonic – the controversial concept of the synthetic *a priori* as set out in the *Critique of pure reason*. Kant maintained that knowledge must rest on judg-ments separate from the contingencies of experience (*a priori*) and yet the predicate must contain something more than is analytically contained in the subject (synthetic). In Beckett's post-trilogy works there are many examples of this type of synthetic *a priori*, most obviously in works such as *All strange away*, *Imagination dead imagine* and *The lost ones* with their would-be scientific, detached observers of various fictional experiments. These investi-gations of the fictional world are far from being merely formal (*a priori*) exercises; even when the recording consciousness is primarily interested in manipulating the 'something there' discovered in the creative act for his own ends, he is still testifying to his own need for form. This calculated approach may be life-denying for creatures such as the 'little people' in *The lost ones*, but it is not the killing opposition of 'no's knife in yes's wound', as found in *Texts for nothing* (*CSP*, 115).

The most important development in the post-trilogy prose involves somehow giving voice to the 'somethings' or creatures trapped in the time-less world of the literary artifact. Their strivings for a language which could express their existence necessitates a passionate engagement with issues of referentiality, of being in time. Beckett's ontological synthesis in works such as *Lessness*, with its 'categories' through which the text runs in its various 'disorders', and *Company* where, 'with what judgment remained' (*NO*, 17), the 'one in the dark' begins to imagine (*NO*, 8), has strong traces of Kantian terminology. Not reason but the imagination is, however, now the deciding factor; a 'Critique of pure imagination' can bring about a very different kind of order. Of the great modern philosophers Heidegger argued that Kant's first *Critique* points to the central function of the imagination so far as the affirmation of being is concerned, but that Kant failed to recognize this and in the second edition reduced the imagination to a mere function of the understanding.[40] Beckett and Heidegger meet in a remarkably similar critique of Kant. The differences between the situations of the philosopher and the poet must also be noted: whereas Heidegger can affirm that temporality as the being of *Dasein* should replace Kant's 'pure reason', Beckett cannot make such an essentially straightforward declaration. His fictional world is at least one stage removed from an existential situation; therefore, Beckett must seek the language which could *mediate* this distantiation between would-be self and would-be world. Beckett said that he did not understand the distinction Heidegger and Sartre had made between existence and being; their language was 'too philosophical'[41] for him (a more polite version of the Unnamable's 'They must consider me sufficiently stupefied with all their balls about being and existing', *T* 320). As I have argued elsewhere, Beckett does indeed make such distinctions in his own later work.[42] He had, however, first to deal with the fundamental realities of the author–other relationship – the true synthetic *a priori* in his writing – before he could deal with vital coincidences between the literary world and our world.

In contemporary literary theory, the reliance on linguistic models has brought about the abandonment of the question of the referent, now dismissed as a logocentric fallacy. Yet Beckett's abiding concern was for the problem of reference, of how language relates to reality, a question which was formerly the domain of the philosopher, but which, in our 'end of philosophy' era, has been taken up by others, perhaps most notably the creator of fictional worlds. Carla Locatelli's work in this area has made a major contribution to Beckett studies, especially to the question of the philosophical nature of Beckett's work. In *Unwording the world*, Locatelli argues rigorously to show how 'Beckett's unwording probes into issues of the cultural encoding of meaning, not only to denounce the conventions of literary discourse, but to reveal the epistemological function of linguistic representation, and the intrinsic hermeneutic quality of our being.'[43] Her main thesis is that 'Beckett's writing constitutes a movement from representations to the representation of representations [. . .] by so doing, Beckett is probing into what today seems the elementary structure of our interpretation of reality as the simplest, basic mode of our being in the world.'[44] Locatelli's argument is seminal and students interested in Beckett's later prose will find it especially useful; its resolution of certain theoretical dilemmas pointed out by Iain Wright should help to give a new direction to the whole issue of the role of philosophy in Beckett's work and the perspectives which the critic might adopt towards it.

Throughout Beckett's career, the driving need was somehow to find the means of reconstructing the referent. The 'Said nohow on' of *Worstward Ho* (*NO*, 128) – which ends the opening paragraph and is by itself the last paragraph – is Beckett's most succinct statement of how he sought to do so. He achieved this 'saying' via a complex series of negatives which effected, however minimally, an affirmation of the relationship of language and being. Without the 'know how' (or *techné*) of Western systematization of thought, Beckett, by working his own way through its contradictions and impasses, formulated in some of his later works a new poetic logic, a 'new no', a 'nohow' that allows for human presence in language. 'Try again. Fail again. Fail better' (*NO*, 101), hammers home the point; conation, from *conari*, to try. Witness this 'syntax of weakness' (what I have termed in this discussion 'Kantian syntax'): 'Never by naught be nulled. Unnullable least. Say that best worse. With leastening words say least best worse' (*NO*, 118). 'Naught not best worse' runs counter to a great deal of Beckett criticism that was based, in large part, on a misreading of how Beckett made use of the philosophical tradition. If naught truly were best worse, it would long ago have terminated Beckett's fundamental premise: 'On'.

NOTES

1 Martin Esslin, 'Samuel Beckett', *Encyclopaedia Britannica macropaedia*.
2 Thomas Trezise, *Into the breach*, ix.
3 Ibid., 9.
4 Iain Wright, '"What matter who's speaking?"', 71–2.
5 Lawrence Harvey, *Poet and critic*, 267–8.
6 Michael Mooney, 'Presocratic Scepticism', 223.
7 Brian Coffey, 'Memory Murphy's maker: some notes on Samuel Beckett', *Threshold*, 17 (1963), 33.
8 John Fletcher, 'Samuel Beckett and the philosophers', 47; Ruby Cohn, *Samuel Beckett: the comic gamut* (New Brunswick: Rutgers University Press, 1962), 56–9; Sylvie Debevec Henning, *Beckett's critical complicity: carnival, contestation, and tradition* (University Press of Kentucky, 1988), 29. Henning mentions the parallel between Murphy's three zones and Spinoza's ways to salvation, but does not develop any details or larger implications (50). My discussion of Spinoza should be compared with that of Laura Barge in *God, the quest, the hero*. Barge sees Murphy's zones as 'rough Beckettian approximations of Spinoza's three levels of knowledge' and regards the problem of 'divinity' posed by the third zone as 'defined in Manichean terms' (241–54). David H. Hesla in his discussion of *Watt* also refers to Spinoza's three kinds of knowledge (*The shape of chaos*, 76).
9 See *Spinoza selections*, ed. John Wild (New York: Scribner's Sons, 1930), xxiii.

Parallels have most often been drawn with chapter 6 of Descartes's *The meditations concerning first philosophy*, 'Of the existence of corporeal things and of the real distinction between the mind and body (of man).'

10 'Spinoza, Benedict (Baruch), *The encyclopedia of philosophy*, ed. Paul Edwards (London: Collier-Macmillan, 1967), 532.

11 Ibid., 535.

12 *Spinoza selections*, 'Ethic', 180 (Proposition xxxv, Second Part, 'Of the nature and origin of the mind').

13 Ibid., 185 (Proposition xl).

14 Ibid., Introduction, lii.

15 Ibid., (Proposition xvii, Corollary, Fifth Part, 'Of the power of the intellect, or of human liberty').

16 Ibid., Introduction, lviii.

17 Beckett's *Whoroscope* (1930) deals more with the life of Descartes than it does with his philosophy, but turns on the connections (or lack of) between his life and thought. See Lawrence Harvey, ibid., 3–66.

18 The characterization of Quigley is itself a type of 'double Dutch': Quigley in some ways is parallel to Spinoza; in other ways he is identified with Holland Mean Time, which would explain his 'demented' association with money. See Sighle Kennedy, *Murphy's bed*, 160. Beckett refers indirectly to Spinoza in *Malone dies*: 'One day I took counsel of an Israelite on the subject of conation' (*T*, 200).

19 Vivian Mercier, *Beckett/Beckett*, 166.

20 Fletcher, 'Samuel Beckett and the philosophers', 55

21 See the footnotes in David H. Hesla, *The shape of chaos*, and Lawrence Harvey, *Poet and critic*. John Pilling, in 'From a (W)horoscope to *Murphy*', *The ideal core of the onion: reading Beckett archives*, ed. John Pilling and Mary Bryden (Reading: Beckett International Foundation, 1992), 15–18, discusses Beckett's extensive notations in the *Murphy* notebook on his reading of Kant.

22 Coffey, 'Memory Murphy's maker', 33–4. James Knowlson, in conversation, corrected the date to December 1937. The edition of Kant Beckett received was that of the Berlin Academy, 1923. Beckett's set of Kant's works is unannotated and is now in private hands.

23 Beckett's comments to Gabriel d'Aubarède, *Nouvelles littéraires* (Paris, 16 February 1961).

24 The poem is quoted *in toto* in Lawrence Harvey, *Poet and critic*, 208.

25 Immanuel Kant, *Critique of judgment*, trans. with an introduction, Werner S. Pluhar (Indianapolis: Hackett, 1987), 74.

26 Ibid., 98.

27 Ibid., 227.

28 Ibid., 228.

29 Ibid., 229–30.

30 The 'as if' of nature's purposiveness is a key concept in Part II of the *Critique of judgment*, 'Critique of teleological judgment'. The great Kant scholar Hans Vaihinger developed systematically the 'fictional' dimensions of 'as if'; see my *Reconstructing Beckett*, 181.

31 Cf. Beckett in the second of the *Three dialogues with Georges Duthuit*: 'The stars are undoubtedly superb, as Freud remarked on reading Kant's cosmological proof of the existence of God' (*PTD*, 112).

32 Interview with Michael Haerdter, cited in Dougald McMillan and Martha Fehsenfeld, *Beckett in the theatre* (New York: Riverrun Press, 1988), 230–1. Beckett refers to the *scibile* in his review of Pound's *Make it new* (*D*, 78).

33 Two prime examples of philosophers to whom Beckett makes extensive reference but whose influence is essentially for ironic counterpoint or structural convenience are Leibniz and Berkeley. With reference to the latter, note particularly the *esse est percipi* note for *Film* and *Three dialogues* which echoes a Berkeleyan title.

34 'Samuel Beckett and Cartesian emblems', 25–104. What Morot-Sir did for the 'Cartesian' question needs to be done with reference to the influence of Fritz Mauthner's language critique on Beckett, an approach which many critics have found attractive. It is obvious, however, that Mauthner's radical nominalism can by no means be an adequate one-to-one means of explaining Beckett's complex approach to language and questions of expression.

35 Three critics who have adopted explicitly Hegelian approaches: Hans-Joachim Schulz, '*This hell of stories*'; Eugene Kaelin, *The unhappy consciousness*; Lance St John Butler, *Samuel Beckett and the meaning of being*.

36 G. W. F. Hegel, *The phenomenology of mind*, trans. with an introduction by J. B. Baillie (New York: Harper and Row, 1967), 27.

37 Ibid., 40–1.

38 Arthur Schopenhauer, *The world as will and representation*, trans. E. F. J. Payne (New York: Dover Publications, 1969), vol. I, xv, 501.

39 Beckett's comments to Lawrence Harvey; see *Poet and critic*, 247–9.

40 See Martin Heidegger, *Kant and the problem of metaphysics*, trans. James S. Churchill (Bloomington: Indiana University Press, 1972).

41 Beckett's distinction as made to Tom F. Driver, 'Beckett by the Madeleine', *Columbia University Forum* 4.3 (1961), 22.

42 See *Reconstructing Beckett*, 31–2.

43 Carla Locatelli, *Unwording the world*, x.

44 Ibid., 29.

RECOMMENDED READING

Barge, Laura, *God, the quest, the hero: thematic structures in Beckett's fiction*, Chapel Hill: University of North Carolina Press, 1988.

Ben-Zvi, Linda', 'Fritz Mauthner for *Company*', *Journal of Beckett Studies*, 9 (1984), 65–88.

Bernal, Olga, *Langage et fiction dans les romans de Beckett*, Paris: Nouvelle revue française, 1970.

Butler, Lance St John, *Samuel Beckett and the meaning of being: a study in ontological parable*, London: Macmillan, 1984.

Coe, Richard N., *Samuel Beckett*, New York: Grove Press, 1964.

Cohn, Ruby, 'Philosophical fragments in the works of Samuel Beckett', in *Samuel Beckett: a collection of critical essays*, ed. Martin Esslin, Englewood Cliffs, N.J.: Prentice-Hall, 1965.

Dobrez, L. A. C., *The Existential and its exits: literary and philosophical perspectives on the works of Beckett, Ionesco, Genet and Pinter*, New York: St Martin's Press, 1986.

Esslin, Martin, Introduction, *Samuel Beckett: a collection of critical essays*, Englewood Cliffs, N.J.: Prentice-Hall, 1965.

Fitch, Brian T., *Reflections in the mind's eye: reference and its problematization in twentieth-century French fiction*, University of Toronto Press, 1991.

Fletcher, John, 'Samuel Beckett and the philosophers', *Comparative Literature*, 17 (1965), 43–56.

Harvey, Lawrence, *Samuel Beckett: poet and critic*, Princeton University Press, 1970.

Hesla, David H., *The shape of chaos: an interpretation of the art of Samuel Beckett*, Minneapolis: University of Minnesota Press, 1971.

Kaelin, Eugene, *The unhappy consciousness: the poetic plight of Samuel Beckett*, Boston: Kulwer, 1982.

Kenner, Hugh, *Samuel Beckett*, New York: Grove Press, 1961.

Kennedy, Sighle, *Murphy's bed: a study of real sources and surreal associations in Samuel Beckett's first novel*, Lewisburg: Bucknell University Press, 1971.

Kern, Edith, *Existential thought and fictional technique: Kierkegaard, Sartre, and Beckett*, New Haven: Yale University Press, 1970.

Locatelli, Carla, *Unwording the world: Samuel Beckett's prose works after the Nobel Prize*, Philadelphia: University of Pennsylvania Press, 1990.

Mercier, Vivian, *Beckett/Beckett*, New York: Oxford University Press, 1977.

Mintz, Samuel I., 'Beckett's *Murphy*: a "Cartesian novel"', *Perspective*, 2.3 (1959), 156–65.

Mooney, Michael, 'Presocratic scepticism: Samuel Beckett's *Murphy* reconsidered', *ELH*, 49 (1982), 214–34.

Morot-Sir, Edouard, 'Samuel Beckett and Cartesian emblems', in *Samuel Beckett: the art of rhetoric*, ed. Edouard Morot-Sir, Howard Harper, Dougald McMillan, Chapel Hill: University of North Carolina Press, 1976.

Murphy, P. J., *Reconstructing Beckett: language for being in Samuel Beckett's fiction*, University of Toronto Press, 1990.

Norris, Christopher, *Spinoza and the origins of modern critical theory*, Oxford: Basil Blackwell, 1991.

Pilling, John, *Samuel Beckett*, London: Routledge and Kegan Paul, 1976, chapter 5.

Rosen, Stephen J., *Samuel Beckett and the pessimistic tradition*, New Brunswick, N. J.: Rutgers University Press, 1976.

Schulz, Hans-Joachim, *'This hell of stories': a Hegelian approach to the novels of Samuel Beckett*, The Hague: Mouton, 1973.

Trezise, Thomas, *Into the breach: Samuel Beckett and the ends of literature*, Princeton University Press, 1991.

Wright, Iain, '"What matter who's speaking?"': Beckett, the authorial subject and contemporary critical theory', *Southern Review*, 16.1 (1983), 59–86.

FURTHER READING

These lists are supplementary to the 'Recommended reading' attached to each essay, the details of which are not repeated here. The secondary literature on Beckett, of which what follows is only a selection, is now of formidably large proportions, and shows no signs of diminishing in volume in the aftermath of his death.

Reference works and bibliographies

Admussen, Richard, *The Samuel Beckett manuscripts: a study*, Boston: G. K. Hall, 1979.

Andonian, Cathleen Carlotta, *Samuel Beckett: a reference guide*, Boston: G. K. Hall, 1989.

Davis, Robin J., Jackson R. Bryer, Melvin J. Friedman and Peter C. Hoy, *Samuel Beckett*, calepins de bibliographie, Paris: Minard, 1971.

Federman, Raymond and John Fletcher, *Samuel Beckett: his works and his critics*, Berkeley and Los Angeles: University of California Press, 1970.

Knowlson, James, S. E. Gontarski and Dougald McMillan (eds.), *The theatrical notebooks of Samuel Beckett*, London: Faber and Faber, 1992 –   .

Murphy, P. J., Konrad Schoell, Rolf Breuer and Werner Huber, *Critique of Beckett criticism: a guide to research in English, French and German*, Columbia, S.C.: Camden House, forthcoming.

O'Brien, Eoin, *The Beckett country*, London: Faber and Faber/Black Cat Press, 1986.

No symbols where none intended: a catalogue of books, manuscripts and other materials, described by Carlton Lake, Austin, Texas: Humanities Research Center, University of Texas, 1984.

Samuel Beckett an exhibition, catalogue by James Knowlson, foreword by A. J. Leventhal, London: Turret Books, 1971.

The Samuel Beckett collection, catalogue by Mary Bryden, James Knowlson and Peter Mills, Reading: Whiteknights Press, forthcoming.

Special numbers of journals devoted to Samuel Beckett

Centrepoint: a journal of interdisciplinary studies, 4.2 (Fall 1981).
College Literature, 8.3 (Fall 1981).
Critique, 519–20 (August–September 1990).
Europe, 770–771 (June–July 1993).
Irish University Review, 14.1 (1984).

James Joyce Quarterly, 8 (Summer 1971).
Journal of the Australian Universities Language and Literature Association, 55 (May 1981).
Journal of Beckett Studies, 1–12 (1976–89); (n.s.) 1–   (1992–   ).
Journal of Modern Literature, 6.1 (February 1977).
L'Esprit créateur, 11 (Fall 1971).
Modern Drama, 9.3 (December 1966); 19.3 (September 1976); 25.3 (September 1982); 26.4 (December 1983); 28.1 (March 1985).
Modern Fiction Studies, 29.1 (Spring 1983).
Perspective, 2.3 (1959).
Review of Contemporary Fiction, 7.2 (Summer 1987).
Revue d'esthétique, numéro hors-série (March 1986).
Romance Studies, 11 (Winter 1987).

Collections of essays

Acheson, James and Kateryna Arthur (eds.), *Beckett's later fiction and drama: texts for Company*, London: Macmillan, 1987.

Astier, Pierre, Morris Beja and S. E. Gontarski (eds.), *Samuel Beckett: humanistic perspectives*, Columbus: Ohio State University Press, 1983.

Ben-Zvi, Linda (ed.), *Women in Beckett: performance and critical perspectives*, Urbana: University of Illinois Press, 1990.

Bishop, Tom and Raymond Federman (eds.), *Samuel Beckett*, Paris: Cahiers de l'Herne, 1976.

Brater, Enoch (ed.), *Beckett at 80/Beckett in context*, New York: Oxford University Press, 1986.

Butler, Lance St John and Robin J. Davis (eds.), *Rethinking Beckett: a collection of critical essays*, London: Macmillan, 1990.

Chevigny, Gale Bell (ed.), *Twentieth century interpretations of 'Endgame'*, Englewood Cliffs, N.J.: Prentice-Hall, 1969.

Cohn, Ruby (ed.), *Samuel Beckett: a collection of criticism*, New York: McGraw-Hill, 1975.

Davis, Robin J., and Lance St John Butler (eds.), *'Make sense who may': essays on Samuel Beckett's later works*, Gerrards Cross: Colin Smythe, 1989.

Esslin, Martin (ed.), *Samuel Beckett* (Twentieth century views), Englewood Cliffs N.J., Prentice-Hall, 1965.

Friedman, Alan Warren, Charles Rossman and Dina Sherzer (eds.), *Beckett Translating/Translating Beckett*, University Park: Pennsylvania State University Press, 1987.

Friedman, Melvin J. (ed.), *Samuel Beckett now*, University of Chicago Press, 1970.

Gontarski, S. E. (ed.), *On Beckett: essays and criticisms*, New York: Grove Press, 1986.

McCarthy, Patrick A., *Critical essays on Samuel Beckett*, Boston: G. K. Hall, 1986.

Morot-Sir, Edouard, Howard Harper, Dougald McMillan (eds.), *Samuel Beckett: the art of rhetoric*, Chapel Hill: University of North Carolina Press, 1976.

O'Hara, J. D. (ed.), *Twentieth century interpretations of 'Molloy', 'Malone dies', 'The Unnamable'*, Englewood Cliffs, N.J.: Prentice-Hall, 1970.

Smith, Joseph H. (ed.), *The world of Samuel Beckett*, Baltimore: Johns Hopkins University Press, 1991.

Worth, Katharine (ed.), *Beckett the shape changer*, London: Routledge and Kegan Paul, 1975.

As no other dare fail: a tribute on Samuel Beckett's 80th birthday by his friends and admirers, London: John Calder, 1986.

Beckett at sixty, London: Calder and Boyars, 1967.

General studies

Ehrhard, Peter, *Anatomie de Samuel Beckett*, Basle: Birkhäuser Verlag, 1976.

Fletcher, John, *Samuel Beckett's art*, London: Chatto and Windus, 1967.

Gluck, Barbara Reich, *Beckett and Joyce: friendship and fiction*, Lewisburg: Bucknell University Press, 1979.

Jacobsen, Josephine and Frederick J. Mueller, *The testament of Samuel Beckett*, London: Faber and Faber, 1976.

Janvier, Ludovic, *Pour Samuel Beckett*, Paris: Editions de Minuit, 1966.

Samuel Beckett par lui-même, Paris: Seuil, 1969.

Scott, Nathan A., *Samuel Beckett*, Bowes and Bowes, 1965.

Studies of Beckett's drama

Hale, Jane Alison, *The broken window: Beckett's dramatic perspective*, West Lafayette: Purdue University Press, 1987.

Völker, Klaus (ed.), *Beckett in Berlin*, Berlin: Edition Hentrick, 1986.

Webb, Eugene, *The plays of Samuel Beckett*, Seattle: University of Washington Press, 1972.

Studies of Beckett's prose fiction

Amiran, Eyal, *Wandering and home: Beckett's metaphysical narrative*, University Park: Pennsylvania State University Press, 1993.

Büttner, Gottfried, *Samuel Beckett's novel 'Watt'*, trans. Joseph Dolan, Philadelphia: University of Pennsylvania Press, 1984.

Finney, Brian H., *Since 'How it is': a study of Samuel Beckett's later fiction*, London: Covent Garden Press 1972.

Fitch, Brian T., *La trilogie de Beckett*, Paris: Minard, 1977.

Fletcher, John, *The novels of Samuel Beckett*, London: Chatto and Windus, 1964.

Levy, Eric P., *Beckett and the voice of species*, Dublin: Gill and Macmillan, 1980.

Rabinovitz, Rubin, *Innovation in Samuel Beckett's fiction*, Urbana: University of Illinois Press, 1992.

Schurman, Susan, *The solipsistic novels of Samuel Beckett*, Cologne: Paul Rugenstein, 1987.

Sherzer, Dina, *Structure de la trilogie de Beckett*, The Hague: Mouton, 1976.

Webb, Eugene, *Samuel Beckett: a study of his novels*, Seattle: University of Washington Press, 1970.

Books with chapters on Beckett

Albright, Daniel, *Representation and the imagination: Beckett, Kafka, Nabokov and Schoenberg*, University of Chicago Press, 1981.

Bishop, Lloyd, *Romantic irony in French literature: from Diderot to Beckett*, Nashville: Vanderbilt University Press, 1989.

Blau, Herbert, *The eye of prey: subversions of the postmodern*, Bloomington: Indiana University Press, 1987.

Bruns, Gerald L., *Modern poetry and the idea of language*, New Haven: Yale University Press, 1974.

Currie, Robert, *Genius: an ideology in literature*, London: Chatto and Windus, 1974.

Ellmann, Richard, *Four Dubliners: Oscar Wilde, James Joyce, W. B. Yeats, Samuel Beckett*, London: Hamish Hamilton, 1987.

Garner, Stanford B., *The absent voice: narrative comprehension in the theater*, Urbana: University of Illinois Press, 1989.

Iser, Wolfgang, *Prospecting: from reader response to literary anthropology*, Bloomington: Indiana University Press, 1989.

Kenner, Hugh, *The stoic comedians: Flaubert, Joyce and Beckett*, London: W. H. Allen, 1964.

Moorjani, Angela B., *The aesthetics of loss and lessness*, London: Macmillan, 1992.

INDEX OF WORKS BY BECKETT

GENERAL INDEX

Adorno, Theodor W. 84, 132
Albee, Edward 215
Apollinaire, Guillaume 185
Arikha, Avigdor 14, 181n
Aristophanes 124
Aristotle 71
Ashcroft, Peggy 95
Asmus, Walter A. 68, 197
Augustine 75, 80, 82, 110

Bacon, Francis 233
Bair, Deirdre 68, 134
Balzac, Honoré de *Louis Lambert* 218
Barfield, Owen 51
Barthes, Roland 219
Beckett, John 130–2
Beckett, May 83
Beethoven, Ludwig van 7, 139
Behan, Brendan 69
Ben-Zvi, Linda 134–5, 140
Berkeley, George 72, 82, 136, 239n
Bertrand, Aloysius *Gaspard de la nuit* 186
Blake, William 51
Böhme, Jakob 45, 55
Bohm, David 56
Bordewijk, Cobi 199
Bowles, Patrick 213
Bruno, Giordano 2
Bynum, Brenda 202, 206

Calder, John 219
Calderón 6
Capra, Fritjof 45, 56
Casement, Patrick 216
Cervantes, Miguel de 29
Chabert, Pierre 93, 128
Chamfort 185, 194
Chekhov, Anton 68
Cluchey, Rich 90, 92–3

Coffey, Brian 229
Cohn, Ruby 95, 100, 225
Coleridge, Samuel Taylor 55, 63, 74, 107
Connor, Steven 97, 102
Conrad, Peter 50
Coover, Robert 125
Corbin, Henri 53
Corneille, Pierre xvi
Craig, George 218
Cunard, Nancy 185

Dandieu, Arnaud 6
Dante 23, 38, 43, 78, 113, 121, 145, 150, 152–5, 162, 163n, 170
    Inferno 27, 113, 121, 145, 152–5, 159–60, 162
    Paradiso 23
    Purgatorio 67, 78, 152
Democritus 224, 227–9
Derrida, Jacques 219, 223
Descartes, René 44–5, 47–8, 52–5, 61–2, 81–2, 178, 222, 226, 229, 238n
Deschevaux-Dumesnil, Suzanne xvi, xix, xx, 67
Devlin, Denis 8
Dickens, Charles 40n
    Great expectations 30, 39, 40n
Doré, Gustave 149–50
Duckworth, Colin 67
Duthuit, Georges 9, 12–13, 18–19

Eisenstein, Sergei 134
Eliot, George
    Middlemarch 39
Eliot, T. S.
    The waste land 33, 187
Epstein, Alvin 199
Esslin, Martin 12, 126–7, 212, 222
Eubulides 80–1

Fallis, Richard 217

247